Ordnance Survey

STREET ATLAS
Tyne
and Wear

GW00419123

Contents

PHILIP'S

First edition published 1996
Reprinted in 1998, 1999 by

Ordnance Survey®   and   George Philip Ltd., a division of
Romsey Road   Octopus Publishing Group Ltd
Maybush   2-4 Heron Quays
Southampton   London
SO16 4GU   E14 4JP

ISBN 0-540-06370-3 (hardback)
ISBN 0-540-06371-1 (spiral)

To the best of the Publishers' knowledge, the information in this atlas was
correct at the time of going to press. No responsibility can be accepted
for any errors or their consequences.

The representation in this atlas of a road, track or path is no evidence
of the existence of a right of way.

**The mapping between pages 1 and 121 (inclusive) in this atlas is
derived from Ordnance Survey® OSCAR® and Land-Line® data, and
Landranger® mapping.**

Ordnance Survey, OSCAR, Land-line and Landranger are registered trade
marks of Ordnance Survey, the national mapping agency of Great Britain.

Printed and bound in Spain by Cayfosa

Key to map symbols

Motorway	
Primary Routes (Dual carriageway and single)	
A Roads (Dual carriageway and single)	
B Roads (Dual carriageway and single)	
C Roads (Dual carriageway and single)	
Minor Roads	
Roads under construction	
County boundaries	
All Railways	
Track or private road	
Gate or obstruction to traffic (restrictions may not apply at all times or to all vehicles)	
All paths, bridleways, BOAT's, RUPP's, dismantled railways, etc.	

The representation in this atlas of a road, track or path is no evidence of the existence of a right of way

174	Adjoining page indicator

Acad	Academy	Mon	Monument
Cemy	Cemetery	Mus	Museum
C Ctr	Civic Centre	Obsy	Observatory
CH	Club House	Pal	Royal Palace
Coll	College	PH	Public House
Ex H	Exhibition Hall	Resr	Reservoir
Ind Est	Industrial Estate	Ret Pk	Retail Park
Inst	Institute	Sch	School
Ct	Law Court	Sh Ctr	Shopping Centre
L Ctr	Leisure Centre	Sta	Station
LC	Level Crossing	TH	Town Hall/House
Liby	Library	Trad Est	Trading Estate
Mkt	Market	Univ	University
Meml	Memorial	YH	Youth Hostel

British Rail station	
Private railway station	
Bus, coach station	
Ambulance station	
Coastguard station	
Fire station	
Police station	
Casualty entrance to hospital	
Churches, Place of worship	
Hospital	
Information Centre	
Parking	
Post Office	
Public Convenience	
Important buildings, schools, colleges, universities and hospitals	
River Soar	Water Name
Stream	
River or canal (minor and major)	
Water Fill	
Tidal Water	
Woods	
Tyne and Wear Metro	

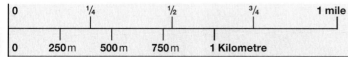

The scale of the maps is 5.52 cm to 1 km (3¹/₂ inches to 1 mile)

The small numbers around the edges of the maps identify the 1 kilometre National Grid lines

IV

Key to map pages

SOUTH SHIELDS

TYNEMOUTH

WHITLEY BAY

JARROW

WALLSEND

NEWCASTLE

AMBLE

ASHINGTON

NEWBIGGIN-BY-THE-SEA

MORPETH

BLYTH

BEDLINGTON

PONTELAND

Corbridge

RYTON

Warkworth
Newton on the Moor
Acklington
Broomhill
Felton
East Thirston
Ulgham
Widdrington
Cresswell
Ellington
Lynemouth
Cambois
East Sleekburn
Pegswood
Bothal
Hepscott
Hebron
Mitford
Bebside
Seaton Sluice
Seaton Delaval
New Hartley
Backworth
Shiremoor
Cramlington
Longbenton
Seaton Burn
Wide Open
Dinnington
Horton Grange
Berwick Hill
Stannington
Saltwick
Whalton
Belsay
Higham Dykes
Darras Hall
Heddon-on-the-Wall
Harlow Hill
Stamfordham
Colwell
Ridsdale
Kirkwhelpington
Scots' Gap
Hartburn
Longhorsley
Forestburn Gate
Rothbury
Thropton
Sharperton
Alwinton
Otterburn
Otterburn Camp
Elsdon
Billsmoor Park
Bellingham
Wark
Newbrough
Acomb
Sandhoe

River Coquet
River Wansbeck
River North Tyne
South Tyne
Tyne

A1
A68
A697
A696
A1068
A189
A197
A192
A1058
A191
A193
A19
A69
A6079

1 2 3 4 5 6 7 8 9 10 11 12 13 14 15 16 17 18 19 20 21 22 23 24 25 26 27 28 29 30 31 32 33 34 35 36 37 38 39 40 41 42 43 44 45 46 47 48 49 50 51 52

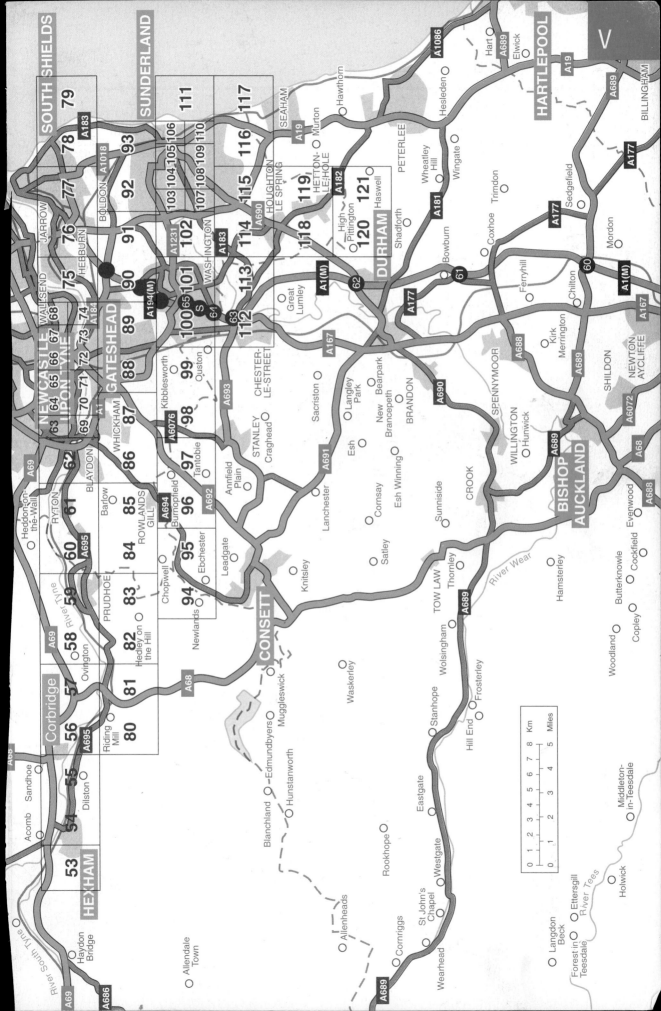

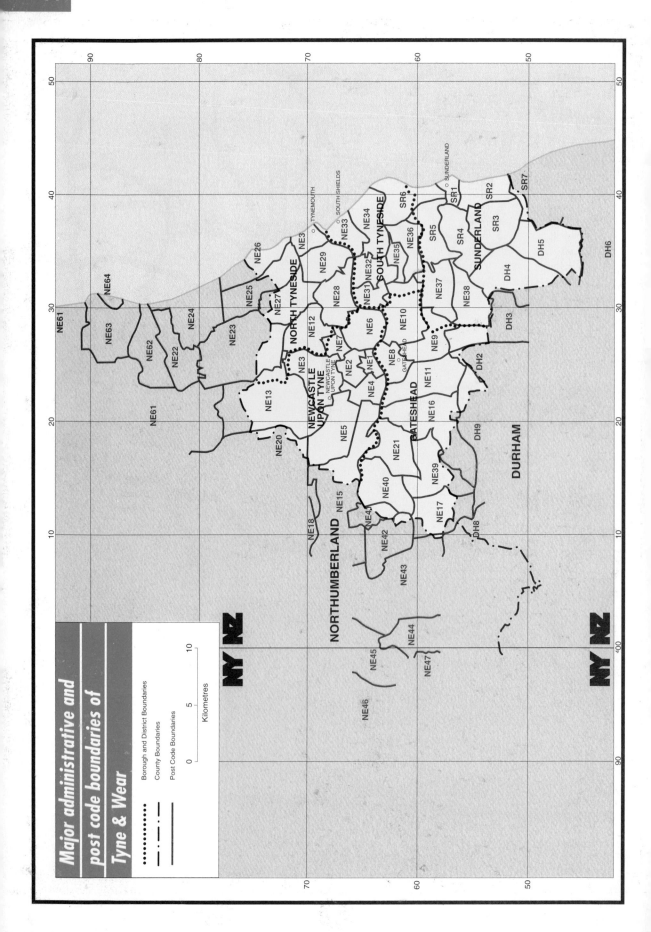

Major administrative and post code boundaries of Tyne & Wear

Borough and District Boundaries
County Boundaries
Post Code Boundaries

Kilometres
0   5   10

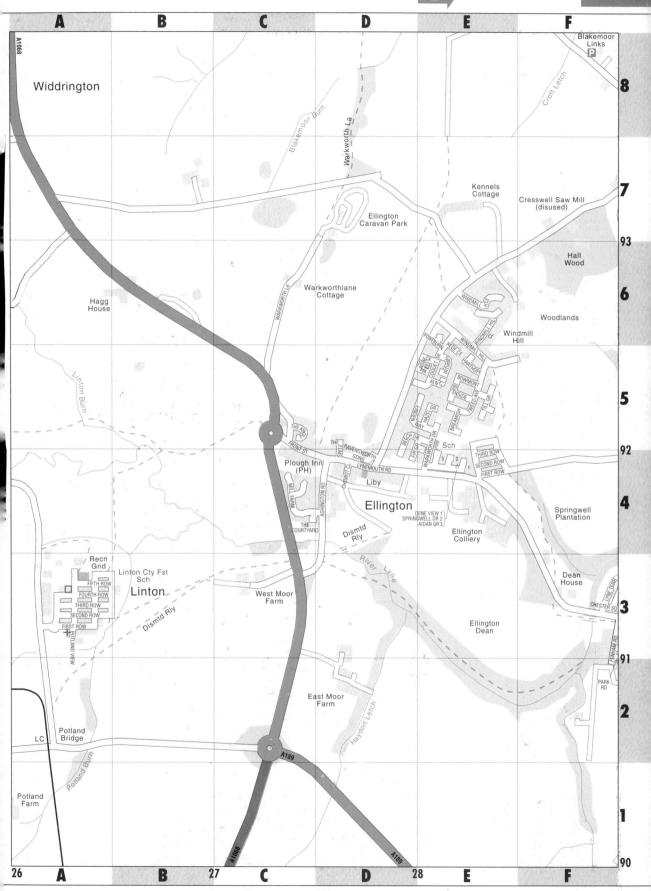

A B C D E F

Widdrington

Blakemoor
Links

8

Blakemoor Burn

Warkworth La

Croft Letch

7

Kennels
Cottage

Cresswell Saw Mill
(disused)

93

Hall
Wood

Ellington
Caravan Park

Woodlands

6

Warkworthlane
Cottage

WARKWORTH LA

Hagg
House

WINDMILL HTS
WINDMILL HILL
WINDMILL CL
Windmill
Hill

Linton Burn

FONTBURN
REDE CT
SMITH
HARTHOPE

BECK RD
COQUET DR
IRTHING
ALN CT

RENINGTON
WANSBECK WAY
WASEL GR

BOWMONT
FENSIDE
TWEED AVE
TILL GR

BREAMISH

5

THE KYL

THE ELMS
RAVENSWORTH
GDNS

Sch

FRONT ST

WARKWORTH DR

THIRD ROW
SECOND ROW
FIRST ROW

92

Plough Inn
(PH)

3 2 1

CHEVIOT CL

LYNEMOUTH RD

Liby

MILL FARM

ASHINGTON RD

BECK DR
FIR GR

Ellington

DENE VIEW 1
SPRINGWELL DR 2
AIDAN GR 3

Springwell
Plantation

4

THE
COURTYARD

Dismtd
Rly

Ellington
Colliery

River Lyne

Dean
House

Recn
Gnd

LYNE TERR

CHESTER SQ

Linton Cty Fst
Sch

FIFTH ROW
FOURTH ROW
THIRD ROW
SECOND ROW
FIRST ROW

Linton

West Moor
Farm

Ellington
Dean

3

Dismtd Rly

FENHAM RD

91

POTLAND VIEW

East Moor
Farm

PARK
RD

2

LC

Potland
Bridge

Haydon Letch

A189

Potland Burn

Potland
Farm

1

90

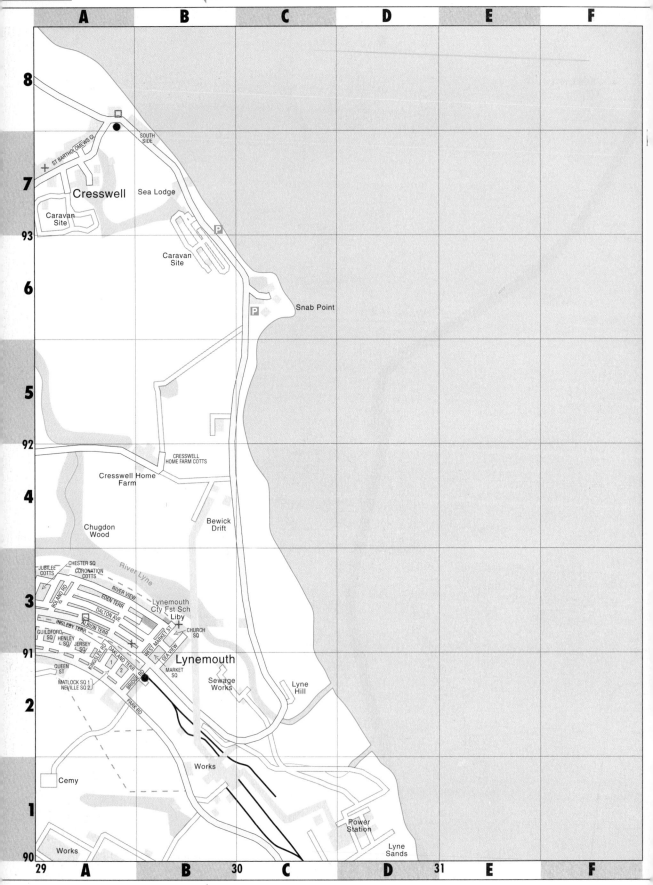

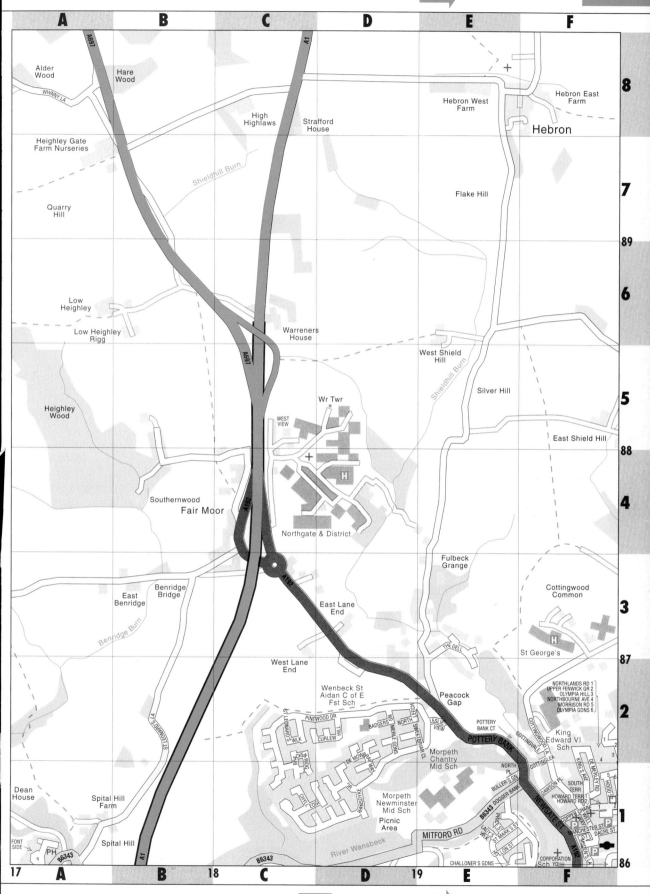

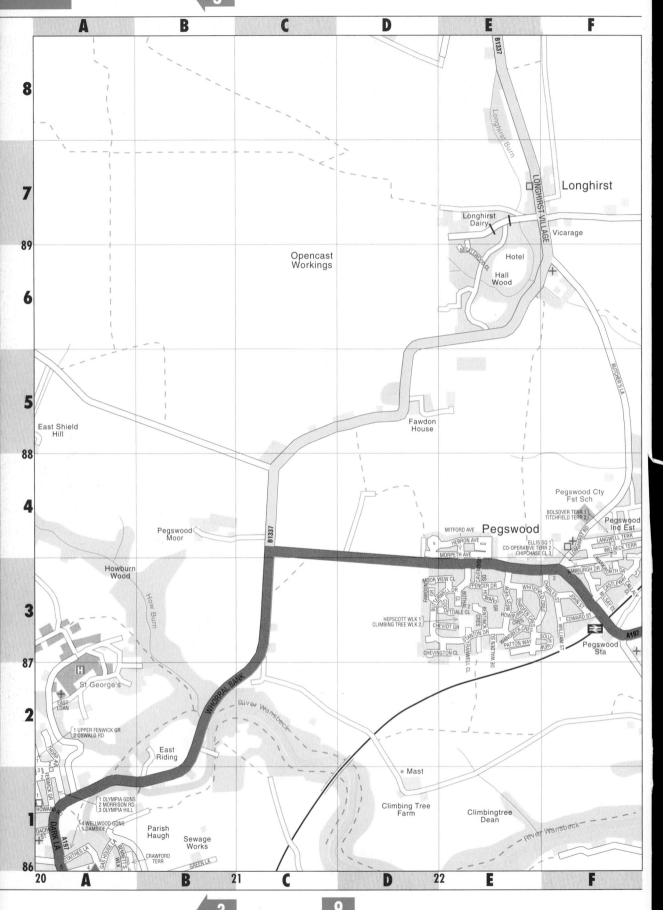

A B C D E F

8

7

89

6

5

88

4

3

87

2

1

86

20 21 22

B1337

Longhirst Burn

LONGHIRST VILLAGE

Longhirst

Longhirst
Dairy

Vicarage

Opencast
Workings

MICKLEWOOD CL

Hotel

Hall
Wood

BUTCHER'S LA

East Shield
Hill

Fawdon
House

Pegswood Cty
Fst Sch

BOLSOVER TERR 1
TITCHFIELD TERR 2

Pegswood
Ind Est

MITFORD AVE

Pegswood

ELLIS SQ 1
CO-OPERATIVE TERR 2
CHIPCHASE CL 3

LANGWELL TERR

WELBECK TERR

B1337

Pegswood
Moor

HEBRON AVE

MORPETH AVE

LONGHIRST RD

WARWORTH DR

BAMBURGH DR

CASTLE WAY

BELSAY CL

Howburn
Wood

How Burn

MOOR VIEW CL

SPENCER DR

BUTTERWELL DR

FAWDON GR

DEERBOLT CL

BOTHAL
CL

HOWARD GR

WEST AVE

WHITEFIELD CRES

CHARLES ST

JOHN ST

HEPSCOTT WLK 1
CLIMBING TREE WLK 2

CHEVIOT GR

HOWBURN CRES

STANTON DR

BENTINCK CRES

WANSBECK CRES

EDWARD ST

WILLIAM ST

SOUTH
AVE

PATTON WAY

CHEVINGTON CL

TRANWELL CL

DEERBOLT AVE

A197

Pegswood
Sta

St George's

EAST
LOAN

1 UPPER FENWICK GR
2 OSWALD RD

WHORRAL BANK

River Wansbeck

East
Riding

Mast

THORP AVE

Climbing Tree
Farm

Climbingtree
Dean

River Wansbeck

FENWICK GR

HOWARD RD

1 OLYMPIA GDNS
2 MORRISON RD
3 OLYMPIA HILL

4 WELLWOOD GDNS
5 DAMSIDE

Parish
Haugh

Sewage
Works

DARK LA

A197

DACRE
ST

STAITHES LA

GAS HOUSE LA

BENNETT'S
WLK

CRAWFORD
TERR

GREEN LA

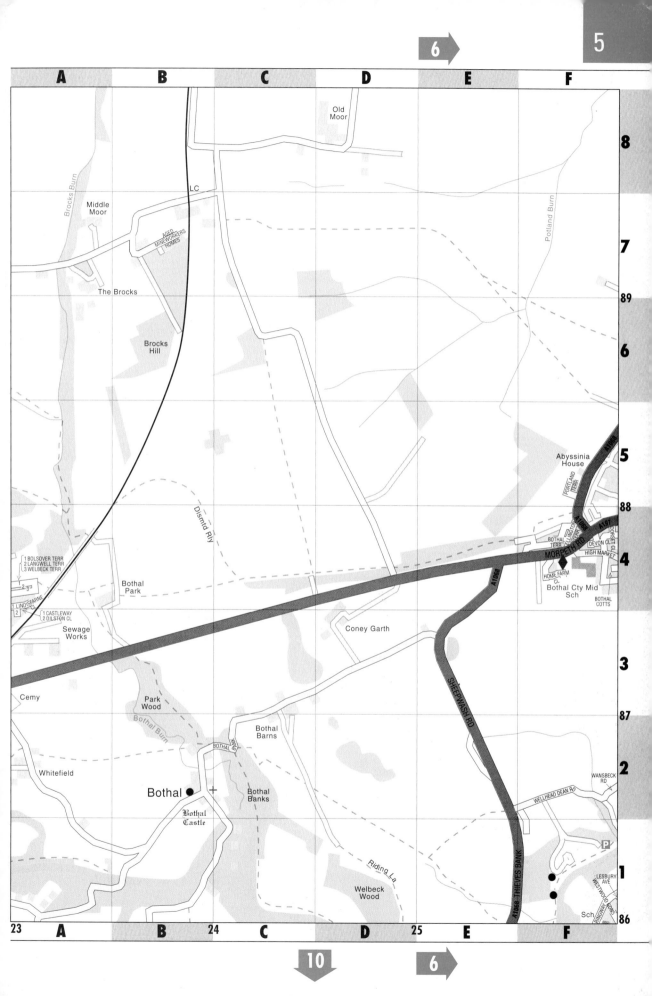

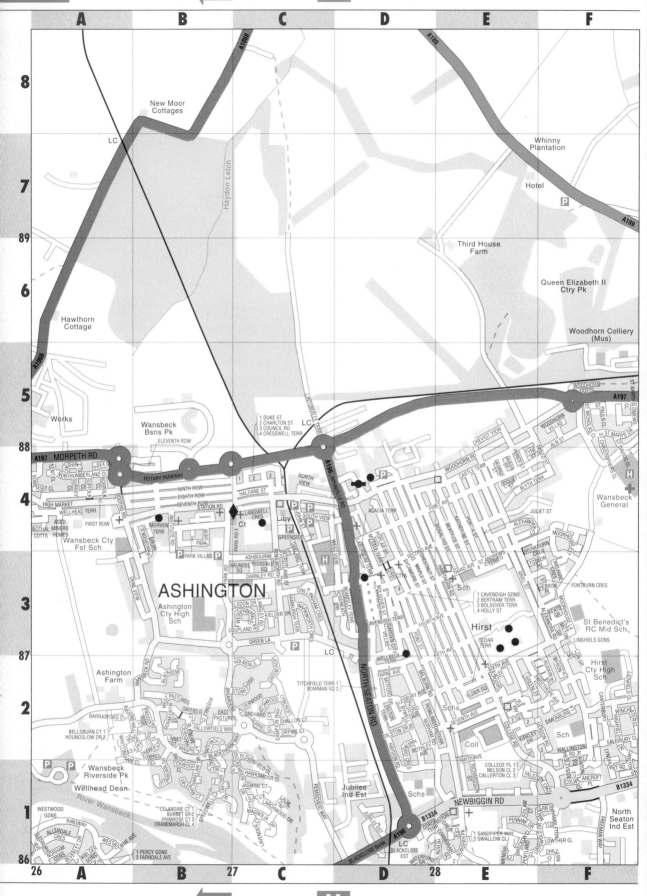

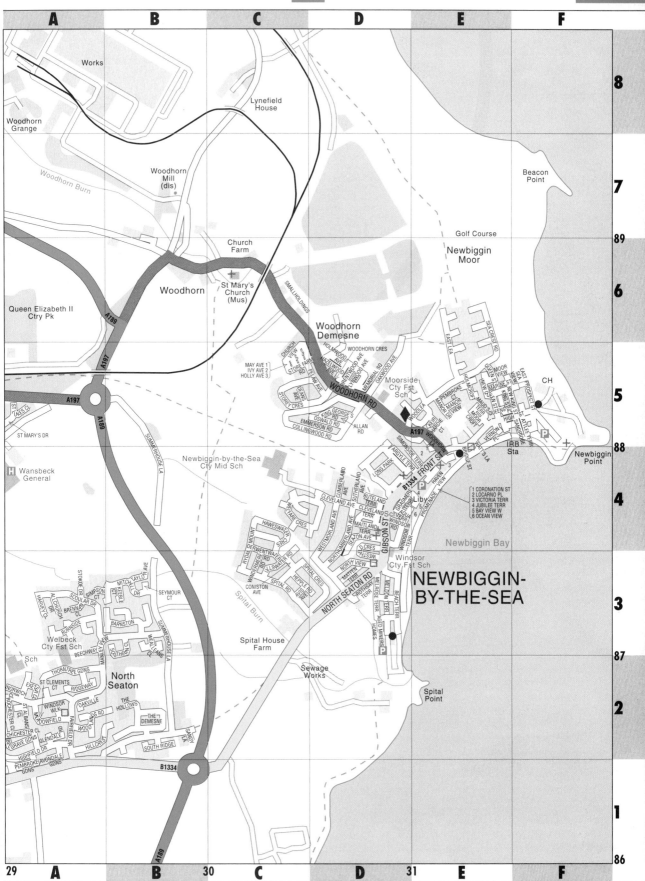

Works

Lynefield
House

Woodhorn
Grange

Woodhorn Burn

Woodhorn Mill
(dis)

Beacon
Point

Church
Farm

Newbiggin
Moor

Golf Course

Woodhorn

St Mary's
Church
(Mus)

SMALLHOLDINGS

Queen Elizabeth II
Ctry Pk

Woodhorn
Demesne

CH

EAST LEA

SEA CRES RD

Moorside
Cty Fst
Sch

EAST PROSPECT TER

ST CRES CL

MAY AVE 1
IVY AVE 2
HOLLY AVE 3

WOODHORN RD

ST MARY'S DR

Newbiggin
Point

IRB
Sta

Newbiggin-by-the-Sea
Cty Mid Sch

Wansbeck
General

FRONT ST

1 CORONATION ST
2 LOCARNO PL
3 VICTORIA TERR
4 JUBILEE TERR
5 BAY VIEW W
6 OCEAN VIEW

Lib'y

Newbiggin Bay

Windsor
Cty Fst Sch

SUMMERHOUSE LA

NEWBIGGIN-
BY-THE-SEA

NORTH SEATON RD

Welbeck
Cty Fst Sch

Sch

North
Seaton

Spital Burn

Spital House
Farm

Sewage
Works

Spital
Point

THE
HOLLOWS

THE
DEMESNE

SOUTH RIDGE

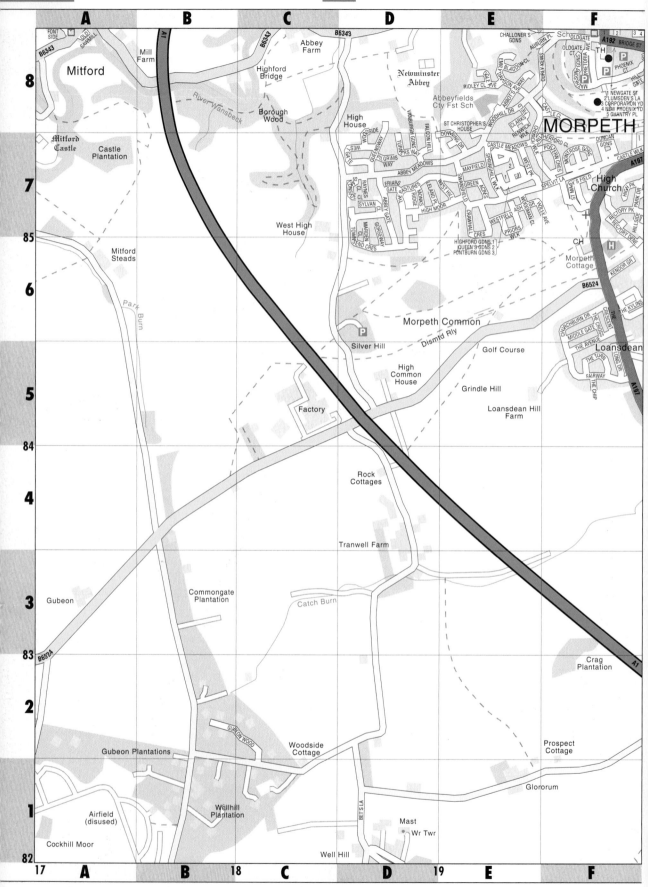

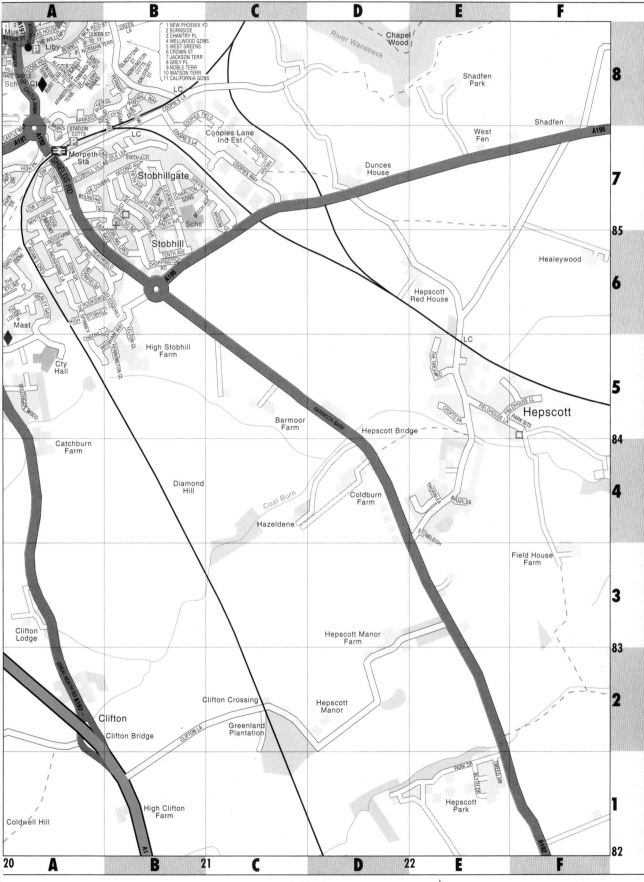

A B C D E F

8
7
85
6
5
84
4
3
83
2
1
82

20 A B 21 C D 22 E F

1 NEW PHOENIX YD
2 BURNSIDE
3 CHANTRY PL
4 WELLWOOD GDNS
5 WEST GREENS
6 CROWN ST
7 JACKSON TERR
8 GREY PL
9 NOBLE TERR
10 WATSON TERR
11 CALIFORNIA GDNS

Mus
Liby
Sch Ct
Morpeth Sta
Stobhillgate
Stobhill
High Stobhill Farm
Cty Hall
Mast
The Lodge
Merley Gate
Catchburn Farm
Diamond Hill
Barmoor Farm
Coal Burn
Hazeldene
Coldburn Farm
Clifton Lodge
Clifton
Clifton Bridge
Clifton Crossing
Clifton La
Greenland Plantation
High Clifton Farm
Coldwell Hill
Hepscott Manor Farm
Hepscott Manor
Hepscott Park
Field House Farm
Hepscott
Fieldhouse La
Park Site
Crofts Pk
Hepscott Red House
Hepscott Bridge
LC
The Orchard
Thornlea
Briarlea
Stoneleigh
Healeywood
West Fen
Shadfen
Shadfen Park
Chapel Wood
River Wansbeck
Dunces House
Coopies Lane Ind Est
Coopies Field
Coopies La
Shields Rd
A196
A197
A192
A1
Great North Rd A1197
Park Dr
Tweed Dr
Blyth Dr

4
10
14
10

A   B   C   D   E   F

8

Ringway
Cty Fst Sch
THNG BANK SHEEPWASH CO
A1068
Sheepwash
GLEBE
FARM
MITFORD
Beverley
DR
HILL TOP CL
HORSLEY
MELDON GDNS
Bothal
Riding
HILLCREST AVE
PARKWAY
WALTON DR
WASHINGTON
NORTHWAY
Schs
River Wansbeck
SOUTH
VIEW
SYCAMORE RD
DENE AVE
SARABEL AVE
ROTHBURY
RUTHERFORD
SCHOOL AVE
CROSSLEASH
BACK MOWBRAY TERR
SHEEPWASH BANK
COLERIDGE CT
STAKEFORD LA
A1068
ALCHESTER RD
South Lodge
A196
RIVERSIDE AVE
WEST AVE
PINE AVE
NORTH AVE
CENTRAL AVE
ASH AVE
BOTHAL AVE
LABURNUM
FERN CT
BYRON
AVE
FREEHOLD
FORD TERR
LOVIAN
TERR
COLERIDGE RD
MOWBRAY
TERR

7

Paddock
Hall
North
Farm
JOHNSONS
VILLAS
MORPETH RD
THE
SQUARE
BROADWAY
HIGH ST
Guide Post

85

South
Farm
East
Choppington
Liby
GLADEWELL CT
GREENFIELD DR
MEADOW BANK DR
UNDERHILL DR
ACREFORD CT
HIGH ST
NORTH MORPETH PAR
A1068
SOUTH PAR
HIGH ST

6

Whinney Hill
Farm
Choppington
Cty Prim Jnr
& Inf Schs
EASTGREEN
EASTGATE
WEST
GREEN
EASTGATE

5

Choppington
KINGS PK

84

The
Travellers Rest
(PH)
CHURCH RD
WINDSOR TERR
Scotland Gate
MARLBOROUGH
FRANCES
VILLE
GLEBE
TERR
WINDSOR TERR

4

Hepscott Burn
Sleek Burn
Willow Bridge
Lord Clyde
(PH)
BARRINGTON RD
LC

Burnthouse
Wood

Netherton Letch
Tip

3

Burnt
House
Windmill
Farm

83

Glebe Farm
CHOPPINGTON RD

2

Lanchester GN
OCRHAM CL
TREE DR
TREE DR
ASH
Howard
House
NETHERTON LA
CENTURIAN
AUGUSTA
CHICHESTER RD
CORCHESTER RD
ROWAN CL
CEDAR CL
Bedlington
Meadowdale
Cty Mid Sch
THE CREST
THE WYNDING
GLEBE
CHERRY
TREE CL
HASSOPWAY
MAPLE CL
Blue House
Farm
ALNWICK CL
DURHAM CL
DUNSTANBURGH
BARNARD
RICHMOND CL
CLOVERDALE
MEADOW CT
COURT RD
SWIFTDALE
HYLTON CL
ROSEDALE
BRIARDALE
GLEBE
JOHN BROWN CT
PIT COTTS
OAKAPPLE CL

1

WILLIAM ALLAN
HOMES
WHITE
LEA AVE
FORSTER AVE
NORTH RIDGE
SCHALKSMUHLE RD
MILNE CT
Liby
Ct

West Farm
NETHERTON LA
NORTH FARM
B1331
NORTH RIDGE
MEADOWDALE
CRES
RIDGE VILLAS
NETHERTON
DALE
RIDGE TERR
DEANERY
BURDON TERR
CUMBERLAND
AVE
WESTMORLAND AVE
A1068
GLEBE RD
B1331
WOOLSINGTON
CT
Cemy
Schs
Sch
P

82

23   A   B   24   C   D   25   E   F

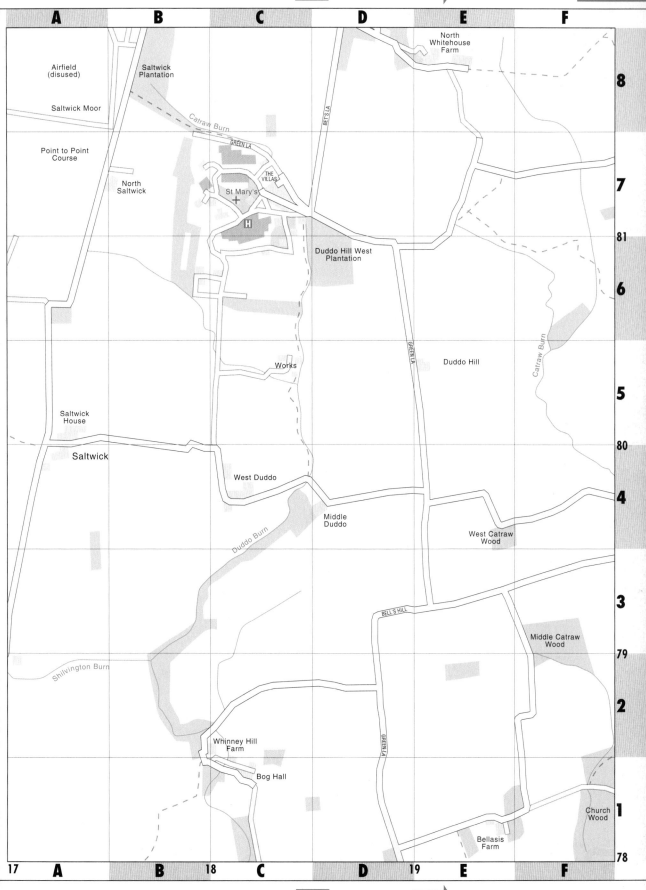

A B C D E F

Airfield (disused)

Saltwick Plantation

Saltwick Moor

Catraw Burn

GREEN LA

BET'S LA

North Whitehouse Farm

8

Point to Point Course

THE VILLAS

7

North Saltwick

St Mary's

81

H

Duddo Hill West Plantation

6

GREEN LA

Works

Duddo Hill

Catraw Burn

5

Saltwick House

80

Saltwick

West Duddo

4

Middle Duddo

West Catraw Wood

Duddo Burn

BELL'S HILL

3

Middle Catraw Wood

Shilvington Burn

79

2

Whinney Hill Farm

GREEN LA

Bog Hall

Church Wood

1

Bellasis Farm

78

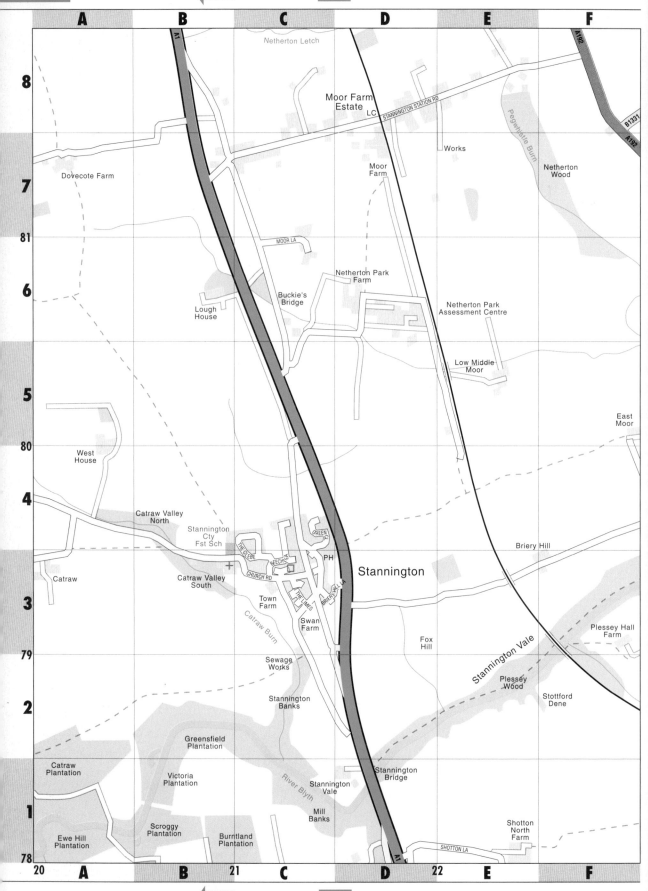

A	B	C	D	E	F

8

Netherton Letch

Moor Farm Estate

LC
STANNINGTON STATION RD

Works

A192

B1331

A192

7
Dovecote Farm

Moor Farm

Netherton Wood

Pegwhistle Burn

81
MOOR LA

6
Lough House

Buckie's Bridge

Netherton Park Farm

Netherton Park Assessment Centre

Low Middle Moor

5
West House

East Moor

80

4
Catraw Valley North

Stannington Cty Fst Sch

Briery Hill

Catraw

Catraw Valley South

THE GLEBE

CHURCH RD

BEECH AV

GREEN LA

PH

Stannington

3
Catraw Burn

Town Farm

Swan Farm

THE LIMES

BRIERDENE LA

Fox Hill

Stannington Vale

Plessey Hall Farm

79
Sewage Works

Plessey Wood

Stottford Dene

2
Stannington Banks

Greensfield Plantation

River Blyth

Stannington Bridge

Catraw Plantation

Victoria Plantation

Stannington Vale

1
Mill Banks

Shotton North Farm

Ewe Hill Plantation

Scroggy Plantation

Burntland Plantation

A1

SHOTTON LA

78

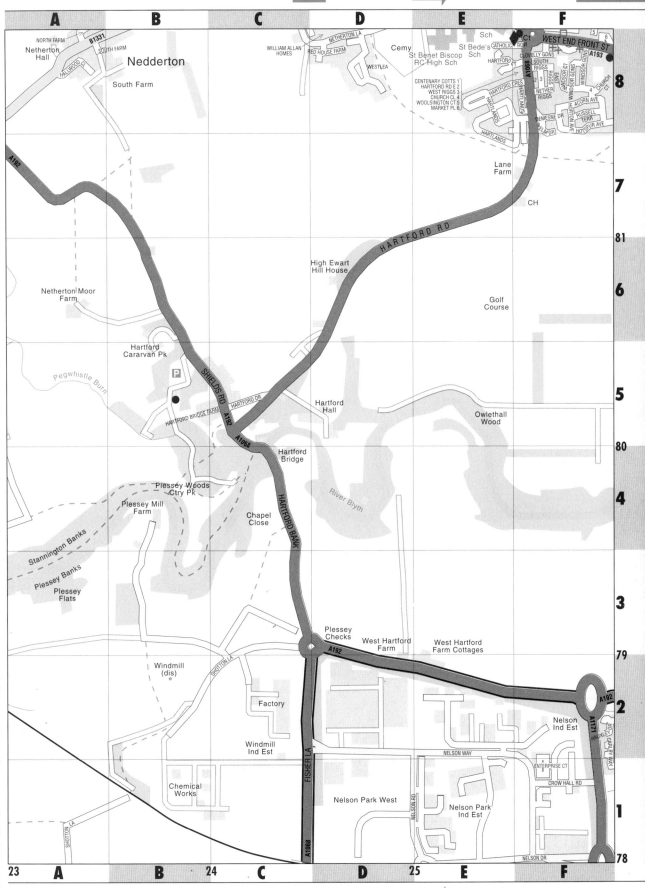

A B C D E F

North Farm
B1331
SOUTH FARM
Netherton
Hall
YALLWOOD CT

Nedderton

South Farm

WILLIAM ALLAN
HOMES
NETHERTON LA
RED HOUSE FARM
WESTLEA
Cemy
Sch
St Benet Biscop
RC High Sch
St Bede's
Sch
HARTFORD CT
WEST END FRONT ST
A193
5   6
CATHOLIC
ROW
CLOVELLY GDNS
SOUTH
RIGGS
NETHER
RIGGS
EAST RIGGS
WINDSOR GDNS
HORTON AVE
WINDSOR GDNS
CHURCH
CT
8

CENTENARY COTTS 1
HARTFORD RD E 2
WEST RIGGS 3
CHURCH CL 4
WOOLSINGTON CT 5
MARKET PL 6
HARTFORD CRES
HARTLANDS
DEMESNE DR
RUSSELL
TERR
ACORN AVE
ARTHUR AVE

HARTLANDS

A192

Lane
Farm

7

CH

HARTFORD RD
81

High Ewart
Hill House

Golf
Course
6

Netherton Moor
Farm

Hartford
Cararvan Pk
P
SHIELDS RD
HARTFORD DR
A192
Pegwhistle Burn
Hartford
Hall
Owlethall
Wood
5

A1068
Hartford
Bridge
80

Plessey Woods
Ctry Pk
HARTFORD BANK
River Blyth
4

Plessey Mill
Farm
Chapel
Close

Stannington Banks
Plessey Banks
Plessey
Flats
3

Plessey
Checks
A192
West Hartford
Farm
West Hartford
Farm Cottages
79

Windmill
(dis)
SHOTTON LA
A192
A1171
Nelson
Ind Est
CARLBY WAY
2

Factory
FISHER LA
NELSON WAY
ENTERPRISE CT
CROW HALL RD

Windmill
Ind Est
NELSON RD
Nelson Park
Ind Est
1

Chemical
Works
A1068
Nelson Park West
SHOTTON LA
NELSON DR
78

23 A B 24 C D 25 E F

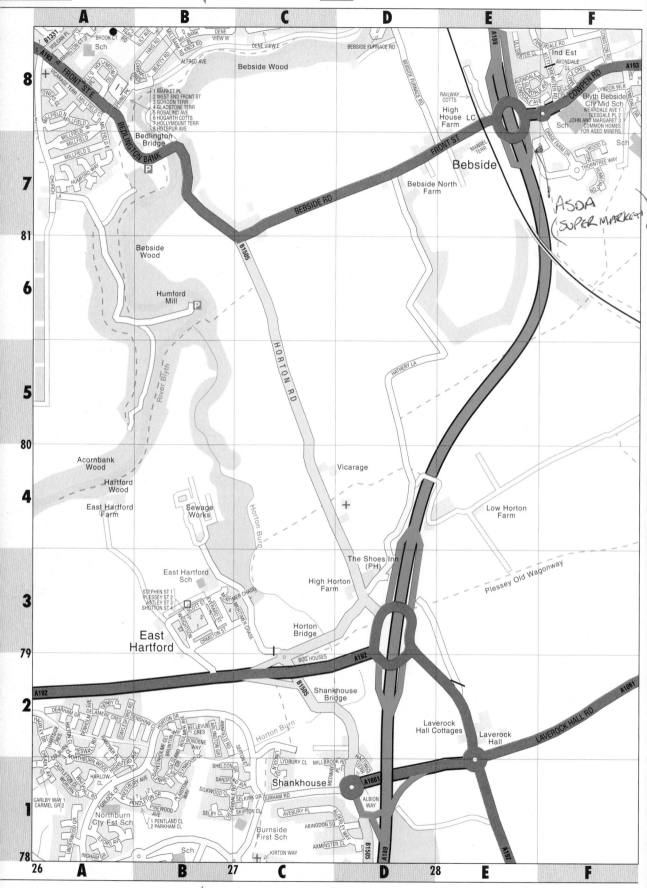

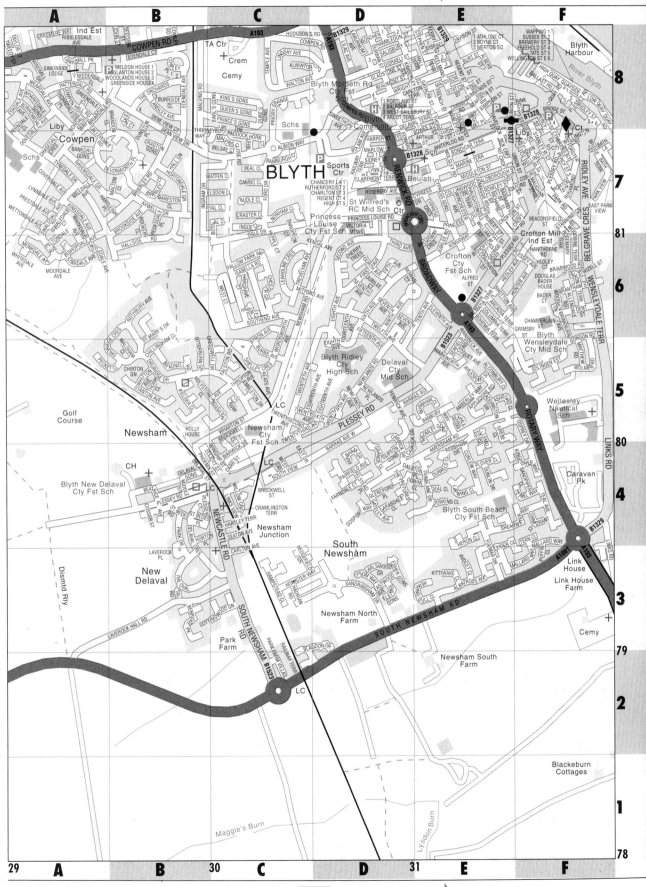

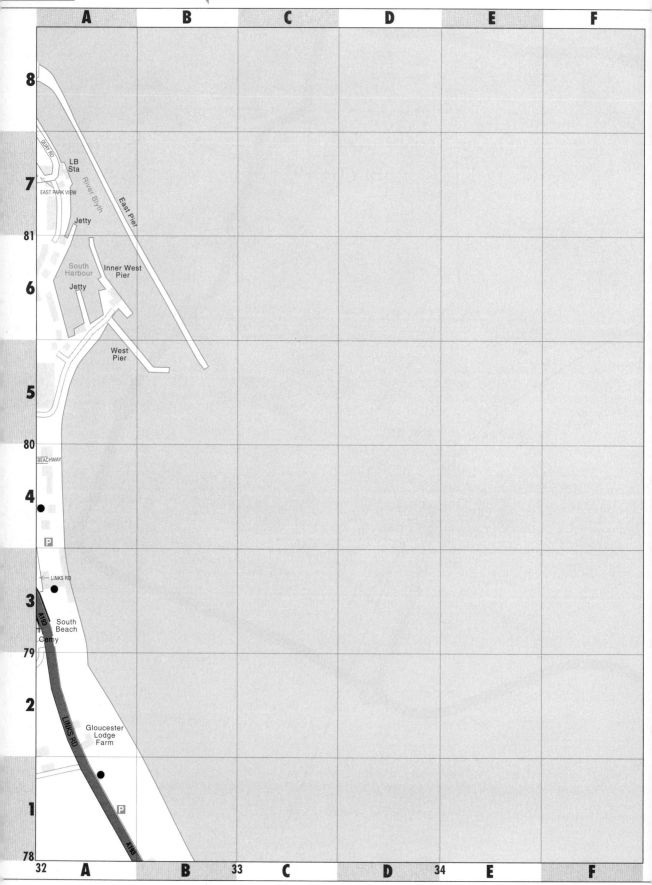

A | B | C | D | E | F

8

QUAY RD
LB Sta
River Blyth
East Park View
East Pier
7
Jetty
81
South Harbour
Inner West Pier
Jetty
6
West Pier
5
80
BEACHWAY
4
P
LINKS RD
3
A193
South Beach
Cemy
79
2
LINKS RD
Gloucester Lodge Farm
P
1
A193
78

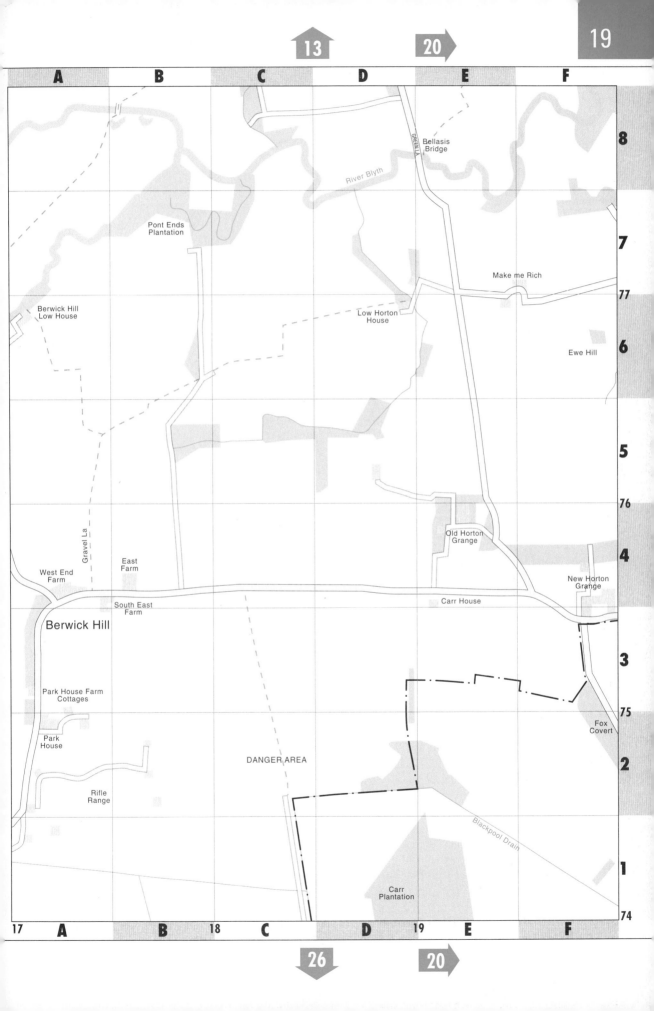

A B C D E F

8

Bellasis
Bridge

GREEN LA

River Blyth

7

Pont Ends
Plantation

Make me Rich

77

Berwick Hill
Low House

Low Horton
House

6

Ewe Hill

5

76

Old Horton
Grange

Gravel La

4

East
Farm

West End
Farm

New Horton
Grange

South East
Farm

Carr House

Berwick Hill

3

Park House Farm
Cottages

75

Fox
Covert

Park
House

DANGER AREA

2

Rifle
Range

Blackpool Drain

1

Carr
Plantation

74

A B C D E F

8

Ewe Hill

Blagdon Lake

New Kennels

Shotton

Shotton South Farm

SHOTTON LA

A1

Lake Plantation

Election Plantation

Home Farm

New Cottages

Coal Wood

7

Lake Wiseman

Old Kennels

North Wood

Cascade Dene

77

Twist Plantation

Bog House

Blagdon Hall

Shotton Edge

Snitter Burn

Fusilier Plantation

6

Grove Pond

Blagdon Park

North Wood

Deer Park Wood

LEGGES DR

SOUTH DR

Thornhill Cottage

5

Shotton Grange

Park House

76

Milkhope Ctr

Milkhope Plantation

4

Hoys Wood

Shotton Edge South

A1

3

Brenkley

North Farm

Crow Wood

Seven Mile House

75

South Brenkley

East Brenkley Farm

Opencast Workings

2

Trinidad Plantation

Gardener's Houses Farm

1

Carr Grange Farm

74

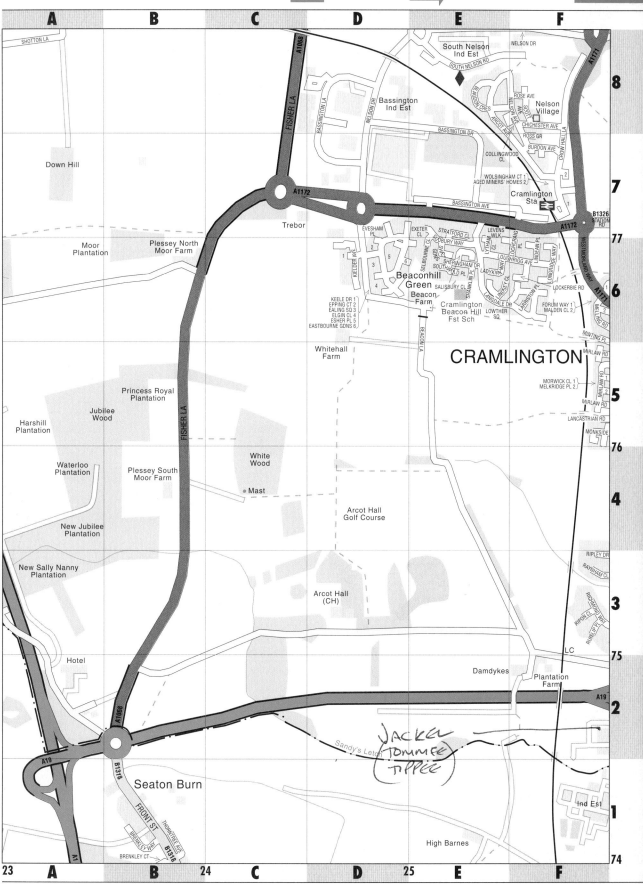

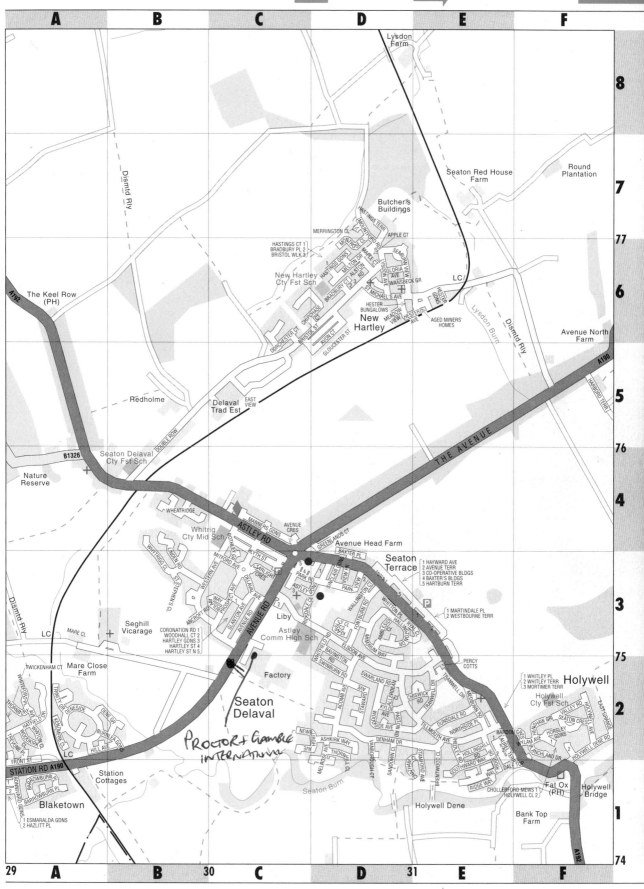

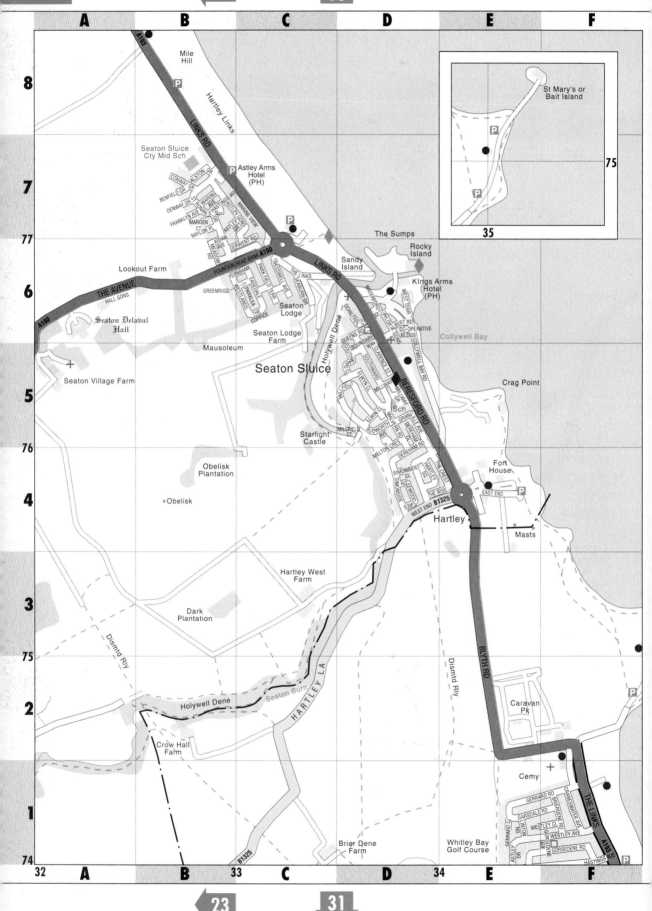

A   B   C   D   E   F

8

7

77

6

5

76

4

3

75

2

1

74

32   A   B   33   C   D   34   E   F

St Mary's or
Bait Island

75

35

Mile
Hill

Hartley Links

Seaton Sluice
Cty Mid Sch

Astley Arms
Hotel
(PH)

CONWAY GR   ALSTON GR

BENFIELD GR

DENWAY GR

FRANKLYN AVE   ST WARING

MARDEN   TOWN'S   HASTINGS AVE

CT   HOLMAN'S DR   ASTLEY GDNS

NAYLOR PL   MARINE VIEW

AIDAN   DERWENT RD

MEADOW   AVE

Lookout Farm

THE AVENUE

HALL GDNS

A190

Seaton Delaval
Hall

Seaton Village Farm

Mausoleum

FOUNTAIN HEAD BANK   A190

FERNBANK

GREENRIGG

WESTLANDS   PARK FIELD TERR

EASEDALE   CRESSWELL AVE

THE   PARKLEA   THE SEABURN GR

COPPICE   THE LINKS

Seaton
Lodge

Seaton Lodge
Farm

The Sumps

Sandy
Island

Rocky
Island

Kings Arms
Hotel
(PH)

WATERFORD CL   WEST TERR

DOHN FRY CL

QUEENS RD   BERT RD

BOUNDARY   CO-OPERATIVE
WAY   BLDGS

SOUTHWARD   CLARENCE ST

ELWIN GR   COLLYWELL BAY RD

Collywell Bay

Seaton Sluice

Holywell Dene

Starlight
Castle

FALL FIELD

MILFIELD
CT

ELWIN CL

BLOXWORTH   MILLWAY

AVE   MILLWAY

MALVERN RD

MELTON CRES   GRANVILLE AVE

DEREHAM RD

Sch

BERESFORD RD

Crag Point

Obelisk
Plantation

• Obelisk

SIMONSIDE   DEREHAM RD

CL   HARTLEY

SIMONSIDE   ROSEWOOD   THE CREST

TERR   AVE   THE RISE

Sch

WEST END   B1325

Hartley

Fort
House

EAST END

Masts

Dismtd Rly

Hartley West
Farm

Dark
Plantation

HARTLEY LA

Holywell Dene

Seaton Burn

Dismtd Rly

BLYTH RD

Caravan
Pk

Crow Hall
Farm

Cemy

THE LINKS

GERRARD RD   CRANSWATER RD

GARSDALE RD   BRIERDENE RD

GERRARD CT   WESTLEY CL

ASTLEY   LINTON   WESTLEY AVE

DR   RD   GORSEDENE

GORSEDENE RD

Brier Dene
Farm

Whitley Bay
Golf Course

B1325

HASTINGS AVE

A193

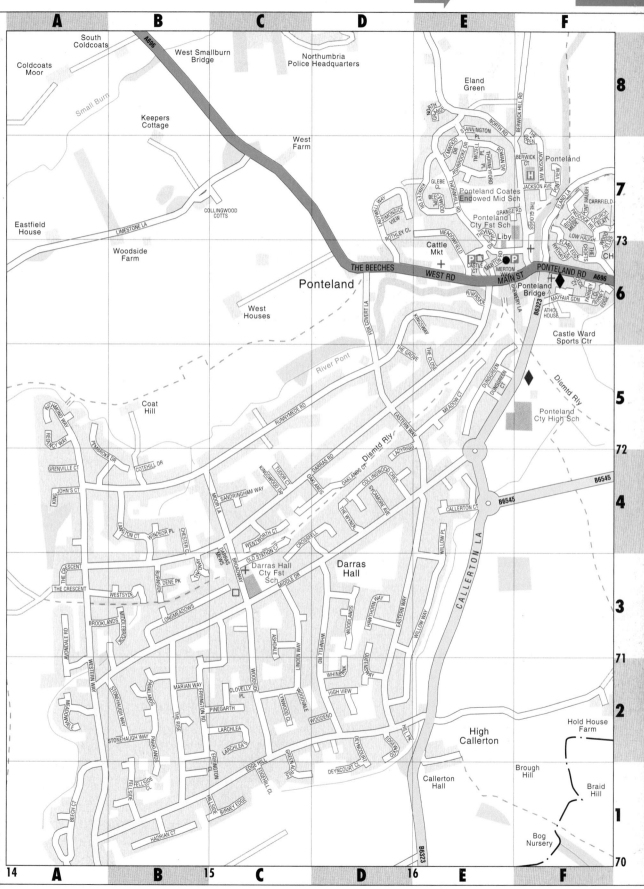

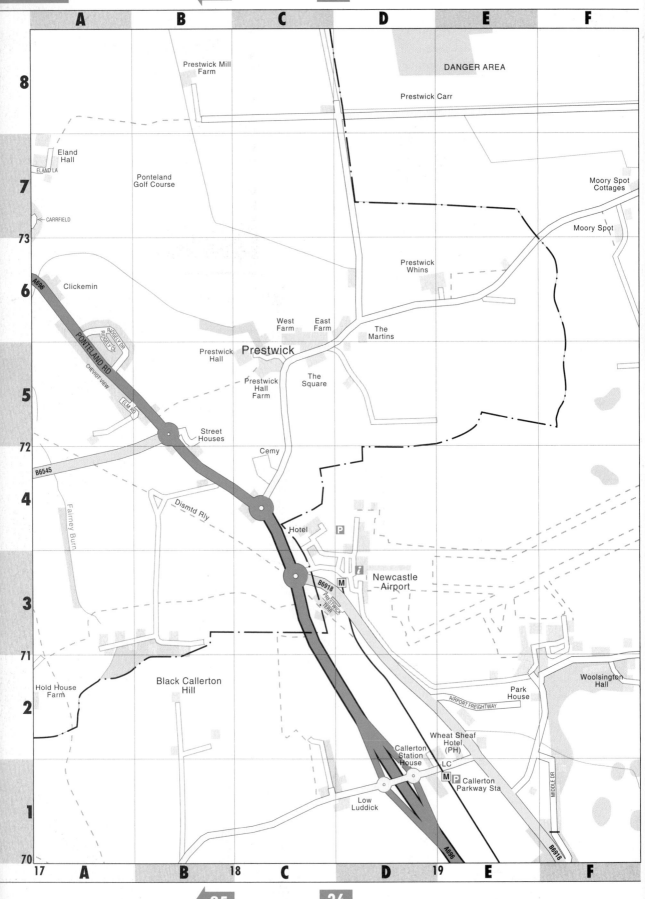

A B C D E F

8

DANGER AREA

Prestwick Mill
Farm

Prestwick Carr

Eland
Hall
ELAND LA

7

Ponteland
Golf Course

Moory Spot
Cottages

CARRFIELD

73

Moory Spot

Prestwick
Whins

6

A696

Clickemin

PONTELAND RD

RUDGELY DR
RIDGELY CL

CHEVIOT VIEW

ELM A6

West
Farm

East
Farm

The
Martins

Prestwick
Hall

Prestwick

5

Prestwick
Hall
Farm

The
Square

Street
Houses

72

Cemy

B6545

4

Dismtd Rly

Fairney Burn

Hotel

P

B6918

Prestwick Terr

M

i

Newcastle
Airport

3

71

Hold House
Farm

Black Callerton
Hill

AIRPORT FREIGHTWAY

Park
House

Woolsington
Hall

2

Wheat Sheaf
Hotel
(PH)

Callerton Station
House

LC

M P Callerton
Parkway Sta

MIDDLE DR

1

Low
Luddick

A696

B6918

70

17 A B 18 C D 19 E F

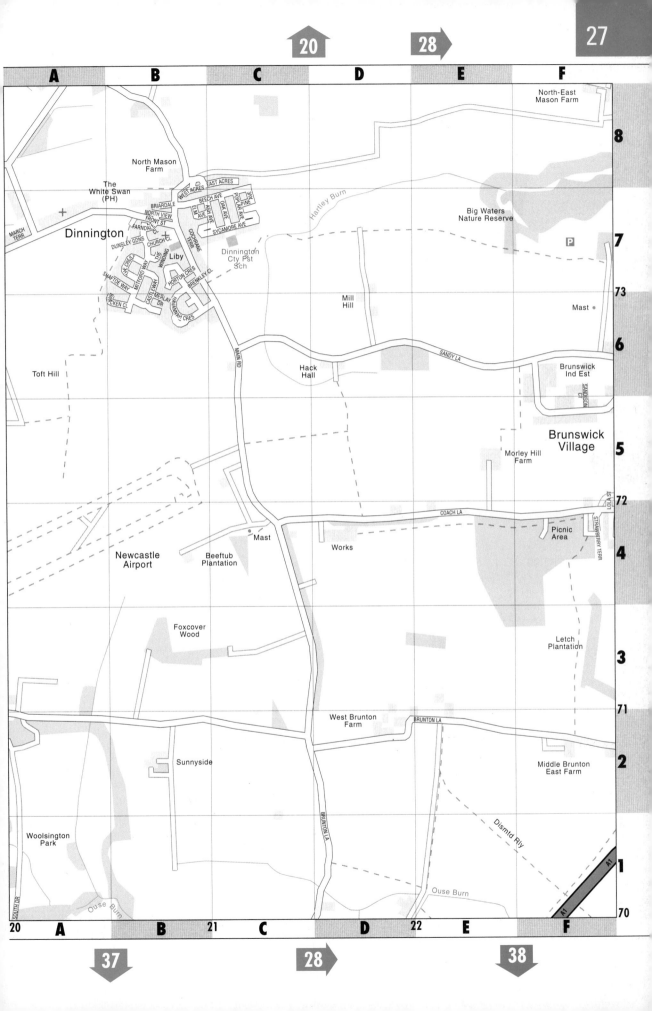

A   B   C   D   E   F

North-East
Mason Farm

8

North Mason
Farm

The
White Swan
(PH)

BRIARDALE

NORTH VIEW

FRONT ST

FARNDALE

CL

WEST ACRES   EAST ACRES

BEECH AVE

ELM AVE

ASH AVE

OAK AVE

POPLAR AVE

PINE AVE

SYCAMORE AVE

Hartley Burn

Big Waters
Nature Reserve

P

7

Dinnington

Liby

DUNSLEY GDNS

CHURCH CL

THE WINDING

Dinnington
Cty Fst
Sch

73

MARCH
TERR

COCHRANE TERR

Mill
Hill

Mast

NE CRESC

MITFORD WAY

SHAFTOE WAY

CASTLE WAY

MERLAY DR

HANNAH CRES

HORTON CRES

BRENKLEY CL

6

BRACKEN CL

MAIN RD

Hack
Hall

SANDY LA

Brunswick
Ind Est

Toft Hill

SANDISON CT

Brunswick
Village

5

Morley Hill
Farm

IVY LO

72

COACH LA

Picnic
Area

STRAWBERRY TERR

Newcastle
Airport

Mast

Beeftub
Plantation

Works

4

Foxcover
Wood

Letch
Plantation

3

71

West Brunton
Farm

BRUNTON LA

Sunnyside

Middle Brunton
East Farm

2

BRUNTON LA

Dismtd Rly

A1

1

Woolsington
Park

SOUTH DR

Ouse Burn

Ouse Burn

A1

70

A B C D E F

8

West Field

Holywell Grange Farm

7

Fenwick's Close Farm

73

East Holywell

6

West Holywell

Cemy

Brierdene Burn

West Farm

B1322

Middle Farm

THOMAS TAYLOR COTTS

ST JOHN'S CL

MELROSE AVE

CHURCH RD

ASHBOURNE

LC

Dismtd Rly

FISHER RD

5

BACKWORTH LA

KILLINGWORTH LA B1317

CASTLE SQ

KILLINGWORTH MK

Recn Gd

Backworth Fst Sch

RUSHBURY CT

GARNLEY SQ

SHREWSBURY DR

TELFORD CL

STRETTON WAY

SKIPTON CL

SHANKLIN CT

STRETFORD CL

CLARA AVE 1
LOWER CRONE ST 2
UPPER CRONE ST 3
BRIDGE TERR 4
EARSDON VIEW 5

A19

72

ECCLESTON CL

MORLEY PL 6
HUGH AVE 7
CHARLES AVE 8
JAMES AVE 9

Recn Gd

BYWELL GR

Shiremoor Mid Sch

HECTOR ST

SOUTH ST

WARK AVE

A186

4

Golf Course

Backworth

Holystone Farm

Moor View

Moor Edge Farm

MOOR EDGE RD

ANN ST 1
HARROW ST 2

GRANGE AVE

Shiremoor Sta

M

ETAL CL

ETAL CRES

MID FIELD AVE

PARK AVE

AGED MINERS HOMES

PARK GR

B1317

1 GARFIELD CL
2 HARWOOD DR

HARTSIDE CRES

HARLOW AVE

HALTON DR

ST MARKS CT 1
CO-OPERATIVE TERR 2

BOYNE GDNS

ABBEY

FORD CRES

ELSBURY AVE

BAMBURGH CRES

BELFORD TERR

BEACHLEY

AIDED MINERS HOMES

BRANDON AVE

MATFEN AVE

PARK RD

SIMONSIDE WAY

East House Farm

HAYDON GDNS 1
HAVELOCK RD 2

HARLE RD

STATION RD

EMERSON PL

KIRKLAND WLK

STANTON CT

FELTON CL

CRASTER AVE

FARNE RD

BEAL

WITTON RD

FARNE RD

PARK LA

PARK RD

CORSLEY AVE

CHILLINGHAM AVE

3

Dismtd Rly

St Edmunds Aided Prim Sch

Shiremoor Fst Sch

BRENKLEY AVE

CARMICHAEL

KIRKLEY RD

BRUNTON GR

ANGERTON AVE

HARBOTTLE TERR

71

Killingworth Moor

Holystone Farm

Holystone Cty Prim Sch

A186

Prospect Hill Farm

B1322

NEW YORK RD

BENTON RD

CRAMLINGTON AVE

BRUNSWICK RD

ST ALBANS VIEW

PARK LA

BRUNSWICK SQ

Hypermarket

2

WINDSOR PL

HOLYSTONE DR

DEVONSHIRE PL

PH

A191

A191

BENTON RD

PH

1 NORTH TERR
2 ECCLES TERR
3 CARLISLE TERR
4 BUDDLE TERR
5 MAUD TERR
6 LAMB TERR
7 GRIFFITH TERR
8 TAYLOR TERR
9 EARSDON TERR
10 CRAMLINGTON TERR
11 CO-OPERATIVE TERR
12 PRESTON TERR

The Allotment

+

Algernon Ind Est

A191

1 PALMERSVILLE
2 CO-OPERATIVE TERR
3 CLARABAD TERR
4 BANISTER DR
5 THORNTON TERR
6 ELIZABETH CT
7 ELIZABETH DR
8 KELVIN PL
9 ROSEBERRY GRANGE

WESLEY WAY

ST CUTHBERT'S RD

Holystone

WHITLEY RD

WEST ST

TURNER ST

BACKWORTH TERR 1
HOLYWELL TERR 2
RYTON TERR 3

West Allotment

1

LAUREL AVE

Palmersville

LAUREL END

Palmersville Sta

WESLEY DR

Benton Square Ind Est

Benton Square

WESLEY CT

ST AIDAN'S SQ

ST AIDAN'S AVE

B1505

FEETHAM CT

GREAT LIME RD

M

B1505

A191

A19

70

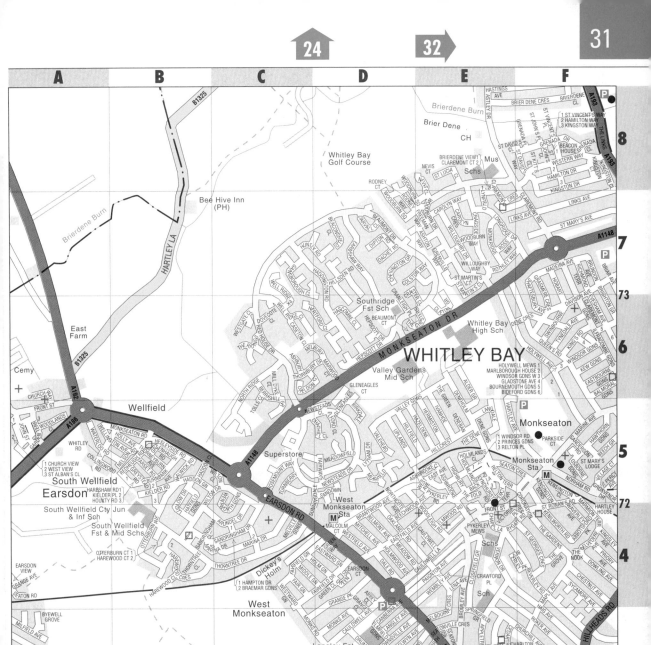

Grid reference letters (top): A B C D E F

Grid reference numbers (right): 8 73 7 6 5 72 4 71 3 2 1 70

Brierdene Burn
Brier Dene CH
Whitley Bay Golf Course
Bee Hive Inn (PH)
Brierdene Burn
HARTLEY LA
B1325
East Farm
Cemy
A1192
B1325
CHURCH FRONT ST
South Wellfield
Earsdon
Wellfield
Monkseaton Rd
A1186
WHITLEY BAY
Southridge Fst Sch
Whitley Bay High Sch
Valley Gardens Mid Sch
Monkseaton
Monkseaton Sta
Parkside
Superstore
Newsteads
West Monkseaton Sta
EARSDON RD
A1148
South Wellfield Cty Jun & Inf Sch
South Wellfield Fst & Mid Schs
Dickey's Holm
West Monkseaton
Byewell Grove
Milfield Ave
Park Gr
Horsley Cres
Glenvdale Ave
Matfen Ave
Ye Robin Hood Inn (PH)
Murton
North Farm
Moorlands
Langley Fst Sch
Woodlawn Sch
Murton Steads Farm
Star of the Sea RC Prim Sch
Monkseaton High Sch
Preston Gate
SEATONVILLE RD
SHIELDS RD
A191
HILL HEADS RD
Foxhunters Light Ind Site
Crawford PL
The Wheatsheaf Inn (PH)
New York
Rake House Farm
RAKE LA
North Tyneside General
H
Billy Mill LA
Blandford Rd
NEW YORK RD
New York Way
Norham Rd N
Greenlea
A192
A1148

Grid reference letters (bottom): A B C D E F

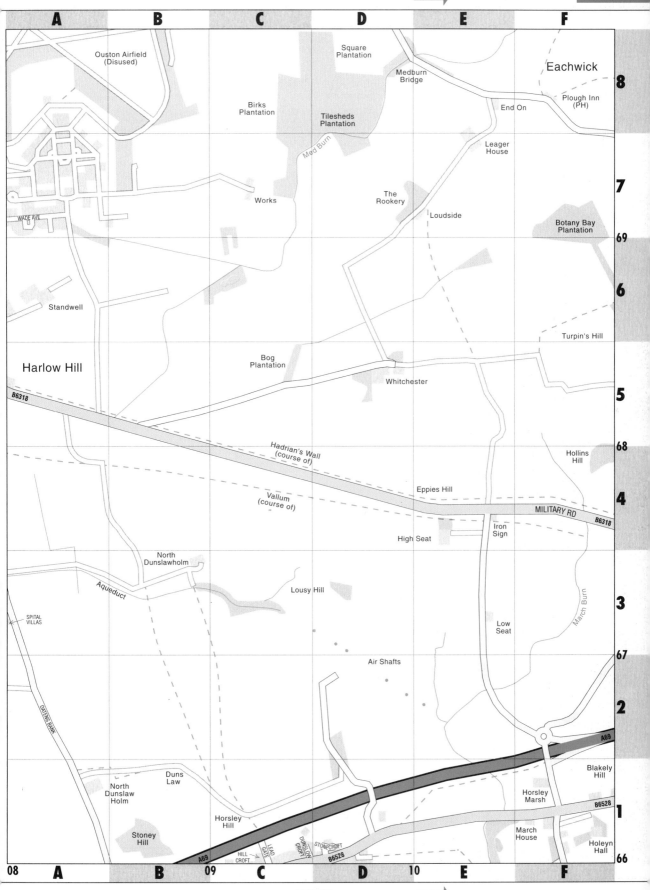

A B C D E F

Ouston Airfield
(Disused)

Square
Plantation

Medburn
Bridge

Eachwick

Plough Inn
(PH)

8

Birks
Plantation

Tilesheds
Plantation

End On

Med Burn

Leager
House

7

WADE AVE

Works

The
Rookery

Loudside

Botany Bay
Plantation

69

Standwell

6

Harlow Hill

Bog
Plantation

Whitchester

Turpin's Hill

B6318

Hollins
Hill

5

68

Hadrian's Wall
(course of)

Eppies Hill

MILITARY RD

B6318

4

Vallum
(course of)

High Seat

Iron
Sign

North
Dunslawholm

Aqueduct

Lousy Hill

Low
Seat

March Burn

3

SPITAL
VILLAS

67

Air Shafts

2

OATENS BANK

A69

North
Dunslaw
Holm

Duns
Law

Blakely
Hill

Horsley
Marsh

B6528

Horsley
Hill

March
House

1

Stoney
Hill

A69

HILL
CROFT

LEAD
GATE

DUNSLOW
CROFT

STONECROFT

B6528

Holeyn
Hall

66

08 A B 09 C D 10 E F

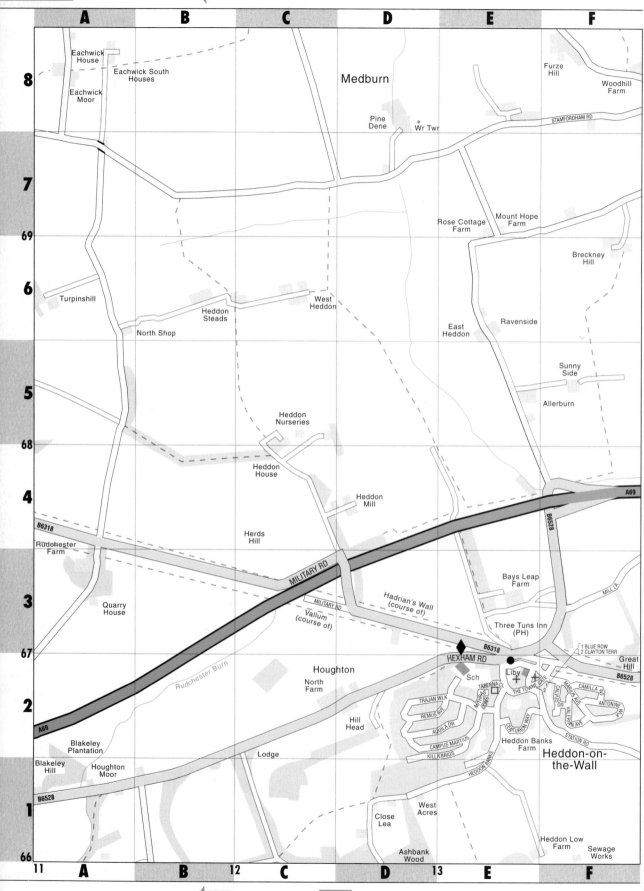

33

A **B** **C** **D** **E** **F**

8

Eachwick House

Eachwick South Houses

Medburn

Furze Hill

Woodhill Farm

Eachwick Moor

Pine Dene

Wr Twr

STAMFORDHAM RD

7

Rose Cottage Farm

Mount Hope Farm

69

Breckney Hill

6

Turpinshill

Heddon Steads

West Heddon

East Heddon

Ravenside

North Shop

Sunny Side

Allerburn

5

Heddon Nurseries

68

Heddon House

4

Heddon Mill

A69

B6318

B6528

Rudchester Farm

Herds Hill

MILITARY RD

Bays Leap Farm

MILL LA

3

Quarry House

MILITARY RD

Hadrian's Wall (course of)

Three Tuns Inn (PH)

Vallum (course of)

67

Rudchester Burn

HEXHAM RD

B6318

Great Hill

1 BLUE ROW
2 CLAYTON TERR

B6528

Houghton

North Farm

Sch

Liby

CAMILLA RD

ANTONINE

2

TRAJAN WLK

REMUS AVE

AQUILA DR

CAMPUS MARTIUS

KILLIEBRIGS

MITHRAS

TABERNA CL

THE TOWNE GATE

CENTURION WAY

MARIUS AVE

CALVUS DR

VALERIAN AVE

STATION RD

Heddon Banks Farm

Heddon-on-the-Wall

A69

Blakeley Plantation

Hill Head

Lodge

HEDDON BANKS

Blakeley Hill

Houghton Moor

West Acres

1

B6528

Close Lea

Ashbank Wood

Heddon Low Farm

Sewage Works

66

33 60

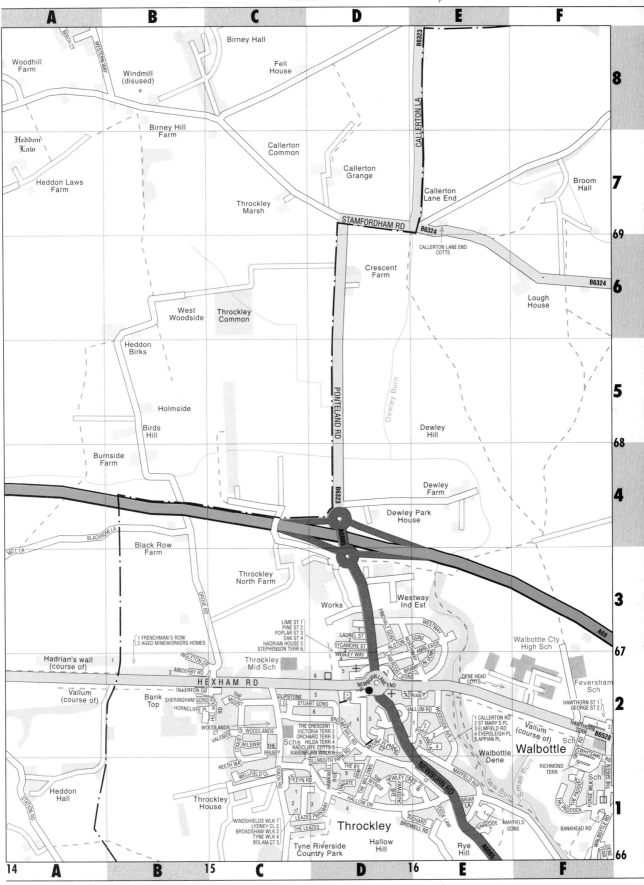

A B C D E F

8
7
69
6
5
68
4
3
67
2
1
66

Woodhill Farm
WESTERN WAY
BEECH CT
Windmill (disused)
Heddon Law
Heddon Laws Farm
Birney Hall
Fell House
Birney Hill Farm
Callerton Common
Callerton Grange
CALLERTON LA
B6323
Callerton Lane End
Broom Hall
Throckley Marsh
STAMFORDHAM RD
B6324
CALLERTON LANE END COTTS
B6324
West Woodside
Throckley Common
Crescent Farm
Lough House
Heddon Birks
Dewley Burn
Holmside
Dewley Hill
Birds Hill
PONTELAND RD
Burnside Farm
Dewley Farm
BLACKROW LA
WILL LA
Black Row Farm
B6323
Dewley Park House
DROVE RD
A6085
Throckley North Farm
Westway Ind Est
WESTWAY
A69
Works
LIME ST 1
PINE ST 2
POPLAR ST 3
OAK ST 4
HADRIAN HOUSE 5
STEPHENSON TERR 6
LAUREL ST
SYCAMORE ST
WESLEY WAY
FINCHALE GDNS
ALSTON GDNS
LANECROSS
AMBLESIDE
BRAMPTON GDNS
Walbottle Cty High Sch
Feversham Sch
Hadrian's wall (course of)
INGLETON DR
AINDERBY RD
Throckley Mid Sch
NEWBURN LANE END
P
HADRIAN
DENE HEAD COTTS
HAWTHORN ST 1
GEORGE ST 2
HAWTHORN TERR
B6528
1 FRENCHMAN'S ROW
2 AGED MINEWORKERS HOMES
HEXHAM RD
OLLERTON DR
STATION RD
Vallum (course of)
Bank Top
SHERINGHAM GDNS
HORNCLIFFE PL
THE MOUNT
HILL HOUSE RD
CLIPSTONE CL
STUART GDNS
BROOMHILL RD
VALLUM RD
WOODSIDE AVE
PORTLAND RD
1 CALLERTON RD
2 ST MARY'S PL
3 ELMFIELD RD
4 EVERSLEIGH PL
5 APPIAN PL
Valium (course of)
Walbottle
WOODLANDS CT
VALESIDE
COOLEY GR
WOODLANDS
WILSWAY
THE BRIARY
THE CRESCENT 1
VICTORIA TERR 2
ORCHARD TERR 3
HILDA TERR 4
RADCLIFFE COTTS 5
RAVENBURN WALK 6
Schs
MAUN PLEASANT
NEWBURN RD
MAYFIELD AVE
New Burn
Small Burn
Walbottle Dene
GROVE RD
WHITEHALL RD
Richmond Terr
THE PADDOCK
REETH WA
WELLFIELD CL
COACH RD
LEYN RD
HAWKWELL RISE
LYNGATE
THE WILLOWS
THE WYND
HEWLEY CRES
THE BY
THE CAUSEWAY
BRIAR LA
FOSSE LAW
KIRKSIDE
MAYFIELD GDNS
FORGE WLK
THE GREEN
WALBOTTLE RD
DENE RD
Heddon Hall
Throckley House
WINDSHIELDS WLK 1
LYDNEY CL 2
BROADSHAW WLK 3
TYNE WLK 4
BOLAM CT 5
LEAZES PKWAY
HALLOW DR
THE LEAZES
Throckley
RICHARD BROWELL RD
Hallow Hill
Rye Hill
BANKHEAD RD
THE PADDOCK
Sch
A6085
Tyne Riverside Country Park

14 A B 15 C D 16 E F

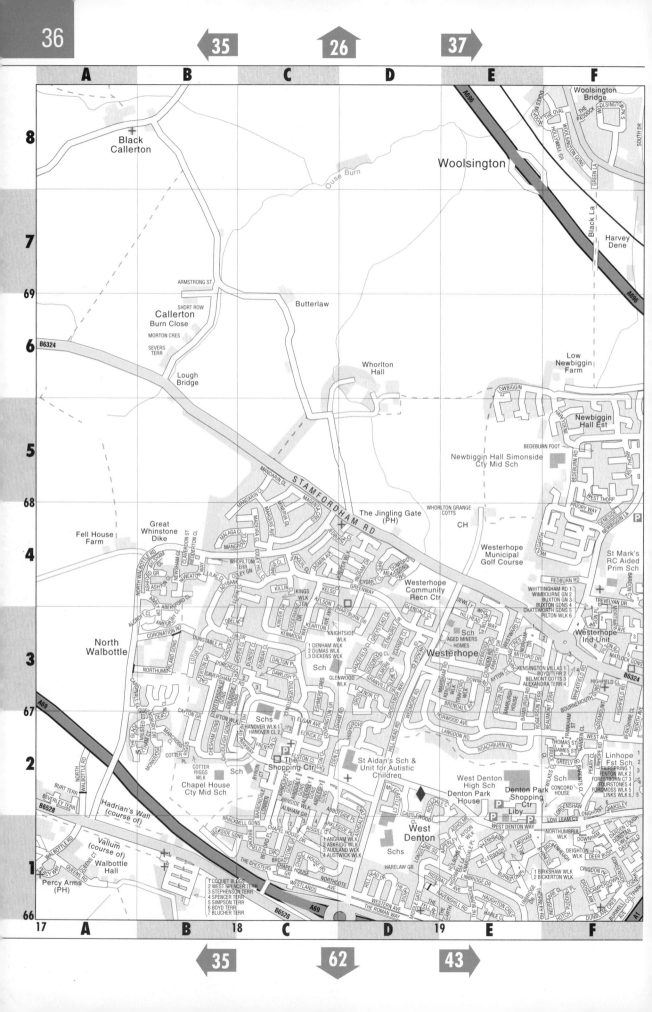

8 Black Callerton
Woolsington
Woolsington Bridge
THE OVAL
THE PADDOCK
WOOLSINGTON PK S.
WOOLSINGTON GDNS
HOLLYWELL LA
SOUTH DR
WOOLSINGTON DR
THE
Ouse Burn

7 Black La
Harvey Dene
A696

69 ARMSTRONG ST
SHORT ROW
Callerton
Burn Close
Butterlaw
Low Newbiggin Farm
MORTON CRES

6 B6324
SEVERS TERR
Lough Bridge
Whorlton Hall
HARECROFT
Newbiggin Hall Est
NEWBIGGIN
BEDEBURN FOOT
BEDEBURN RD
WEST THORP
BEDE BURN
WEST THORP

5 STAMFORDHAM RD
Newbiggin Hall Simonside Cty Mid Sch
PRIORY WAY
DENESIDE
NEWBIGGIN LA
P

68 MANDARIN CL
MANDARIN L
MAGENTA CRES
WHORLTON GRANGE COTTS
CH
Westerhope Municipal Golf Course
St Mark's RC Aided Prim Sch

4 Fell House Farm
Great Whinstone Dike
The Jingling Gate (PH)
MINERVA AVE
MADEIRA CL
MARQUIS CL
CLAVERDON ST
NEWSHAM CL
MEDBERTON CL
WHORLTON TERR
LILAC CL
COLEY GN
MALAGA CL
MANGROVE
JASMIN AVE
JEDBURG
MOTHER WLK
INGRAM DR
CLINFORD CL
MEADOWS
REDBURN RD
WHITTINGHAM RD 1
WIMBOURNE GN 2
BUXTON GN 3
BUXTON GDNS 4
CHATSWORTH GDNS 5
PILTON WLK 6
TREVELYAN DR
ASHTON GR
ASHFORD GR
NORTH WALBOTTLE RD
AYSHAM
LIYBANK
GREENWAY
CYGNET CL
Westerhope Community Recn Ctr
DEWLEY
HILLHEAD WAY
WHOL
HILLHEAD

3 North Walbottle
ABERCROMBY
ABBEY DR
AMESFORD
KILLIN
KINGS WLK
KELSO
KELSON TERR
KELSON
HARTBURN DR
Westerhope
GRACEFIELD CL
Sch
Aged Miners Homes
KENSINGTON VILLAS 1
BOYD TERR 2
BELMONT COTTS 3
ALEXANDRA TERR 4
B6324
HIGHFIELD
MATLOCK GDNS
Westerhope Ind Unit
ALCROFT CL
CORONATION RD
DUNSTABLE PL
LOTUS CL
KINVER DR
KIDDERMINSTER
RELIA
KNIGHTSIDE WLK
GRESTEAD CL
GLENWOOD WLK
GARNER CL
GLENDALE CL
DEWLEY
MARSHALL CT
DILSTON DR
BAMBURGH
BAMBURGH CL
ROGERSON TERR
BEAUMONT TERR
BOURNEMOUTH GDNS
HIGHFIELD RD
1 DENHAM WLK
2 DUMAS WLK
3 DICKENS WLK
NORTHUMBERLAND GDNS
NORTHUMB
CADOGAN
DORCHES
CAVERSHAM
DUNBAR
DALTON PL
DAWLISH PL
Sch
GRANVILLE DR
DOWNEND
AYTON CL
KENDAL CL
TRAFFORD CL
WEDMORE RD
HILL HEAD RD
NORWOOD AVE
LANGDON RD
MITFORD DR
WESTWOOD CT
CASEMOUNT CT
BERKSHIRE CT
NORTH AVE
MATLOCK GDNS

2 CAYTON GR
CHEDWORTH GDNS
CHILDCLEIGH GDNS
COLDISS
CLIFTON PL
ELGAR AVE
ELRICK CL
FRENCH CL
EDDINGTON GR
ESHMERE CRES
GREE
GLENWOOD WLK
ENOR CT
GROSS
Sch
BRENDALE CL
DAISY CL
ROACHBURN RD
BRUCE
THOMAS ST
JAMES ST
GREELY RD
WEST AVE
PEARY CL
WILKES CL
SCH
CONCORD HOUSE
Linhope Fst Sch
FAIRSPRING 1
FENTON WLK 2
FORRESTDON WLK 3
FOURSTONES 4
FORDMOSS WLK 5
LINKS WLK 6
THE GLADE
MILSTED CL
QUO
DEANS
MARCROSS
MONKRIDGE
COTTER RIGGS
CAROMELL CL
COTTER RIGGS PL
COTTER RIGGS WLK
BYRON
ESHELBY
ELSTON CL
P
The Shopping Ctr
St Aidan's Sch & Unit for Autistic Children
MILLESTONE
West Denton High Sch
Denton Park House
West Denton Shopping Ctr
P
P
Liby
P
LOW LEAM CT
WEST DENTON WAY
NORTHUMBRIA
DOWNHAM
CRENSHAW PL
LONGHIRST
BARKSLEY
CONSTANTINE

1 Percy Arms (PH)
WALBOTTLE RD
QUEENS CT
PERCY WAY
BURT TERR
REVERLEY TERR
NORTH WALBOTTLE RD
B6528
Hadrian's Wall (course of)
Vallum (course of)
Walbottle Hall
BRACKNELL GDNS
BECKSIDE GDNS
Chapel House Cty Mid Sch
BARROWBURN
BROOKFIELD GR
BEDFORD PL
Sch
ALNHAM GR
ABBOTSIDE PL
ARKLESIDE PL
AISGILL
Sch
1 ANGRAM WLK
2 ASKRIGG WLK
3 AUDLAND WLK
4 AUSTWICK WLK
CHAPEL HOUSE DR
THE CHESTERS
CHAPEL HOUSE RD
NORTHCOTE AVE
BROAD
West Denton
HARELAW GR
LONE SQ
Schs
MILECASTLE
CASTLEWOOD CL
RIDSDALE CL
ASHOLME
APERLEY
AYDON
HOLBURN
KNARESDALE PL
KIRKHEADS
ALLERWASH
BELSAY
AIGHAM
LINBRIDGE DR
BURNSTONES
DEIGHTON WLK
DEER BUSH
DARDEN LOUGH
DUNSTAN
DAYSHIELD
1 BIRKSHAW WLK
2 BICKERTON WLK
CRIGDON WLK
CAMPERDOWN
CROSSWAY
CONSTANCE
HOTCH
PUDDING
DUNBAR
AVE
COTTERAM

66 1 COQUET BLDGS
2 WEST SPENCER TERR
3 STEPHENSON TERR
4 SPENCER TERR
5 SIMPSON TERR
6 BOYD TERR
7 BLUCHER TERR
WESTLANDS
THE CHESTERS
B6528
A69
WESTERN AVE
THE ROMAN WAY
MIDDLE GATE
HILL TOP
THE GARTH
THE FELL
RAVENSHILL RD
HAUGHTON CRES
HARLE CL
THE BURNSIDE
LINDISFARNE

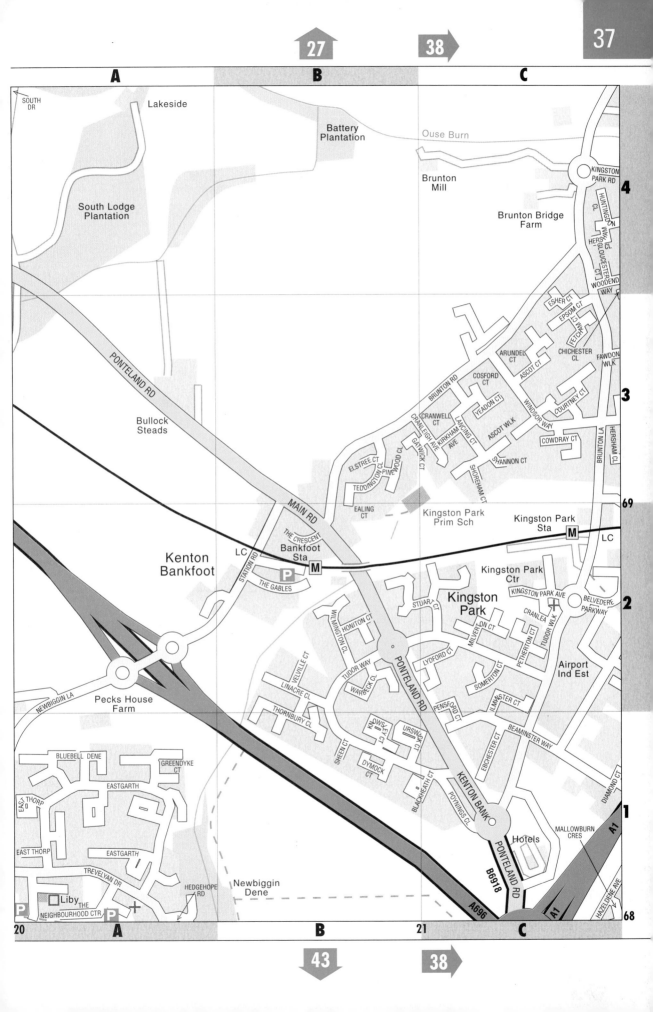

A
B
C

SOUTH DR
Lakeside
Battery Plantation
Ouse Burn
Brunton Mill
4
KINGSTON PARK RD
South Lodge Plantation
Brunton Bridge Farm
HUNTINGTON CL
HERSHAM CL
GLOUCESTER CT
WOODEND WAY
ESHER CT
EPSOM CT
CHETCH CT
PONTELAND RD
ARUNDEL CT
ASCOT CT
CHICHESTER CL
FAWDON WLK
Bullock Steads
BRUNTON RD
COSFORD CT
COURTNEY CT
3
CRANWELL CT
YEADON CT
WINDSOR WAY
CRANLEIGH AVE
KIRKHAM AVE
LANCING CT
ASCOT WLK
COWDRAY CT
BRUNTON LA
HERSHAM CL
ELSTREE CT
PINEWOOD CL
GATWICK CT
SHOREHAM CT
SHANNON CT
TEDDINGTON CL
MAIN RD
EALING CT
69
Kingston Park Prim Sch
Kingston Park Sta
THE CRESCENT
M
LC
Kenton Bankfoot
STATION RD
LC
Bankfoot Sta
M
Kingston Park Ctr
KINGSTON PARK AVE
BELVEDERE PARKWAY
2
THE GABLES
Kingston Park
CRANLEA
TUDOR WLK
WILMINGTON CL
HONITON CT
STUART CT
MILVERTON CT
PETHERTON CT
Airport Ind Est
NEWBIGGIN LA
Pecks House Farm
VELVILLE CT
TUDOR WAY
PONTELAND RD
LYDFORD CT
SOMERTON CT
ILMINSTER CT
LINACRE CL
WARBECK CL
PENSFORD CT
BEAMINSTER WAY
THORNBURY CL
SHEEN CT
KNOWS LEY CT
URSWICK CT
DYMOCK CT
EBCHESTER CT
BLUEBELL DENE
GREENDYKE CT
EASTGARTH
BLACKHEATH CT
KENTON BANK
DIAMOND CT
EAST THORP
POYNINGS CL
1
A1
EAST THORP
EASTGARTH
Hotels
MALLOWBURN CRES
TREVELYAN DR
HEDGEHOPE RD
Newbiggin Dene
PONTELAND RD
P
Liby
THE NEIGHBOURHOOD CTR
P
B6918
A696
A1
HAZELDENE AVE
68

20
A
B
21
C

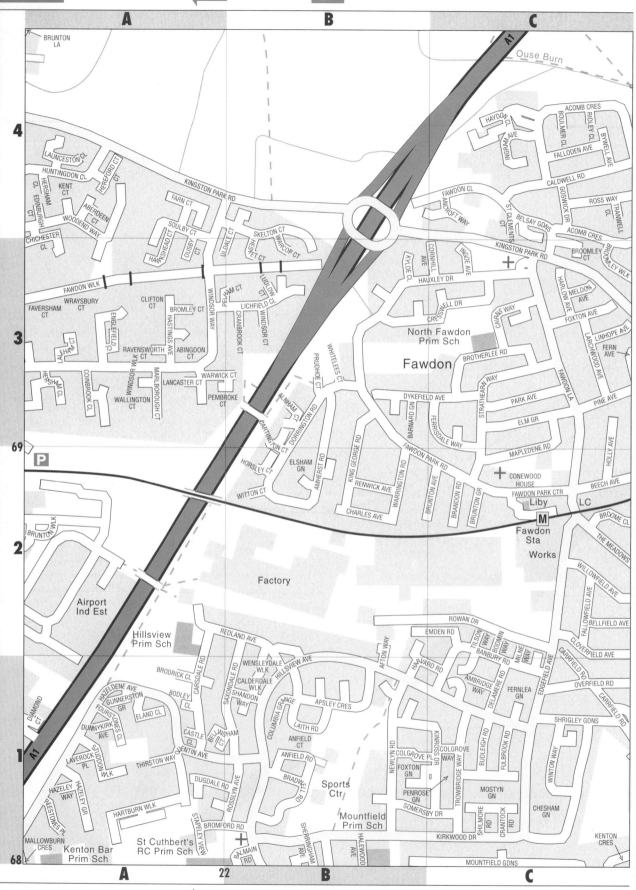

A B C

4

3

69

P

2

1

68

BRUNTON LA

A1

Ouse Burn

LAUNCESTON CL
HUNTINGDON CL
HERSHAM CL
EDINBURGH CT
CHICHESTER CL
KENT CT
HEREFORD CT
ABERDEEN CT
WOODEND WAY
FARN CT
SOULBY CT
HAWKSHEAD CT
OUSBY CT
HESKET CT
SKELTON CT
WARCOP CT
KINGSTON PARK RD

FAWDON WLK
FAVERSHAM CT
WRAYSBURY CT
ENGLEFIELD RD
CLIFTON CT
BROMLEY CT
HASTINGS AVE
WINDSOR WAY
PELHAM CT
CRANBROOK CT
WINDSOR CT
LICHFIELD CL
LUDLOW
LALEHAM CT
RAVENSWORTH CT
ABINGDON CT
HERSM CL
COINBROOK CL
WINDSOR RD
MARLBOROUGH CT
LANCASTER CT
WALLINGTON CT
PEMBROKE CT
WARWICK CT

HORSLEY CT
WITTON CT
CARTINGTON CT
ALNHAM CT
DORRINGTON RD
PRUDHOE CT
WHITELEES CT
ELSHAM GN
AMHERST RD
KING GEORGE RD
RENWICK AVE
WARRINGTON RD
CHARLES AVE

BRUNTON WLK
Airport Ind Est
Hillsview Prim Sch

DIAMOND CT
A1

Factory

HAZELDENE AVE
GUNNERSTON GR
FOURSTONES CL
DUNNYKIRK AVE
ELAND CL
LAVEROCK PL
STUDDON WLK
HAZELEY WAY
HAZELEY GR
REDSTONES PL
MALLOWBURN CRES
Kenton Bar Prim Sch
HARTBURN WLK

BRODRICK CL
CARSDALE RD
REDLAND AVE
SAXONDALE RD
WENSLEYDALE WLK
CALDERDALE WLK
HILLSVIEW AVE
SHANDON WAY
BODLEY CL
BELL CL
WIGHAM CT
CASTLE CL
QUENTIN AVE
THIRSTON WAY
DUGDALE RD
COLUMBIA GRANGE
LAITH RD
APSLEY CRES
ANFIELD CT
ANFIELD RD
BRADWELL RD
ROSSLYN AVE
STAPELEY VIEW
BROMFORD RD
BALMAIN RD
St Cuthbert's RC Prim Sch
SHERINGHAM AVE

AFTON WAY
HARVARD RD
ROWAN DR
EMDEN RD
NEWLYN RD
COLGROVE PL
COLGROVE WAY
FOXTON GN
PENROSE GN
KINROSS DR
SOMERSBY DR
TROWBRIDGE WAY
KIRKWOOD DR
Sports Ctr
Mountfield Prim Sch
HALEWOOD AVE
MOUNTFIELD GDNS
KENTON CRES

North Fawdon Prim Sch
Fawdon

HAYDON CL
INGRAM AVE
ACOMB CRES
BOULMER CL
RIDLEY CL
BYWELL AVE
FALLODEN AVE
CALDWELL RD
GOSWICK DR
ROSS WAY
TRANWELL CL
BELSAY GDNS
ST CLEMENTS CT
ACOMB CRES
BROOMLEY CT
BROOMLEY WLK
KINGSTON PARK RD
FAWDON CL
ANCROFT WAY
KYLOE CL
CORNHILL AVE
HAUXLEY DR
INGOE AVE
CRESSWELL DR
CAIRNS WAY
HARLOW AVE
MELDON AVE
FOXTON AVE
LINHOPE AVE
FERN AVE
LARCHWOOD AVE
BROTHERLEE RD
DYKEFIELD AVE
STRATHEARN WAY
PARK AVE
FAWDON LA
PINE AVE
BARNARD GN
FERRISDALE WAY
ELM GR
MAPLEDENE RD
HOLLY AVE
BRUNTON AVE
BRANDON RD
BRUNTON GR
CONEWOOD HOUSE
FAWDON PARK CTR
Liby
LC
BEECH AVE
M
Fawdon Sta
Works
BROOME CL
THE MEADOWS
WILLOWFIELD AVE
FALLOWFIELD AVE
BELLFIELD AVE
CLOVERFIELD AVE
CARRFIELD RD
OVERFIELD RD
EDGEFIELD AVE
CARRFIELD RD
SHRIGLEY GDNS
TILSON WAY
BODMIN WAY
MILNE WAY
BANBURY RD
AMBRIDGE WAY
DELAMERE RD
FERNLEA GN
BUDLEIGH RD
FULBROOK RD
WINTON WAY
MOSTYN GN
SHILMORE RD
CRANTOCK RD
CHESHAM GN

A 22 B C

37

44

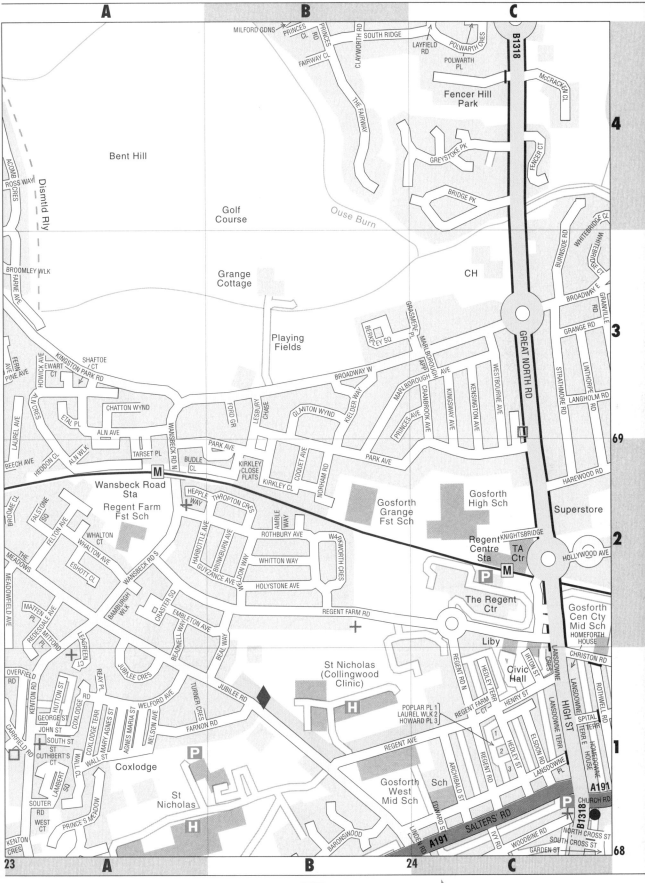

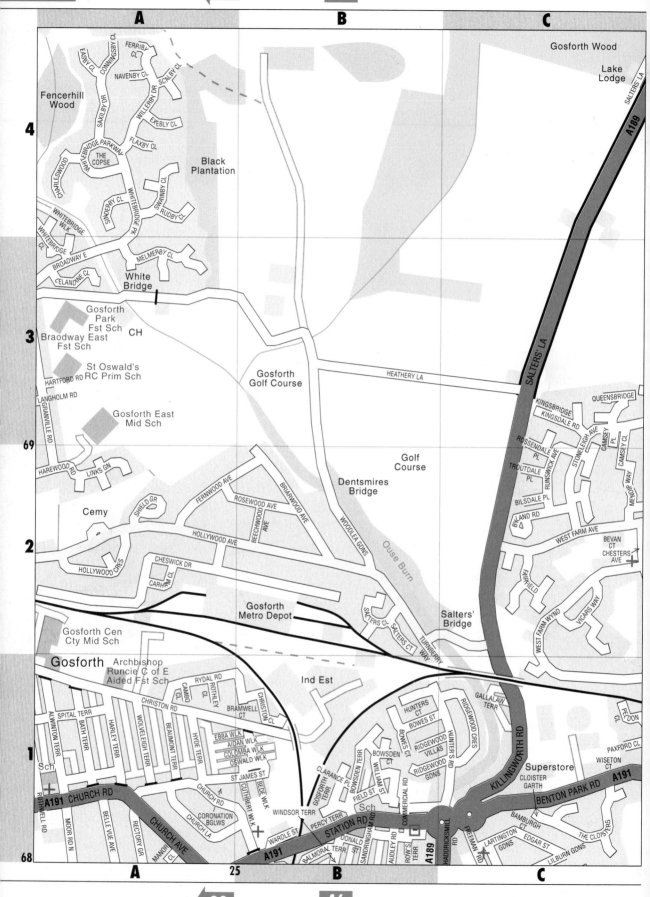

Gosforth Wood

Lake Lodge

Fencerhill Wood

EASBY CL
CONNINGSBY CL
FERRIBY CL
NAVENBY CL
WILLERBY DR
SCALBY CL
SAXILBY DR
EXEBLY CL
WHITEBRIDGE PARKWAY
FLAXBY CL
THE COPSE
CHARLESWOOD
SINDERBY CL
WHITEBRIDGE PK
SWANBY CL
RUDBY CL
WHITEBRIDGE WLK
WHITEBRIDGE CL
BROADWAY E
MELMERBY CL
CELANDINE CL

Black Plantation

White Bridge

Gosforth Park Fst Sch
CH
Braodway East Fst Sch

HARTFORD RD
LANGHOLM RD
GRANVILLE RD
HAREWOOD RD
LINKS GN

St Oswald's RC Prim Sch

Gosforth East Mid Sch

Cemy

SHIELD GR
FERNWOOD AVE
ROSEWOOD AVE
BRIARWOOD AVE
BEECHWOOD AVE
WOODLEA GDNS
HOLLYWOOD AVE
HOLLYWOOD CRES
CHESWICK DR
CARHM CL

Gosforth Golf Course

HEATHERY LA

Gosforth Metro Depot

Golf Course

Dentsmires Bridge

Ouse Burn

SALTERS CL
SALTERS CT
TURNBERRY WAY

Salters' Bridge

SALTERS LA

A189

KINGSBRIDGE
QUEENSBRIDGE
KINGSDALE RD
ROSSENDALE PL
RUNSWICK AVE
STONELEIGH AVE
CAMSEY PL
CAMSEY CL
TROUTDALE PL
BILSDALE PL
MENDIP WAY
BYLAND RD
WEST FARM AVE
BEVAN CT
CHESTERS AVE
FAIRFIELD
WEST FARM WYND
VICARS WAY

Gosforth Cen Cty Mid Sch

Gosforth
Archbishop Runcie C of E Aided Fst Sch

Ind Est

ALNWINTON TERR
SPITAL TERR
BATH TERR
HARLEY TERR
WOLVELEIGH TERR
BEAUMONT TERR
HYDE TERR
CHRISTON RD
CAMBO CL
RYDAL RD
ROTHLEY CL
BRAMWELL CT
CHRISTON CL
EBBA WLK
AIDAN WLK
COLOMBA WLK
OSWALD WLK
ST JAMES ST
CHURCH RD
CUTHBERT WLK
BEDE WLK
WINDSOR TERR
CLARANCE PL
GOSFORTH TERR
BOWSDEN TERR
PERCY TERR
FIELD ST
WILLIAM ST
BOWSDEN CT
BOWES ST
HUNTERS CT
BOWES ST
RIDGEWOOD VILLAS
HUNTERS RD
RIDGEWOOD GDNS
RIDGEWOOD CRES
GALLALAW TERR
KILLINGWORTH RD

Superstore

CLOISTER GARTH
BENTON PARK RD
A191

PELDON CL
PAXFORD CL
WISETON CT
BAMBURGH CT
EDGAR ST
LARTINGTON GDNS
THE CLOISTERS
LILBURN GDNS

Sch

A191
CHURCH RD
ROTHWELL RD
MOOR RD N
BELLE VUE AVE
RECTORY GR
MANOR CL
CHURCH AVE
CORONATION BGLWS
CHURCH LA
WARDLE ST
A191
BALMORAL TERR
STATION RD
DONALD ST
SANDRINGHAM RD
AUDLEY RD
ROWS TERR
COMMERCIAL RD
A189
HADDRICKSMILL
FREEMAN RD

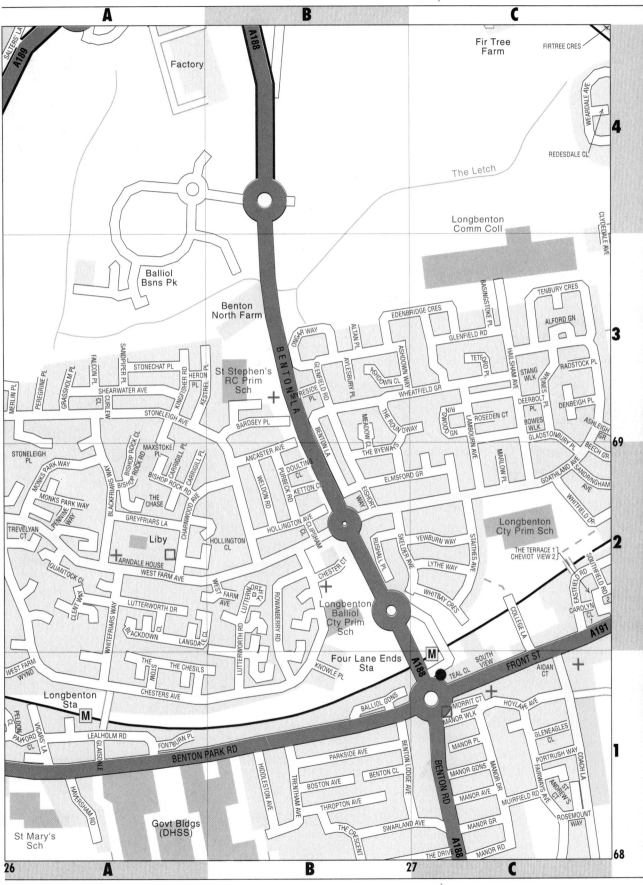

A   B   C

Fir Tree Farm

FIRTREE CRES

WEARDALE AVE

4

REDESDALE CL

The Letch

Longbenton Comm Coll

CLYDEDALE AVE

A189

SALTERS' LA

A188

Factory

Balliol Bsns Pk

Benton North Farm

TENBURY CRES

ALFORD GN

BASINGSTOKE PL

Edenbridge Cres

Glenfield Rd

3

ONGAR WAY

ALTAN PL

AYLESBURY PL

ASHDOWN WAY

HAILSHAM AVE

STANG WLK

RADSTOCK PL

MERLIN PL

PEREGRINE PL

GRASSHOLM PL

FALCON PL

SANDPIPER PL

STONECHAT PL

SHEARWATER AVE

CURLEW

KINGFISHER RD

HERON PL

KESTREL PL

St Stephen's RC Prim Sch

MYRESIDE PL

GLENFIELD RD

WHEATFIELD GR

MEADOW CL

THE BYEWAYS

TETFORD PL

DONKIN RD

JONES WLK

DEERBOLT PL

RIN GDN

BOWES WLK

GLADSTONBURY PL

DENBEIGH PL

ASHLEIGH GR

BEECH GR

STONELEIGH AVE

BARDSEY PL

ANCASTER AVE

WELDON RD

PURBECK RD

DOULTING CL

KETTON CL

THE ROUNDWAY

ROSEDEN CT

LAMBOURN AVE

69

STONELEIGH PL

MONKS PARK WAY

MONKS PARK WAY

PENNINE WAY

BLACKFRIARS WAY

BISHOP ROCK CL

BISHOP ROCK RD

BISHOP ROCK RD

CARRIGILL PL

CARRIGILL PL

CHARNWOOD AVE

THE CHASE

GREYFRIARS LA

HOLLINGTON CL

Liby

ARNDALE HOUSE

HOLLINGTON AVE

CLIPSHAM CL

CHESTER CT

ELMSFORD GR

EISHORT WAY

RUSHALL PL

SKELDER AVE

YEWBURN WAY

MARLOW PL

GOATHLAND AVE

SANDRINGHAM AVE

WHITFIELD DR

Longbenton Cty Prim Sch

2

TREVELYAN CT

QUANTOCK CL

CLEVE WAY

WHITEFRIARS WAY

WEST FARM AVE

WEST FARM AVE

LUTTERWORTH DR

LUTTERWORTH RD

LUTTERWORTH CL

ROWANBERRY RD

Longbenton Balliol Cty Prim Sch

LYTHE WAY

STAITHES AVE

THE TERRACE 1
CHEVIOT VIEW 2

EASTFIELD RD

SOUTHFIELD RD

CAROLYN CL

A191

BLACKDOWN

LANGDALE CL

THE STOW

THE CHESILS

CHESTERS AVE

KNOWLE PL

Four Lane Ends Sta

WHITBAY CRES

M

TEAL CL

SOUTH VIEW

FRONT ST

AIDAN CT

COLLEGE LA

Longbenton Sta

M

WEST FARM WYND

PEFTON CL

PAXFORD CL

VICARS LA

GLAISDALE

LEALHOLM RD

FONTBURN PL

BENTON PARK RD

HAVERSHAM RD

St Mary's Sch

Govt Bldgs (DHSS)

HIDDLESTON AVE

TRENTHAM AVE

PARKSIDE AVE

BOSTON AVE

BENTON CL

THROPTON AVE

THE CRESCENT

SWARLAND AVE

BENTON LODGE AVE

BALLIOL GDNS

MANOR WLK

MORRIT CT

MANOR PL

MANOR GDNS

MANOR AVE

MANOR DR

MANOR GR

MANOR RD

BENTON RD

A188

HOYLAKE AVE

GLENEAGLES CL

PORTRUSH WAY

FAIRWAYS AVE

MUIRFIELD AVE

ST ANDREW'S CT

COACH LA

ROSEMOUNT WAY

1

68

A188

THE DRIVE

A188

BENTON LA

BENTON LA

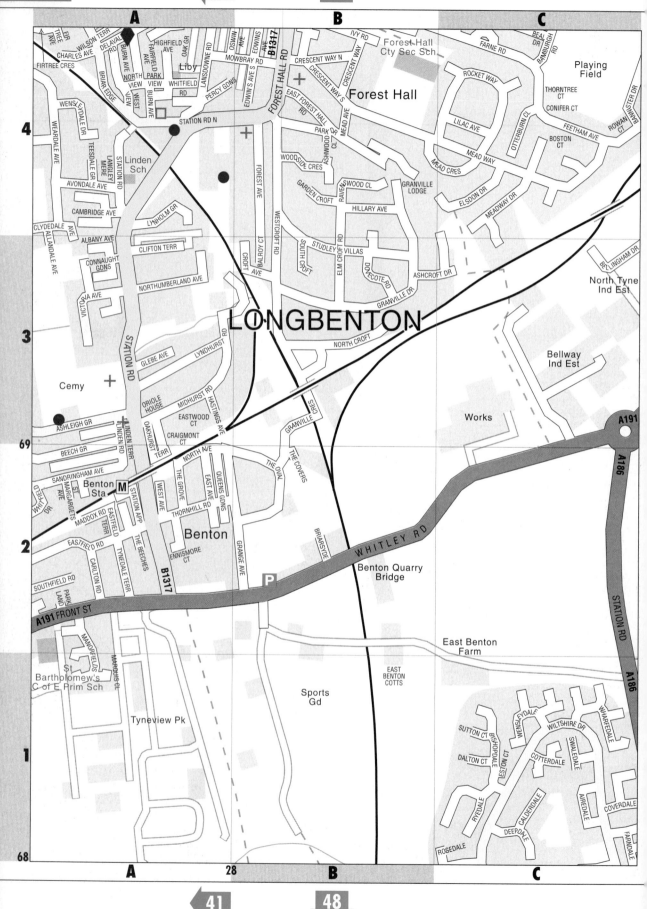

A   B   C

EIR TREE AVE
WILSON TERR
CHARLES AVE
DELAVAL RD
BURN AVE
FIRTREE CRES
HIGHFIELD AVE
FAIRFIELD AVE
OAK GR
LANSDOWNE RD
MOWBRAY RD
OSWIN AVE
EDWINS AVE
B1317
CRESCENT WAY N
IVY RD
FARNE RD
BEAL DR
BAMBURGH RD
Playing Field

Liby
NORTH VIEW
BURN AVE
WEST VIEW
WHITFIELD RD
PERCY GDNS
EDWIN'S AVE S
FOREST HALL RD
EAST FOREST HALL RD
CRESCENT WAY S
CRESCENT WAY
Forest Hall Cty Sec Sch
Forest Hall
ROCKET WAY
THORNTREE CT
CONIFER CT
ROWAN CT
BANNISTER DR

4

WENSLEYDALE DR
WEARDALE AVE
TEESDALE GR
BRIAR EDGE
LANGLEY MERE
Linden Sch
STATION RD N
FOREST AVE
PARK DR
ASHWOOD CL
MEAD AVE
LILAC AVE
MEAD WAY
MEAD CRES
GRANVILLE LODGE
ELSDON DR
MEADWAY DR
OTTERBURN CL
BOSTON CT
FEETHAM AVE

AVONDALE AVE
CAMBRIDGE AVE
LYNHOLM GR
STATION RD
WOODSIDE CRES
GARDEN CROFT
RAVENSWOOD CL
HILLARY AVE
GRANVILLE DR

CLYDEDALE AVE
ALLANDALE AVE
ALBANY AVE
CONNAUGHT GDNS
CLIFTON TERR
NORTHUMBERLAND AVE
VICTORIA AVE
BALROY CT
CROFT AVE
WESTCROFT RD
SOUTH CROFT
STUDLEY VILLAS
ELM CROFT RD
DOVECOTE RD
ASHCROFT DR
NORTH TYNE Ind Est
BELLINGHAM DR

3

Cemy
GLEBE AVE
ORIOLE HOUSE
LYNDHURST
MIDHURST RD
HASTINGS AVE
NORTH CROFT
Bellway Ind Est
A191

ASHLEIGH GR
BEECH GR
SANDRINGHAM AVE
EASTWOOD CT
CRAIGMONT CT
OAKHURST TERR
NORTH AVE
Works
A186

69

LINDEN TERR
LINDEN RD
THE GROVE
EAST AVE
QUEENS GDNS
THE OVAL
GRANVILLE
THE COVERS
GRANVILLE RD

WHITFIELD DR
ST MARGARET'S AVE
MADDOX RD
EASTFIELD TERR
STATION APP
WEST AVE
THORNHILL RD
Benton Sta M
BRIARSYDE
WHITLEY RD

2

SOUTHFIELD RD
PARK LANE
CARLTON RD
THE BEECHES
TYNEDALE TERR
EASTFIELD RD
ENNISMORE CT
Benton
GRANGE AVE
B1317
P
Benton Quarry Bridge
STATION RD
A186

A191 FRONT ST
MANORFIELDS
MARQUIS CT
East Benton Farm

St Bartholomew's C of E Prim Sch
Tyneview Pk
Sports Gd
EAST BENTON COTTS
SUTTON CT
BISHOPDALE CT
WENSLEYDALE CT
WILTSHIRE DR
WHARFEDALE
DALTON CT
ELSTON CT
COTTERDALE
SWALEDALE

1

ROSEDALE
RYEDALE
DEEPONE
CALDERDALE
AIREDALE
COVERDALE
FARNDALE

68

LONGBENTON

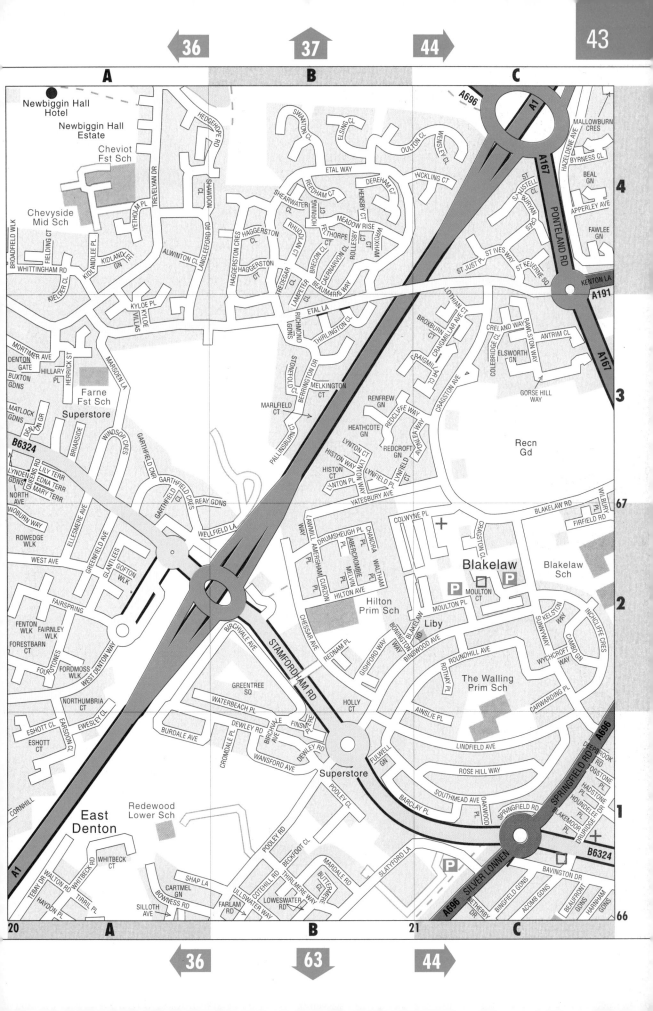

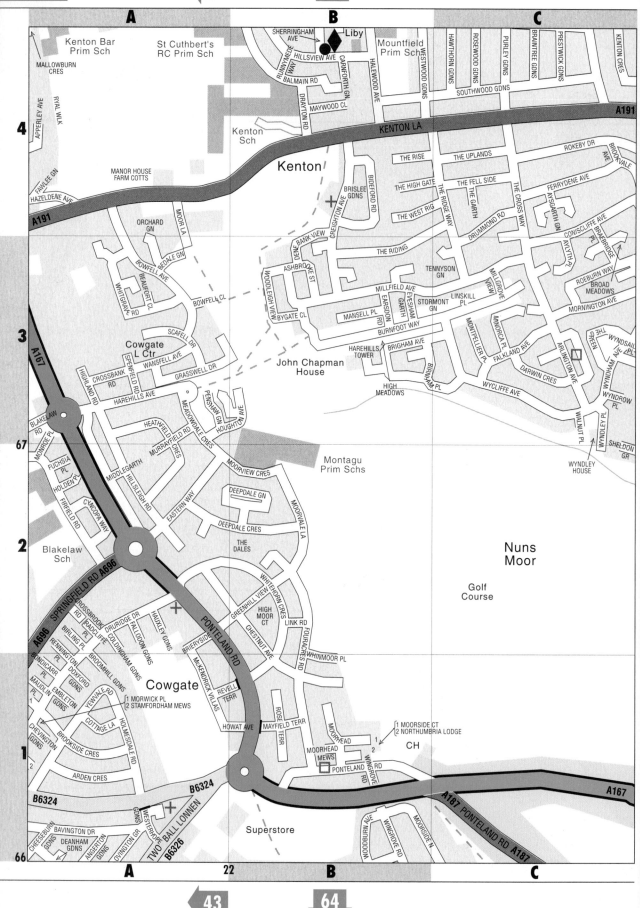

Kenton Bar
Prim Sch

St Cuthbert's
RC Prim Sch

Liby

Mountfield
Prim Schs

MALLOWBURN
CRES

SHERRINGHAM
AVE

HILLSVIEW AVE

CARNFORTH GN

HALEWOOD AVE

WESTWOOD GDNS

HAWTHORN GDNS

ROSEWOOD GDNS

PURLEY GDNS

BRAINTREE GDNS

PRESTWICK GDNS

KENTON CRES

APPERLEY AVE

RYAL WLK

FAWLEE GN

HAZELDENE AVE

RUNNYMEDE TWAY

BALMAIN RD

DRAYTON RD

MAYWOOD CL

SOUTHWOOD GDNS

4

A191

KENTON LA

A191

Kenton
Sch

Kenton

MANOR HOUSE
FARM COTTS

ORCHARD
GN

MOOR LA

BEDALE GN

BOWFELL AVE

BEAUFORT CL

WHITDRAKE
RD

BOWFELL CL

SCAFELL DR

WANSFELL AVE

GRASSWELL DR

WOODLEIGH VIEW

DENE BANK VIEW

ASHBROOKE ST

BYGATE CL

CREIGHTON AVE

BRISLEE
GDNS

BIDEFORD RD

MANSELL PL

EARSDON
GARTH

MILLFIELD AVE

EVESHAM
GARTH

BURNFOOT WAY

THE RISE

THE HIGH GATE

THE WEST RIG

THE RIDING

THE UPLANDS

THE FELL SIDE

THE RIDGE WAY

THE GARTH

DRUMMOND RD

STORMONT
GN

TENNYSON
GN

LINSKILL
PL

THE CROSS WAY

MILLGROVE VIEW

ROKEBY DR

FERRYDENE AVE

AYSGARTH GN

CONISCLIFFE AVE

ALYTH PL

BRAEBRIDGE
PL

ROEBURN WAY

MORNINGTON AVE

BROAD
MEADOWS

BROOKVALE
AVE

Cowgate
L Ctr

CROSSBANK
RD

HIGHLAND RD

SPENFIELD RD

HAREHILLS AVE

PENSHAW GN

HOUGHTON AVE

John Chapman
House

HAREHILLS
TOWER

BRIGHAM AVE

HIGH
MEADOWS

BIRNHAM
PL

MONTPELLIER PL

AMORCA PL

FALKLAND AVE

DARWIN CRES

WYCLIFFE AVE

ARLINGTON AVE

THE
GREEN

WYNDSAIL
PL

WYNDHAM AVE

WYNDROW
PL

WALNUT PL

WYNLEY PL

SHELDON
GR

3

A167

BLAKELAW
RD

MONROE PL

FUCHSIA
PL

HOLDEN PL

CYNCOPA WAY

FIRFIELD RD

MIDDLEGARTH

HILLSLEIGH RD

HEATHFIELD GARTH

MURRAYFIELD RD

MEADOWDALE CRES

EASTERN WAY

MOORVIEW CRES

MOORVALE LA

DEEPDALE GN

DEEPDALE CRES

THE
DALES

Montagu
Prim Schs

WYNDLEY
HOUSE

67

Blakelaw
Sch

SPRINGFIELD RD A696

A696

CROSSBROOK
RD

RADCLIFFE
PL

BIRLING PL

BROOMHILL GDNS

DRURIDGE DR

COLDINGHAM GDNS

FALLOON GDNS

HAUXLEY GDNS

BRIERYSIDE

PONTELAND RD

GREENHILL VIEW CRES

WHITEHORN CRES

HIGH
MOOR
CT

CHESTNUT AVE

LINK RD

FOURACRES RD

WHINMOOR PL

Nuns
Moor

Golf
Course

2

RENNINGTON GDNS

DOXFORD
GDNS

BONDICARR
GDNS

MAUDLIN
PL

EMBLETON
GDNS

YEWVALE RD

COTTAGE LA

McKENDRICK VILLAS

REVELL
TERR

1 MORWICK PL
2 STAMFORDHAM MEWS

Cowgate

HOWAT AVE

MAYFIELD TERR

ROSE
TERR

MOORHEAD

MOORHEAD
MEWS

WINGROVE RD

PONTELAND

1 MOORSIDE CT
2 NORTHUMBRIA LODGE

CH

CHEVINGTON
GDNS

BROOKSIDE CRES

HOLMESDALE RD

ARDEN CRES

1

B6324

B6324

GDNS

WESTHOPE

TWO BALL LONNEN

B6326

CHEESEBURN
GDNS

BAVINGTON DR

DEANHAM
GDNS

ANGERTON
GDNS

OVINGTON GR

Superstore

WOODBURN AVE

WINGROVE RD

MOORSIDE N

A187 PONTELAND RD

A167

A187

66

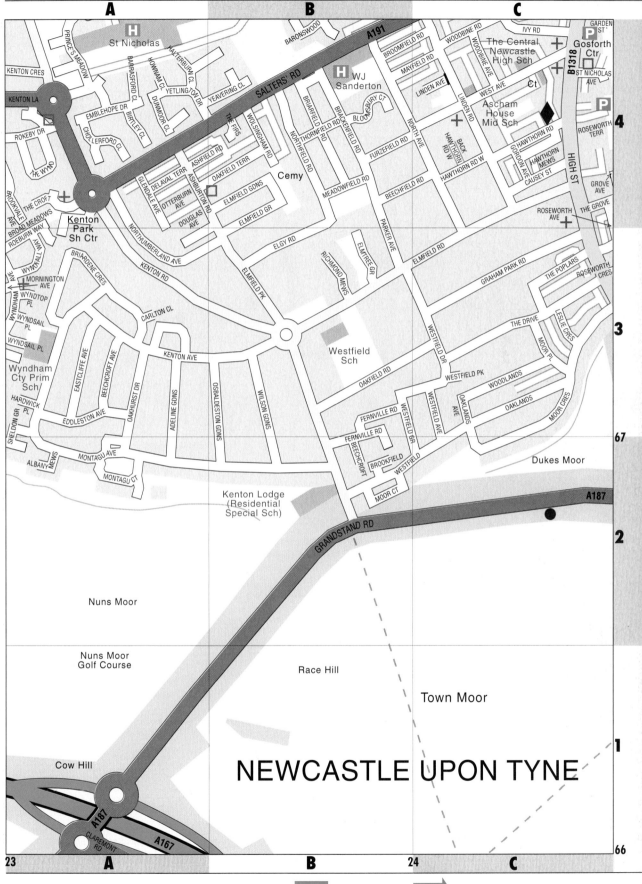

NEWCASTLE UPON TYNE

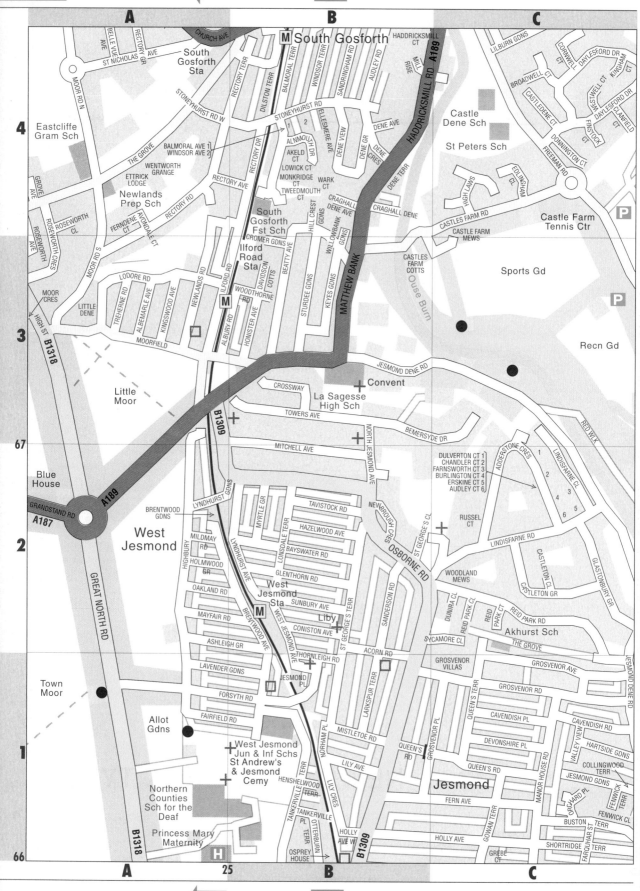

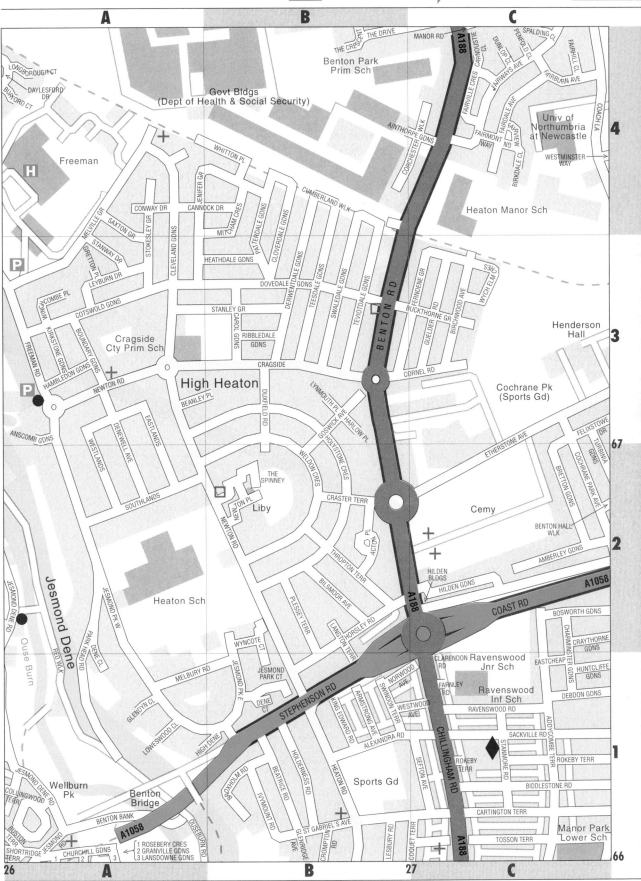

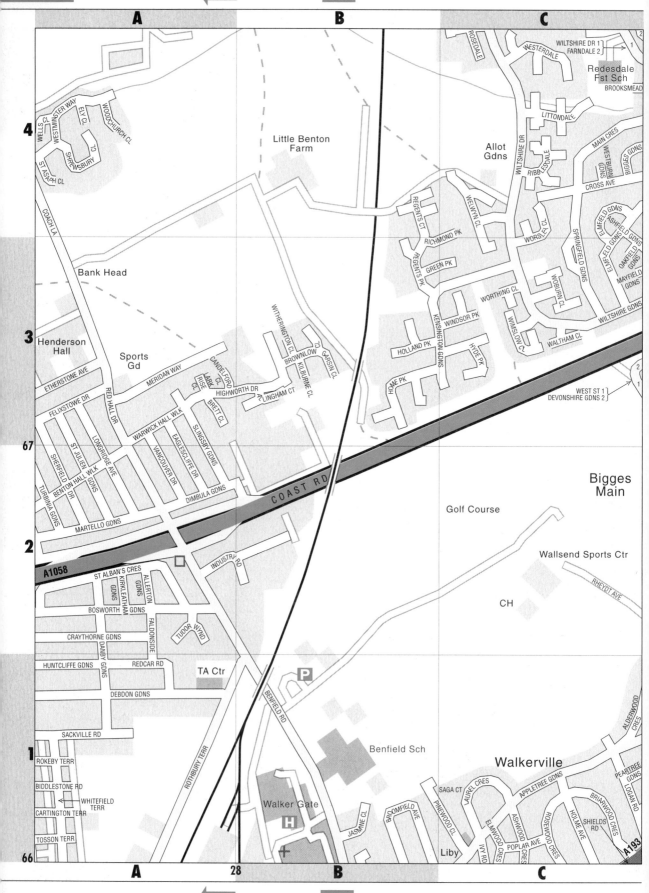

A   B   C

Little Benton Farm

WILTSHIRE DR 1
FARNDALE 2

ROSEDALE

WESTERDALE

Redesdale Fst Sch

BROOKSMEAD

LITTONDALE

Allot Gdns

WILTSHIRE DR

RIBBLESDALE

MAIN CRES

WESTBURN GDNS

BIGGES GDNS

CROSS AVE

4

WELLS CL

WESTMINSTER WAY

ELY CL

WOODCHURCH CL

SHREWSBURY CL

ST ASAPH CL

COACH LA

REGENTS CT

RICHMOND PK

REGENTS PK

GREEN PK

WELWYN CL

WORSLEY CL

WOBURN CL

WINSLOW CL

ELMFIELD GDNS

ASHFIELD GDNS

ELMFIELD GDNS

OAKFIELD GDNS

MAYFIELD GDNS

SPRINGFIELD GDNS

WILTSHIRE GDNS

Bank Head

3

Henderson Hall

Sports Gd

ETHERSTONE AVE

FELIXSTOWE DR

RED HALL DR

MERIDAN WAY

CANDELFORD CL

LARK RISE

HIGHWORTH DR

BRETT CL

LINGHAM CT

WITHERINGTON CL

BROWNLOW CL

KILBURNIE CL

GARSIN CL

HOLLAND PK

HOME PK

KENSINGTON GDNS

WINDSOR PK

HYDE PK

WORTHING CL

WALTHAM CL

WEST ST 1
DEVONSHIRE GDNS 2

67

SHERFIELD

TURBINIA GDNS

ST JULIEN

BENTON HALL WLK

LONGRIDGE AVE

WARWICK HALL WLK

VANCOUVER DR

EAGLESCLIFFE DR

SLINGSBY GDNS

DIMBULA GDNS

MARTELLO GDNS

COAST RD

Bigges Main

Golf Course

Wallsend Sports Ctr

RHEYDT AVE

2

A1058

ST ALBAN'S CRES

INDUSTRIAL RD

CH

ALLERTON GDNS

KIRKLEATHAM GDNS

BOSWORTH GDNS

FALDONSIDE

CRAYTHORNE GDNS

TUDOR WYND

DANBY GDNS

HUNTCLIFFE GDNS

REDCAR RD

DEBDON GDNS

TA Ctr

P

BENFIELD RD

SACKVILLE RD

1

ROKEBY TERR

BIDDLESTONE RD

WHITEFIELD TERR

CARTINGTON TERR

TOSSON TERR

ROTHBURY TERR

Walker Gate

H

Benfield Sch

Walkerville

SAGA CT

LAUREL CRES

APPLETREE GDNS

PINEWOOD CL

BROMFIELD AVE

POPLAR AVE

ELMWOOD CRES

ASHWOOD CRES

ROSEWOOD CRES

HOLME AVE

IVY RD

JASMINE CL

Liby

ALDERWOOD CRES

PEARTREE GDNS

LOGAN RD

BRIARWOOD CRES

SHIELDS RD

A193

66

A   28   B   C

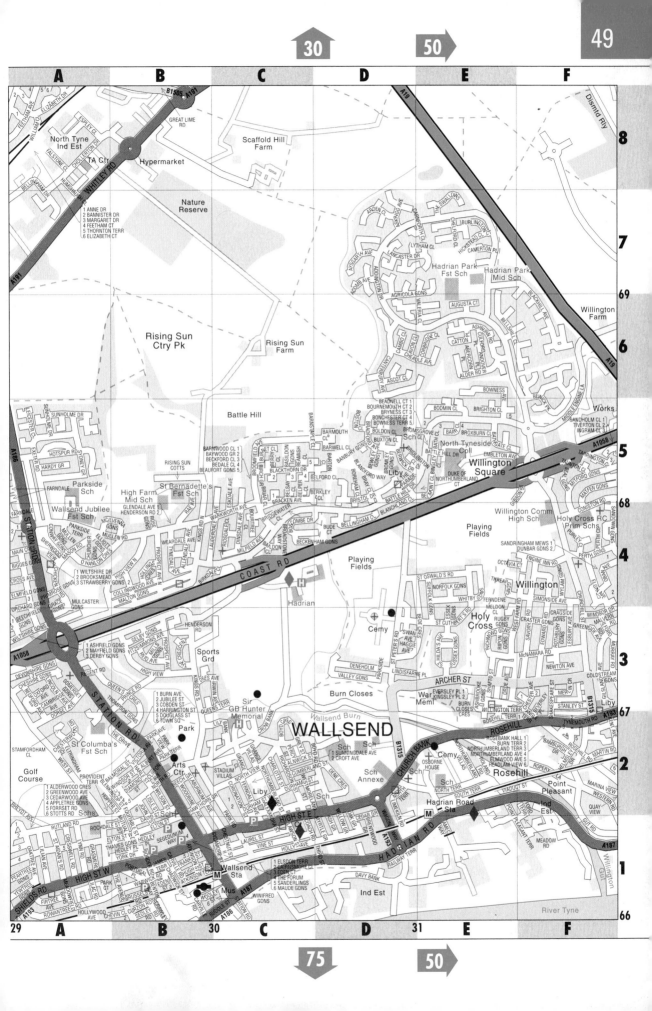

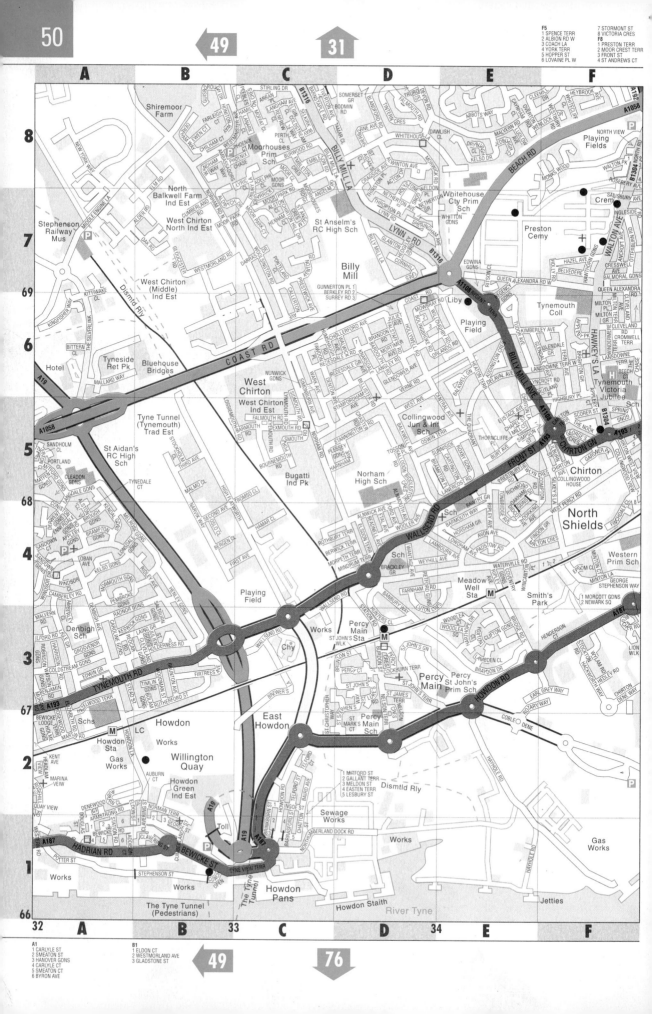

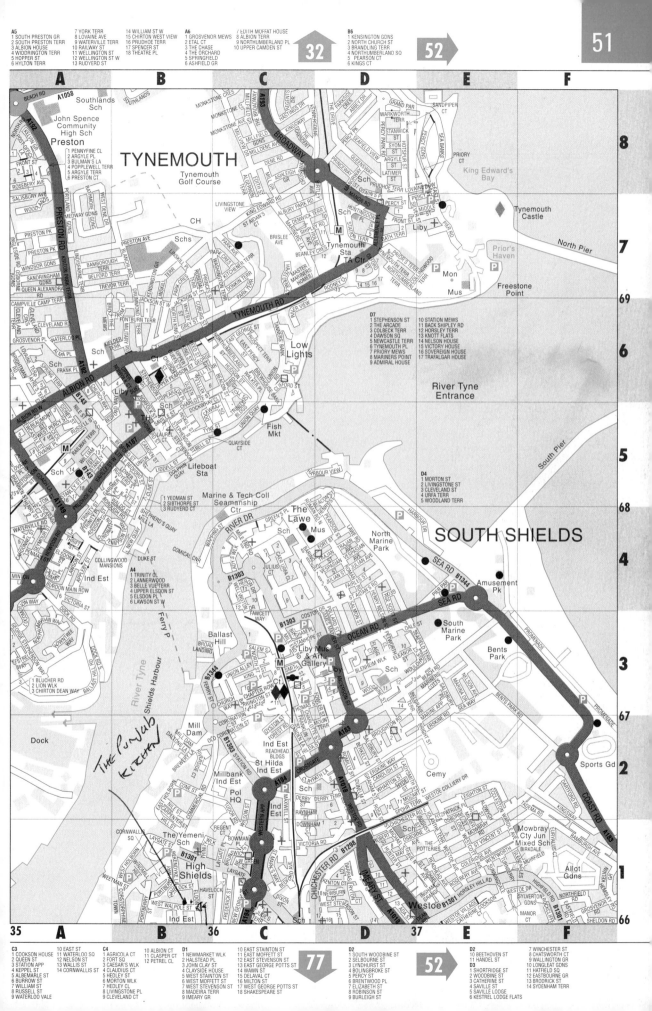

A5
1 SOUTH PRESTON GR
2 SOUTH PRESTON TERR
3 ALBION HOUSE
4 WIDDRINGTON TERR
5 HOPPER ST
6 HYLTON TERR
7 YORK TERR
8 LOVAINE AVE
9 BULMAN'S LA
10 POPPLEWELL TERR
11 RAILWAY ST
12 WELLINGTON ST
13 RUDYERD ST
14 WILLIAM ST W
15 CHIRTON WEST VIEW
16 PRUDHOE TERR
17 SPENCER ST
18 THEATRE PL

A6
1 GROSVENOR MEWS
2 ETAL CT
3 THE CHASE
4 THE ORCHARD
5 SPRINGFIELD
6 ASHFIELD GR
7 EDITH MOFFAT HOUSE
8 ALBION TERR
9 NORTHUMBERLAND PL
10 UPPER CAMDEN ST

B6
1 KENSINGTON GDNS
2 NORTH CHURCH ST
3 BRANDLING TERR
4 NORTHUMBERLAND SQ
5 PEARSON CT
6 KINGS CT

32 52

D7
1 STEPHENSON ST
2 THE ARCADE
3 COLBECK TERR
4 DAWSON SQ
5 NEWCASTLE TERR
6 TYNEMOUTH PL
7 PRIORY MEWS
8 MARINERS POINT
9 ADMIRAL HOUSE
10 STATION MEWS
11 BACK SHIPLEY RD
12 HORSLEY TERR
13 KNOTT FLATS
14 NELSON HOUSE
15 VICTORY HOUSE
16 SOVEREIGN HOUSE
17 TRAFALGAR HOUSE

D4
1 MORTON ST
2 LIVINGSTONE ST
3 CLEVELAND ST
4 URFA TERR
5 WOODLAND TERR

A4
1 TRINITY CL
2 LANNERWOOD
3 BELLE VUE TERR
4 UPPER ELSDON ST
5 ELSDON PL
6 LAWSON ST

1 BLUCHER RD
2 LION WLK
3 CHIRTON DEAN WAY

C3
1 COOKSON HOUSE
2 QUEEN ST
3 STATION APP
4 KEPPEL ST
5 ALBEMARLE ST
6 BURROW ST
7 WILLIAM ST
8 RUSSELL ST
9 WATERLOO VALE
10 EAST ST
11 WATERLOO SQ
12 NELSON ST
13 WALLIS ST
14 CORNWALLIS ST

C4
1 AGRICOLA CT
2 FORT SQ
3 CAESAR'S WLK
4 CLAUDIUS CT
5 HEDLEY ST
6 MORTON WLK
7 HEDLEY CL
8 LIVINGSTONE PL
9 CLEVELAND CT
10 ALBION CT
11 CLASPER CT
12 PETREL CL

D1
1 NEWMARKET WLK
2 HALSTEAD PL
3 JOHN CLAY ST
4 CLAYSIDE HOUSE
5 WEST STAINTON ST
6 WEST MOFFETT ST
7 WEST STEVENSON ST
8 MADEIRA CT
9 CLEVELAND CT
10 EAST STAINTON ST
11 EAST STEVENSON ST
13 EAST GEORGE POTTS ST
14 WAWN ST
15 DELAVAL CT
16 MILTON ST
17 WEST GEORGE POTTS ST
18 SHAKESPEARE ST

D2
1 SOUTH WOODBINE ST
2 SELBOURNE ST
3 LYNDHURST ST
4 BOLINGBROKE ST
5 PERCY ST
6 BRENTWOOD PL
7 ELIZABETH ST
8 ROBINSON ST
9 BURLEIGH ST

D2
10 BEETHOVEN ST
11 HANDEL ST

D3
1 SHORTRIDGE ST
2 WOODBINE ST
3 CATHERINE ST
4 SAVILLE ST
5 SAVILLE LODGE
6 KESTREL LODGE FLATS

7 WINCHESTER ST
8 CHATSWORTH CT
9 WALLINGTON GR
10 LONGLEAT GDNS
11 HATFIELD SQ
12 EASTBOURNE GR
13 BRODRICK ST
14 SYDENHAM TERR

77 52

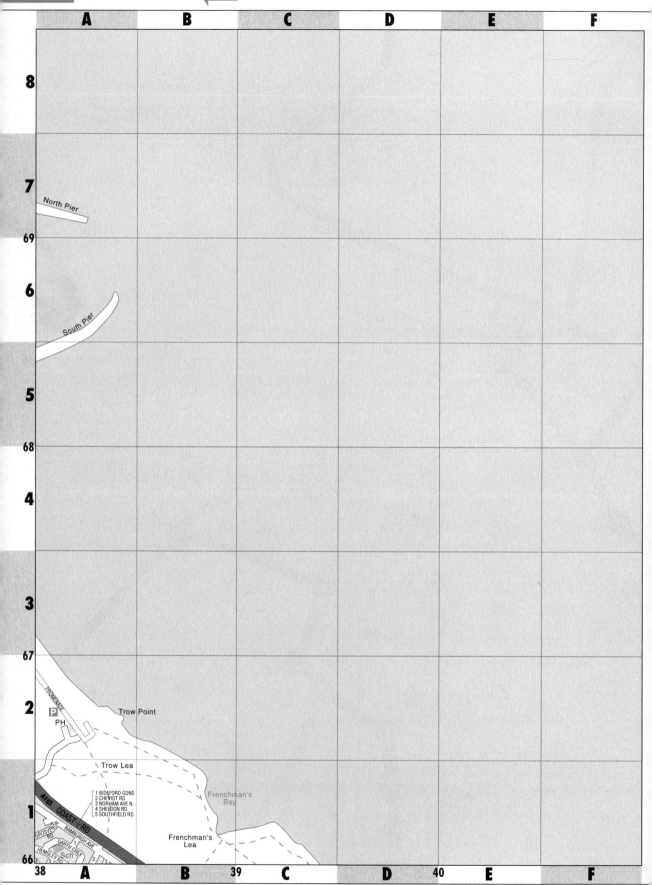

North Pier

South Pier

PROMENADE

P

PH

Trow Point

Trow Lea

Frenchman's
Bay

1 BIDEFORD GDNS
2 CHEVIOT RD
3 NORHAM AVE N
4 SHEUDON RD
5 SOUTHFIELD RD

A183 COAST RD

GROSVENOR RD

BAMBURGH AVE

GARTH CRES

HEMSLEY RD

Sch

Frenchman's
Lea

A · B · C · D · E · F

8
7
65
6
5
64
4
63
3
2
1
62

Alnmouth Terr

Coastley Burnfoot Farm

Warden

Burnfoot Wood

West Boat

Kingshaw Haugh

River Tyne

Old Bridge End

Westwood House

A69

B6531

Highwood Farm

Cemy

Golf Course

LC

SPITAL LA

CH

Caravan Site

High Wood

Highside

The Shaws Farm

Shaws La

Cobbler's Hall

MILLFIELD GDNS 1
QUATRE BRAS 2
MILLFIELD CT 3
WESTBOURNE GR 4
PORTLAND TERR 5

THE LINK
DUKES RD
LEAZES LA

BROADWAY GDNS

EILANSGATE

Sch

QUEENS WAY

LEAZES LA

LEAZES PK

GLEN TERR

WINDSOR TERR

WOODBINE TERR

MILLFIELD

PARK AVE

Caravan Site

Plain Trees Farm

LEAZES CRES 6
HIGH BURSWELL 7
BURNLAND TERR 8
LEAZES TERR 9
WESTFIELD CL 10

OSBORNE AVE

FREE

HEATHER HILL

Low Gate Cty Prim Sch

Low Gate

Summerrods West Farm

SHAWS LA

Leazes

BEECH AVE

BEECH HILL

ALEXANDRA CRES

HELL POOL LA

WHITBY

ALEXANDRA TERR

B6531

CRESCENT

SHAFTOE LEAZES

B6305

SOUTH KINGS

Queen Elizabeth High Sch

TYNEDALE TERR

FAIRFIELD

Summerrods

ALLENDALE RD

MAIDENS CROFT

B6305

HEXTOL TERR

Breckon Hill

Cockshaw Burn

Summerrods Dean

Woodley Field Farm

CANON SAVAGE DR

St Josephs RC Mid Sch

CAUSEY

HEXTOL

WEST HEXTOL CL

VALEBROOK

ST PAULS RD

Blossom Hill

High House Farm

HIGHFORD LA

HENDERSON

DERBY DR

BENSON DR

ST MATTHEWS

ST JOHNS RD

EASTGATE RD

B6305

IVESON

PATTERSON CL

BISHOPTON WAY

THE CL

CAUSEY HILL RD

Nichols Dean

Low Yarridge

Highford

BIRCH CL

ASH CL

ELM CL

DICKSON CL

CONNISCLIFFE CT

THE OAKS

CAUSEY HILL WAY

WYDON PK

HEXHAM

ARMSTRONG

RIDLEY DR

ROBSON DR

BURNSIDE

Barn End

PERCY CL

CLOUGH DR

MILBURN CL

SCOTT CL

CHARLTON CL

West Plantation

Caravan Site

Benson's Fell

Green Hill

High Yarridge

Rot Sike

Hexham Race Course

Plover Hill

90 · A · B · 91 · C · D · 92 · E · F

A · B · C · D · E · F

8 Riding Farm

Acomb

Target House

Birkey Burn

East Oakwood Farm

Oakwood

Anick

West Oakwood

FAIRFIELD CRES

EAST OAKWOOD

OAKWOOD

The Rat (PH)

Anick Grange

7 The Hermitage

A69

OAKWOOD BANK

Bank Foot

A69

65 Golf Course

Tyne Green

CH

A6079

Bridge End

Bridge End Ind Est

The Oaklands

Harwood Meadows

6 TYNE GREEN RD

LC

P

Tyne Green Country Park

Haugh Lane Ind Est

Factory

1 CHURCH ROW
2 MARKET PL
3 PUDDING MEWS
4 ST MARY'S WYND
5 ST MARY'S CHARE
6 MEAL MKT

STATION RD

Tyne Mills Ind Est

Tyne Mills

Hexham Sta

Sewage Wks

5 Sch

ALBION TERR

HOLY ISLAND

GARDEN TERR

ALEMOUTH RD

Wentworth L Ctr

P WENTWORTH PL

Broomhaugh Island

Anickgrange Haugh

River Tyne

1 PEARSON'S TERR
2 MILLFIELD TERR
3 WESTBOURNE GR
4 FENWICK GR
5 KINGSGATE
6 DUNWOODIE TERR
7 COCKSHAW CT
8 GIBSON PL

Abbey

The Liby

Seal

Mus

HALL ORCHARD RD

A6079

DEAN ST

PETH HEAD

DENE AVE

DENE PK

A695

64 B6531

B6305

BATTLE HILL CATTLE MARKET

PRIESTPOPPLE

B6305

A695

Hexham General

Hexham Priory Sch

EAST WOODLANDS

EASTFIELDS

Craneshaugh

4 HENCOTES

St CUTHBERTS

Sch

GAPRIGG

War Memorial

H EASTGATE

Hexham Cty Mid Sch

PESCOTT CL

MAIDEN'S WLK

KENT GR

REDE AVE

H

Hexham General

BROOMHAUGH

RADCLIFFE RD

BYWELL AVE

DILSTON AVE

LANGLEY

EDGEWOOD

MONKS MEADOWS

FAIRWOOD

EASTWOOD

EASTWOOD GRANGE CT

Craneshaugh

Bogle Hole

1 MONK'S TERR
2 WOODLANDS
3 WOODSIDE
4 CHURCHLANDS
5 ELDON RD
6 GLANTON RD

Cock Wood

PRIESTLANDS RD

PRIESTLANDS DR

ST GEORGE'S

SOUTH PK

BOUNDARY CT

GREEN BANK

HILLCREST DR

Hexham East Cty Fst Sch

1 ASHWOOD RD
2 WOODLEA CRES

Delegate Hall

3 Hackwood Park Sch

GALLOWS BANK

TYNEVIEW TERR

QUARRY EDGE

WEST VIEW TERR

Halfmile Wood

Duke's House

HACKWOOD PK

Gallowsbank Wood

Golden Hill

63 High Shield

LONGBROW

Coalpits Flat

Dukeshouse Wood

2 Mount Pleasant

Loughbrow

Oakerlands Farm

Milking Hill

Sunnyside Plantation

1 Black House

CAUSEY HILL RD

Oakerlands House

Sunnyside

Devil's Water

B6306

62

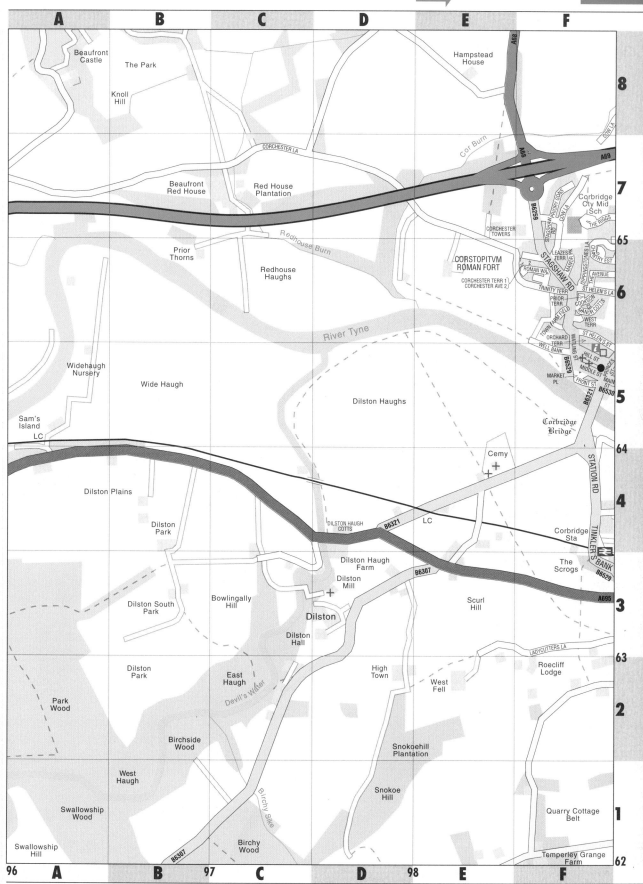

A B C D E F

8

7

65

6

64

5

64

4

63

3

63

2

1

62

Beaufront
Castle

The Park

Knoll
Hill

Hampstead
House

CORCHESTER LA

Beaufront
Red House

Red House
Plantation

Redhouse Burn

Cor Burn

A69

A69

B6259

Corbridge
Cty Mid
Sch

THE RIGGS

CHANTRY EST

CORCHESTER
TOWERS

STAGSHAW PRIORY GDNS

CON LA

Prior
Thorns

Redhouse
Haughs

CORSTOPITVM
ROMAN FORT

CORCHESTER TERR 1
CORCHESTER AVE 2

LEAZES TERR

STAGSHAW RD

ROMAN WA

PRIOR
TERR

TRINITY TERR

MANOR

RUPPINGSTONES LA

AVENUE

ST HELEN'S LA

COOKSTON

MANOR COTTS

WEST
TERR

CHANTRY EST

Widehaugh
Nursery

Wide Haugh

River Tyne

Dilston Haughs

TOWN FARM FIELD

ORCHARD
TERR

WELL BANK

WATLING ST

ST HELEN'S ST

HILL ST

i

B6529

MARKET
PL

FRONT ST

MIDDLE ST

PRINCES ST

MAIN ST

B6530

Corbridge
Bridge

Sam's
Island

LC

Cemy

B6321

STATION RD

Dilston Plains

LC

Corbridge
Sta

TINKLER'S BANK

B6529

Dilston
Park

DILSTON HAUGH
COTTS

B6321

The
Scrogs

Dilston Haugh
Farm

Dilston
Mill

B6307

Scurl
Hill

A695

Dilston South
Park

Bowlingally
Hill

Dilston

Dilston
Hall

High
Town

West
Fell

Roecliff
Lodge

LADYCUTTERS LA

Dilston
Park

East
Haugh

Devil's Water

Snokoehill
Plantation

Park
Wood

Birchside
Wood

Birchy Sike

Snokoe
Hill

Quarry Cottage
Belt

West
Haugh

Swallowship
Wood

Birchy
Wood

B6307

Swallowship
Hill

Temperley Grange
Farm

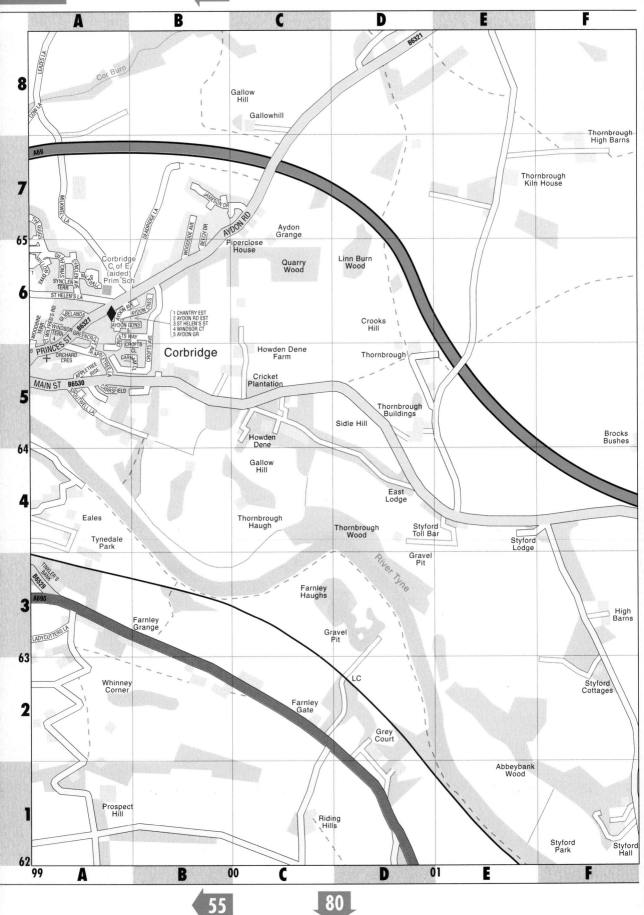

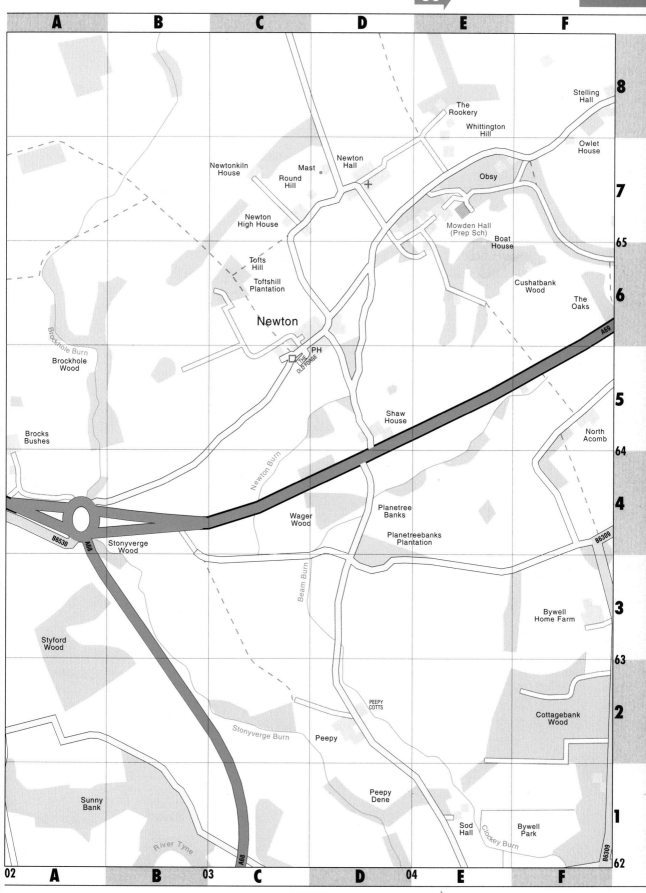

A   B   C   D   E   F

8

Stelling Hall

The Rookery

Whittington Hill

Owlet House

Newtonkiln House

Mast

Newton Hall

Obsy

7

Round Hill

Newton High House

Mowden Hall (Prep Sch)

Boat House

65

Tofts Hill

Cushatbank Wood

The Oaks

6

Toftshill Plantation

Newton

A69

Brockhole Burn

Brockhole Wood

PH
THE OLD FORGE

5

Shaw House

Brocks Bushes

North Acomb

64

Newton Burn

Wager Wood

Planetree Banks

4

Stonyverge Wood

B6530

A68

Planetreebanks Plantation

B6309

Beam Burn

Bywell Home Farm

3

Styford Wood

63

PEEPY COTTS

Cottagebank Wood

2

Stonyverge Burn

Peepy

Sunny Bank

Peepy Dene

Bywell Park

1

River Tyne

A68

Sod Hall

Clookey Burn

B6309

62

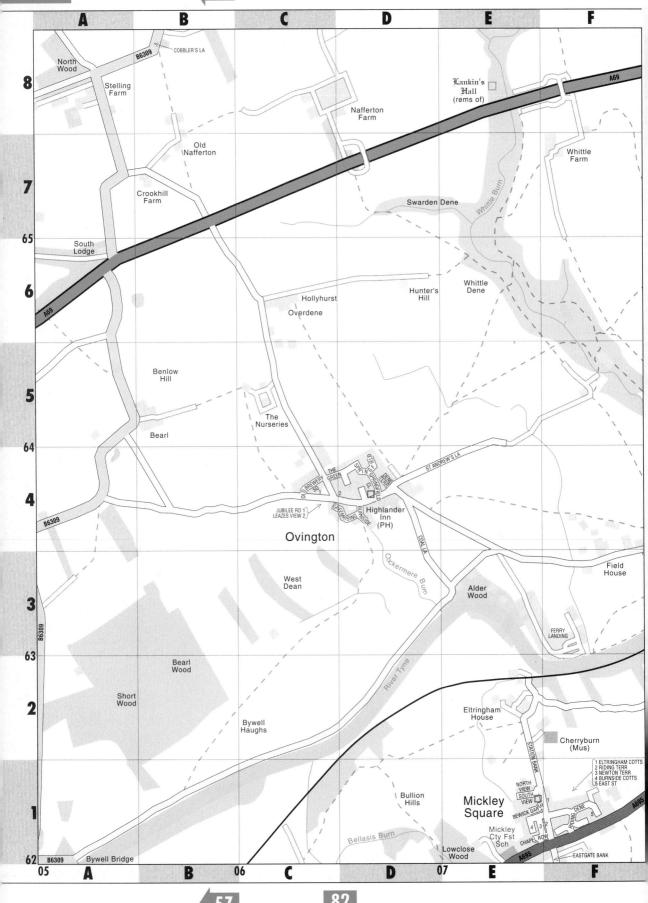

A   B   C   D   E   F

B6309

COBBLER'S LA

North Wood

Stelling Farm

Old Nafferton

Nafferton Farm

Lankin's Hall (rems of)

A69

Whittle Farm

Crookhill Farm

Whittle Burn

Swarden Dene

South Lodge

A69

Hollyhurst

Overdene

Hunter's Hill

Whittle Dene

Benlow Hill

The Nurseries

Bearl

ST ANDREW'S LA

OLD SPRINGFIELD

DENE TERR

THE GREEN

OLD BREWERY SQ

SPRINGFIELD

CL

Highlander Inn (PH)

JUBILEE RD 1
LEAZES VIEW 2

GREENRISING

BURNSIDE

Ovington

COAL LA

Field House

West Dean

Ockermere Burn

Alder Wood

FERRY LANDING

B6309

Bearl Wood

River Tyne

Short Wood

Eltringham House

Bywell Haughs

Cherryburn (Mus)

STATION BANK

1 ELTRINGHAM COTTS
2 RIDING TERR
3 NEWTON TERR
4 BURNSIDE COTTS
5 EAST ST

Bullion Hills

Mickley Square

NORTH VIEW

SOUTH VIEW

BEWICK BANK

RIDING DENE

A695

Bellasis Burn

Mickley Cty Fst Sch

CHAPEL ROW

Lowclose Wood

EASTGATE BANK

B6309   Bywell Bridge

A695

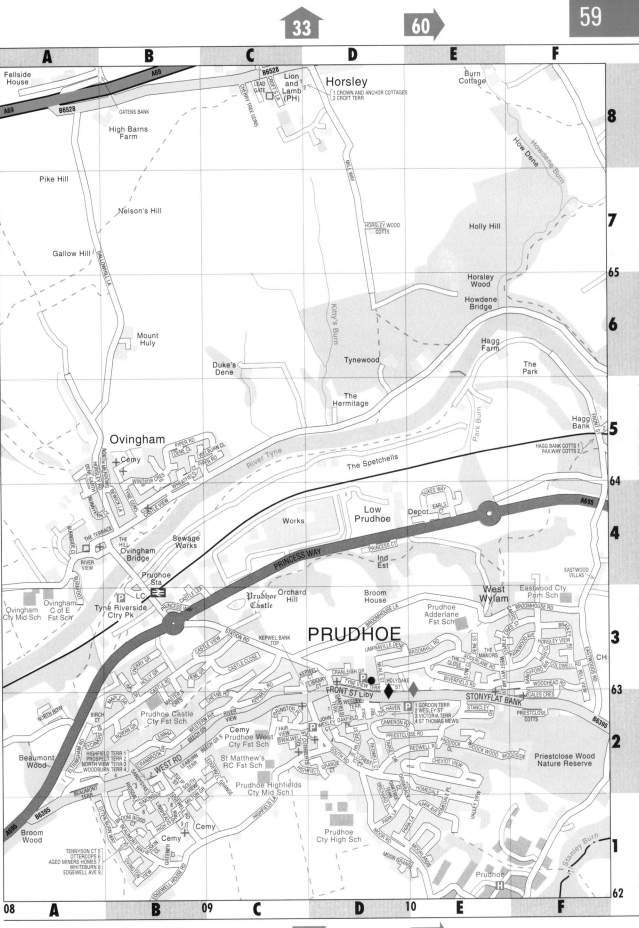

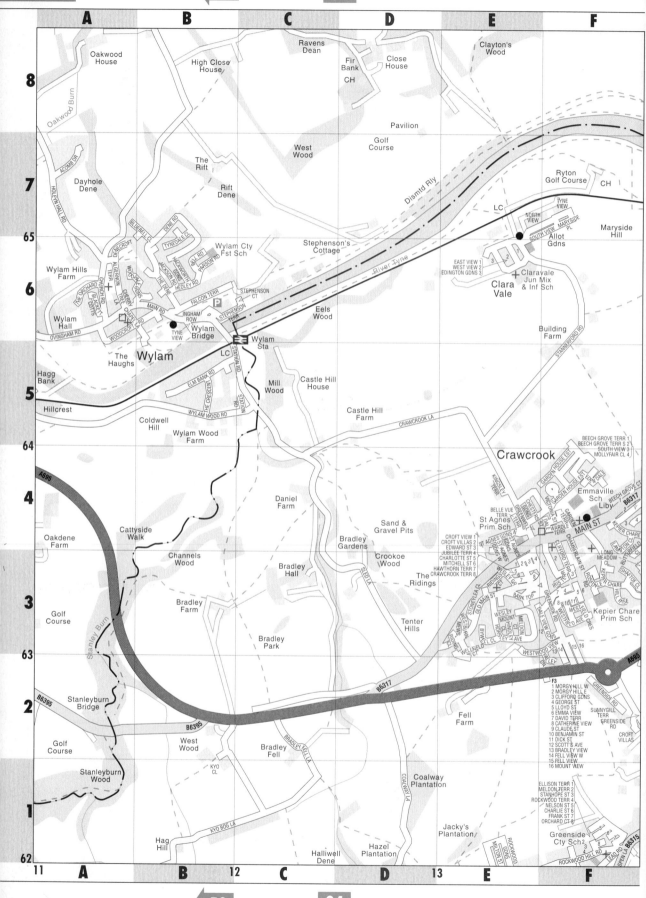

35
62

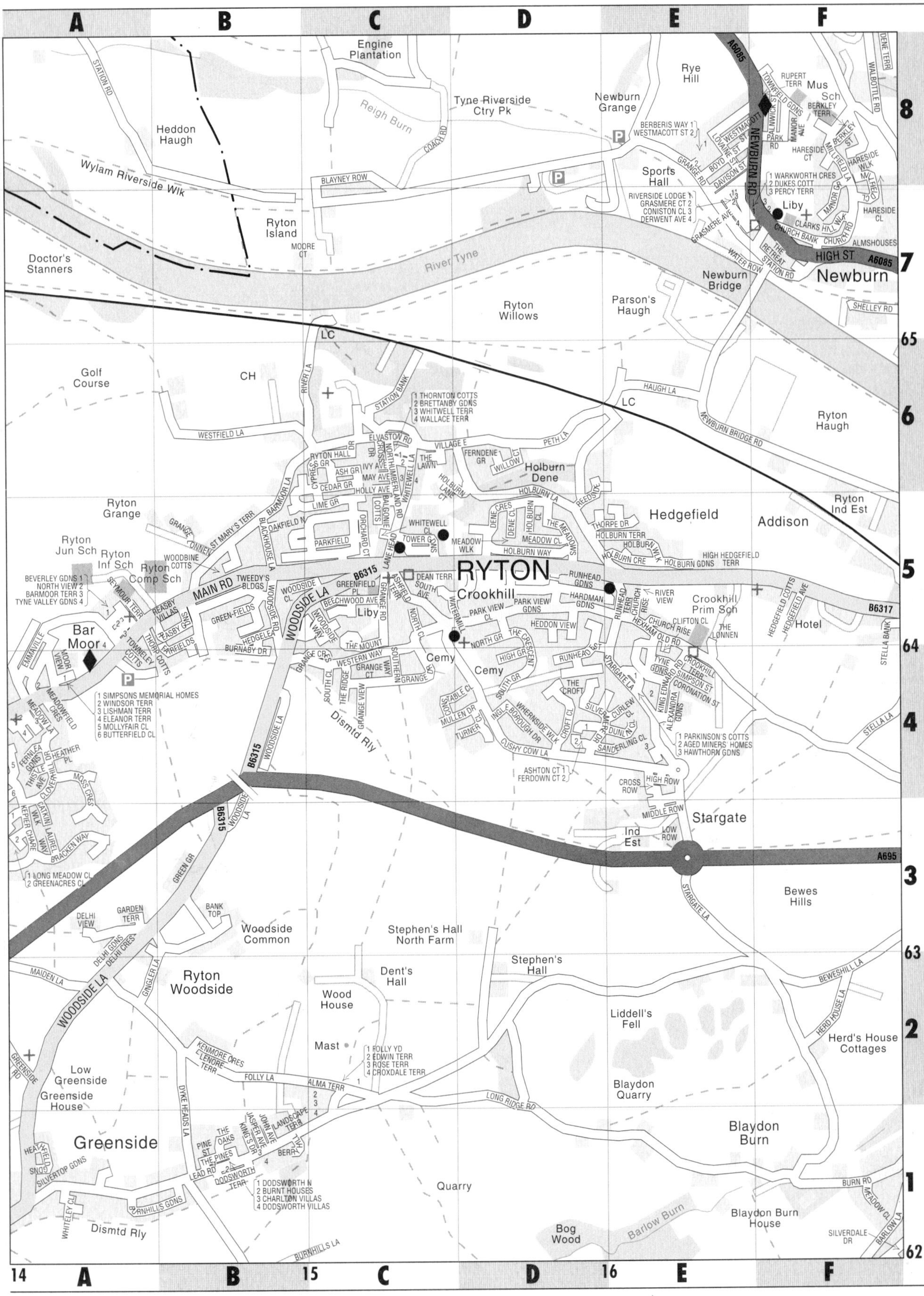
A
B
C
D
E
F
8
7
65
6
5
64
4
3
63
2
1
62
14
15
16
Engine Plantation
Reigh Burn
Tyne Riverside Ctry Pk
Newburn Grange
Rye Hill
Heddon Haugh
Wylam Riverside Wlk
STATION RD
COACH RD
BLAYNEY ROW
Ryton Island
MOORE CT
Doctor's Stanners
River Tyne
Sports Hall
BERBERIS WAY 1
WESTMACOTT ST 2
RIVERSIDE LODGE 1
GRASMERE CT 2
CONISTON CL 3
DERWENT AVE 4
GRANGE RD
GRASMERE AVE
BOYD ST
DAVISON ST
LOVAINE ST
WESTMACOTT ST
A6085
NEWBURN RD
RUPERT TERR
Mus
Sch
BERKLEY TERR
TOWNFIELD GDNS
ALNWICK ST
PARK RD
MANOR AVE
HARESIDE CT
BERKLEY ST
HARESIDE WLK
MILLFIELD
1 WARKWORTH CRES
2 DUKES COTT
3 PERCY TERR
Liby
CLARKS HILL WLK
CHURCH BANK
CHURCH RD
MANOR GR
HARESIDE CL
ALMSHOUSES
HIGH ST
WALBOTTLE RD
DENE TERR
THE RETREAT
STATION RD
WATER ROW
Newburn Bridge
Newburn
SHELLEY RD
Ryton Willows
Parson's Haugh
LC
Golf Course
CH
RIVER LA
STATION BANK
1 THORNTON COTTS
2 BRETTANBY GDNS
3 WHITWELL TERR
4 WALLACE TERR
HAUGH LA
NEWBURN BRIDGE RD
Ryton Haugh
WESTFIELD LA
ELVASTON RD
RYTON HALL DR
CROSSLEA
NORTHUMBERLAND RD
WHITEWELL LA
VILLAGE E
FERNDENE GR
WILLOW
PETH LA
THE LAWN
ASH GR
IVY AVE
MAY AVE
HOLLY AVE
CYPRESS GR
CEDAR GR
LIME GR
BARMOOR LA
Holburn Dene
HOLBURN LANE CT
HOLBURN LA
REEDSIDE
Ryton Grange
ST MARY'S TERR
GRANGE
LONNEN
OAKFIELD N
BLACKHOUSE LA
BALGONIE COTTS
ORCHARD CT
PARKFIELD
WHITEWELL CL
TOWER GDNS
MEADOW WLK
DENE CRES
DENE CL
HOLBURN CL
THE MEADOWS
MEADOW CL
HOLBURN WAY
THORPE DR
HOLBURN TERR
HOLBURN WLK
HOLBURN CRES
HOLBURN GDNS
Hedgefield
Addison
Ryton Ind Est
HIGH HEDGEFIELD TERR
Ryton Jun Sch
Ryton Inf Sch
Ryton Comp Sch
WOODBINE COTTS
TWEEDY'S BLDGS
BEVERLEY GDNS 1
NORTH VIEW 2
BARMOOR TERR 3
TYNE VALLEY GDNS 4
SEYMOUR TERR
MAIN RD
B6315
LANE HEAD
RYTON
DEAN TERR
RUNHEAD GDNS
RIVER VIEW
Crookhill
Prim Sch
B6317
HEDGEFIELD COTTS
HEDGEFIELD AVE
Hotel
STELLA BANK
REASBY VILLAS
REASBY GDNS
GREEN-FIELDS
WOODSIDE RD
WOODSIDE CL
WOODSIDE LA
GREENFIELD PL
ASHFIELD TERR
SOUTH AVE
BEECHWOOD AVE
GRANGE RD
Liby
WATERMILL
PARK VIEW CL
PARK VIEW GDNS
HARDMAN GDNS
RUNHEAD TERR
CHURCH RISE
CHURCH
HEXHAM OLD RD
CLIFTON CL
THE LONNEN
HEDDON VIEW
Bar Moor
MOOR VIEW
EMMAVILLE
THORP COTTS
TOWNELEY COTTS
FAIRFIELDS
HEDGELEA
BURNABY DR
WOODSIDE WAY
THE MOUNT
NORTH CL
NORTH GR
THE CRESCENT
HIGH GR
RUNHEAD EST
STARGATE LA
TYNE GDNS
SIMPSON ST
CROOKHILL TERR
CORONATION ST
KING EDWARD RD
1 SIMPSONS MEMORIAL HOMES
2 WINDSOR TERR
3 LISHMAN TERR
4 ELEANOR TERR
5 MOLLYFAIR CL
6 BUTTERFIELD CL
GRANGE CRES
WESTERN WAY
GRANGE CT
SOUTHERN WAY
GRANGE
Cemy
SOUTH CL
THE RIDGE
GRANGE VIEW
CONSTABLE CL
MULLEN DR
TURNER CL
SOUTH GR
INGLEBOROUGH DR
WHERNSIDE WLK
THE CROFT
CROFT CL
SILVERMERE DR
CURLEW CL
DUNLIN CL
SANDERLING CL
ALEXANDRA GDNS
CUSHY COW LA
1 PARKINSON'S COTTS
2 AGED MINERS' HOMES
3 HAWTHORN GDNS
ASHTON CT 1
FERDOWN CT 2
MEADOWFIELD CRES
MEADOW LA
FERNLEA GDNS
THISTLE AVE
CLOVERHILL DR
HEATHER PL
MOSS CRES
KEPIER CHARE
GATKIN WLK
LAUREL
BRACKEN WAY
1 LONG MEADOW CL
2 GREENACRES CL
Dismtd Rly
STELLA LA
CROSS ROW
HIGH ROW
MIDDLE ROW
Stargate
Ind Est
LOW ROW
A695
STARGATE LA
Bewes Hills
GREEN GR
GARDEN TERR
BANK TOP
DELHI VIEW
DELHI GDNS
DELHI CRES
Woodside Common
Stephen's Hall North Farm
Stephen's Hall
MAIDEN LA
GINGLER LA
Ryton Woodside
Dent's Hall
Wood House
BEWESHILL LA
HERD HOUSE LA
Liddell's Fell
Herd's House Cottages
WOODSIDE LA
Mast
1 FOLLY YD
2 EDWIN TERR
3 ROSE TERR
4 CROXDALE TERR
KENMORE CRES
LENORE TERR
FOLLY LA
ALMA TERR
LONG RIDGE RD
Blaydon Quarry
Low Greenside
Greenside House
GREENSIDE RD
DYKE HEADS LA
Greenside
THE OAKS
PINE ST
THE PINES
JASPER AVE
KING'S DR
JOHN AVE
LANDSCAPE TERR
BERRY
LEAD RD
DODSWORTH TERR
1 DODSWORTH N
2 BURNT HOUSES
3 CHARLTON VILLAS
4 DODSWORTH VILLAS
Quarry
Blaydon Burn
HEATHFIELD GDNS
SILVERTOP GDNS
WHITELEY CL
BURNHILLS GDNS
Dismtd Rly
Bog Wood
Barlow Burn
Blaydon Burn House
BURN RD
MEADOW CL
BARLOW LA
SILVERDALE DR
BURNHILLS LA

85
62

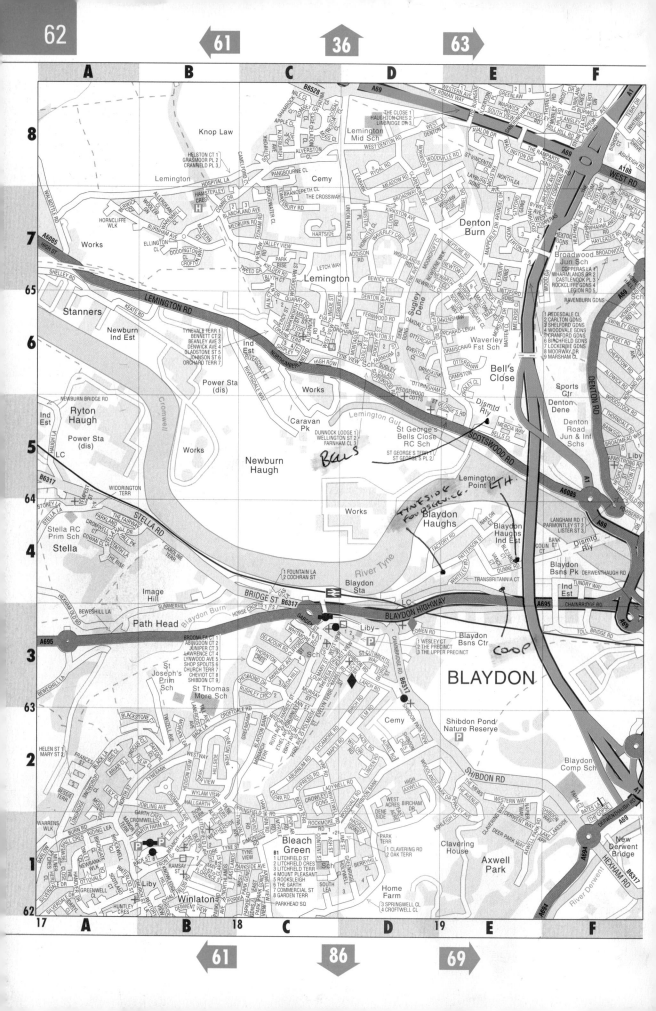

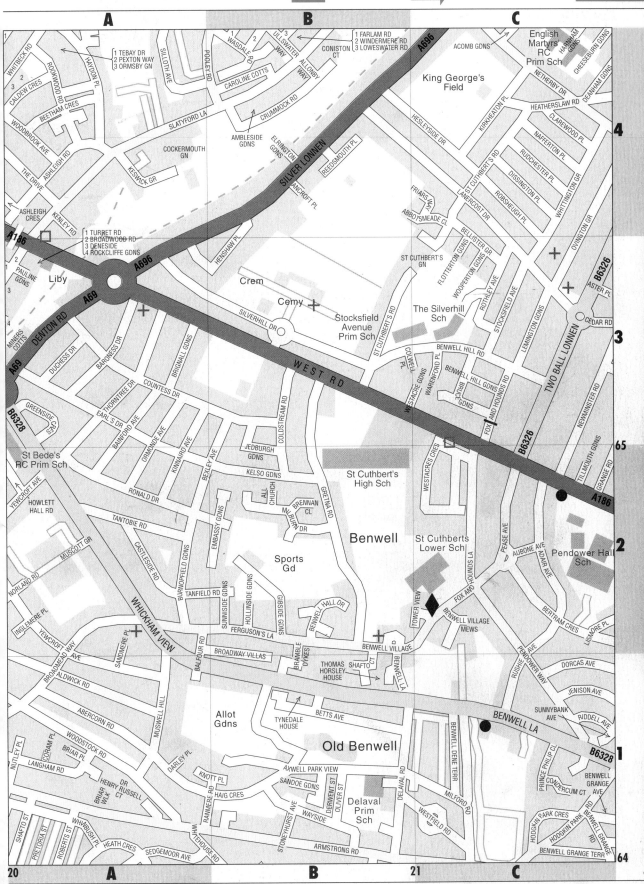

A B C

1 TEBAY DR
2 PEXTON WAY
3 ORMSBY GN

1 FARLAM RD
2 WINDERMERE RD
3 LOWESWATER RD

WHITBECK RD
CALDEW CRES
ROOKWOOD RD
BEETHAM CRES
HAYDON PL
POOLEY RD
WASDALE RD
SILLOTH AVE
CAROLINE COTTS
ULLSWATER WAY
ALLONBY WAY
CONISTON CT
A696
ACOMB GDNS

English Martyrs' RC Prim Sch
CHEESEBURN GDNS
HARNHAM GDNS

WOODBROOK AVE
ASHLEIGH RD
SLATFORD LA
CRUMMOCK RD
ELRINGTON GDNS

King George's Field
NETHERBY DR
DEANHAM GDNS

THE DRIVE
KESWICK GR
COCKERMOUTH GN
AMBLESIDE GDNS
SILVER LONNEN
REEDSMOUTH PL
HESLEYSIDE DR
KIRKHEATON PL
HEATHERSLAW RD
CLAREWOOD PL
NAFFERTON PL
RUDCHESTER PL
DISSINGTON PL

4

ASHLEIGH CRES
KENLEY RD
HENSHAW PL
ANCROFT PL
FRIARS WAY
ABBOTSMEADE CL
ST CUTHBERT'S RD
LANERCOST DR
BELLISTER GR
ROBSHEUGH PL
WHITTINGTON GR
OVINGTON GR

A186
1 TURRET RD
2 BROADWOOD RD
3 DENESIDE
4 ROCKCLIFFE GDNS

Liby
PAULINE GDNS
A696
A69
DENTON RD
Crem
Cemy
ST CUTHBERT'S GN
FLOTTERTON GDNS
WOOPERTON GDNS
ROTHLEY AVE
BELLISTER GR
B6326
ASTER PL

MINERS COTTS
A69
B6328
GREENSIDE CRES
DUCHESS DR
BARONESS DR
BRIGNALL GDNS
SILVERHILL DR
Stocksfield Avenue Prim Sch
The Silverhill Sch
BENWELL HILL RD
STOCKSFIELD AVE
LEMINGTON GDNS
CEDAR RD
TWO BALL LONNEN
NEWMINSTER RD

3

HORNTREE DR
COUNTESS DR
WEST RD
COLWELL PL
WESTACRE GDNS
BENWELL HILL GDNS
BENWELL HILL RD
BRUCE GDNS
FOX AND HOUNDS RD
B6326
TILLMOUTH GDNS
GRANGE RD

EARL'S DR
BAINFORD AVE
ORMONDE AVE
KINNAIRD AVE
BEXLEY AVE
JEDBURGH GDNS
COLDSTREAM RD
WESTACRES CRES
65

St Bede's RC Prim Sch
RONALD DR
KELSO GDNS
St Cuthbert's High Sch
A186

YEWCROFT AVE
HOWLETT HALL RD
TANTOBIE RD
EMBASSY GDNS
ALL CHURCH
BRENNAN CL
M.BURN DR
GRETNA RD
Benwell
St Cuthberts Lower Sch
PEASE AVE
AUBONE AVE
ADAIR AVE
Pendower Hall Sch

MUSCOTT GR
CASTLESIDE RD
Sports Gd
BERTRAM CRES
LISMORE PL

2

NORLAND RD
BURNOPFIELD GDNS
TANFIELD RD
SUNNISIDE GDNS
HOLLINSIDE GDNS
GIBSIDE GDNS
BENWELL HALL DR
TOWER VIEW
FOX AND HOUNDS LA
Benwell Village Mews
RUSSHIE AVE
PENDOWER WAY
DORCAS AVE

INGLEMERE PL
YEWCROFT AVE
WHICKHAM VIEW
SANDMERE PL
FERGUSON'S LA
BRAMBLE DYKES
BENWELL VILLAGE
BENWELL LA
JENISON AVE

BROADMEAD WAY
ALDWICK RD
BALFOUR RD
BROADWAY VILLAS
Thomas Horsley House
SHAFTO CT
SUNNYBANK AVE
RIDDELL AVE

ABERCORN RD
MUSWELL HILL
Allot Gdns
TYNEDALE HOUSE
BETTS AVE
BENWELL DENE TERR
BENWELL LA
B6328

1

NUTLEY PL
CORAM PL
WOODSTOCK RD
BRIAR PL
LANGHAM RD
DARLEY PL
KNOTT PL
Old Benwell
AXWELL PARK VIEW
DELAVAL RD
MILFORD RD
PRINCE PHILIP CL
CONDERCUM CT
Benwell Grange Ave

HENRY RUSSELL CT
DR
BRIAR WLK
RANMERE RD
HAIG CRES
SANDOE GDNS
OLIVER ST
DERWENT ST
Delaval Prim Sch
WESTFIELD RD

SHAFTO ST
PRETORIA ST
ROBERTS ST
WHV.BUSH PL
HEATH CRES
WHITEHOUSE RD
SEDGEMOOR AVE
STONEYHURST AVE
WAYSIDE
ARMSTRONG RD
HODGKIN PARK CRES
HODGKIN PARK RD
BENWELL GRANGE RD
BENWELL GRANGE TERR
64

20 A B 21 C

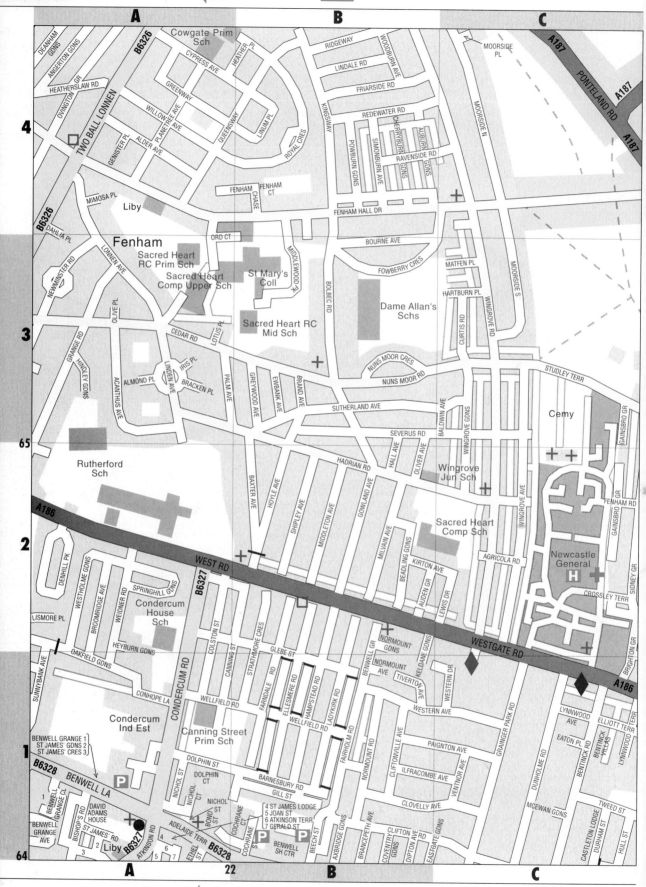

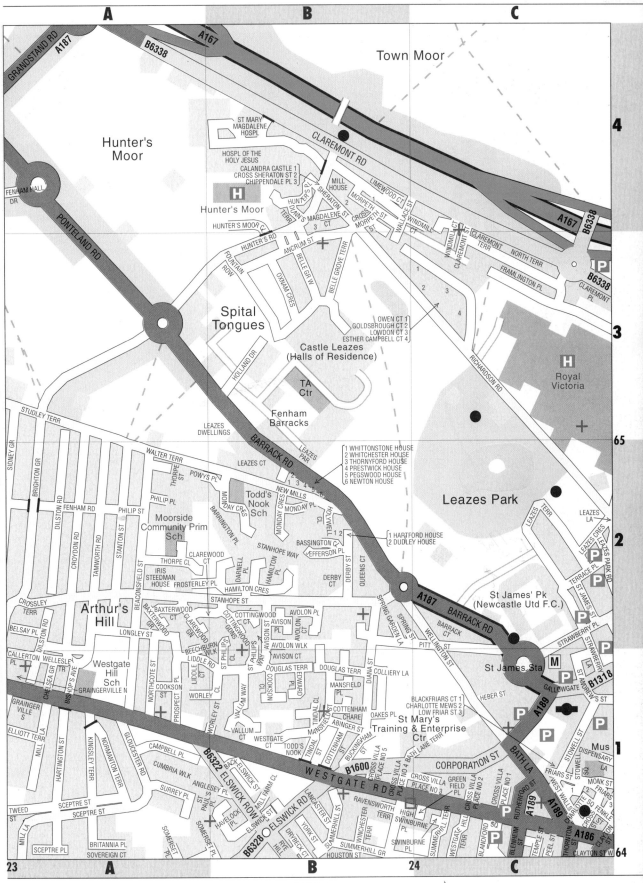

Town Moor

Hunter's
Moor

FENHAM HALL DR

GRANDSTAND RD
A187
B6338
A167

PONTELAND RD

ST MARY MAGDALENE HOSPL
HOSPL OF THE HOLY JESUS
CALANDRA CASTLE 1
CROSS SHERATON ST 2
CHIPPENDALE PL 3

CLAREMONT RD

H
Hunter's Moor

HUNTER'S MOOR C

HUNTER'S RD

FOUNTAIN ROW

ANCRUM ST

OXNAM CRES

BELLE GR W

BELLE GROVE TERR

HUNTER'S PL
DUAN'S TERR
SHERATON PL
MAGDALENE CT
3
CROSS MORPETH ST

MORPETH ST
MORPETH PL
WALLACE ST
WINDMILL

MILL HOUSE

LIMEWOOD CT

WINDMILL CT
WINDMILL CT
CLAREMONT TERR
NORTH TERR

FRAMLINGTON PL

A167
B6338

P
B6338
CLAREMONT PL

Spital
Tongues

HOLLAND DR

Castle Leazes
(Halls of Residence)

TA
Ctr

Fenham
Barracks

LEAZES DWELLINGS

BARRACK RD

LEAZES PAR

OWEN CT 1
GOLDSBROUGH CT 2
LOWDON CT 3
ESTHER CAMPBELL CT 4

1
2
3
4

RICHARDSON RD

H
Royal
Victoria

65

1 WHITTONSTONE HOUSE
2 WHITCHESTER HOUSE
3 THORNYFORD HOUSE
4 PRESTWICK HOUSE
5 PEGSWOOD HOUSE
6 NEWTON HOUSE

LEAZES CT

NEW MILLS
1 2 3 4 5 6

Leazes Park

LEAZES TERR

LEAZES CRES
LEAZES LA

LEAZES CRES
LEAZES PARK RD

2

TERRACE PL
P

STUDLEY TERR
SIDNEY GR
BRIGHTON GR

WALTER TERR

THORPE ST
POWYS PL
PHILIP PL

Todd's
Nook
Sch

MONDAY CRES
BARRINGTON PL
MONDAY CRES

MONDAY PL
HOLMWELL CL

1 2

1 HARTFORD HOUSE
2 DUDLEY HOUSE

St James' Pk
(Newcastle Utd F.C.)

ST JAMES PL

P

STRAWBERRY PL

DILSTON RD
FENHAM RD
PHILIP ST

Moorside
Community Prim
Sch

STANTON ST

CLAREWOOD CT
THORPE CL

DARNELL PL
IRIS STEEDMAN HOUSE
FROSTERLEY PL

STANHOPE WAY
HAMILTON ST
HAMILTON CRES
STANHOPE ST

BASSINGTON CL
EFFERSON PL

DERBY ST
DERBY CT
QUEENS CT

SPRING GARDEN LA
SPRING ST

A187
BARRACK RD

BARRACK CT

P

P

STRAWBERRY LA
ST ANDREW'S ST

P
B1318

CROYDON RD
TAMWORTH RD

CROSSLEY TERR
BELSAY PL
DILSTON RD

Arthur's
Hill

BEACONSFIELD ST
BAXTERWOOD CT
BAXTERWOOD GR

LONGLEY ST

CLAREWOOD GN
BEECHBURN WLK
LIDDLE RD

ST PHILIPS
ST PHILIPS

COTTINGWOOD
COTTINGWOOD GDNS
COTTINGWOODS
AVISON ST
AVISON PL
AVOLON PL
AVOLON WLK
AVISON CT

WELLINGTON ST
PITT ST

St James' Sta

GALLOWGATE

M

P

P

SK
SK

CALLERTON PL
WELLESLE
CHELSEA GR TR

Westgate
Hill
Sch

GRAINGERVILLE N

NORTHCOTE ST
COOKSON ST
PROSPECT ST

WILLIAM WAY
WORLEY ST

DOUGLAS TERR
EDWARD PL
DOUGLAS TERR
MANSFIELD PL

DIANA ST
COLLIERY LA

BLACKFRIARS CT 1
CHARLOTTE MEWS 2
LOW FRIAR ST 3

HEBER ST

A189

P

Mus

GRAINGER VILLE S
ELLIOTT TERR
MILL LA
HARTINGTON ST
KINGSLEY TERR

BISHOP'S AVE

VALLUM WAY
VALLUM CT

TINDAL CL
TINDAL ST
MANSFIELD ST
COTTENHAM CHARE

WESTGATE CT
TODD'S NOOK
ABINGER ST
BUCKINGHAM ST
OAKES PL

St Mary's
Training & Enterprise
Ctr

CORPORATION ST

FRIARS ST
STOWELL ST

Dispensary
LA
MONK ST
FRIARS

1

TWEED ST
MILL LA
SCEPTRE ST
SCEPTRE ST

GLOUCESTER RD
CAMPBELL PL
CUMBRIA WLK
SURREY PL
SOMERSET PL

B6322 ELSWICK ROW

BACK ELSWICK ST
MILL FARM CL
ANGLESEY PL
ST PAUL'S PL
HAVELOCK PL
ELSWICK ROW

ELSWICK RD
LANCASTER ST
YORK ST

B1600

WESTGATE RD

CROSS VILLA PLACE NO 5
CROSS VILLA PLACE NO 4
CROSS VILLA PLACE NO 3
CROSS VILLA PLACE NO 2
CROSS VILLA PLACE NO 1

RAVENSWORTH TERR
WINCHESTER TERR
HIGH SWINBURNE PL
SWINBURNE ST

GREEN FIELD PL

SUMMERHILL TERR
SUMMERHILL GR

SUMMERHILL ST
HOUSTON ST

WESTGATE TERR

BATH LA
WEST WALLS

BLANDFORD SQ
BLENHEIM ST

THORNTON ST
CHARLOTTE SQ
CROSS ST

RUTHERFORD ST

A189
A189

P

A186
CLAYTON ST W
64

SCEPTRE PL
BRITANNIA PL
SOVEREIGN CT

SOMERSET PL

B6328
DRYBECK CT
RYE HILL
PEEL ST
TEMPLE ST

CLAYTON ST

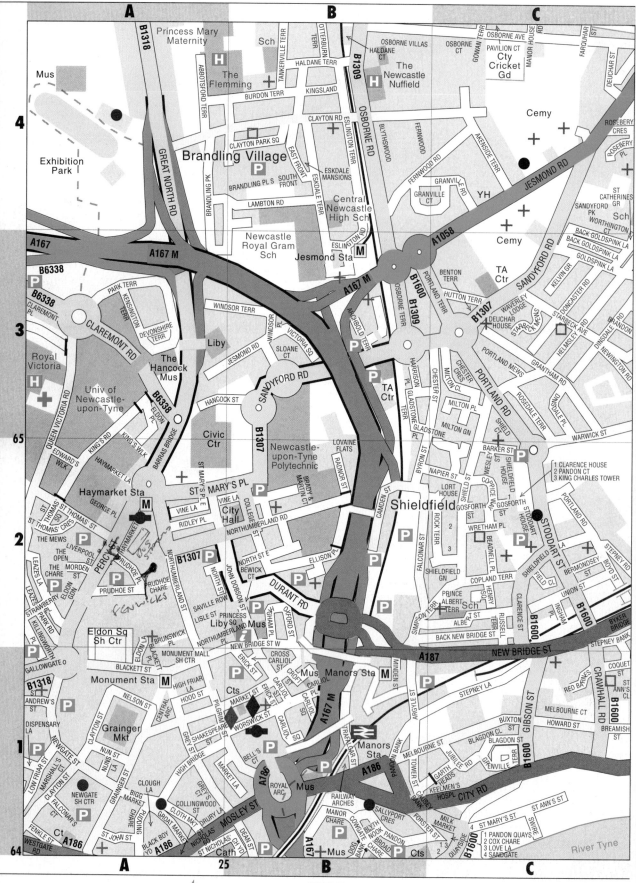

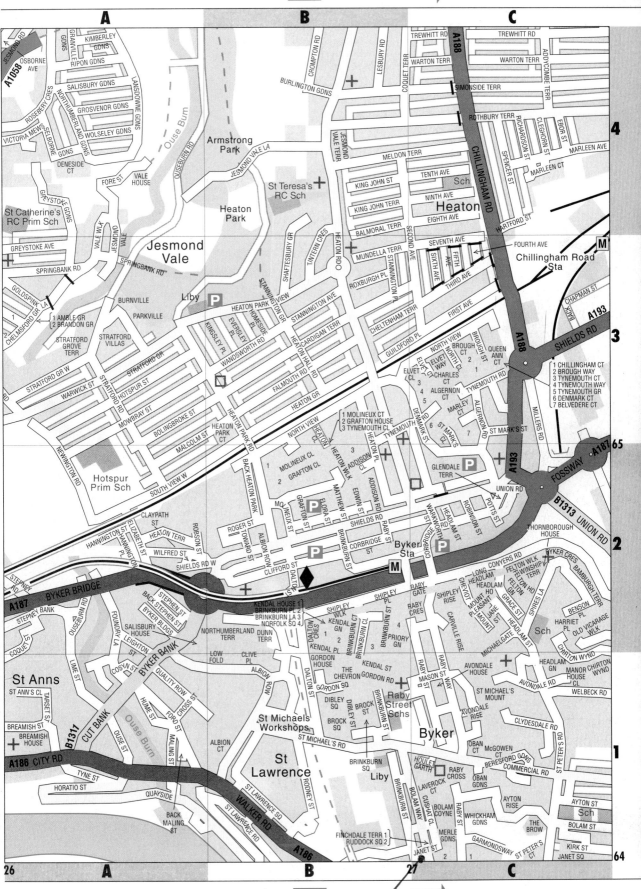

47

68

A   B   C

4

3

65

2

1

64

67
48
75

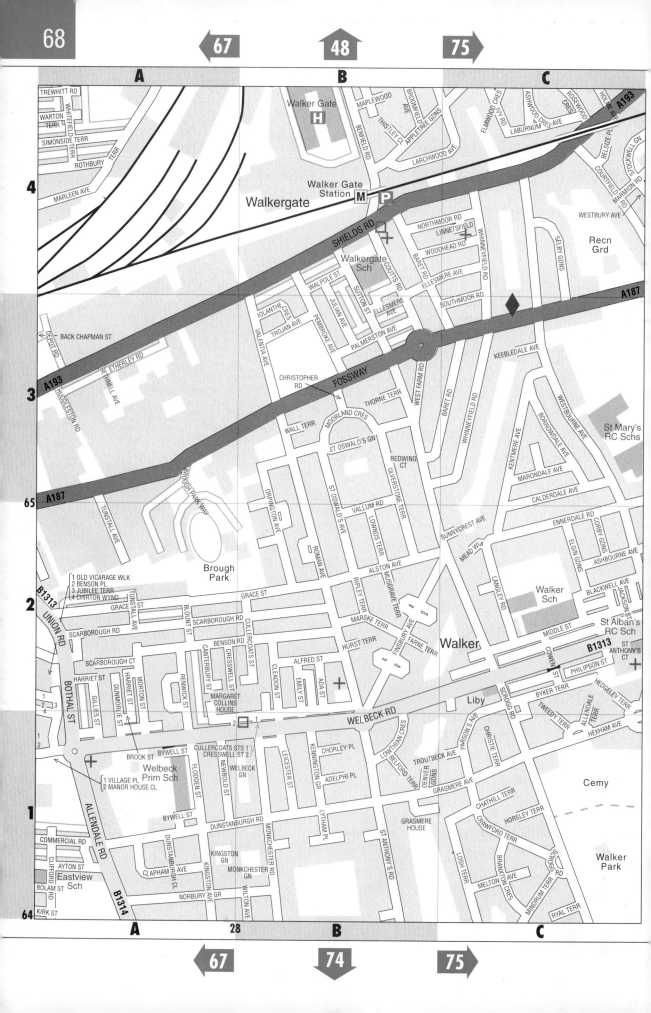

A   B   C

TREWHITT RD
WARTON TERR
WHITEFIELD TERR
SIMONSIDE TERR
ROTHBURY TERR

Walker Gate
H

MAPLEWOOD
BROOMFIELD AVE
THISTLEY CL
APPLETREE GDNS
ELMWOOD CRES
IVY RD
ASHWOOD CRES
ASHWOOD AVE
ROSEWOOD CRES
HOLME AVE A193
BELSIZE PL
STOCKWELL GN
MARMION RD
COURTFIELD RD

4
MARLEEN AVE
BENFIELD RD
LARCHWOOD AVE
LABURNUM CRES
WESTBURY AVE
Recn Grd

Walker Gate
Station
M P
Walkergate
SHIELDS RD
NORTHMOOR RD
LINNETSFIELD
WHINNEYFIELD RD
SELBY GDNS

Walkergate
Sch
WOODHEAD RD
COUTTS RD
BARET RD
ELLESMERE AVE
SOUTHMOOR RD
A187

BACK CHAPMAN ST
WALPOLE ST
SUTTON ST
ELLESMERE AVE
PALMERSTON AVE
KEEBLEDALE AVE

DEPOT RD
BETHERLEY RD
BETHNELL AVE
IOLANTHE CRES
TROJAN AVE
VALENTIA AVE
JULIAN AVE
PEMBROKE AVE
West Farm Rd
WEST FARM RD
St Mary's
RC Schs

3 A193
HUDDLESTON RD
CHRISTOPHER RD
FOSSWAY
THORNE TERR
BARET RD
WHINNEYFIELD RD
KENTMERE AVE
BORROWDALE AVE
WESTBOURNE AVE
MARONDALE AVE
CALDERDALE AVE

WALL TERR
MOORLAND CRES
ST OSWALD'S GN
REDWING CT
ENNERDALE RD
CORBY GDNS
ASHBOURNE AVE

65 A187
BROUGH PARK WAY
ORPINGTON AVE
ST OSWALD'S AVE
VALLUM RD
LOWNDS TERR
ULVERSTONE TERR
SUNNYCREST AVE
MEAD WLK
ELGIN GDNS
BLACKWELL AVE
JACKSON'S

TUNSTALL AVE
Brough Park
ROMAN AVE
ALSTON AVE
LANGLEY RD
Walker
Sch
MIDDLE ST

1 OLD VICARAGE WLK
2 BENSON PL
3 JUBILEE TERR
4 CHIRTON WYND
GRACE ST
RIPLEY TERR
MARSKE TERR
MUSGRAVE TERR
FINSBURY AVE
FARNE TERR
St Alban's
RC Sch
St
ANTHONY'S
CT

2 B1313
UNION RD
GRACE ST
TUNSTALL AVE
SCARBOROUGH RD
BLOUNT ST
SCARBOROUGH RD
CULLERCOATS ST
HURST TERR
Walker
COWEN ST
B1313
PHILIPSON ST

SCARBOROUGH CT
BENSON RD
CANTERBURY ST
CRESSWELL ST
CLEADON ST
ALFRED ST
ADA ST
EMILY ST
Liby
SCROGG RD
BYKER TERR
HEDGELEY TERR

HARRIET ST
MORTON ST
RENWICK ST
Margaret
Collins
House
WELBECK RD
LONTHIAN CRES
PARSON'S AVE
CHRISTIE TERR
TWEEDY TERR
ALLENDALE TERR
HEXHAM AVE

BOTHAL ST
GILLIES ST
DUNMORLIE ST
HARRIET ST
BROOK ST
BYWELL ST
CULLERCOATS STS 1
CRESSWELL ST 2
CHORLEY PL
KENNINGTON GR
BELFORD TERR
TROUTBECK AVE
GRASMERE AVE
CHATHILL TERR
HORSLEY TERR
Cemy

1 VILLAGE PL
2 MANOR HOUSE CL
Welbeck
Prim Sch
FLODDEN ST
NEWBOLD ST
WELBECK GN
LEICESTER ST
ADELPHI PL
DENVER GDNS
Grasmere
House
CRAWFORD TERR
Walker
Park

1
BYWELL ST
DUNSTANBURGH RD
MONCKCHESTER RD
LYTHAM PL
ST ANTHONY'S RD
LOSH TERR
MELTON AVE
SCROGG RD
MINDRUM TERR

COMMERCIAL RD
AYTON ST
ALLENDALE RD
DUNSTANBURGH CL
KINGSTON GN
BRANXTON CRES
RYAL TERR

CLIFFORD ST
Eastview
Sch
CLAPHAM AVE
KINGSTON AVE
MONCKCHESTER GN
WILTON AVE

BOLAM RD
64 KIRK ST
B1314
NORBURY GR

A   28   B   C

67
74
75

A

B

C

PRETORIA ST
WHITFIELD RD
ROBERTS ST
HEATH CRES
SEDGEMOOR AVE
HILLSIDE CRES
LITTLE WAY
CRANBROOK PL
CRANBROOK RD
CRANBROOK RD
DELAVAL RD
FOREST RD
ARMSTRONG RD
HODGKIN PARK RD
SHAFTO ST
LIGHTWOOD AVE
LIGHTWOOD AVE
WHITEHOUSE RD
CROSSHILL RD
DELAVAL GDNS
WOODLAND CRES
HOLMLAND
SOUTH BENWELL RD

Scotswood
ST MARGARET S RD
ST MARGARET'S RD
Delaval
EGERTON ST

A695
CONWOOD RD
DELAVAL RD
WHITEHOUSE RD

4

Paradise

Works
SCOTSWOOD RD
A695

Works

A695

Works

River Tyne

Works

Derwenthaugh Marina

3

A695
DERWENTHAUGH RD
RIVERSIDE WAY
RIVERSIDE WAY
MANDELA WAY

A114
Derwent Haugh
A114
SCOTSWOOD VIEW

DERWENTHAUGH RD
GIBSIDE WAY
MAPLE ROW

63

A695

River Derwent
P
P
P

A69
PINETREE WAY
HOLLINSIDE RD
P
P

2

Allot Gdns
LONG RIGG
Hotel
P
P
ℹ
The Metrocentre

A1
LONGRIGG RD
ALLISON CT

The Sands Ind Est
B6317
1 SPENCERS BANK
2 HOOD ST
3 BREWERY LA
4 JUBILEE TERR
MILLER'S LA
ST MICHAEL'S WAY

SANDS RD
LYNDHURST TERR
Swalwell

1

3 2 1
BREWERY BANK
CROWLEY RD
MARKET LA
A1

B6317 HEXHAM RD
4
NAPIER RD
PARK TERR
MASEFIELD AVE
COALWAY LAN
COLBECK AVE
ENFIELD AVE
SHIELD AVE

SWALWELL BANK
P
QUALITY ROW RD
AXWELL TERR
RIDLEY GDNS
RICHMOND AVE
CLAVERING RD
LUMLEY AVE
GROSVENOR AVE
OAKLANDS
BEVERLEY DR

B6317
Whickham Ind Est
MARLBORO AVE

62

20

A

B

21

C

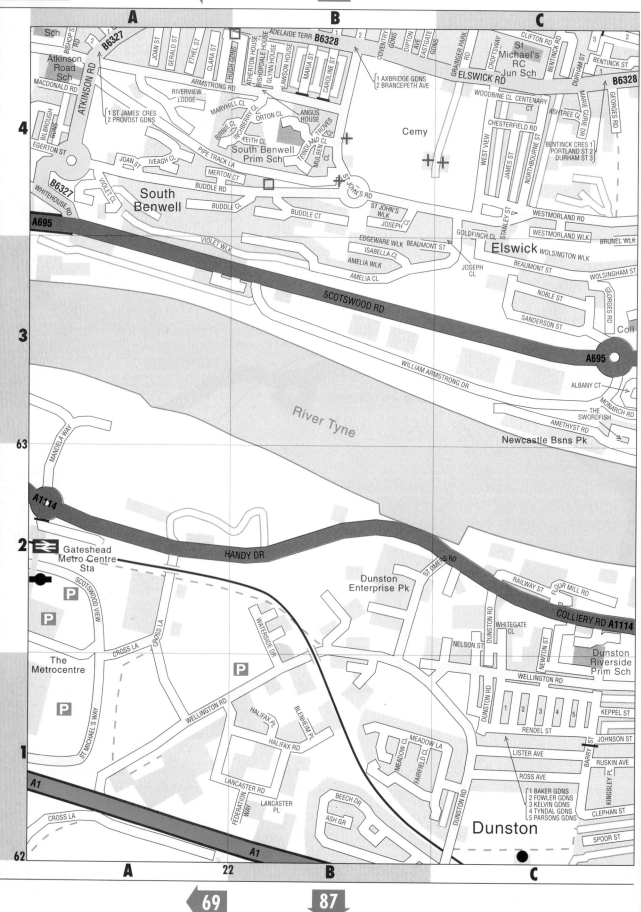

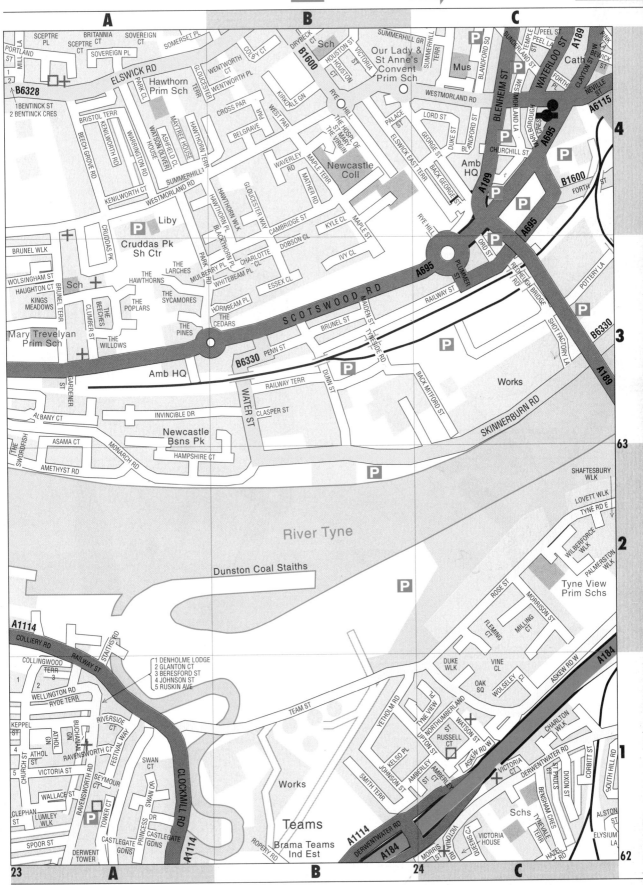

A   B   C

SCEPTRE PL
BRITANNIA CT
SOVEREIGN CT
PORTLAND ST
MILL LA
SCEPTRE CT
SOVEREIGN PL
SOMERSET PL
DRYBECK
Sch
SUMMERHILL GR
SUMMERHILL TERR
P
PEEL ST
PEEL ST
A189
PINK LA

B6328
ELSWICK RD
Hawthorn Prim Sch
PARK CL
WENTWORTH CT
COLBY CT
B1600
HOUSTON ST
HOUSTON CT
VICTORIA ST
Our Lady & St Anne's Convent Prim Sch
Mus
BLANDFORD SQ
SUNDERLAND ST
WEST MORLAND CRES
FORTH PL
WATERLOO ST
CLAYTON ST W
BEWICK ST
Cath

1 Bentinck St
2 Bentinck Cres
GLOUCESTER TERR
WENTWORTH PL
CROSS PAR
KIRKDALE GN
WEST PAR
RYE HILL
WESTMORLAND RD
BLENHEIM ST
CHURCHILL ST
P
P
A6115

BRISTOL TERR
KENILWORTH RD
WARRINGTON RD
WATSON OLIVER HOUSE
ASHFIELD CL
HAWTHORN TERR
MAYTREE HOUSE
HAWTHORN WLK
BELGRAVE
WAVERLEY RD
MAPLE TERR
MATHER RD
THE HOSP OF ST MARY THE VIRGIN
Newcastle Coll
PALACE ST
LORD ST
GEORGE ST
DUKE ST
BLANDFORD ST
A189
Amb HQ
P
P
FORTH ST
NEVILLE ST
4

BEECH GROVE RD
SUMMERHILL
WESTMORLAND RD
KENILWORTH CT
GLOUCESTER WAY
HAWTHORN WLK
CAMBRIDGE ST
BLACKTHORN PL
Liby
P
Cruddas Pk Sh Ctr
KYLE CL
MAPLE ST
ELSWICK EAST TERR
BACK GEORGE ST
RYE HILL
ORD ST
P
B1600
FORTH
FORTH ST

BRUNEL WLK
WOLSINGHAM ST
HAUGHTON CT
BRUNEL TERR
KINGS MEADOWS
Sch
THE HAWTHORNS
THE LARCHES
MULBERRY RD
PARK RD
CHARLOTTE CL
WHITEBEAM PL
ESSEX CL
IVY CL
DOBSON CL
A695
PLUMMER ST
P
REDHEUGH BRIDGE RD
POTTERY LA
P
B6330
A189

Mary Trevelyan Prim Sch
THE BEECHES
CLUMBER ST
THE SYCAMORES
THE POPLARS
THE CEDARS
HORNBEAM PL
SCOTSWOOD RD
BRUNEL ST
MAIDEN ST
TYNESIDE RD
RAILWAY ST
SHOT FACTORY LA
3

THE SWORDFISH
THE WILLOWS
THE PINES
Amb HQ
B6330
PENN ST
DUNN ST
P
P
BACK MITFORD ST
Works

GARDENER ST
ALBANY CT
ASAMA CT
MONARCH RD
INVINCIBLE DR
WATER ST
CLASPER ST
RAILWAY TERR
SKINNERBURN RD
63

ASAMA CT
AMETHYST RD
Newcastle Bsns Pk
HAMPSHIRE CT
P
SHAFTESBURY WLK

River Tyne
LOVETT WLK
TYNE RD E

Dunston Coal Staiths
P
WILBERFORCE WLK
PALMERSTON WLK
2

ROSE ST
MORRISON ST
Tyne View Prim Schs

A1114
COLLIERY RD
STAITHS RD
RAILWAY ST
1 Denholme Lodge
2 Glanton Ct
3 Beresford St
4 Johnson St
5 Ruskin Ave
FLEMING CT
MILLING CT
A184

COLLINGWOOD TERR
1
2
3
DUKE WLK
VINE CL
OAK SQ
WOLSELEY CL
ASKEW RD W

WELLINGTON RD
RYDE TERR
TEAM ST
YETHOLM RD
TYNE VIEW PL
NORTHUMBERLAND ST
WATSON ST
CHARLTON WLK
CHARLTON WLK

KEPPEL ST
RIVERSIDE CT
BUCHANAN GN
ATHOL GN
RAVENSWORTH CT
FESTIVAL WAY
KELSO PL
UPTON ST
RUSSELL CT
ASKEW RD W
VICTORIA CT
DERWENTWATER RD
ST PAULS
DIXON ST
CORBITT ST
SOUTH HILL RD

CHURCH ST
ATHOL ST
VICTORIA ST
SEYMOUR CT
SWAN CT
SWAN DR
CASTLEGATE
CASTLEGATE GDNS
SMITH TERR
JOHNSON ST
AMBERLEY ST
AMBERLEY CT
VICTORIA CT
BENSHAM CRES
TYNEDALE TERR
HAZEL RD
ALSTON ST
ELYSIUM LA

CLEPHAN ST
LUMLEY WLK
WALLACE ST
TOWER CT
PRINCESS DR
CLOCKMILL RD
A1114
Works
Teams
Brama Teams Ind Est
A1114
DERWENTWATER RD
A184
MORRIS ST
VICTORIA RD
QUEENS RD
Schs
Victoria House
62

SPOOR ST
DERWENT TOWER
P
ROPERY RD

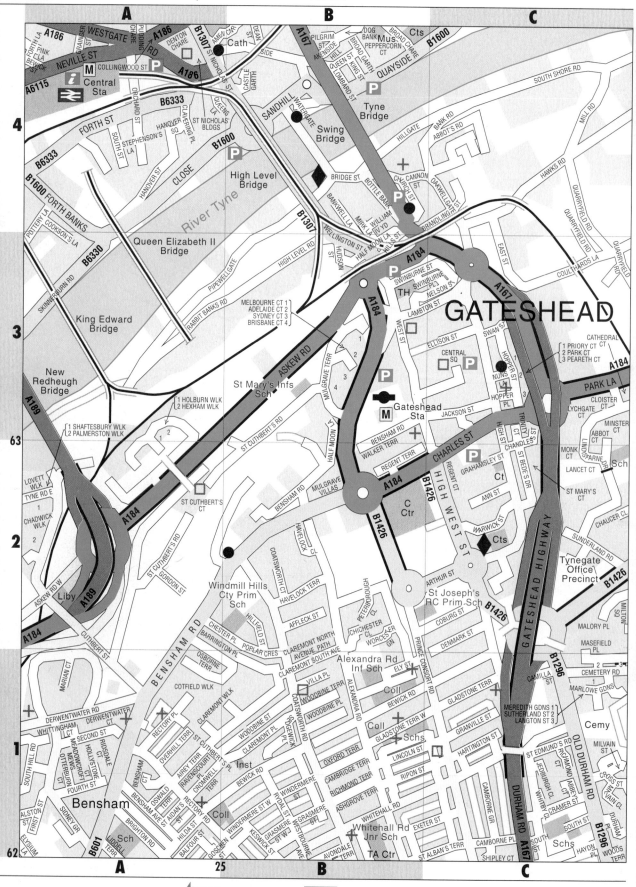

A B C

A186 RAINIER WESTGATE A186 B1307 ST NICHOLAS AMEN CNR DEAN PILGRIM DOG BANK Mus Cts
FORTH LA PINK PUDDING Cath SIDE AKENSIDE PEPPERCORN CT BROAD CHARE B1600
PINK CLA CHARE RD HILL QUEEN ST BROAD GARTH CT QUAYSIDE
BEWICK NEVILLE ST M COLLINGWOOD ST P A186 CASTLE GARTH QUEEN ST KING ST LOMBARD ST

A6115 i Central B6333 SANDHILL WATERGATE Tyne P SOUTH SHORE RD
Sta ORCHARD ST QUEENS Swing Bridge
FORTH ST CLAVERING PL ST NICHOLAS' Bridge HILLGATE BANK RD MILL RD
STEPHENSON'S HANOVER BLDGS Swing ABBOT'S RD
B6333 LA SQ Bridge BRIDGE ST CHURCH CANNON ST
SOUTH ST CLOSE High Level B1600 BOTTLE BANK P OAKWELLGATE HAWKS RD QUARRYFIELD RD
B6333 HANOVER ST Bridge BANKWELL LA WILLIAM BRANDLING QUARRYFIELD RD
B1600 FORTH BANKS B1307 MIRK LA IV YD EAST ST COULTHARDS LA QUARRYFIELD RD
POTTERY LA River Tyne HALF MOON LA HILLS ST
COOKSON'S LA B6330 WELLINGTON ST HUDSON A184 SWINBURNE ST A167
B6330 Queen Elizabeth II HIGH LEVEL RD SWINBURNE GATESHEAD
SKINNERBURN RD Bridge PIPEWELLGATE TH PL NELSON ST
RABBIT BANKS RD P LAMBTON ST CATHEDRAL
New MELBOURNE CT 1 A184 WEST ST ELLISON ST SWAN 1 PRIORY CT
Redheugh ADELAIDE CT 2 ASKEW RD CENTRAL ST 2 PARK CT
Bridge SYDNEY CT 3 MULGRAVE TERR SQ P 3 PEARETH CT
A189 BRISBANE CT 4 1 HOPPER A184
63 St Mary's Infs 2 NUNS CT PARK LA
Sch 3 HOPPER CLOISTER
1 HOLBURN WLK 4 P PL LYCHGATE CT
2 HEXHAM WLK M Gateshead JACKSON ST HIGH ST MINSTER
1 SHAFTESBURY WLK 1 Sta BENSHAM RD TRINITY ABBOT CT
2 PALMERSTON WLK 2 1 WALKER TERR CHARLES ST CHANDLESS ST BEDE'S DR CT Sch
LOVETT ST CUTHBERT'S RD REGENT TERR P GRAHAMSLEY ST ST MARY'S LINDISFARNE
WLK A184 Ct LANCET CT CT
TYNE RD E BENSHAM RD B1426 ANN ST MONK CHAUCER CL
CHADWICK MULGRAVE C HIGH WEST ST REGENT CT CT
WLK 2 ST CUTHBERT'S VILLAS Ctr WARWICK Cts SUNDERLAND
A184 CT HAVELOCK B1426 ST Tynegate RD
2 ST CUTHBERT'S RD HAVELOCK CL ARTHUR ST Office B1426
ASKEN RD W GORDON ST COATSWORTH CT Precinct
Liby A189 HAVELOCK TERR St Joseph's GATESHEAD HIGHWAY
A184 CUTHBERT ST Windmill Hills RC Prim Sch B1426 MALORY PL
Cty Prim CHESTER PL PETERBOROUGH COBURG ST MILTON
BENSHAM RD Sch HILLFIELD ST CL CHICHESTER DENMARK ST SQ MASEFIELD
BARRINGTON PL POPLAR CRES CL WORCESTER B1296 PL
MARIAN CT OSBORNE AFFLECK ST GN Alexandra Rd 2 CEMETERY RD
TERR CLAREMONT NORTH Inf Sch CAMILLA 1 MARLOWE
COTFIELD WLK AVENUE PATH VILLA PL ELY ST Coll MEREDITH GDNS 1 GDNS
CLAREMONT SOUTH AVE WOODBINE ST BEWICK RD GLADSTONE TERR SUTHERLAND ST 2 Cemy
DERWENTWATER RD WOODBINE PL ALEXANDRA RD Coll GRANVILLE ST LANGTON ST 3
WHITTINGHAM DERWENTWATER CLAREMONT PL COATSWORTH RD GLADSTONE TERR W HARTINGTON ST OLD DURHAM RD MILVAIN
CT CT YOGWICK PRINCE CONSORT RD Schs ST EDMUND'S RICHMOND ST
SECOND ST RECTORY PL AIRLY TERR OXFORD TERR CAMBRIDGE TERR ST JEDBURGH CL ABBEY RD CROSS B1296
SOUTH HILL RD RIDSDALE OVERHILL TERR ST CUTHBERT'S BEWICK RD RICHMOND TERR LINCOLN ST CAMBORNE GR WHITBY CL VAIN CL DURHAM
HOLLYSTONE CT RAVENSCOURT RYDAL ST RIPON ST CRAMER ST TERR
MEADOWCROFT CROMWELL WINDERMERE ASHGROVE TERR SOUTH ST WOODS
OTTERBURN FOURTH ST HILDA ST TERR WINDERMERE ST W WHITEHALL RD GRASMERE TERR A167 B1296 TERR
Bensham BENSHAM AVE S RECTORY RD Coll GRASMERE Whitehall Rd EXETER ST Schs HAYDN
B601 OSWALD BRIGHTON RD BALFOUR ST GOSCHEN ST Jnr Sch ST ALBAN'S TERR DURHAM RD PL
ELYSIUM SIDNEY GR Sch LIDDELL KESWICK ST WESTBOURNE CAMBORNE GR SHIPLEY CT
LA FIRST ST AVONDALE TA Ctr
62 TERR

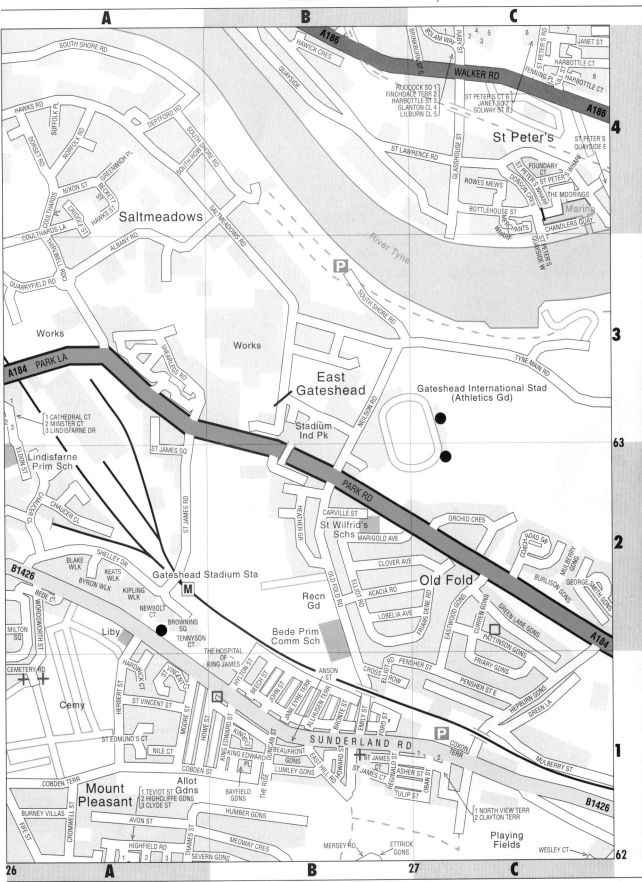

A · B · C

Saltmeadows

SOUTH SHORE RD
HAWKS RD
SUFFOLK PL
DORSET RD
NORFOLK RD
DEPTFORD RD
SOUTH SHORE RD
GREENWICH PL
HAWICK CRES
BRINKBURN ST
BOLAM WAY
RABY ST
JANET ST
ST PETER'S RD
HARBOTTLE CT
WALKER RD
HARBOTTLE CT
NIXON ST
BECKETT
CRIDDLE ST
COULTHARDS LA
COULTHARDS PL
HAWKS RD
ALBANY RD
QUAYSIDE
ST LAWRENCE RD
FENNING PL
RUDDOCK SQ 1
FINCHDALE TERR 2
HARBOTTLE ST 3
GLANTON CL 4
LILBURN CL 5
ST PETER'S CT 6
JANET SQ 7
SOLWAY ST 8
A186

St Peter's

4

THIRLWELL RDO
QUARRYFIELD RD
SALTMEADOWS RD
GLASSHOUSE ST
DOBSON CRES
ST PETER'S WHARF
FOUNDARY CT
ST PETER'S WHARF
ST PETER'S QUAYSIDE E
ROWES MEWS
BOTTLEHOUSE ST
MERCHANTS WHARF
THE MOORINGS
Marina
CHANDLERS QUAY
ST PETER'S QUAYSIDE W

River Tyne

Works

Works

P

SOUTH SHORE RD

3

A184 PARK LA
SHEARLESS RD
TYNE MAIN RD

East Gateshead

Gateshead International Stad (Athletics Gd)

Stadium Ind Pk
ST JAMES SQ
NEILSON RD

63

1 CATHEDRAL CT
2 MINSTER CT
3 LINDISFARNE DR

Lindisfarne Prim Sch

ELDON ST
CHAUCER CL
CHAUCER CL
ST JAMES RD

PARK RD

CARVILLE ST
HEATHER GR
MARIGOLD AVE
ORCHID CRES
COACH ROAD GN
MULBERRY GDNS
GEORGE SMITH GDNS

St Wilfrid's Schs

CLOVER AVE
BURLISON GDNS

2

BLAKE WLK
SHELLEY DR
KEATS WLK
BYRON WLK
KIPLING WLK
ACACIA RD
FRIARS DENE RD
EASTWOOD GDNS
CURREN GDNS
GREEN LANE GDNS

Old Fold

Gateshead Stadium Sta
M

NEWBOLT CT
BROWNING SQ
TENNYSON CT
WORDSWORTH ST
BEDE CT
MILTON SQ

Liby

Recn Gd
OLD FOLD RD
ELLIOT RD
LOBELIA AVE
PATTINSON GDNS
HEPBURN GDNS
GREEN LA
A184

Bede Prim Comm Sch

FRIARY GDNS

THE HOSPITAL OF KING JAMES

CEMETERY RD
HARDWICK CT
VINCENT CT
HYLTON ST
BEECH ST
JOHN ST
JANE EYRE TERR
ANSON ST
ALLHUSEN TERR
BRONTE ST
EMILY ST
FORD ST
CROSS ROW
PENSHER ST
ELLIOT RD
PENSHER ST E
P
COXON TERR
MULBERRY ST

Cemy

ST VINCENT ST
MOORE ST
HOWE ST
KING EDWARD RD
ST EDMUND'S CT
NILE CT
KING EDWARD PL
DUNCAN ST
BEAUFRONT GDNS
EAST HILL RD
HOWARD ST
ST JAMES CT
ST JAMES CT
REGINALD ST
ASHER ST
OBAN ST

SUNDERLAND RD

B1426

1

COBDEN TERR
COBDEN ST
THE RISE
LUMLEY GDNS
BAYFIELD GDNS
TULIP ST

Mount Pleasant

Allot Gdns
1 TEVIOT ST
2 HIGHCLIFFE GDNS
3 CLYDE ST

BURNEY VILLAS
FIFE ST
CROMWELL ST
AVON ST
THAMES ST
HUMBER GDNS
MEDWAY CRES
MERSEY RD
ETTRICK GDNS
WESLEY CT

1 NORTH VIEW TERR
2 CLAYTON TERR

Playing Fields

HIGHFIELD RD
SEVERN GDNS

B1426

62

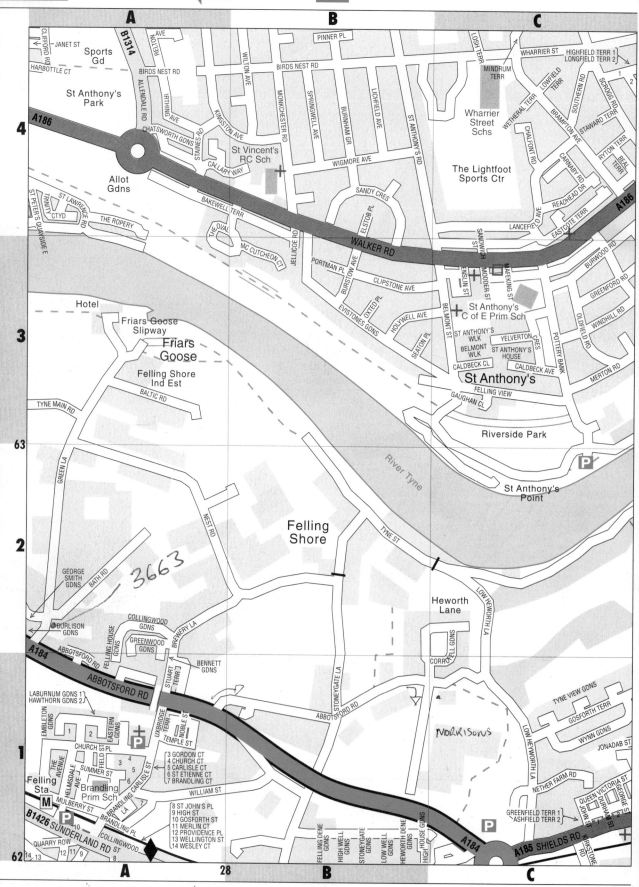

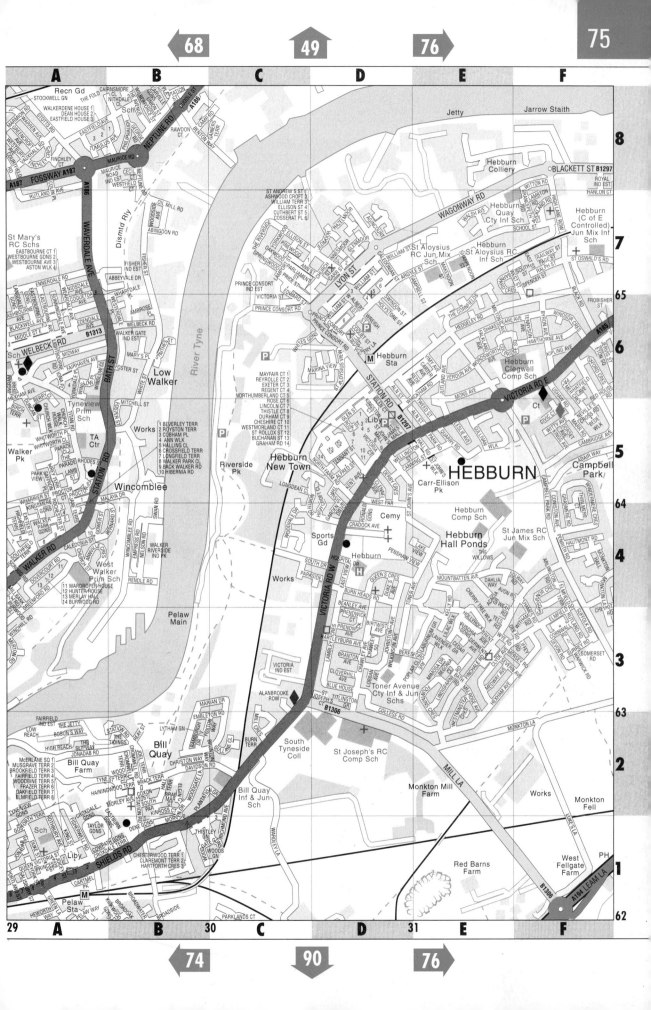

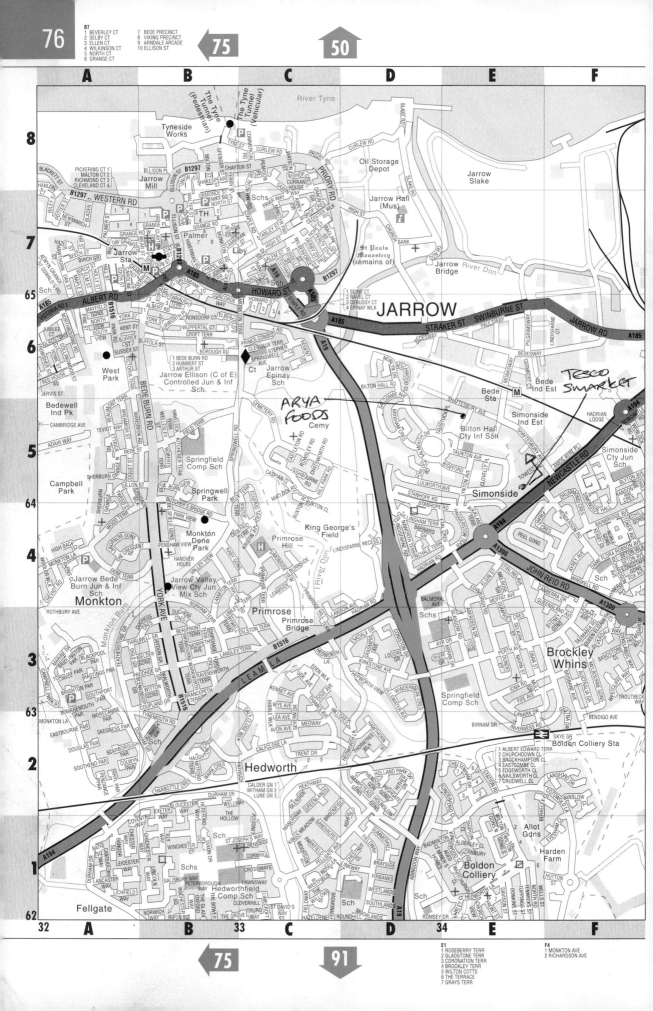

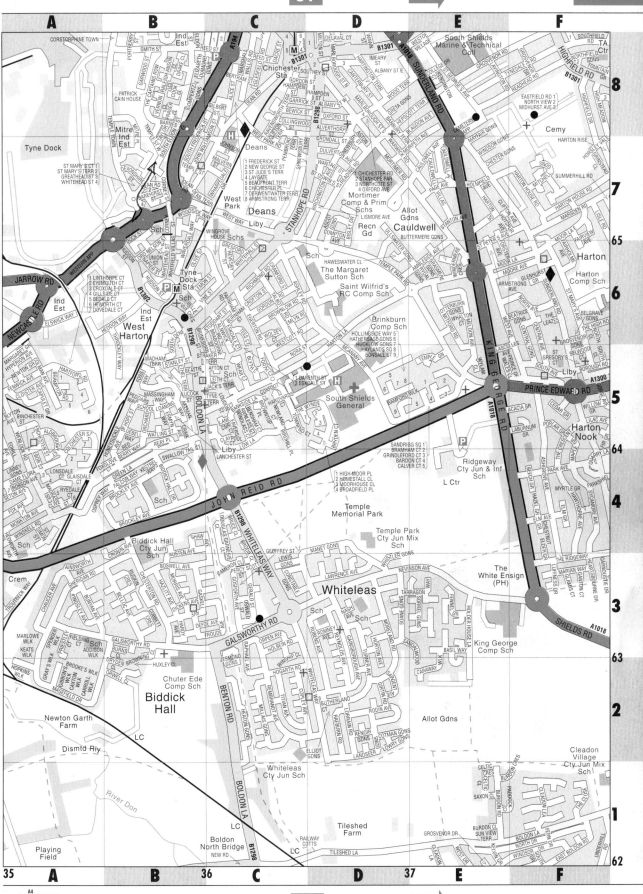

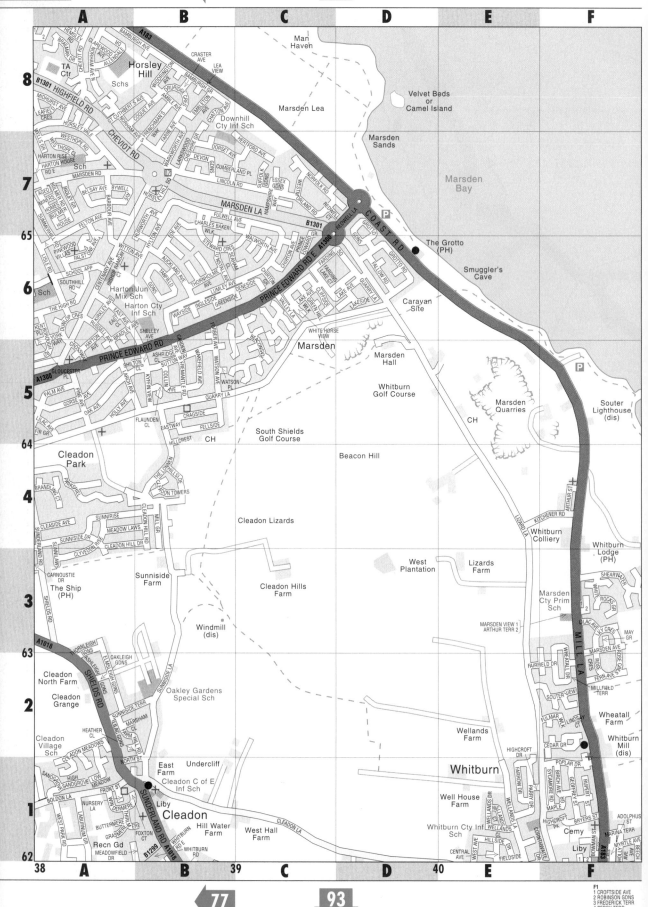

77
52

A B C D E F

8

7

65

6

5

64

4

63

3

2

1

62

77
93

38 A B 39 C D 40 E F

Man Haven

Velvet Beds or Camel Island

Marsden Lea

Marsden Sands

Marsden Bay

Horsley Hill

CRASTER AVE

LEA VIEW

TA Ctr

Schs

B1301 HIGHFIELD RD

CHEVIOT RD

Sch

Downhill Cty Inf Sch

MARSDEN LA

CHARLES BAKER WLK

STEWARD CRES

Harton Jun Mix Sch

Harton Cty Inf Sch

PRINCE EDWARD RD E A1300

B1301

COAST RD

The Grotto (PH)

Smuggler's Cave

Marsden

Caravan Site

WHITE HORSE VIEW

Marsden Hall

Whitburn Golf Course

PRINCE EDWARD RD

A1300

GLOUCESTER PL

PALM AVE

A1018

CRAGSIDE

EASTWAY

FELLSIDE

HILLCREST

CH

CH

Cleadon Park

CLEADON TOWERS

South Shields Golf Course

Beacon Hill

Marsden Quarries

Souter Lighthouse (dis)

ARTHUR ST

KITCHENER RD

LIZARD LA

Whitburn Colliery

MILL LA

Cleadon Lizards

West Plantation

Lizards Farm

Whitburn Lodge (PH)

SHEARWATER

Sunniside Farm

The Ship (PH)

SHIELDS RD

Cleadon Hills Farm

Marsden Cty Prim Sch

MARSDEN VIEW 1
ARTHUR TERR 2

Marsden Ave

A1018

Cleadon North Farm

Cleadon Grange

Windmill (dis)

Oakley Gardens Special Sch

SUNNISIDE LA

SUNNISIDE TERR

Wellands Farm

Wheatall Farm

Whitburn Mill (dis)

Cleadon Village Sch

CLEADON MEADOWS

East Farm

Undercliff

Cleadon C of E Inf Sch

Whitburn

Well House Farm

Whitburn Cty Inf Sch

BOLDON LA

Liby

Cleadon

Hill Water Farm

West Hall Farm

CLEADON LA

B1299

SUNDERLAND RD A1018

B1301

A183

Cemy

Liby

Recn Gd

MEADOWFIELD DR

F1
1 CROFTSIDE AVE
2 ROBINSON GDNS
3 FREDERICK TERR
4 PERCY TERR

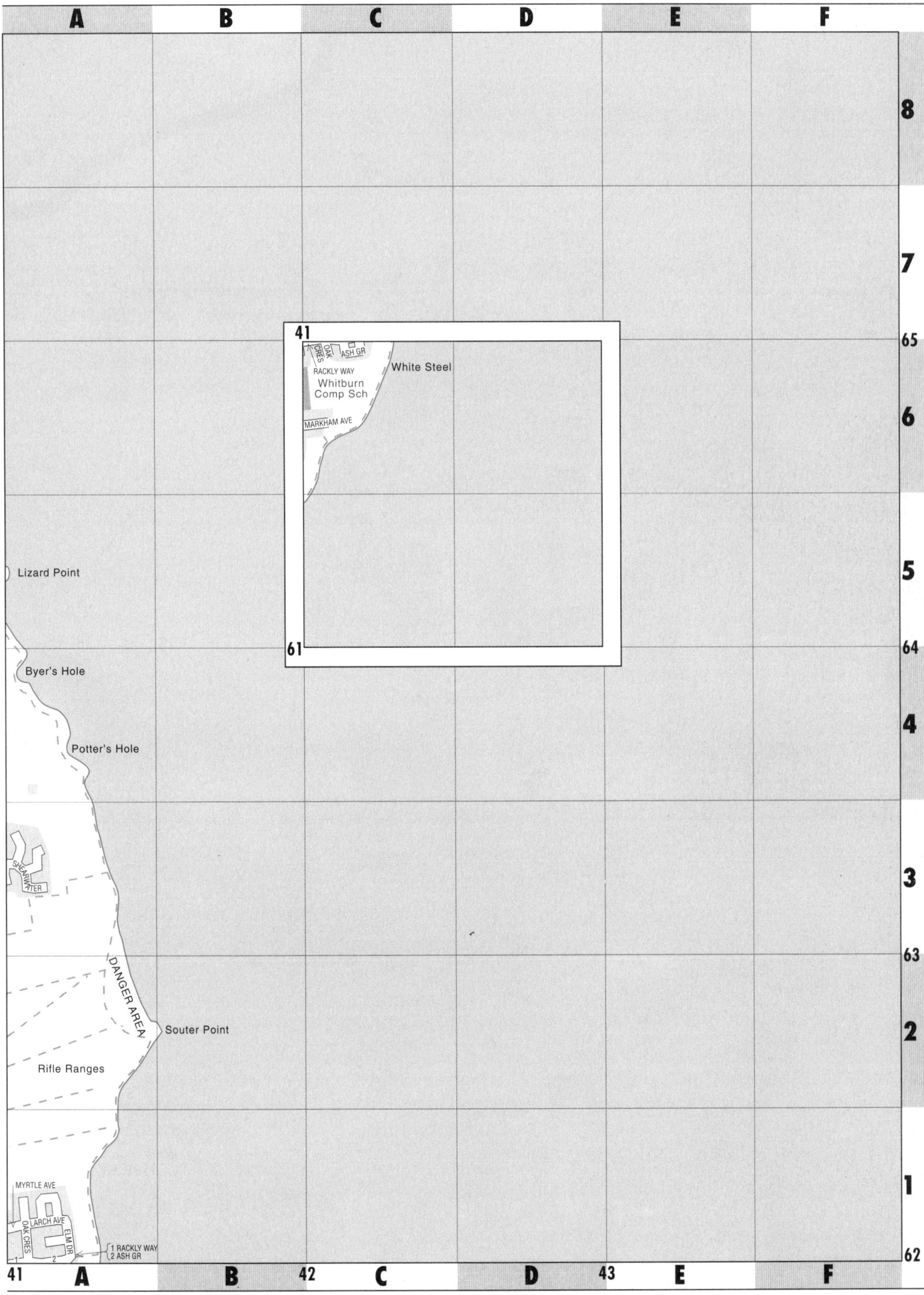

A　　B　　C　　D　　E　　F

8

7

65

6

41

OAK CRES　ASH GR

RACKLY WAY　　White Steel

Whitburn
Comp Sch

MARKHAM AVE

61

5

Lizard Point

64

Byer's Hole

4

Potter's Hole

3

SALTERWATER

63

DANGER AREA

Souter Point

2

Rifle Ranges

1

MYRTLE AVE

LARCH AVE

OAK CRES　ELM DR

1 RACKLY WAY
2 ASH GR

62

41　　A　　B　　42　　C　　D　　43　　E　　F

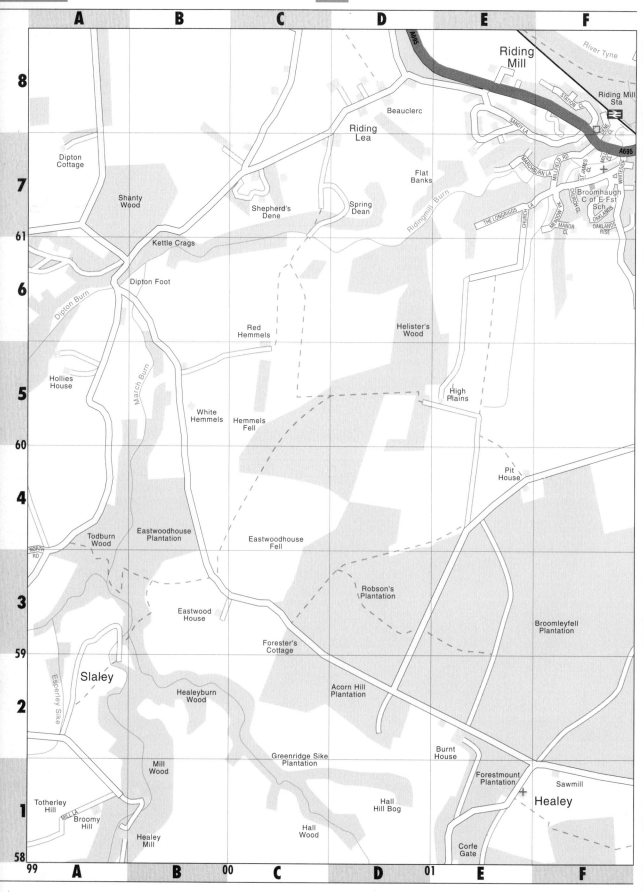

A B C D E F

8

7

61

6

5

60

4

3

59

2

1

58

99 A B 00 C D 01 E F

River Tyne

Riding Mill

Riding Mill Sta

A695

A695

STATION CL

MILL CL

DERE CL

WHITESIDE

ST JAMES CL

CHURCH CL

MILFIELD RD

MARCHBURN LA

SANDY LA

CHURCH LA

MEADOW PK

MANOR CL

OAKLANDS

OAKLANDS RISE

THE LONGRIGGS

Broomhaugh C of E Fst Sch

Beauclerc

Riding Lea

Flat Banks

Ridingmill Burn

Spring Dean

Shepherd's Dene

Helister's Wood

Dipton Cottage

Shanty Wood

Kettle Crags

Dipton Foot

Dipton Burn

March Burn

Red Hemmels

High Plains

Hollies House

White Hemmels

Hemmels Fell

Pit House

60

Todburn Wood

Eastwoodhouse Plantation

Eastwoodhouse Fell

Robson's Plantation

Broomleyfell Plantation

NORTH RD

Eastwood House

Forester's Cottage

Acorn Hill Plantation

Slaley

Esperley Sike

Healeyburn Wood

Greenridge Sike Plantation

Burnt House

Forestmount Plantation

Sawmill

Healey

Mill Wood

Hall Hill Bog

Totherley Hill

MILL LA

Broomy Hill

Healey Mill

Hall Wood

Corfe Gate

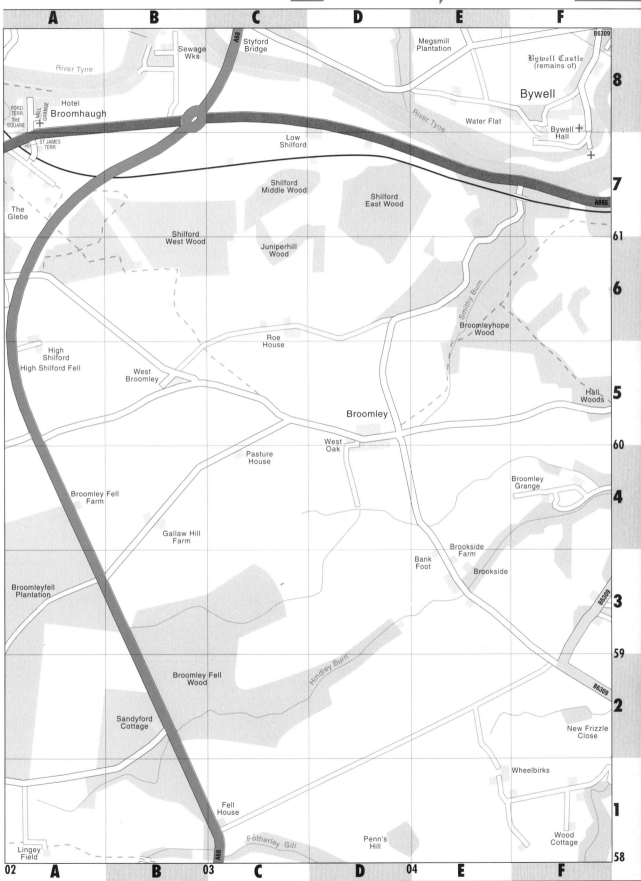

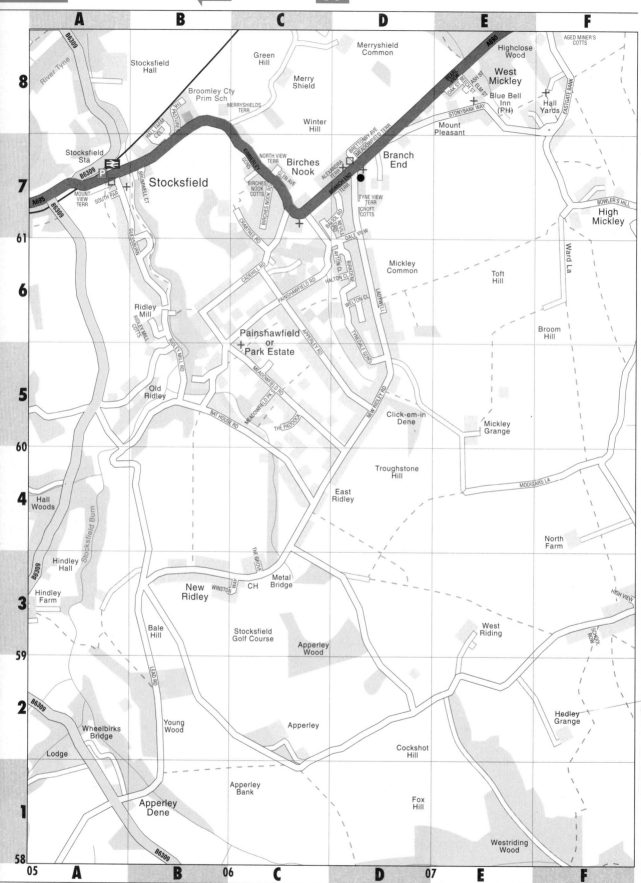

A B C D E F

8

Aged Miner's Cotts

River Tyne

Stocksfield Hall

Green Hill

Merryshield Common

Highclose Wood

West Mickley

Hall Yards

A695

Broomley Cty Prim Sch

MERRYSHIELDS TERR

Merry Shield

Winter Hill

Oak St
Ash St
Beech St
Elm St

Blue Bell Inn (PH)

FASTGATE BANK

HALL FARM CL

STONYBANK WAY

7

Stocksfield Sta

P

Stocksfield

MOUNT VIEW TERR

SOUTH PAR

BRUNWELL CT

B6309

A695

GUESSBURN

NORTH VIEW TERR

KIMBERLEY GDNS

BIRCHES NOOK COTTS

GLEN AVE

Birches Nook

ALEXANDRA TERR

BAZOL RD

NEVILL RD

BRANCH END

BRETTONBY AVE

MEADOWFIELD TERR

Branch End

Mount Pleasant

TYNE VIEW TERR

CROFT COTTS

BOWLER'S HILL

High Mickley

61

6

CADEHILL RD

PAINSHAWFIELD RD

APPERLEY RD

LAYTON CL

HALTON CL

BIRKLANE

WELTON CL

LADYWELL

Mickley Common

Toft Hill

WARD LA

Ridley Mill

RIDLEY MILL COTTS

RIDLEY MILL RD

Painshawfield or Park Estate

TYNEDALE GDNS

Broom Hill

5

Old Ridley

BAT HOUSE RD

MEADOWFIELD PK RD

MEADOWFIELD RD

THE PADDOCK

NEW RIDLEY RD

Click-em-in Dene

Mickley Grange

60

Hall Woods

Stocksfield Burn

Troughstone Hill

MODIGARS LA

4

Hindley Hall

East Ridley

North Farm

B6309

THE GROVE

WINSTON AVE

CH

Metal Bridge

West Riding

HIGH VIEW

3

Hindley Farm

New Ridley

LEAD RD

Bale Hill

Stocksfield Golf Course

Apperley Wood

SCHOOL ROW

Hedley Grange

59

Apperley

2

B6309

Wheelbirks Bridge

Young Wood

Cockshot Hill

Lodge

Apperley Bank

Fox Hill

1

Apperley Dene

Westriding Wood

58

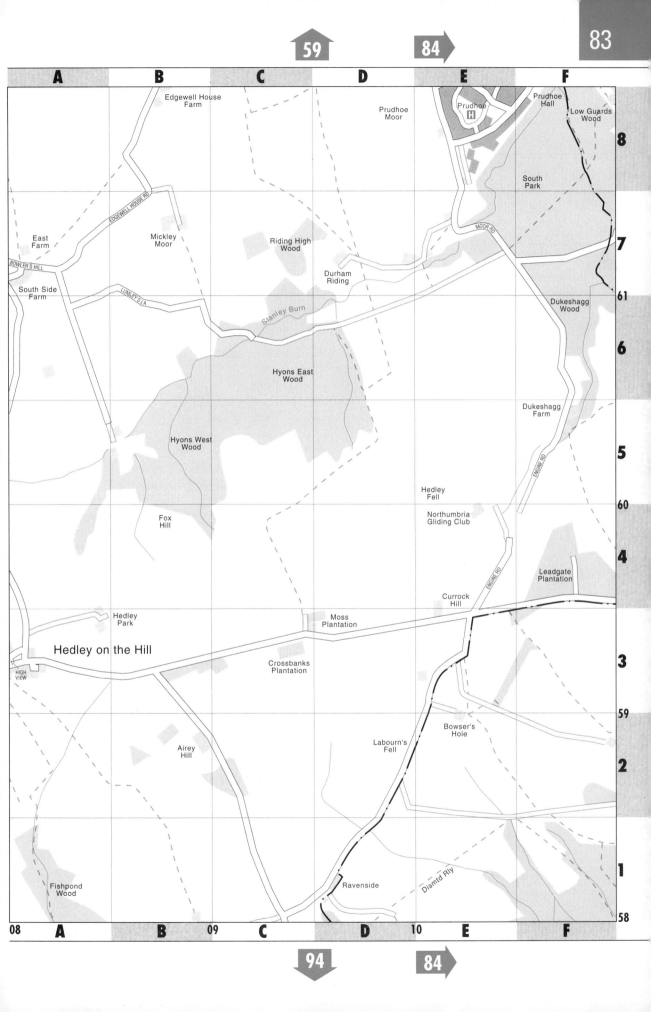

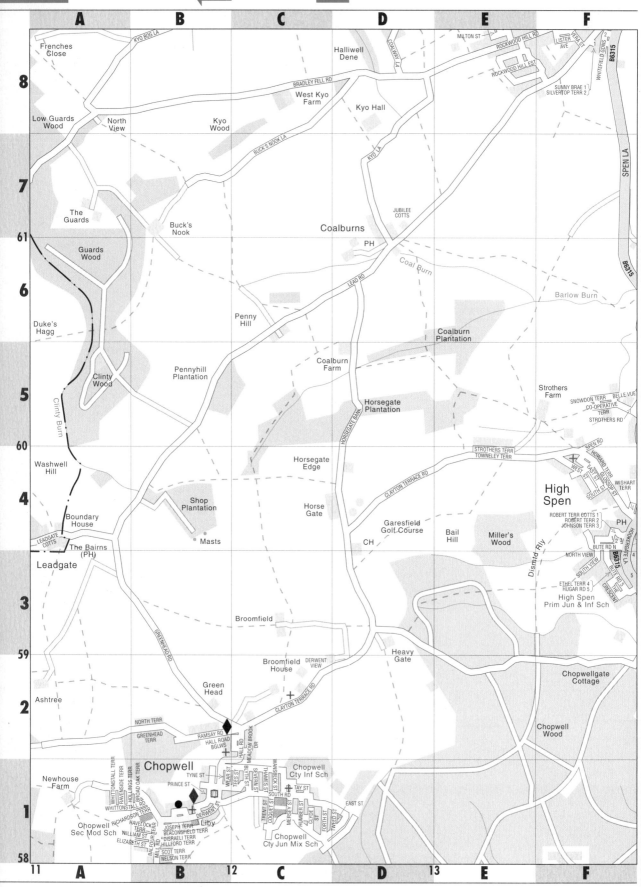

A   B   C   D   E   F

8

Frenches
Close

KYO BOG LA

Halliwell
Dene

MILTON ST

ROCKWOOD HILL RD

LISTER
AVE

VERA ST

WHITEFIELD GDNS

B6315

BRADLEY FELL RD

West Kyo
Farm

ROCKWOOD HILL EST

SUNNY BRAE 1
SILVERTOP TERR 2

Low Guards
Wood

North
View

Kyo
Wood

Kyo Hall

CONWAY LA

SPEN LA

7

The
Guards

Buck's
Nook

BUCK'S NOOK LA

KYO LA

Coalburns

JUBILEE
COTTS

B6315

61

Guards
Wood

PH

6

Duke's
Hagg

Penny
Hill

LEAD RD

Coal Burn

Barlow Burn

Coalburn
Plantation

5

Clinty
Wood

Pennyhill
Plantation

Coalburn
Farm

Strothers
Farm

SNOWDON TERR   BELLE VUE

CO-OPERATIVE
TERR
STROTHERS RD

Clinty Burn

Horsegate
Plantation

HORSEGATE BANK

60

Washwell
Hill

Horsegate
Edge

STROTHERS TERR
TOWNELEY TERR

SPEN RD

HOWARD TERR

WEST ST
EAST ST
GLASSOP ST
SOUTH ST

WISHART
TERR

High
Spen

4

Boundary
House

Shop
Plantation

CLAYTON TERRACE RD

Horse
Gate

Garesfield
Golf Course

Bail
Hill

Miller's
Wood

ROBERT TERR COTTS 1
ROBERT TERR 2
JOHNSON TERR 3

PH

LEADGATE
COTTS

CH

Dismld Rly

BUTE RD N

NORTH VIEW

HOXENGRIEVE LA

B6315

Masts

The Bairns
(PH)

SOUTH VIEW

BUTE RD

CRESCENT

Leadgate

ETHEL TERR 4
HUGAR RD 5

High Spen
Prim Jun & Inf Sch

3

Broomfield

Heavy
Gate

Chopwellgate
Cottage

59

Broomfield
House

DERWENT
VIEW

Chopwell
Wood

2

Ashtree

Green
Head

GREENHEAD RD

CLAYTON TERRACE RD

NORTH TERR

GREENHEAD
TERR

RAMSAY RD

HALL ROAD
BGLWS

HALL RD

MEADOW BROOK
DR

Newhouse
Farm

Chopwell

TYNE ST

WEAR ST
TEES ST
SWAN ST
THAMES ST

Chopwell
Cty Inf Sch

WHITTONSTALL TERR
RAVENSIDE TERR
HOLLINGS TERR
BROAD OAK TERR

PRINCE ST

Liby

TAY ST

SOUTH RD

EAST ST

1

WHITTONSTALL RD
RICHARDSON RD

RAVELOCK
TERR

JOSEPH TERR
BEACONSFIELD TERR
DISRAELI TERR

DERWENT ST

TRENT ST
COQUET ST
MERSEY ST
HUMBER ST
CLYDE ST
FORTH ST
TWEED ST

Chopwell
Sec Mod Sch

WILLIAM ST

ELIZABETH ST

BALFOUR
TERR
HILL RD

HILLFORD TERR

SCOT TERR

NELSON TERR

Chopwell
Cty Jun Mix Sch

58

11   A   B   12   C   D   13   E   F

A B C D E F

8
7
61
6
5
60
4
3
59
2
1
58

SILVERDALE DR 1
WAVERLEY CL 2
HARTSIDE CRES 3
WEST LA 4

Little Brockwell
Brockwell

GLENDALE CL
FARNDALE
MELDON WAY
DENHAM
REDSDALE CT
BEVERLEY CT
KNARESDENE LA
SELBY'S GRAVE

Barlow Letch

Reeley Mires Farm

BURNHILLS LA

Chicken's Wood

BARLOW LA

Reeley Mires West Wood

Reeley Mires Wood

North Farm

Barlow Gill Wood

The Black Horse (PH)

South Farm

Barlow Burn

Norman's Riding Wood

Water Gate Sewage Works

Huntley Gill

Rickless Farm

Barlow

GARESFIELD LA

Winlaton Care Village

Spenside Farm

Martin's Wood

ROGUES LA

Dismtd Rly
Lillycrook Hill

Pawston Birks

BARLOW CRES

BARLOW FELL RD

Barlow Fell

High Thornley

STROTHERS RD

PAWSTON RD

RAMSAY ST
WATSON ST

ASHTREE LA

WEST HIGH HORSE CL

HOLLINHILL LA

AGED MINERS
HOMES
COLLINGDON RD

Dismtd Rly

COLLINGDON GN

WISHART TERR
HIGH SPEN CT

Spen Banks

Sherburn Tower Farm

ASHFIELD CT

SPEN BURN
GREENLEA CL
FELL VIEW
STOKER TERR
DENE
SCHOOL LA
ELMWOOD CRES
HUGAR RD
WOODLANDS CL

SPEN LA

Hookergate Comp Sch

Spen Burn

Sherburn Green Wood

THORNFIELD PL
GLEN CL
CHAPEL VIEW
ASHTREE CL
SHERBURN PARK AVE
SHERBURN GN
PORTHAUGH
AVON CL
A694 LOCHHAUGH RD
Sch
DOWNIES CL
SOUTHWOOD CRES
LILLEY TERR
GOVEN TERR
Sch

THE OAKS
BURNOP TERR
ROBSON TERR

Low Spen

HILLSIDE CL
ROOKSWOOD GDNS
SNIPES DENE
GARESFIELD GDNS
LILLEYCROFT
CARNFORTH GDNS

WOOD TERR

Low Spen Farm

NORWOOD CRES

THORNLEY VIEW

Hooker Gate

HOOKERGATE LA

Low Spen Burn
THE GREEN
BARKWOOD RD
HOLLINSIDE TERR

Caravan and Camp Site

WILLIAM MORRIS AVE
A J COOK'S COTTS
WOODLEA RD
NORTH VIEW W
NORTH VIEW
EVANS ST
DENE VIEW
EAST VIEW
PONTOP VIEW
BROWN ST
MARK ST
SWINDON ST
VALLEY DR
WHINFIELD DR
HIGH ST
LEAZES VIEW
BURNSIDE
WOODLANDS RD

Rowlands Gill

Dismtd Rly

TOWNLEY FIELDS
THE CRESCENT
HOLLYHEN
STATION RD
B6314

ENGEL ST
KIER HARDIE ST
SOUTH VIEW W
HILLCROFT

St Joseph's RC Aided Sch

WELL ST
MARGARET TERR
OLGA TERR
HIGHFIELD RD
WHALEY TERR
VICTORIA TERR

NELL TERR

Highfield

PARK VIEW
STEWARTSFIELD
SOUTH SHERBURN
KILL'S WAY
MIDDLETON AVE
NORMAN RD
Liby
THE AVENUE
THE GROVE
BURNOPFIELD RD B6311
Derwent Wlk

LINTZFORD RD
ALEXANDRA ST
ALBERT ST

Highfield Jun & Inf Schs

WOODSIDE WLK
WHINFIELD WAY
GLENDER TERR
DENE CRES
SMAILES LA
STRATHMORE AVE
STRATHMORE RD B6315

Pallis Burn

Beda Hills

LOW WEST AVE
WEST AVE
CROSS TERR
ORCHARD DENE
DENE RD
DENE AVE
WINDROW
ORCHARD RD

A694 DIPWOOD RD
RIVERSIDE WAY
DERWENT WAY
AGED MINERS' HOMES

STIRLING AVE
STIRLING CT

River Derwent

Derwent Bridge

BUSTY BANK
B6314

14 A B 15 C D 16 E F

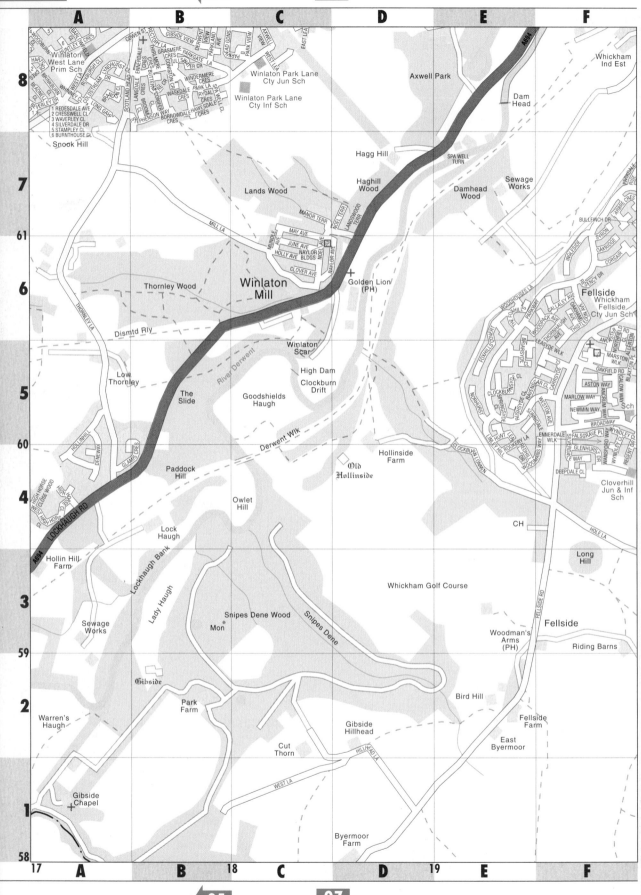

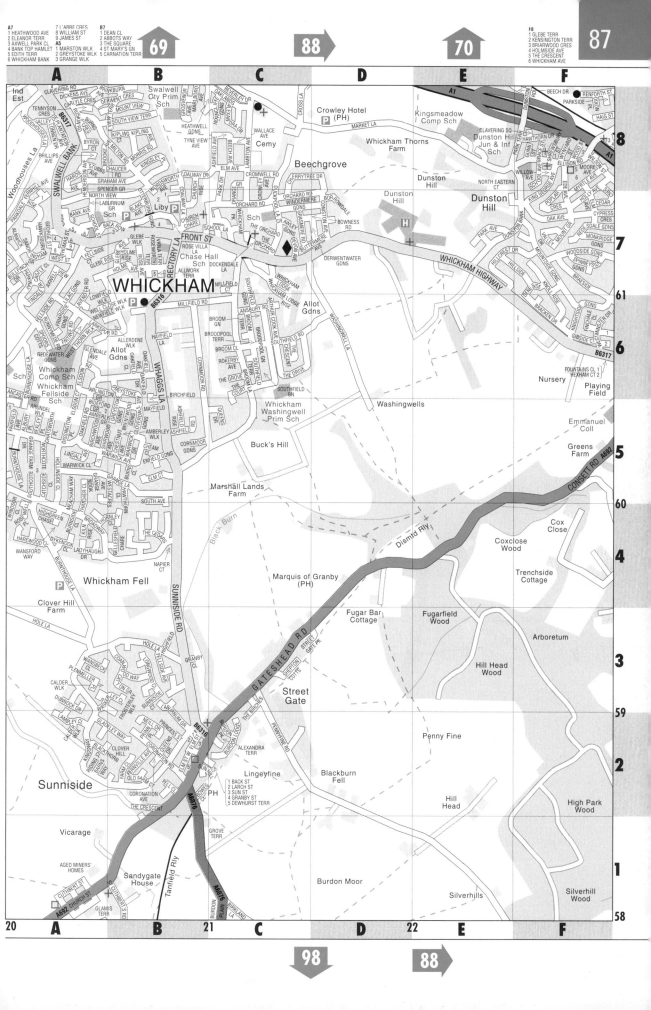

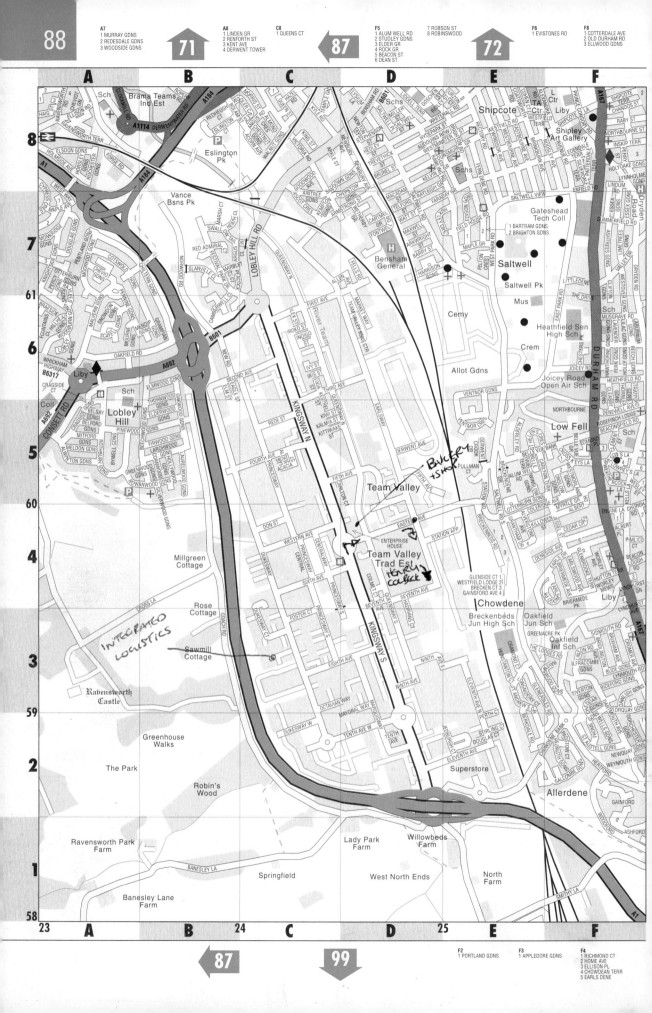

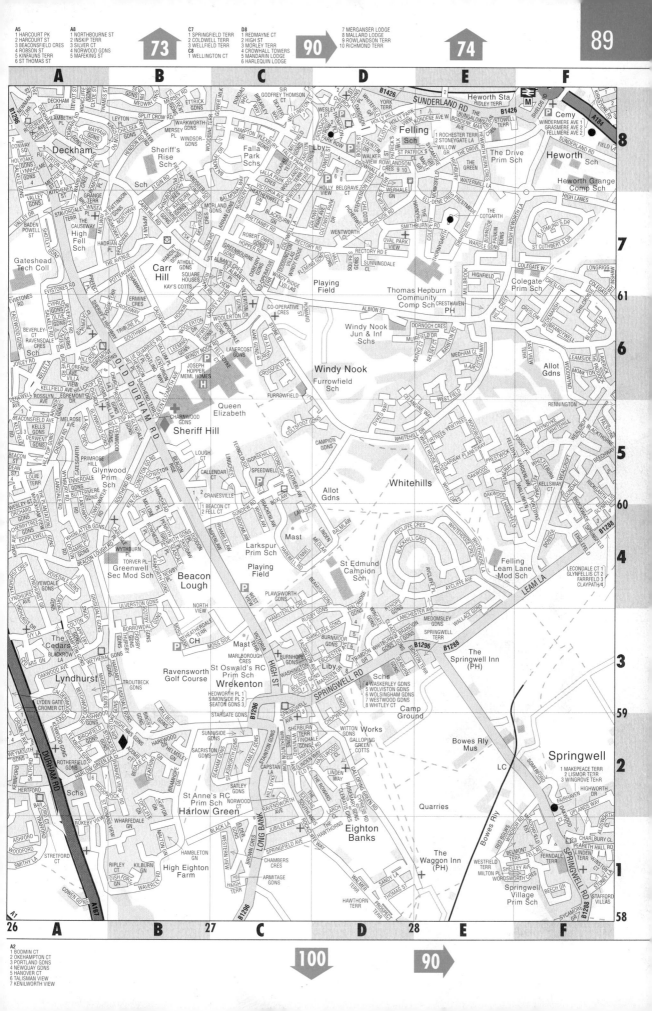

A5
1 HARCOURT PK
2 HARCOURT ST
3 BEACONSFIELD CRES
4 ROBSON ST
5 KINFAUNS TERR
6 ST THOMAS ST

A8
1 NORTHBOURNE ST
2 INSKIP TERR
3 SILVER CT
4 NORWOOD GDNS
5 MAFEKING ST

C7
1 SPRINGFIELD TERR
2 COLDWELL TERR
3 WELLFIELD TERR

C8
1 WELLINGTON CT

D8
1 REDMAYNE CT
2 HIGH ST
3 MORLEY TERR
4 CROWHALL TOWERS
5 MANDARIN LODGE
6 HARLEQUIN LODGE

7 MERGANSER LODGE
8 MALLARD LODGE
9 ROWLANDSON TERR
10 RICHMOND TERR

A2
1 BODMIN CT
2 OKEHAMPTON CT
3 PORTLAND GDNS
4 NEWQUAY GDNS
5 HANOVER CT
6 TALISMAN VIEW
7 KENILWORTH VIEW

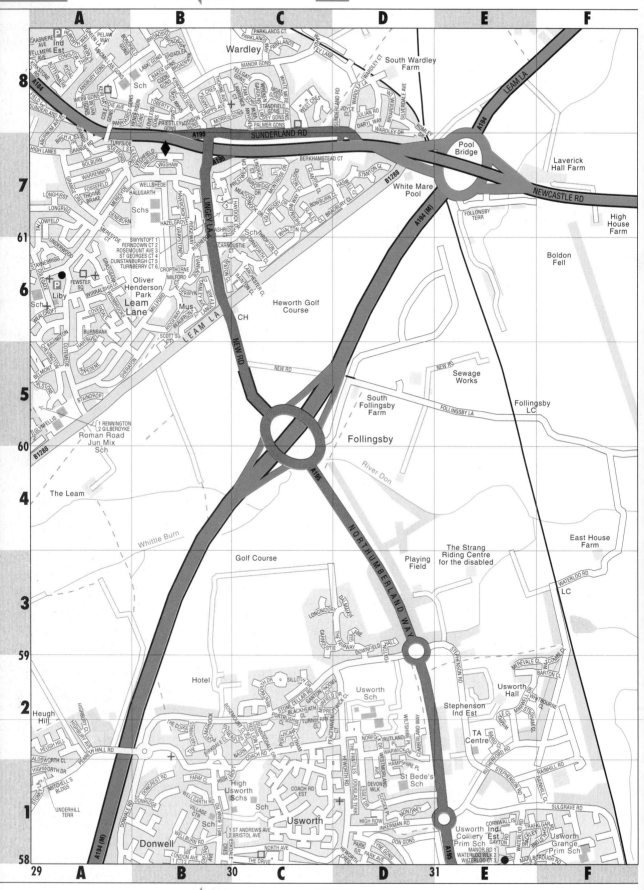

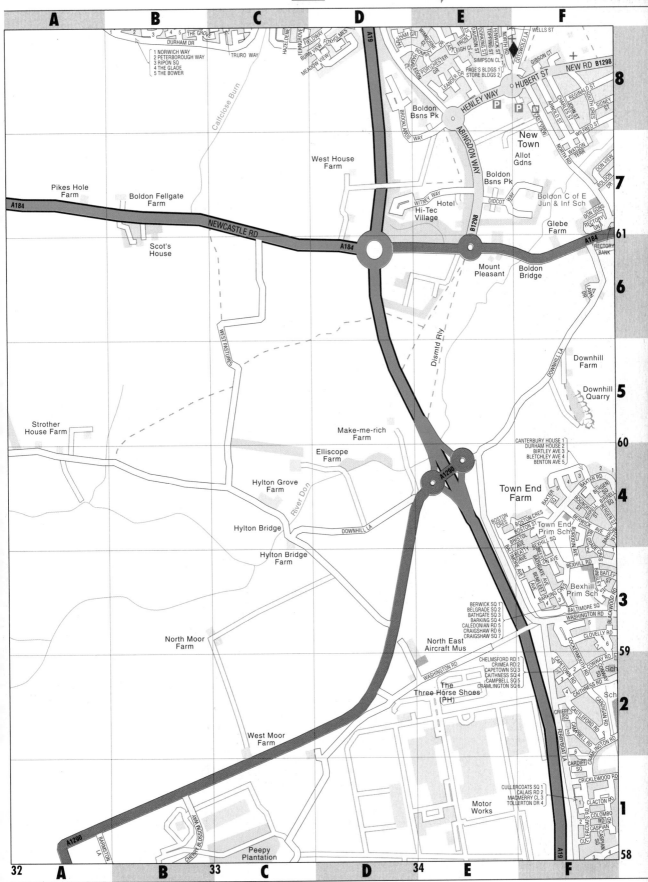

1 NORWICH WAY
2 PETERBOROUGH WAY
3 RIPON SQ
4 THE GLADE
5 THE BOWER

THE GROVE
DURHAM DR
TRURO WAY
HAZE DENE
FERNGROVE
FIELDWAY
MEADOW VIEW
BURN VIEW
FOXHOLMES

WEST HOUSE FARM

Pikes Hole Farm

Boldon Fellgate Farm

NEWCASTLE RD

A184

Scot's House

WEST PASTURES

Strother House Farm

Make-me-rich Farm

Elliscope Farm

Hylton Grove Farm

River Don

Hylton Bridge

DOWNHILL LA

Hylton Bridge Farm

North Moor Farm

West Moor Farm

A1290

BARMSTON LA

CHERRY BLOSSOM WAY

Peepy Plantation

A19

Boldon Bsns Pk
BROOKLANDS WAY

HENLEY WAY
ABINGDON WAY

New Town
WELLS ST
HUBERT ST
NEW RD B1298
PAGE'S BLDGS 1
STORE BLDGS 2
EAST VIEW
GIBSON CT
COTSWOLD LA
NORTH RD

Allot Gdns

Boldon Bsns Pk

WITNEY WAY
DIDCOT WAY
B1298

Hotel
Hi-Tec Village

Boldon C of E Jun & Inf Sch

Glebe Farm

Mount Pleasant

Boldon Bridge

A184
RECTORY BANK

DON VIEW
DON GDNS
RECTORY GN
LAWN DR
DOWNHILL LA

Downhill Farm

Downhill Quarry

Dismtd Rly

A1290

CANTERBURY HOUSE 1
DURHAM HOUSE 2
BIRTLEY AVE 3
BLETCHLEY AVE 4
BENTON AVE 5

Town End Farm

BAXTER RD
BERGEN SQ
BIRTLEY SQ
BOGNOR RD
BERWICK AVE
BORDON AVE

Town End Prim Sch

BOSTON CRES
BRISTOL AVE
BEATTY AVE
BALTIMORE AVE
BEXHILL SQ
BRESCON AVE
BATHGATE SQ

Bexhill Prim Sch

BARKING CRES
BELGRADE AVE
BENCROFT AVE
BATLEY ST
BINGLEY ST
BEXHILL RD
BLACKWOOD RD

BALTIMORE SQ
WASHINGTON RD
CLOVELLY RD

BERWICK SQ 1
BELGRADE SQ 2
BATHGATE SQ 3
BARKING SQ 4
CALEDONIAN RD 5
CRAIGSHAW RD 6
CRAIGSHAW SQ 7

North East Aircraft Mus

CHELMSFORD RD 1
CRIMEA RD 2
CAPETOWN SQ 3
CAITHNESS SQ 4
CAMPBELL SQ 5
CRAMLINGTON SQ 6

WASHINGTON RD

CAPETOWN RD
CONWAY RD
CAITHNESS RD
CONWAY RD
Sch
Sch

The Three Horse Shoes (PH)

CRIEFF SQ
CASTLEFORD SQ
CAMPBELL RD
CARDIGAN RD
CRAMLINGTON RD
FERRYBOAT LA

CULLERCOATS SQ 1
CALAIS RD 2
MACMERRY CL 3
TOLLERTON DR 4

Motor Works

CARDIFF SQ
CRICKLEWOOD RD
CLACTON RD
COLOMBO RD
CASPIAN
CUCKERCOATS RD
CRAMLINGTON RD

A19

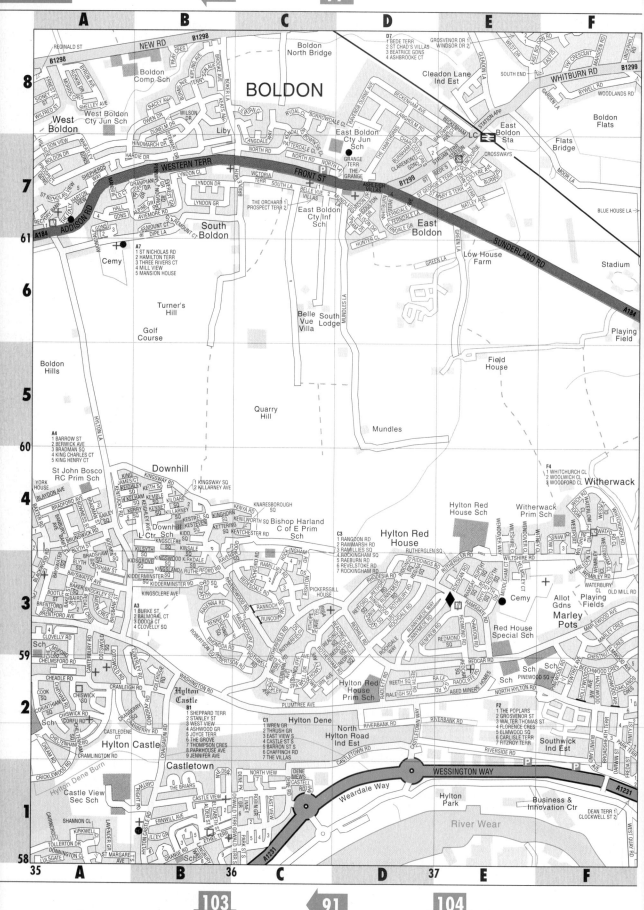

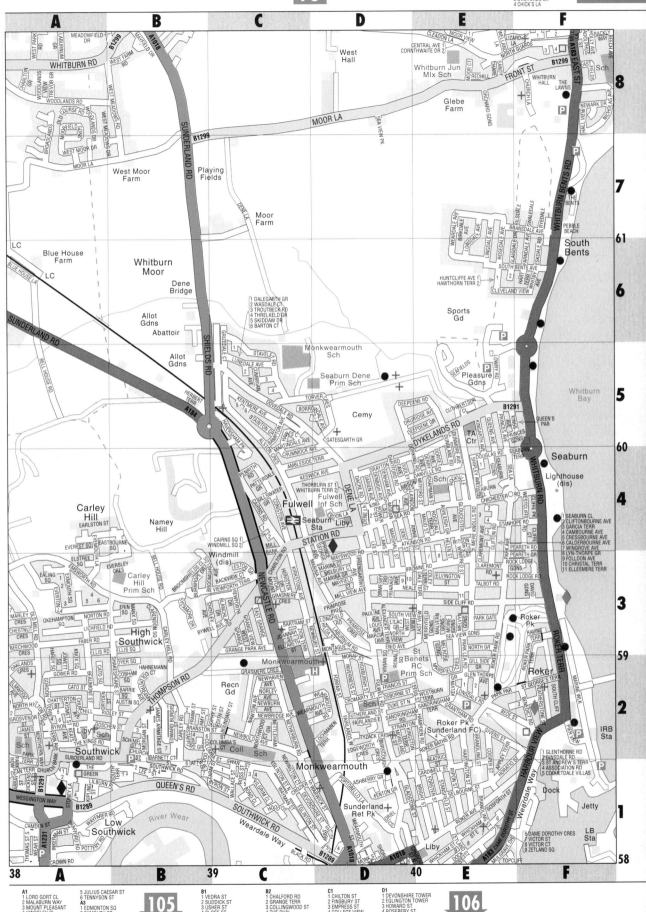

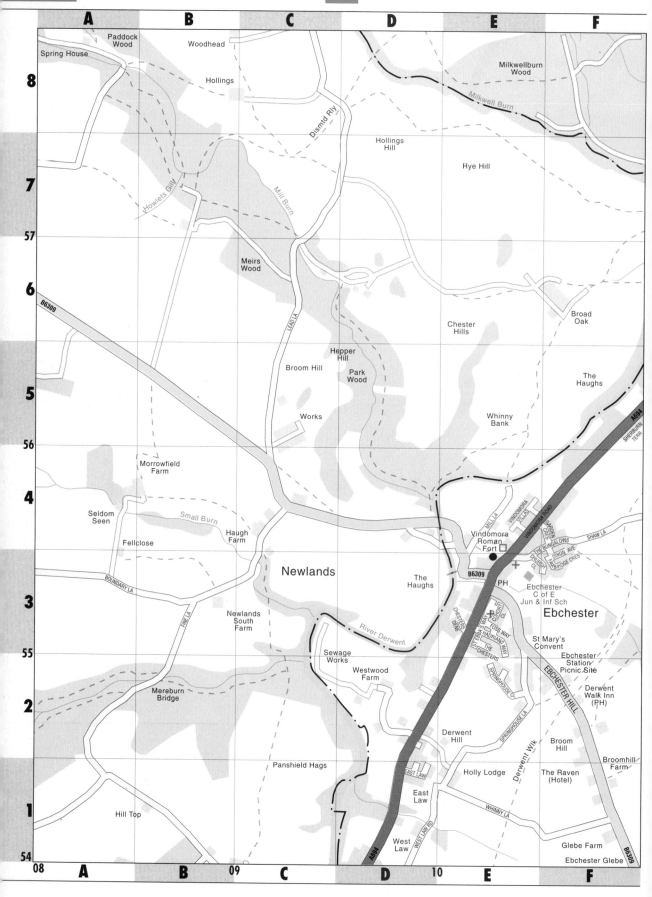

A   B   C   D   E   F

Spring House

Paddock Wood

Woodhead

Hollings

Milkwellburn Wood

Milkwell Burn

8

Dismtd Rly

Hollings Hill

Rye Hill

Howlets Gill

Mill Burn

7

57

Meirs Wood

Broad Oak

6

B6309

LEAD LA

Chester Hills

Hepper Hill

Broom Hill

Park Wood

The Haughs

5

Works

Whinny Bank

A694

SHERBURN TERR

56

Morrowfield Farm

Seldom Seen

Small Burn

Haugh Farm

Vindomora Roman Fort

MILL LA

VINDOMORA VILLAS

VINDOMORA ROAD

THE BUNGALOWS

DIXON AVE

SHAW LA

4

Fellclose

Newlands

The Haughs

B6309

PH

Ebchester C of E Jun & Inf Sch

Ebchester

BOUNDARY LA

FINE LA

Newlands South Farm

River Derwent

CHESTERS DENE

EBBA'S WAY

FOSS WAY

HADRIAN'S WAY

THE CHESTERS

ST MARY'S

St Mary's Convent

3

55

Sewage Works

Westwood Farm

Ebchester Station Picnic Site

SPRINGHOUSE CL

EBCHESTER HILL

Derwent Walk Inn (PH)

Mereburn Bridge

SPRINGHOUSE LA

Derwent Hill

Broom Hill

Derwent Wlk

Broomhill Farm

2

Panshield Hags

EAST LAW

Holly Lodge

The Raven (Hotel)

East Law

A694

WEST LAW RD

WHINNY LA

1

Hill Top

West Law

Glebe Farm

B6309

Ebchester Glebe

54

08   A   B   **09**   C   D   **10**   E   F

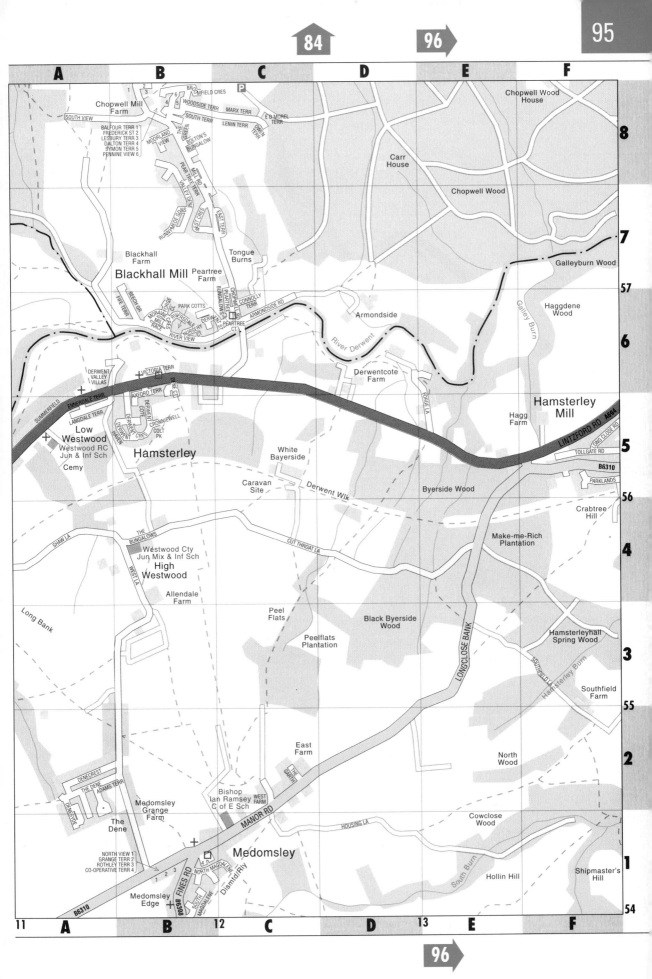

A B C D E F

8 7 57 6 5 56 4 3 55 2 1 54

Chopwell Wood House

Chopwell Mill Farm

SOUTH VIEW

2 1
6 3
4 5

BR CMFIELD CRES
WOODSIDE TERR
SOUTH TERR
MARX TERR
LENIN TERR
E D MOREL TERR
OWEN TERR

P

BALFOUR TERR 1
FREDERICK ST 2
LESBURY TERR 3
DALTON TERR 4
SYMON TERR 5
PENNINE VIEW 6

MOORLAND VIEW
THE GREEN
BOLTON'S BUNGALOW
PEAR TREE TERR
VALLEY DENE
MILL RD
SET CRES
EAST CRES
EAST TERR

Carr House

Chopwell Wood

Blackhall Farm

Tongue Burns

Galleyburn Wood

Blackhall Mill

Peartree Farm

BEECH GR
FIRE TERR
MORALE CRES
MILL RACE
FORGE RIVERSDALE
NURSERY CT
RIVER VIEW
BUNGALOWS
DERN CT
PEARTREE CT
CHOPWELL TERR
CONNOLLY TERR
ARMONDSIDE RD
PARK COTTS
ST

River Derwent

Armondside

Haggdene Wood

Galley Burn

Derwentcote Farm

Hamsterley Mill

LINTZFORD RD A694

Hagg Farm

LONG CLOSE RD
TOLLGATE RD
B6310
PARKLANDS

VICTORIA TERR
DENE CT
AXFORD TERR
DERWENT COTE
CRONNIEWELL CRES
COLT PK

DERWENT VALLEY VILLAS

SUMMERFIELD
ENNERDALE TERR
LANGDALE TERR

Low Westwood
Westwood RC Jun & Inf Sch
Cemy

Hamsterley

White Bayerside

Caravan Site

Derwent Wlk

Byerside Wood

Crabtree Hill

Make-me-Rich Plantation

THE BUNGALOWS
WEST LA
SHAW LA

Westwood Cty Jun Mix & Inf Sch

High Westwood

Allendale Farm

CUT THROAT LA

Black Byerside Wood

LONGCLOSE BANK

Hamsterleyhall Spring Wood

SOUTHFIELD LA

Hamsterley Burn

Southfield Farm

Long Bank

Peel Flats

Peelflats Plantation

East Farm

THE GARTH

North Wood

DENECREST
THE DENE
ADAMS TERR
DENESIDE

Medomsley Grange Farm

Bishop Ian Ramsey C of E Sch
WEST FARM
MANOR RD

HOUSING LA

Cowclose Wood

South Burn

The Dene

NORTH VIEW 1
GRANGE TERR 2
ROTHLEY TERR 3
CO-OPERATIVE TERR 4

FINES RD
NORTH MAGD
MAGDALENE LA
Dismtd Rly

Medomsley

Hollin Hill

Shipmaster's Hill

B6310

Medomsley Edge

B6398
SOUTH
MAGDALENE

11 12 13

A B C D E F

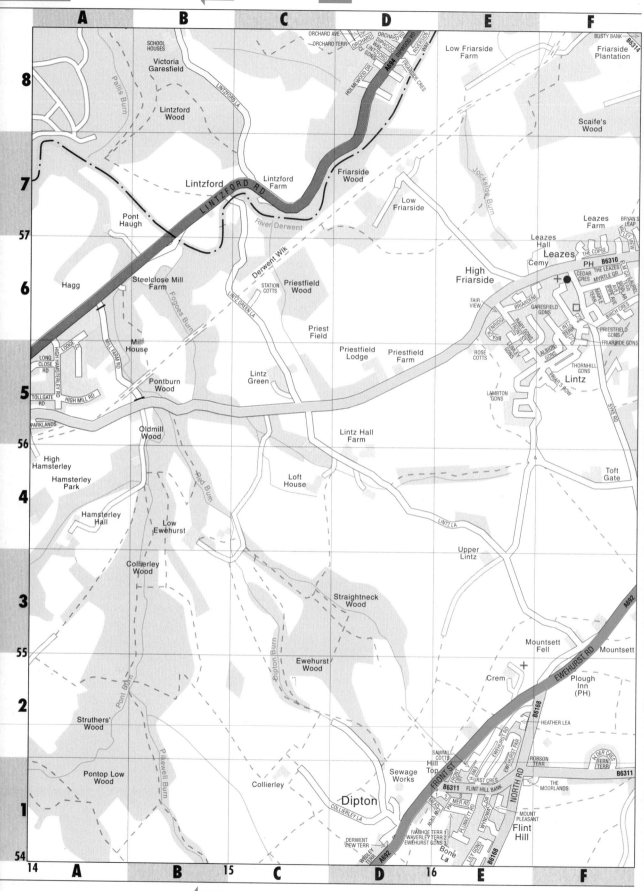

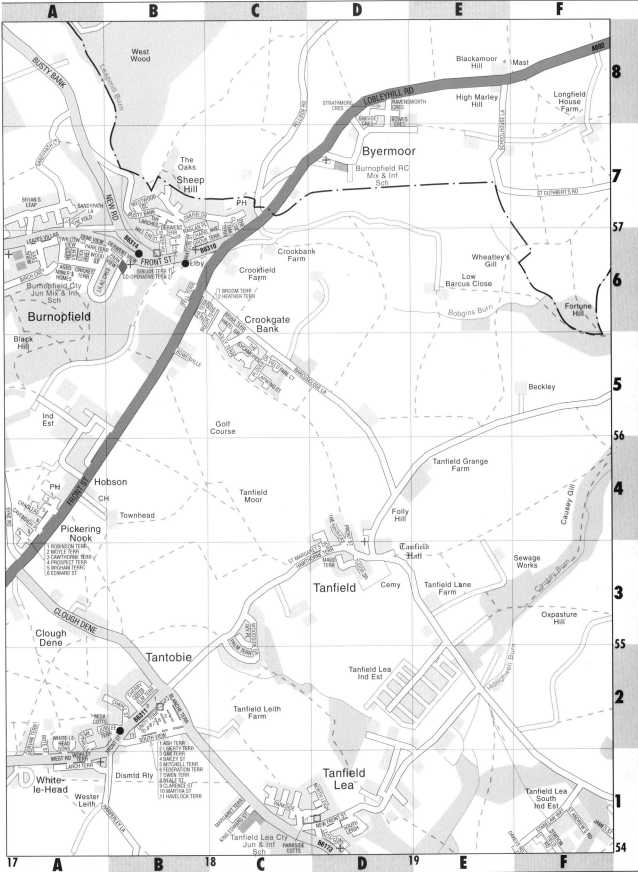

A B C D E F

West Wood

A692

Blackamoor Hill
Mast

LOBLEYHILL RD

Longfield House Farm

STRATHMORE CRES
RAVENSWORTH CRES
GIBSIDE CRES
BOWES CRES

High Marley Hill

SCHOOLHOUSE LA

Byermoor

Burnopfield RC Mix & Inf Sch

ST CUTHBERT'S RD

8

7

57

6

BUSTY BANK

Leapmill Burn

The Oaks

Sheep Hill

PH

FELLSIDE RD

Crookbank Farm

Wheatley's Gill

Low Barcus Close

Fortune Hill

Bryan's Leap

SANDYPATH LA

NEW RD

THE FOLD

WESTWOOD CL

BUSTY BANK

THE LARCHES

DERWENT TERR

OAKFIELDS

RAGLAN PL

CHAPEL AVE

GROVE TERR

THE CLOSE

OAK TERR

DENE VIEW
WILLOW VIEW
EDEN ST
WOOD ST
PARK TERR
PARK VIEW
LILAC CRES

LEAZES VILLAS
EAST VIEW
BIRCH CRES
AGED MINER'S HOMES
CRICKET TERR

DERWENT VIEW

HILL CREST

WATSON ST

B6314

FRONT ST

B6310

Lib'y

GIBSIDE TERR
CO-OPERATIVE TERR 2

FELL TERR

1 BROOM TERR
2 HEATHER TERR

Crookfield Farm

Crookgate Bank

Burnopfield Cty Jun Mix & Inf Sch

Burnopfield

Black Hill

FELL TERR
BEDE TERR
FEN TERR
BRIAR TERR
HAZEL GR
HOLLY TERR

THE SYCAMORES

THE FLOWER GR

FIELD FARE CT

LAPWING CT

BARCUSCLOSE LA

Bobgins Burn

Beckley

BOWESVILLE

Golf Course

56

5

Ind Est

Tanfield Grange Farm

Causey Gill

FRONT ST

PH

SYKE RD

CRAGLEAS & CAVENDISH PL

1
2
3
4
5
6

Hobson

CH

Townhead

Pickering Nook

1 ROBINSON TERR
2 MOYLE TERR
3 CAWTHORNE TERR
4 PROSPECT TERR
5 WIGHAM TERR
6 EDWARD ST

Tanfield Moor

THE HAYRICKS

ST MARGARET'S DR

HAWTHORNE TERR

MAUD TERR

FRONT ST

TUDOR DR

Folly Hill

Tanfield Hall

Cemy

Tanfield Lane Farm

Sewage Works

Causey Burn

Oxpasture Hill

4

56

3

CLOUGH DENE

Clough Dene

Tantobie

Tanfield

55

WOODSIDE GR

IVY PL

PALM TERR

Houghwell Burn

CHERRY COTTS

ELM TERR

CHAPEL ST

B6311

UNITY TERR

BLANCHE TERR

SOUTH VIEW

10 9 8 7 6

BEDA COTTS

JUBILEE TERR

CORVAN TERR

BOTE ST

SYM ST

WHITE-LE-HEAD GDNS

WORLEY TERR

WEST RD

FRONT ST

LARCH TERR

11

1 2
3 4

1 ASH TERR
2 LIBERTY TERR
3 OAK TERR
4 BAILEY ST
5 MITCHELL TERR
6 FEDERATION TERR
7 OWEN TERR
8 NEALE ST
9 CLARENCE ST
10 MARTHA ST
11 HAVELOCK TERR

Tanfield Leith Farm

Tanfield Lea Ind Est

Tanfield Lea

Tanfield Lea South Ind Est

2

1

White-le-Head

Wester Leith

HARPERLEY LA

Dismtd Rly

MARGARET TERR

KING EDWARD TERR

Tanfield Lea Cty Jun & Inf Sch

PARKSIDE

NORTH LEIGH

NEW FRONT ST

PARKSIDE COTTS

LEIGH GDNS

SOUTH LEIGH

B6173

STANLEY WAY

STATION RD

ST ANDREW'S RD

OAKEY'S RD

JAMES ST

54

17 A B 18 C D 19 E F

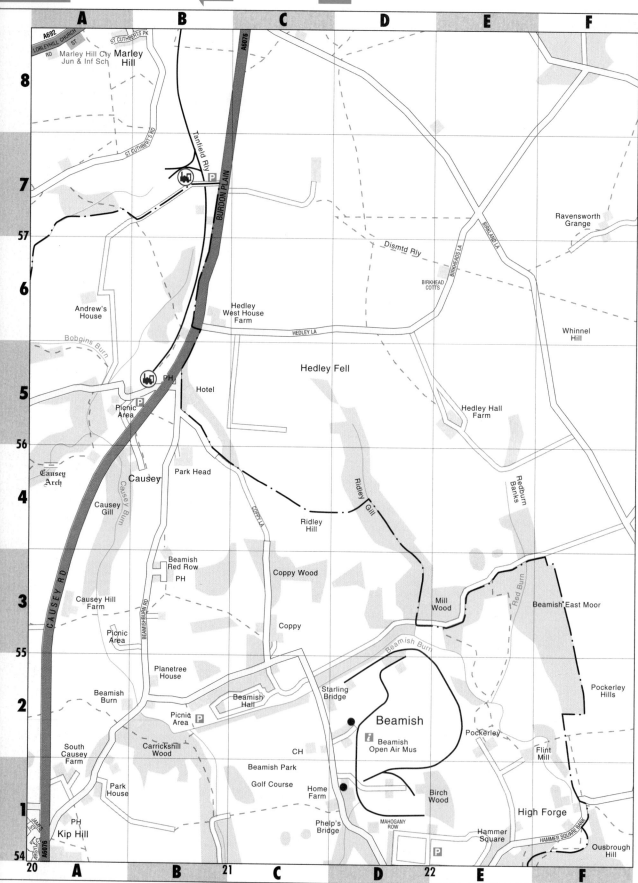

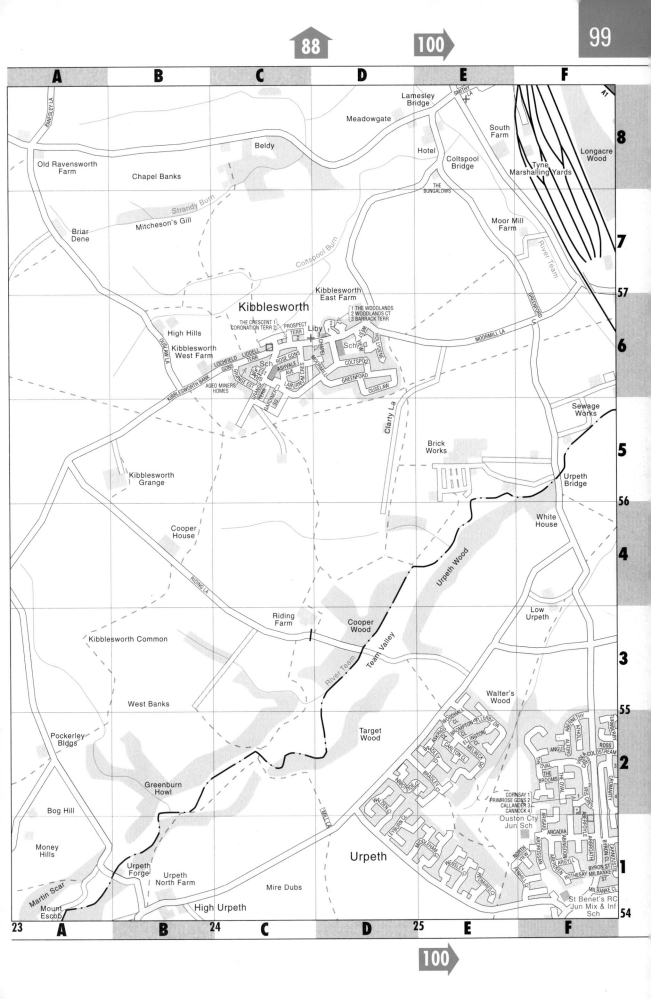

A B C D E F

8

Lamesley Bridge
SMITHY LA

Meadowgate

South Farm

Longacre Wood

Old Ravensworth Farm

Beldy

Hotel

Coltspool Bridge

Tyne Marshalling Yards

Chapel Banks

THE BUNGALOWS

7

Strandy Burn

Mitcheson's Gill

Briar Dene

Coltspool Burn

Moor Mill Farm

River Team

GREENFORD LA

57

Kibblesworth East Farm

1 THE WOODLANDS
2 WOODLANDS CT
3 BARRACK TERR

6

Kibbleworth

High Hills

THE CRESCENT 1
CORONATION TERR 2

PROSPECT TERR

2

Liby

2

3

CHAPEL CL

Sch

HOLLYDENE

WEST VIEW

MOORMILL LA

Kibblesworth West Farm

OUSELAW LA

LOCHFIELD GDNS

LIDDELL TERR

ROSE GDNS

ASHVALE AVE

LABURN CRES

MOORHILL

COLTSPO

GREENFORD

OUSELAW

Sch

GRANGE EST

GARDNER LISO

KIBBLESWORTH BANK

AGED MINERS' HOMES

Clarty La

Sewage Works

5

Kibblesworth Grange

Brick Works

Urpeth Bridge

56

Cooper House

White House

4

RIDING LA

Urpeth Wood

Low Urpeth

Riding Farm

Cooper Wood

Team Valley

River Team

3

Kibblesworth Common

Walter's Wood

55

West Banks

WOODHALL CL
ASKRIGG CL
BROMPTON CL
ELLERBY DR
ELLINGTON CL
MELBECK CL
CARLTON CL

ABERNETHY
ATHOL
ALFORD
ANGUS
VIOLA CRES
COLDSTREAM
TURNBERRY
ROSS

2

Pockerley Bldgs

Target Wood

BRADLEY CL
BRADLEY CL

NABB CL

THE OVAL
THE BROOMS
THE OVAL

IRIS GRO

CROMARTY

3

Greenburn Howl

CORNSAY 1
PRIMROSE GDNS 2
CALLANDER 3
CANNOCK 4

ARISAIG

ARCADIA

ABERFOYLE

ABBROATH

BYRON ST

CARNOUSTIE

MILBANKE ST

Bog Hill

LEYBURN CL

Ouston Cty Jun Sch

P

ABINGDON

NORTH VIEW

ARDROSSAN

ARGYLL

ROTHESAY

MILBANKE CL

1

Money Hills

WHELPCL

MICKLETON CL

WENSLEY CL

PIMPRES CL

PENHILL CL

ST Benet's RC Jun Mix & Inf Sch

Martin Scar

Urpeth Forge

Urpeth North Farm

Mire Dubs

Urpeth

54

Mount Escob

High Urpeth

A B C D E F

8 Low Eighton
PH
Blackim Hill
Mount Lonnen
Mount Rd
LCs
PH
Bowes Rly
Dunkirk
Sheddon's Hill
Havannah
A194(M)
B1296
DURHAM RD
A167
A1
B1288
Donkin Rd

7 NEWCASTLE BANK
A6127
Joseph Hopper Aged Miners Homes
Northside Farm
PH
The Mill House (PH)
Armstrong Ind Est
Long Bank
Whitworth Rd
Armstrong Rd
Lambert Rd

57 Long Acre Farm
The Holly's
Crem Cemy
Windsor Rd
Highfield
Dene Ct
Crathie
Leybourne Hold
Snug Dr
A1
B1288
Black Fell
A194(M)
Herdwghill
Howe
Heatherlaw
Blackwell Rd

6 Longshank La
Works
THE BUNGALOWS 1
KEIR HARDY TERR 2
QUIGLEY TERR 3
LEIGHTON TERR 4
BIRCH TERR 5
ROSEWOOD TERR 6
ASHGROVE TERR 7
ELM TERR 8
Valley View
Lynburn
Windsor Rd
Glamis Villas
Dodds Terr
Dennison Terr
Oliver Cres
Neville Cres
Moore Cres
Gilliland Cres
Selkirk Cres
Birtley East Cty Jun & Inf Sch
North Side
A1231
Black Fell
Knoulberry Rd
Pickershaw
Phoenix Rd
B1288

5 Works
Russell Terr
Lansbury Av
Elisabeth Av
Lansbury Dr
Avon Cres
Mary Ave
Leyton Cres
Layers Rd
Ridgeway
Wilson Ave
Croft
Garside Ave
Ravensworth
C5
1 BIRTLEY VILLAS
2 HUDDART TERR
3 SANDERS GDNS
4 HILLCROFT
5 MOUNT PLEASANT BGLWS
6 PLEASANT PL
7 ST JOSEPH'S CT
8 DOVE CT
Uplands House
A194(M)
B1288
Motel
Junction 65
Crowther Ind Est
Harvey Cl
A1231
Crowther Rd
Featherstone

56 Edward Rd
St Joseph's RC Inf Sch
Ravensworth Rd
Pine St
Mitchell St
Poplar St
King St
B1288
Orchard St
Birtley La
Egton Terr
Mount Pleasant
Felcross
Highbridge
Mount Rd
Primrose Terr
Woodbine Terr
Jasmine Terr
FELL BANK
NEW SOUTH TERR
THE UPLANDS
Hill St
Portobello
A1(M)
Morpeth Cl
Bolam Rd
Greenhead
Chipchase
Prwick

4 Birtley Prim Sch
Ind Est
STATION LA
Gladstone Terr
George St
Queen St
Morris St
Beaconsfield
Beacon Terr
The Avenue
Ruskin Rd
Sheldon St
St John's Grn
South View
Kateregina
Birtley Ravensworth Terrace Cty Jun & Inf Sch
Penshaw Way
Portobello Way
Portland Rd
Shadon Way
Lapwing Cl
Ayton Rd
Ham
C4
1 CRAIG ST
2 BERTRAM ST
3 JONES ST
4 WEST ST
5 DUNELM CL
6 CONSTABLES GARTH
7 ORCHARD PK
8 GROVE COTTS
9 DAISY COTTS
10 MONUMENT TERR
11 ARNDALE HOUSE
12 HARRATON TERR
13 KESTREL CT
BIRTLEY
Liby Sch
P
12
11
Leuchars
Harras Bank

3 Ouston Bank Farm
Rowletch Burn
Works
DURHAM RD
Harrison Ct
Harras Bank
Birtley Lord Lawson Comp Sch
Birtley La
CH
Radcliffe St
St Wilfrid St
1 SWINBURNE PL
2 CHARLES PERKINS MEMORIAL COTTAGE HOMES
NORTH ST 1
CHAPEL ROW 2
Fell Cl
Springvale
West View
Polpero
Penshaw Row
Ayton Prim Sch
P
6
Washington Birtley Service Area
P
1 HOREDEST RD
2 REDWING DR
3 GREENFINCH CL
4 GOLDCREST CL

55 Blue Barns
Westline Ind Est
Birtley Golf Course
Lyvdond Dr
Hartland Dr
Tamerton Dr
Mitigarry
Hawk Terr
Dunvegan
West Penshaw View
Portobello Terr
Glen Luce
Ayton
Redshank Cl
Sandpiper Cl
Martin Cl
Dunnock Dr
Crake Way

2 Turnberry
Tranberry
Calander
Cannock
Cromarty
Ouston
Greenfields
Works
Barley Mow
Birtley Portobello Cty Jun & Inf Sch
Colebrooke
Rosslyn Pl
Kinkstone
Windermere
Thirlmere
Grasmere
Thurso
Hotel
Vigo Wood

1 Milbanke Cl
Byron Cl
Carnoustie
Fairisle
Ross
Carlisle
Ouston Cty Inf Sch
Ouston Spring Farm
Surrey Terr
York Rd
Norfolk Pl
Norfolk Ave
Cambridge Pl
Cheshire Ave
Oxford Rd
Durham Pl
Bedford Ave
Lonsdale
Vigodale
Schs
Kinross Cl
Elgin Cl
Athlone Pl
Dorset Ave
Pembroke Ave
Northumberland Ave
Suffolk Pl
Portree
Lothian Cl
Saddray
Scafell
Hartside
Kirkdale
Lonvick
Garsdale
Junction 64
A1(M) WESTERN HIGHWAY
Vigo La
A1(M)
Kentmere
Rickleton Way
The Chase
Coquet

54

26 A 27 B C D 28 E F

F3
1 WHEATEAR CL
2 FIELDFARE CL
3 STONECHAT CL
4 CORMORANT CL
5 PLOVER CL
6 WHITETHROAT CL
7 TEAL CL
8 WREN CL

D8 1 HEWORTH CRES 2 TYNE GDNS 3 DORCAS TERR 4 WOOD TERR 5 RICHARDSON TERR 6 ARNDALE HOUSE	7 VICTORIA PL 8 HOLYOAKE TERR 9 TREES TERR	**90**

E8
1 CO-OPERATIVE TERR
2 ELLIOTT TERR
3 USWORTH STATION RD
4 WATERLOO CT
5 WELLINGTON CT
6 HASTINGS WLK

102

7 WESTGARTH TERR
8 THOMAS ST
9 ROCK TERR
10 STATION TERR
11 NENE CT
F8
1 COLLINGWOOD CT

2 WELLINGTON WLK
3 NEVILLE CT
4 KENILWORTH CT
5 JOHNSON CT
6 HODGSON TERR

101

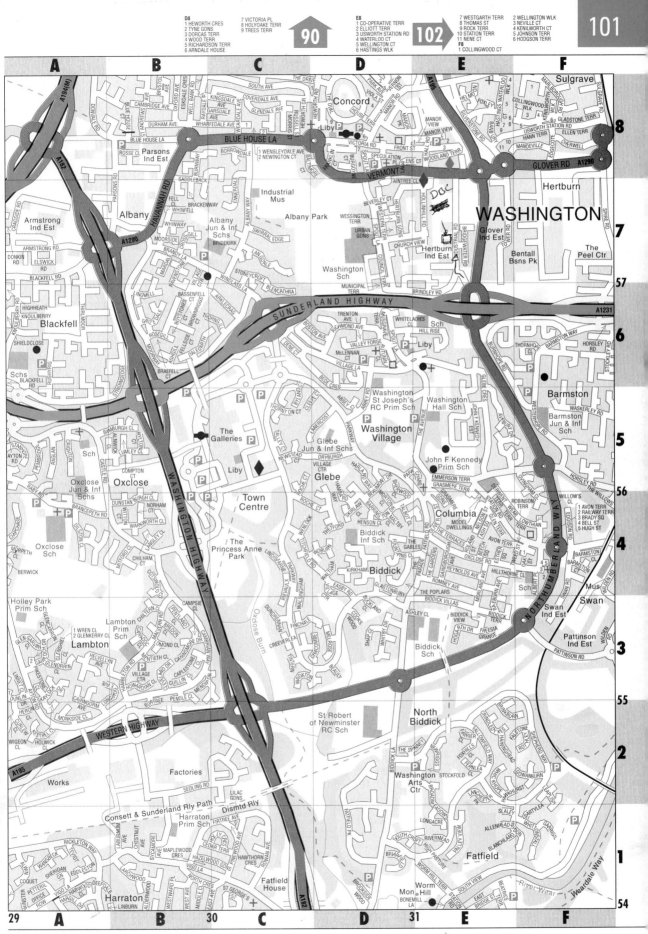

101
91
103

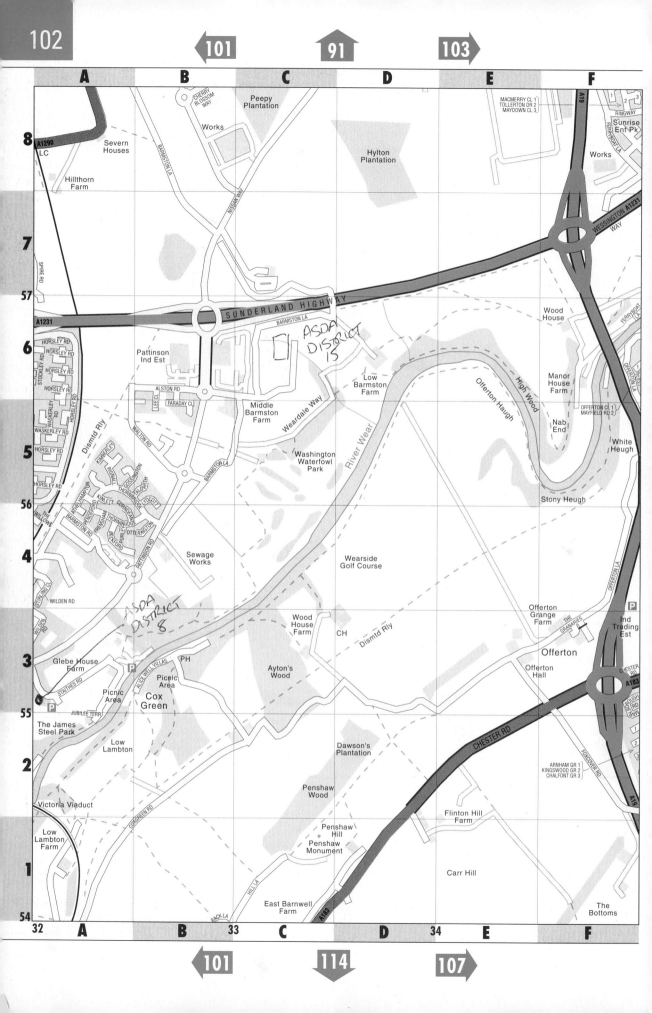

101
114
107

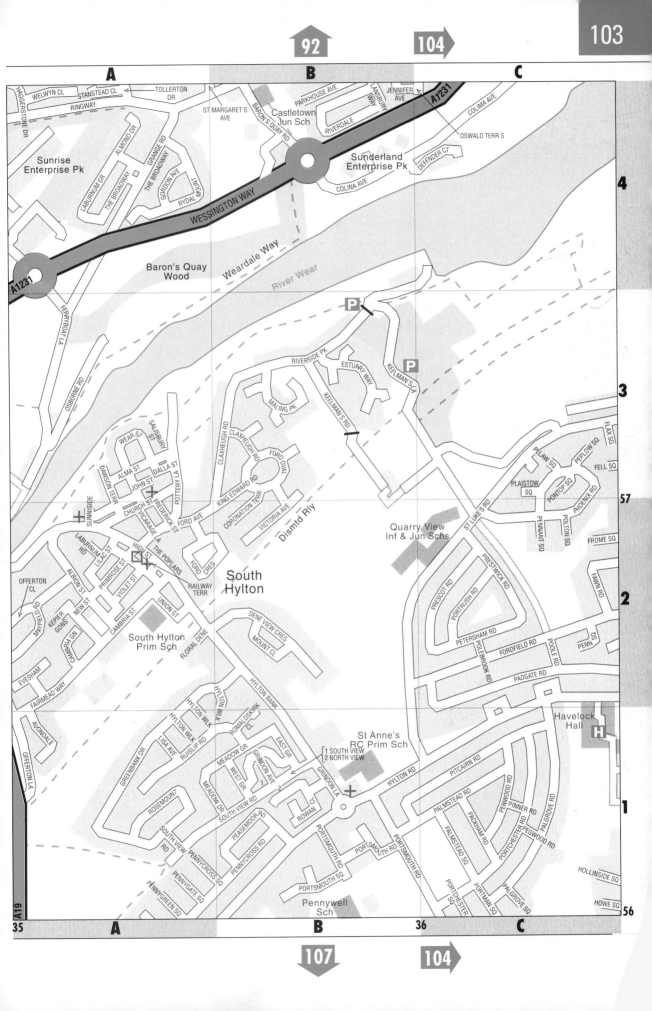

A
B
C

WELWYN CL
STANSTEAD CL
TOLLERTON DR
RINGWAY
HAGGERSTONE DR
ST MARGARET'S AVE
BARON'S QUAY RD
PARKHOUSE AVE
LANSBURY WAY
JENNIFER AVE
A1231
Castletown Jun Sch
RIVERDALE
COLIMA AVE
OSWALD TERR S

Sunrise Enterprise Pk
ALMOND DR
GRANGE RD
THE BROADWAY
GORDON AVE
RYDAL MOUNT
THE BROADWAY
LABURNUM GR
Sunderland Enterprise Pk
COLINA AVE
DEFENDER CT

4

WESSINGTON WAY

A1231

FERRYBOAT LA

Baron's Quay Wood
Weardale Way
River Wear

P

OSBORNE RD

P

RIVERSIDE PK
ESTUARY WAY
KEELMAN'S LA

3

MALING PK
KEELMAN'S RD

FLAX SQ
PEPLOW SQ
PELAW SQ
FELL SQ
PONTOP SQ
PHOENIX RD
PLAISTOW SQ

WEAR ST
SALISBURY ST
CLAXHEUGH RD
CLAXHEUGH RD
FORD OVAL

57

ALMA ST
DALLA ST
JOHN ST
DAWSON TERR
POTTERY LA
KING EDWARD RD
CORONATION TERR
VICTORIA AVE
Dismtd Rly
Quarry View Inf & Jun Schs
ST LUKE'S RD
PENNANT SQ
POLTON SQ
FROME SQ

SUNNISIDE
CHURCH ST
FREDERICK ST
VICARAGE LA
FORD AVE

LABURNUM RD
LILAC ST
HIGH ST
THE POPLARS
FORD CRES
PRESCOT RD
PORTRUSH RD
PRESTWICK RD
FAWN RD

OFFERTON CL
ALBION ST
PRIMROSE ST
South Hylton
PETERSHAM RD
POLEBROOK RD

MYRFIELD RD
NEW ST
VIOLET ST
RAILWAY TERR
PORTSMOUTH RD

2

KEPIER GDNS
CAMBRIA GN
CAMBRIA ST
UNION ST
DENE VIEW CRES
FORDFIELD RD
POOLE RD
PENN SQ

EVESHAM
South Hylton Prim Sch
MOUNT CL
PADGATE RD

FAIRMEAD WAY
FLORAL DENE

AVONDALE
HYLTON WLK
Havelock Hall
H

OFFERTON LA
GREENBANK DR
LISA AVE
RUISLIP RD
ROMALDSKIRK CL
MEADOW GR
EAST GR
St Anne's RC Prim Sch
1 SOUTH VIEW
2 NORTH VIEW
HYLTON RD
PITCAIRN RD
PENWOOD RD
PINNER RD
PALGROVE RD

HYLTON WALK
MEADOW DR
WEST GR
GRINDON AVE
GRINDON LA
PALMSTEAD RD
PACKHAM RD
PORTCHESTER RD
PEGWOOD RD

1

ROSEMOUNT
SOUTH VIEW RD
PEASEMOOR RD
ROWAN CL
PORTSMOUTH RD
PALMSTEAD RD
PORTMAN SQ
PALGROVE SQ

A19
SOUTH VIEW RD
PENNYCROSS SQ
PENNYCROSS RD
PORTSMOUTH SQ
PORTCHESTER SQ
HOLLINSIDE SQ
HOWE SQ

PENNYGATE SQ
PENNYGREEN SQ
Pennywell Sch

56

35
A
B
36
C

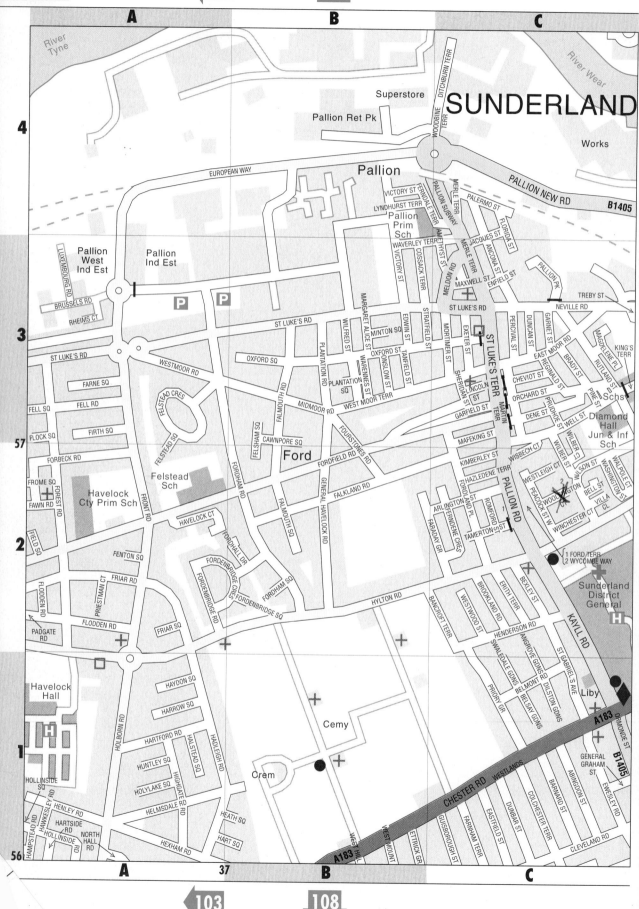

A   B   C

River Tyne

River Wear

4

Superstore
Pallion Ret Pk

DITCHBURN TERR
WOODBINE TERR

SUNDERLAND
Works

PALLION NEW RD
B1405

EUROPEAN WAY

Pallion

VICTORY ST
LYNDHURST TERR

FERNDALE TERR
PALLION SUBWAY
AMETHYST ST
MERLE TERR
MELDON
PALMERMO ST
FLORIDA ST

Pallion West Ind Est
LUXEMBOURG RD
Pallion Ind Est
Pallion Prim Sch
WAVERLEY TERR
VICTORY ST
COSSACK TERR
MERLE TERR
JACQUES ST
ANCONA ST
PALLION PK

MAXWELL ST
ENFIELD ST
TREBY ST
NEVILLE RD

BRUSSELS RD
RHEIMS CT

3

ST LUKE'S RD
WESTMOOR RD
ST LUKE'S RD
MARGARET ALICE ST
WILFRED ST
MINTON SQ
EDWIN ST
STRATFIELD ST
EXETER ST
ST LUKE'S TERR
PERCIVAL ST
DUNCAN ST
GARNET ST
EAST MOOR RD
BRADY ST
MAGDELENE PL
RUTLAND ST
KING'S TERR

FARNE SQ
OXFORD SQ
PLANTATION RD
OXFORD ST
ONSLOW ST
TANFIELD ST
MORTIMER ST
LINCOLN ST
SHERIDAN ST
CHEVIOT ST
ORCHARD ST
PRUDHOE ST
DENE ST
PINE ST
WELL ST
Schs

FELL SQ
FELL RD
FELSTEAD CRES
PLANTATION SQ
WEST MOOR TERR
GARFIELD ST
MARTIN TERR
Diamond Hall Jun & Inf Sch

FIRTH SQ
FELSTEAD SQ
WARENNES ST
MAFEKING ST
WILBER CT
WILBER ST

57

FLOCK SQ
FELSHAM SQ
CAWNPORE SQ
FORDFIELD RD
KIMBERLEY ST
WISBECH CT
WILBERFORCE ST
WASHINGTON ST

FORBECK RD
Felstead Sch
Ford
FOURSTONES RD
HAZLEDENE TERR
PALLION RD
WESTLEIGH CT
BELL ST
WALPOLE CT

FROME SQ
FOREST RD
FAWN RD
Havelock Cty Prim Sch
FORDHAM RD
ARLINGTON GR
FERNDENE CRES
FORDLAND PL
ROMFORD ST
PEACOCK ST W
WOOD
WINCHESTER CT
VILLA CL

2

FIELD SQ
HAVELOCK CT
FALMOUTH SQ
GENERAL HAVELOCK RD
FALKLAND RD
FARADAY GR
TAMERTON ST

1 FORD TERR
2 WYCOMBE WAY

FLODDEN RD
FENTON SQ
FORDHALL DR
FORDENBRIDGE CRES
FORDHAM SQ
HYLTON RD
BANCROFT TERR
WESTWOOD ST
BROOKLAND RD
ERITH TERR
BEXLEY ST
KAYLL RD
Sunderland District General H

PADGATE RD
PRIESTMAN CT
FRIAR RD
FORDENBRIDGE RD
FORDENBRIDGE SQ
HENDERSON RD
ANGROVE GDNS
ST GABRIEL'S AVE

FLODDEN RD
FRIAR SQ
SWALEDALE GDNS
WESTWOOD ST
DILSTON GDNS
Liby
A183
B1405

Havelock Hall
HAYDON SQ
HARROW SQ
PRIORY GR
BELMONT ST
BELSAY GDNS
GENERAL GRAHAM ST

1

H
HOLBORN RD
HARTFORD RD
HADLEIGH RD
Cemy
CHESTER RD
WESTLANDS
ST GABRIEL'S AVE
ABINGDON ST
EWESLEY RD

HOLLINSIDE SQ
HUNTLEY SQ
HALSTEAD SQ
HIGHGATE RD
Crem
DUNBAR ST
COLCHESTER TERR
BARNARD ST
CLEVELAND RD

HOLYLAKE SQ
HELMSDALE RD
HEATH SQ
EASTFIELD ST
FARNHAM TERR
GUISBROUGH ST

HENLEY RD
HARTSIDE RD
NORTH HALL RD
HART SQ
A183
WEST HILL
WEST MOUNT
ETTRICK GR
CHESTER RD

HAMPSTEAD RD
HAWKESLEY RD
HOLLINSIDE RD
HEXHAM RD

56

A   37   B   A183   C

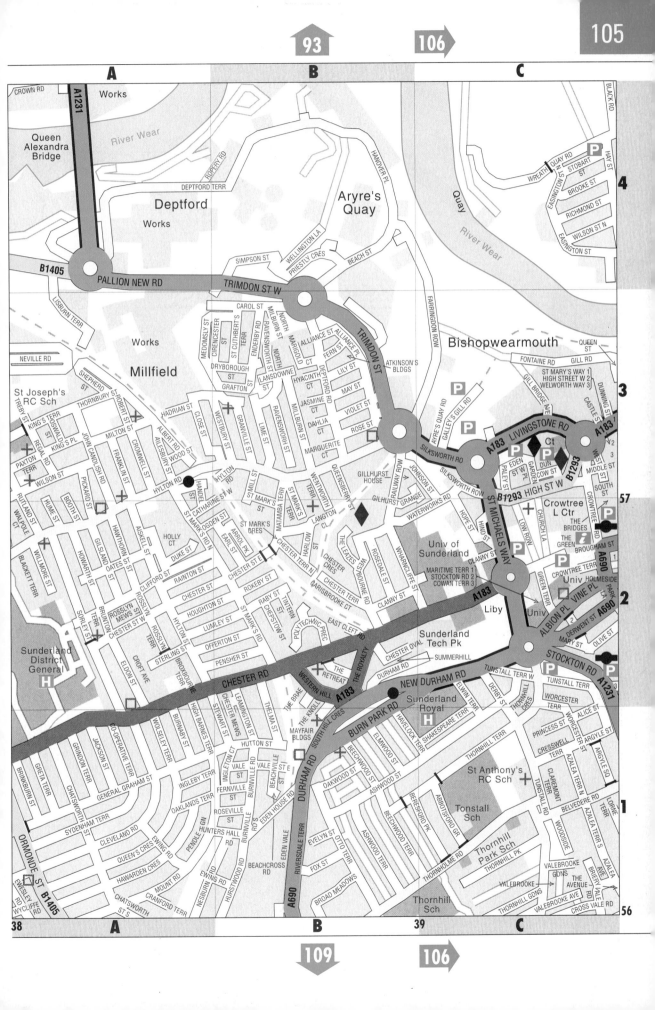

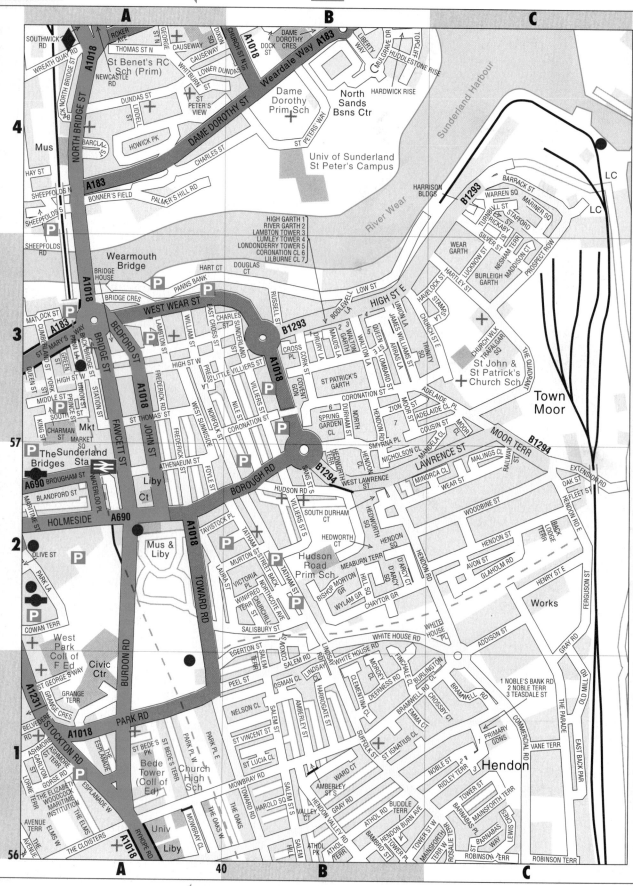

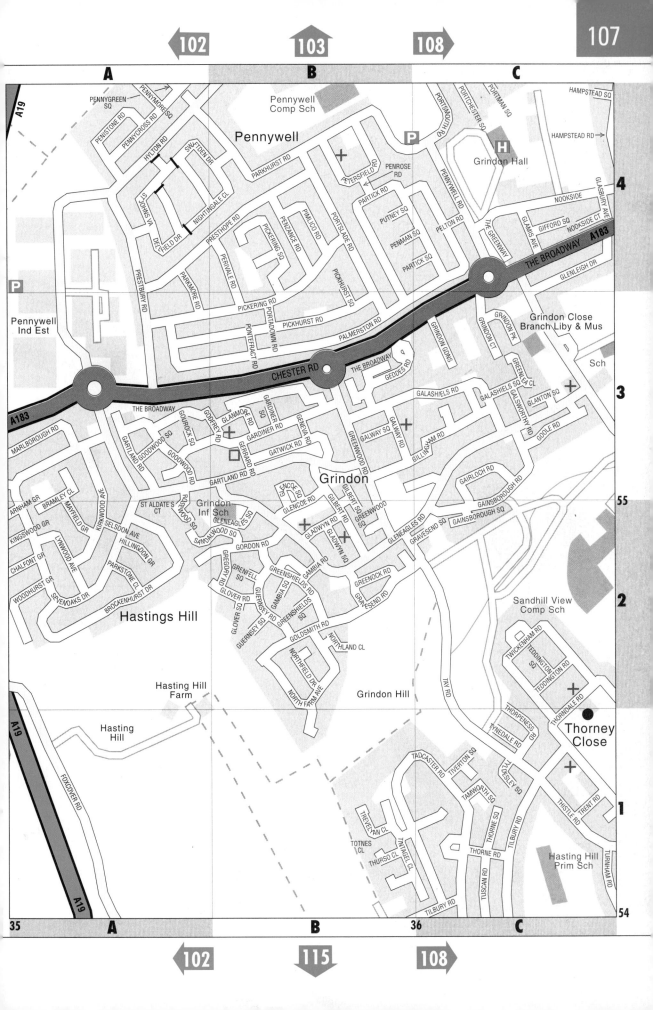

107
104

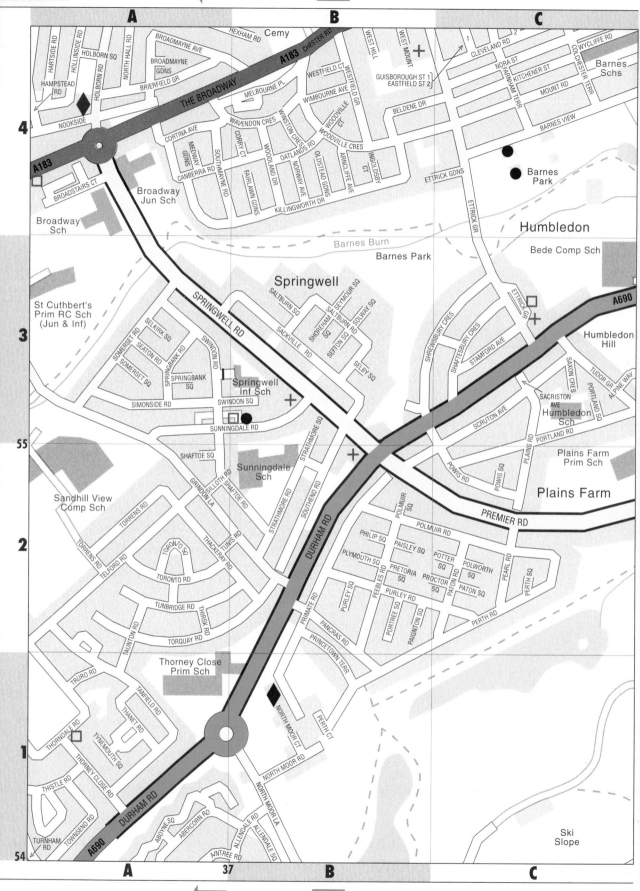

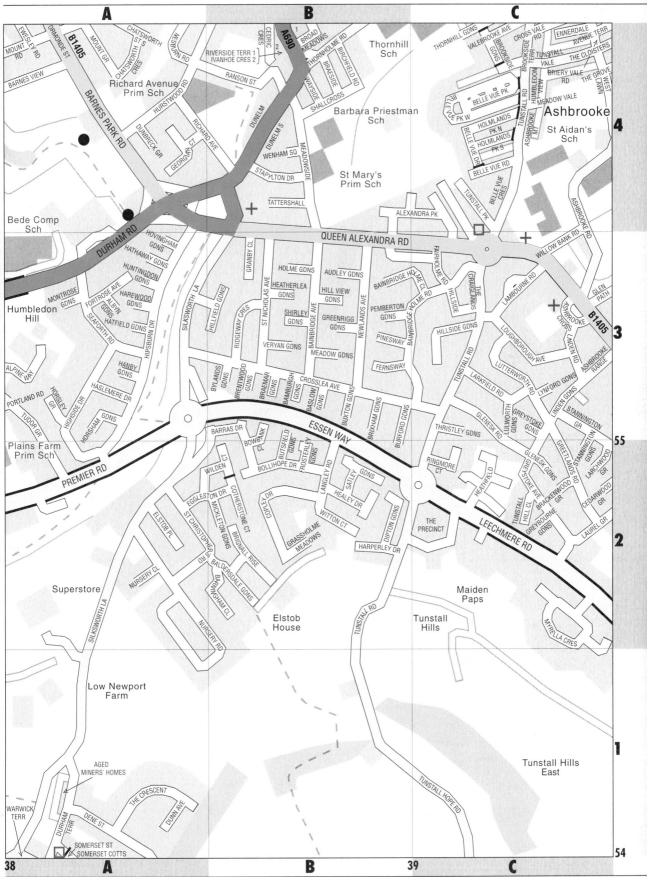

A   B   C

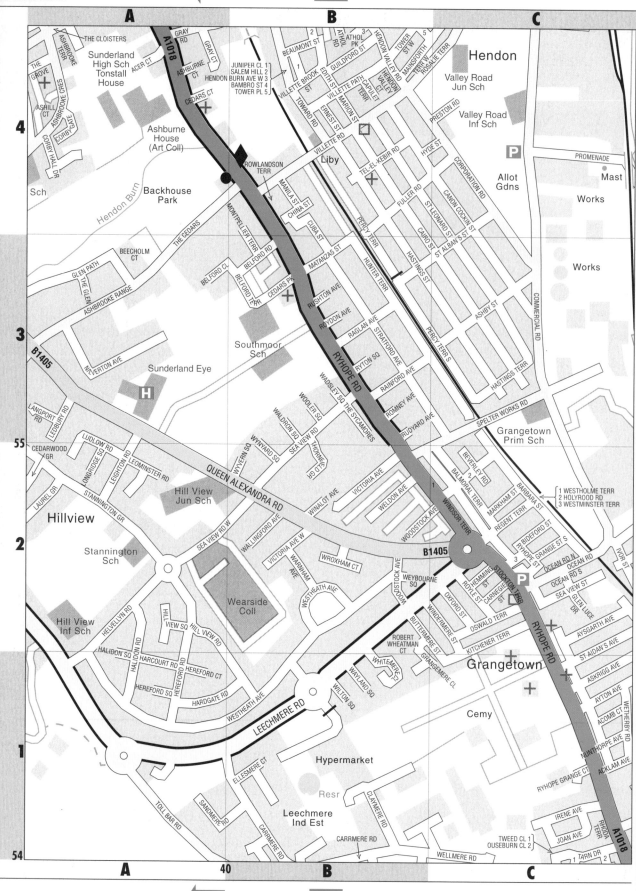

106

Maud's Hole

Hudson Dock

North East Pier

South West Breakwater

Dock

Sewage Works

Roker Pier

North Pier

New South Pier

PROMENADE

SEA BEACH RD

HALCYON HOUSE LA

LC

OCEAN RD

MARGARET ST

1 ST AIDAN'S AVE
2 ASKRIGG AVE

AYTON

APPLEFORTH AVE

WETHERBY RD

ASKERN AVE

ACKLAM AVE

MILLTHORP CL

Salterfen Rocks

RYHOPE RD

A1018

110

117

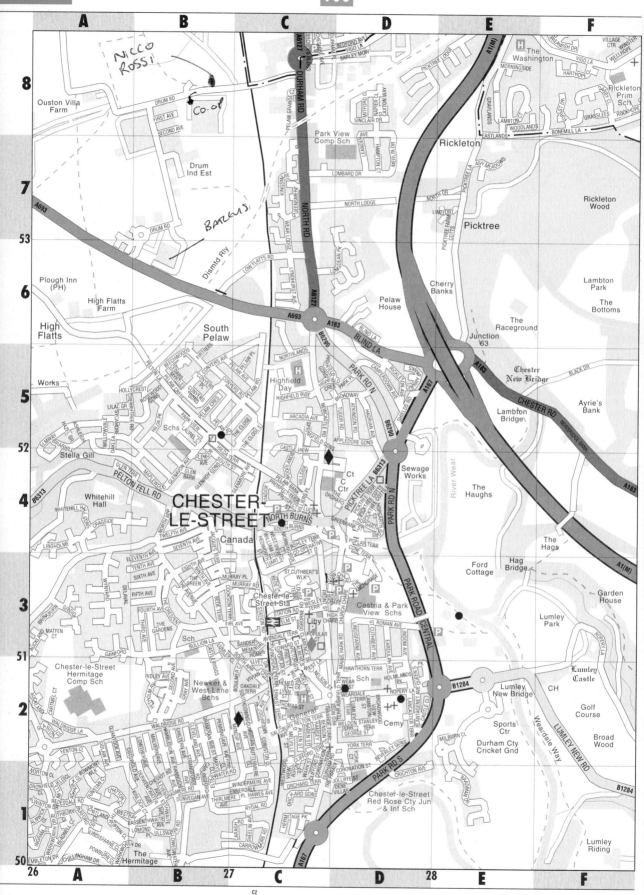

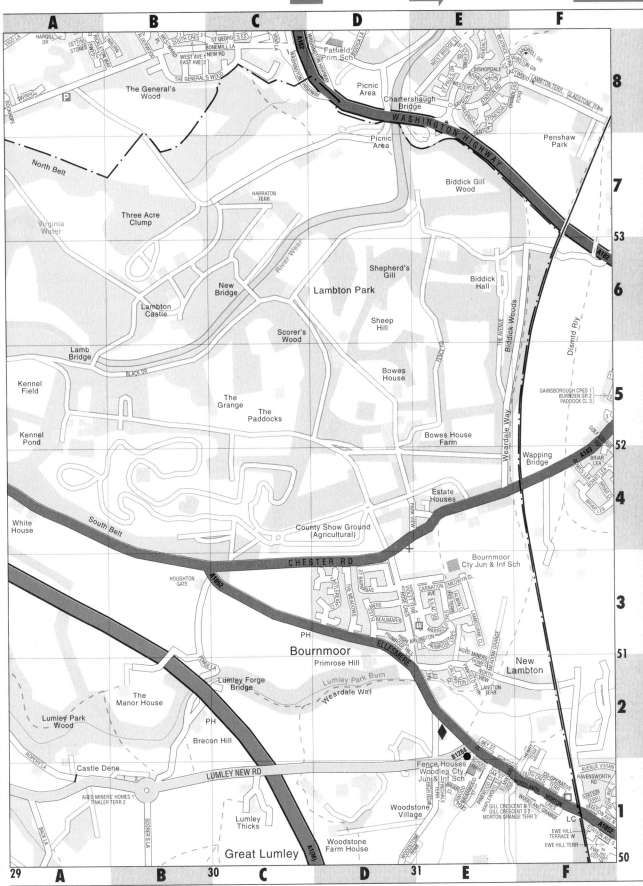

A   B   C   D   E   F

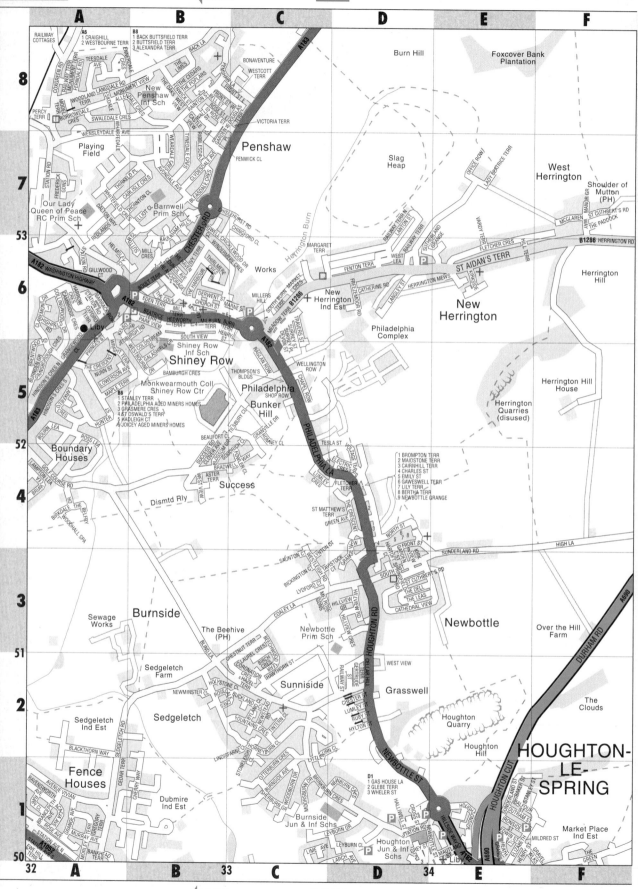

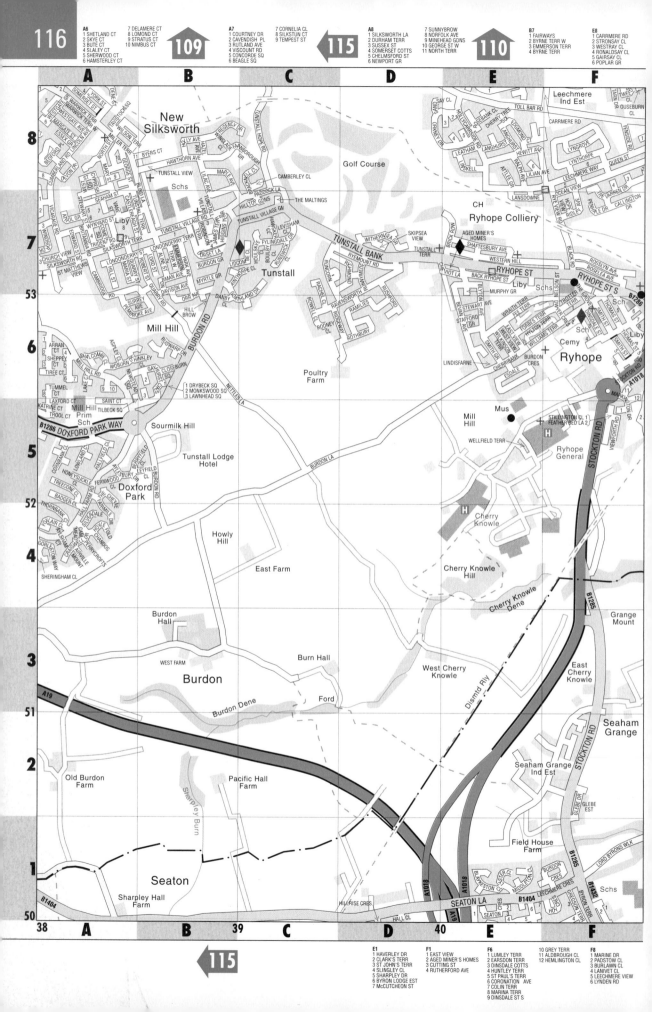

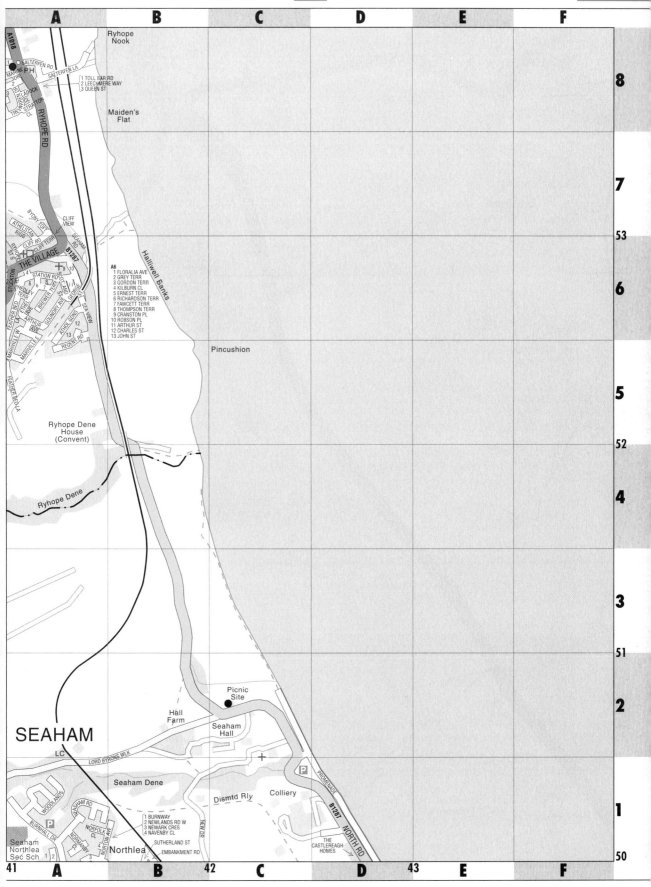

A B C D E F

8
7
53
6
5
52
4
3
51
2
1
50

Ryhope Nook

SALTERFEN RD
SALTERFEN LA
MARINE PH

1 TOLL BAR RD
2 LEECHMERE WAY
3 QUEEN ST

Maiden's Flat

A1018
RYHOPE RD

ATHELSTAN RIGG
BYONY TOFT
CLIFF VIEW
CLIFF RD
CLIFF TERR
THE VILLAGE
B1287
SEAHAM RD

Halliwell Banks

A6
1 FLORALIA AVE
2 GREY TERR
3 GORDON TERR
4 KILBURN CL
5 ERNEST TERR
6 RICHARDSON TERR
7 FAWCETT TERR
8 THOMPSON TERR
9 CRANSTON PL
10 ROBSON PL
11 ARTHUR ST
12 CHARLES ST
13 JOHN ST

STATION RD
STOCKTON RD
HEDLEY TERR
FEATHER RD
ETHE
BREWER TERR
GOUNDRY AVE
GEORGE
ARTHUR AVE
ATHOL GDNS
ATHOL RD
REGENT RD
MARVILLE W
MARVILLE E
SEA VIEW

Pincushion

Ryhope Dene House (Convent)

FEATHER BEDLA

Ryhope Dene

Picnic Site

Hall Farm

Seaham Hall

SEAHAM

LC

LORD BYRONS WLK

Seaham Dene

Dismtd Rly

Colliery

PROMENADE
NORTH RD
B1287

P

1 BURNWAY
2 NEWLANDS RD W
3 NEWARK CRES
4 NAVENBY CL

WOODLANDS
BURNHALL DR
SEAHAM RD
NORFOLK CL
NORMANBY CL
NORTON AVE
NEW DR
SUTHERLAND ST
EMBANKMENT RD

P

Seaham Northlea Sec Sch

Northlea

THE CASTLEREAGH HOMES

41 A 42 B C 42 C 43 D 43 E F 50

A B C D E F

114

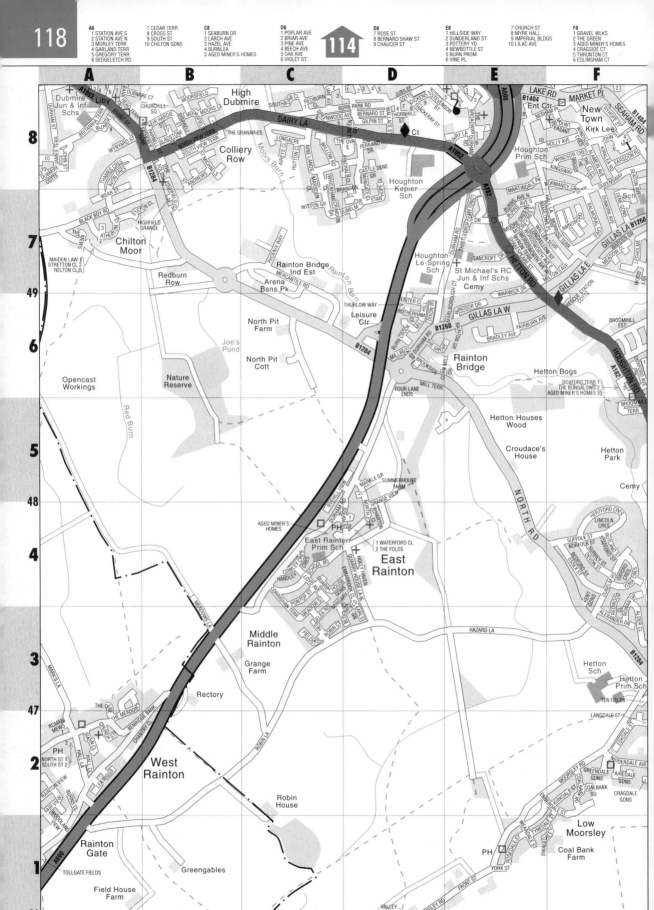

120

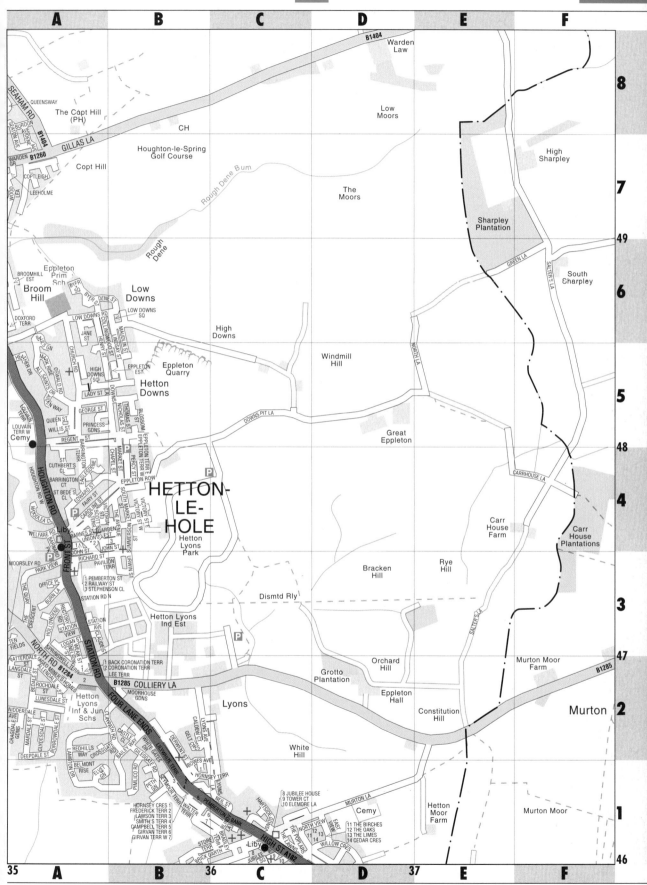

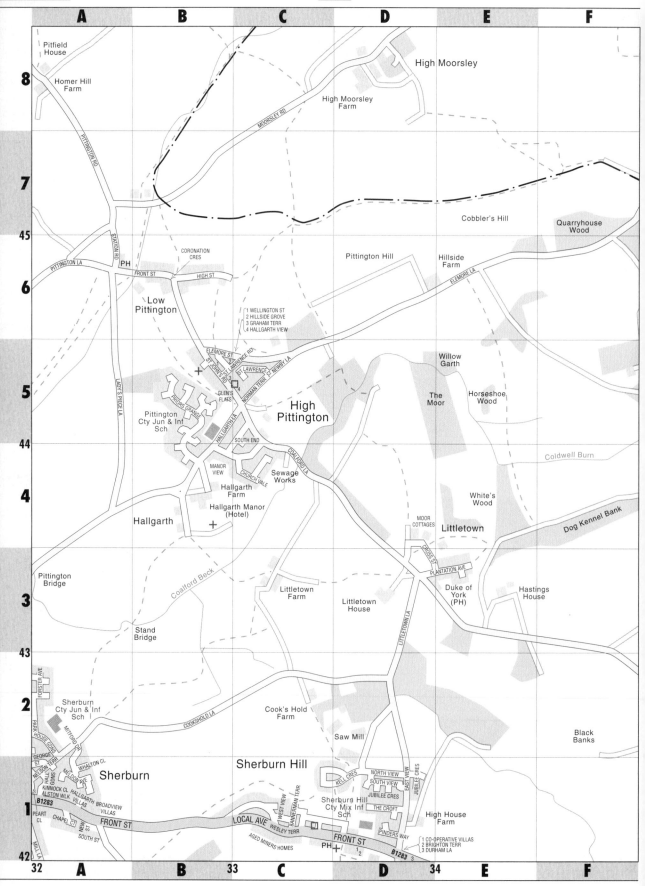

Pitfield House

Homer Hill Farm

High Moorsley

PITTINGTON RD

MOORSLEY RD

High Moorsley Farm

STATION RD

PITTINGTON LA

PH

FRONT ST

HIGH ST

CORONATION CRES

Cobbler's Hill

Quarryhouse Wood

Pittington Hill

Hillside Farm

ELEMORE LA

Low Pittington

1 WELLINGTON ST
2 HILLSIDE GROVE
3 GRAHAM TERR
4 HALLGARTH VIEW

ELEMORE ST
ST JOHN'S RD
LAWRENCE RD
NORMAN TERR
NEWBY LA

ST LAWRENCE

Willow Garth

LADY'S PIECE LA

PRIORS GRANGE

GLEN'S FLATS

HALLGARTH LA

Pittington Cty Jun & Inf Sch

High Pittington

The Moor

Horseshoe Wood

SOUTH END

Coldwell Burn

MANOR VIEW

CHURCH VALE

Sewage Works

COALFORD LA

Hallgarth Farm

White's Wood

Littletown

Hallgarth

Hallgarth Manor (Hotel)

MOOR COTTAGES

Dog Kennel Bank

Pittington Bridge

Coalford Beck

Littletown Farm

Littletown House

CROSS ST

PLANTATION AVE

Duke of York (PH)

Hastings House

Stand Bridge

LITTLETOWN LA

FORSTER AVE

Sherburn Cty Jun & Inf Sch

Cook's Hold Farm

Saw Mill

PARK HOUSE GDNS

MITFORD DR

GEORGE ST
NELSON TERR
HALL GDNS
MELDON AVE
WHALTON CL

Sherburn

KINNOCK CL
ALSTON WLK
HALLGARTH VILLAS
BROADVIEW VILLAS

Sherburn Hill

KELL CRES
NORTH VIEW
SOUTH VIEW
EAST VIEW
JUBILEE CRES
NEW ROW

Black Banks

B1283

PEART CL

CHAPEL CT

NEW LA

SOUTH ST

FRONT ST

LOCAL AVE

WEST VIEW
BANNERMAN TERR
WESLEY TERR

Sherburn Hill Cty Mix Inf Sch

THE CROFT

High House Farm

AGED MINERS HOMES

PH

FRONT ST

PINDERS WAY

B1283

1 CO-OPERATIVE VILLAS
2 BRIGHTON TERR
3 DURHAM LA

MILL LA

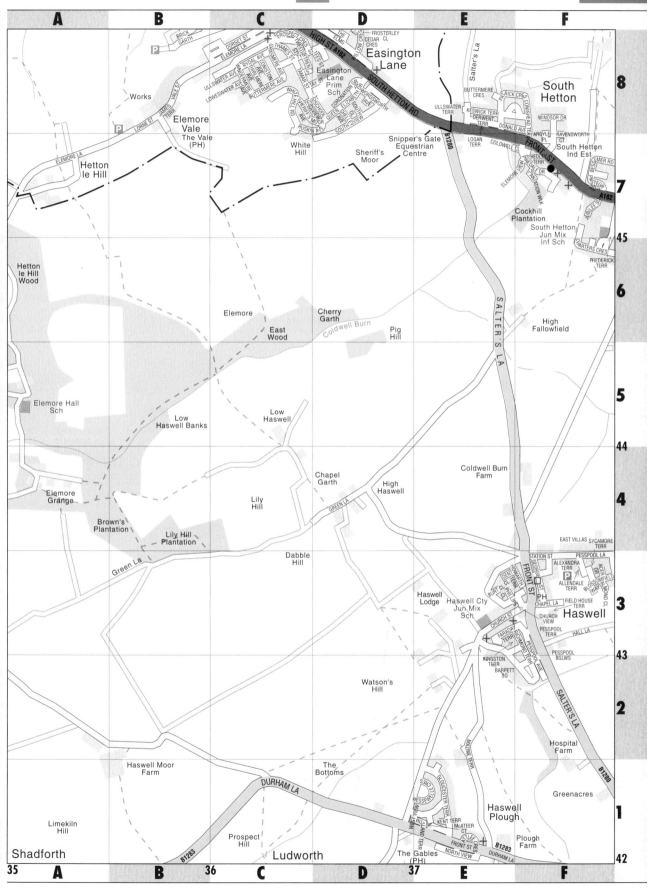

How to use the index

Street names are listed alphabetically and show the locality, the Postcode District, the page number and
a reference to the square in which the name falls on the map page

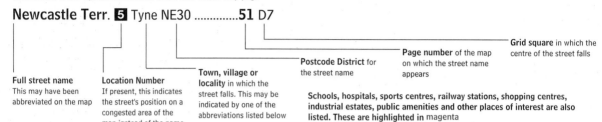

Full street name
This may have been
abbreviated on the map

Location Number
If present, this indicates
the street's position on a
congested area of the
map instead of the name

**Town, village or
locality** in which the
street falls. This may be
indicated by one of the
abbreviations listed below

Postcode District for
the street name

Page number of the map
on which the street name
appears

Grid square in which the
centre of the street falls

Schools, hospitals, sports centres, railway stations, shopping centres,
industrial estates, public amenities and other places of interest are also
listed. These are highlighted in magenta

Abbreviations used in the index

App **Approach**	Cl **Close**	Espl **Esplanade**	Orch **Orchard**	Sq **Square**
Arc **Arcade**	Comm **Common**	Est **Estate**	Par **Parade**	Strs **Stairs**
Ave **Avenue**	Cnr **Corner**	Gdns **Gardens**	Pk **Park**	Stps **Steps**
Bvd **Boulevard**	Cotts **Cottages**	Gn **Green**	Pas **Passage**	St **Street, Saint**
Bldgs **Buildings**	Ct **Court**	Gr **Grove**	Pl **Place**	Terr **Terrace**
Bsns Pk **Business Park**	Ctyd **Courtyard**	Hts **Heights**	Prec **Precinct**	Trad Est **Trading Estate**
Bsns Ctr **Business Centre**	Cres **Crescent**	Ind Est **Industrial Estate**	Prom **Promenade**	Wlk **Walk**
Bglws **Bungalows**	Dr **Drive**	Intc **Interchange**	Ret Pk **Retail Park**	W **West**
Cswy **Causeway**	Dro **Drove**	Junc **Junction**	Rd **Road**	Yd **Yard**
Ctr **Centre**	E **East**	La **Lane**	Rdbt **Roundabout**	
Cir **Circus**	Emb **Embankment**	N **North**	S **South**	

Abbreviations of town, village and rural locality names

Acomb **Acomb** 54 A8	Dgton **Dinnington** ... 27 B7	Hedw **Hedworth** 76 C2	N-u-T **Newcastle-upon-**	S Shs **South**
Annit **Annitsford** 22 B1	Dipton **Dipton** 96 D1	Heps **Hepscott** 9 F5	**Tyne** 45 B1	**Shields** 51 E4
Ashgn **Ashington** 6 B3	Dud **Dudley** 29 A7	H le H **Hetton-le-**	Newl **Newlands** 94 C3	Spring **Springwell** 89 F2
Bworth **Backworth** 30 C4	Duns **Dunston** 70 C1	**Hole** 119 B4	Newt **Newton** 57 C6	Stake **Stakeford** 11 B7
Barlow **Barlow** 85 C6	Each **Eachwick** 33 F8	Hexham **Hexham** 53 E2	N Shs **North Shields** 50 F4	Stann **Stannington** ... 14 D3
Beam **Beamish** 98 D2	Ears **Earsdon** 31 A5	H Pitt **High**	Oak **Oakwood** 54 E8	Stocks **Stocksfield** ... 82 B7
Beb **Bebside** 16 E7	E Lane **Easington**	**Pittington** 120 C5	Ouston **Ouston** 100 A2	Sland **Sunderland** . 104 C4
Bed **Bedlington** 11 A1	**Lane** 121 D8	H Spen **High Spen** 84 F4	Oham **Ovingham** 59 B5	Sunn **Sunniside** 87 A2
B Hill **Berwick Hill** .. 19 A3	E Cram **East**	Holy **Holywell** 23 F2	Oving **Ovington** 58 C4	Tanf **Tanfield** 97 D3
Birt **Birtley** 100 D4	**Cramlington** . 22 E5	Hors **Horsley** 59 D8	Pegs **Pegswood** 4 E4	Tanf L **Tanfield Lea** .. 97 D3
B Mill **Blackhall Mill** 95 B7	E Hart **East Hartford** 16 B3	H-le-Sp **Houghton-le-**	Pens **Penshaw** 114 C7	Tant **Tantobie** 97 B2
Blay **Blaydon** 62 E3	E Rain **East**	**Spring** 114 F1	Pont **Ponteland** 25 D6	Tley **Throckley** 35 D1
Blyth **Blyth** 17 C7	**Rainton** 118 D4	Jarrow **Jarrow** 76 D6	Prest **Prestwick** 26 C5	Tyne **Tynemouth** ... B8 51
Boldon **Boldon** 92 C8	E Sle **East**	Kibble **Kibblesworth** 99 C6	Prud **Prudhoe** 59 D3	Urpeth **Urpeth** 99 D1
Bothal **Bothal** 5 B2	**Sleekburn** 12 A3	Kill **Killingworth** . 29 D3	R Mill **Riding Mill** ... 80 E8	Walb **Walbottle** 35 F2
Bourn **Bournmoor** .. 113 D3	Ebch **Ebchester** 94 F3	Linton **Linton** 1 B3	R Gill **Rowlands Gill** 85 E2	Walls **Wallsend** 49 D2
B Wh **Brockley**	Elling **Ellington** 1 D4	Lbtn **Longbenton** .. 42 E7	Ryhope **Ryhope** 116 F6	Warden **Warden** 53 A8
Whins 76 F3	Fence **Fencehouses** 114 A1	Long **Longhurst** 4 F7	Ryton **Ryton** 61 D5	Wash **Washington** 101 F7
B Vill **Brunswick**	Gates **Gateshead** 72 C3	Lud **Ludworth** 121 C1	Sea **Seaham** 117 A2	W Rain **West**
Village 27 F5	Gr Lum **Great**	Lmth **Lynmouth** 2 B2	Seaton **Seaton** 116 B1	**Rainton** 118 B2
Burdon **Burdon** 116 B3	**Lumley** 113 C1	Medb **Medburn** 34 D8	S Burn **Seaton Burn** . 21 B1	W Sle **West**
Burnop **Burnopfield** .. 97 A6	Green **Greenside** 61 A1	Medom **Medomsley** ... 95 C1	S Del **Seaton**	**Sleekburn** 11 D7
Burns **Burnside** 114 B3	G Post **Guide Post** 10 F7	M Sq **Mickley**	**Deleval** 23 C2	Whick **Whickham** 87 B7
Byer **Byermoor** 97 D7	Hams **Hamsterley** ... 95 B5	**Square** 58 E1	S Slu **Seaton Sluice** 24 C5	Whit **Whitburn** 78 E1
Byw **Bywell** 81 F8	H Mill **Hamsterley**	Mford **Mitford** 8 A8	Seg **Seghill** 22 F1	White **Whiteleas** 77 D3
Cam **Cambois** 12 C5	**Mill** 95 F5	Mpeth **Morpeth** 8 F8	Shadf **Shadforth** ... 121 A1	W Bay **Whitley Bay** .. 31 E6
C le S **Chester-le-**	H Hill **Harlow Hill** ... 33 A5	Murton **Murton** 119 F2	Sherb **Sherburn** 120 A1	Wdton **Widdrington** ... 1 A8
Street 112 B4	Hasw **Haswell** 121 F3	Nedder **Nedderton** 15 B8	S Hill **Sherburn**	W Open **Wide Open** 28 C5
Chopp **Choppington** . 10 E5	Hazle **Hazlerigg** 28 A4	N Herr **New**	**Hill** 120 C1	Win M **Winlaton Mill** 86 C6
Chopw **Chopwell** 84 B1	Heal **Healey** 80 F1	**Herrington** .. 114 E6	S Row **Shiney Row** . 114 B5	Wools **Woolsington** . 36 E8
Clea **Cleadon** 78 B1	Hebb **Hebburn** 75 E5	N Silk **New**	S Slu **Shiremoor** 30 F3	Wylam **Wylam** 60 B5
Crbdge **Corbridge** 56 B5	Hebron **Hebron** 3 F8	**Silksworth** ... 116 B8	Sholt **Sholton** 20 E8	
Cram **Cramlington** . 21 F5	H-o-t-W **Heddon-on-**	N-b-t-S **Newbiggin-by-**	Silk **Silksworth** .. 115 F7	
Craw **Crawcrook** 60 E4	**the-Wall** 34 F2	**the-Sea** 7 E3	Slal **Slaley** 80 A2	
Cress **Cresswell** 2 A7	H o t H **Hedley on**	New **Newbottle** ... 114 E3	S Hett **South**	
	the Hill 83 A3	Newb **Newburn** 61 F7	**Hetton** 121 F8	

A J Cook's Cotts. R Gill NE39 85 B2
Abbay St. Sland SR5 93 A1
Abbey Cl. W Bay NE25 31 D4
Abbey Cl. Wash NE38 101 D5
Abbey Ct. Gates NE8 72 C1
Abbey Dr. Jarrow NE32 76 C7
Abbey Dr. N-u-T NE5 36 B3
Abbey Dr. Tyne NE30 51 D8
Abbey Gate. Mpeth NE61 8 D7
Abbey Meadows. Mpeth NE61 8 D7
Abbey Rd. Wash NE38 101 D5
Abbey Terr. Shire NE27 30 E3
Abbey View. Hexham NE46 54 C4
Abbeyfields Cty Fst Sch. Mpeth NE61 8 E8
Abbeyvale Dr. N-u-T NE6 75 B7
Abbot Ct. Gates NE8 72 C3
Abbot's Rd. Gates NE8 72 C4
Abbot's Way. Mpeth NE61 8 E8
Abbots Cl. Stake NE62 11 B8
Abbots Way. Tyne NE29 50 E8
Abbots Way. Whick NE16 87 B7
Abbotsfield Cl. Silk SR3 115 F5
Abbotsford Gr. Sland SR2 105 C1
Abbotsford Pk. W Bay NE25 31 F4
Abbotsford Rd. Gates NE10 74 A1
Abbotsford Rd. Gates NE10 74 B1
Abbotsford Terr. N-u-T NE2 66 A4
Abbotside Cl. Urpeth DH2 99 D2
Abbotside Pl. N-u-T NE5 36 D2
Abbotsmeade Cl. N-u-T NE5 63 C4
Abbs St. Sland SR5 93 D1
Abercorn Pl. Walls NE28 49 E6
Abercorn Rd. N-u-T NE15 63 A1
Abercorn Rd. Sland SR3 115 D8
Abercrombie Pl. N-u-T NE5 43 B2
Aberdare Rd. Sland SR3 115 E7
Aberdeen. Ouston DH2 99 F1
Aberdeen Ct. N-u-T NE13 38 A4
Aberdeen Dr. B Wh NE32 76 E3
Aberdeen Tower. Sland SR3 115 E8
Aberfoyle. Ouston DH2 99 F1
Abernethy. Ouston DH2 99 F2
Abersford Cl. N-u-T NE5 36 B3
Abingdon. Ouston DH2 99 F1
Abingdon Ct. Blay NE21 62 C3
Abingdon Ct. N-u-T NE3 38 A3
Abingdon Rd. N-u-T NE6 75 B7
Abingdon Sq. Cram NE23 16 C1
Abingdon St. Sland SR4 104 C1
Abingdon Way. Boldon NE35 & NE36 91 E7
Abinger St. N-u-T NE4 65 B1
Aboyne Sq. Sland SR3 108 A1
Acacia Ave. Fence DH4 114 A1
Acacia Gr. Hebb NE31 75 E4
Acacia Gr. S Shs NE34 77 F5
Acacia Rd. Gates NE10 73 B2
Acacia St. Gates NE11 88 C5
Acacia Terr. Ashgn NE63 6 D3
Acanthus Ave. N-u-T NE4 64 A3
Acer Ct. Sland SR2 110 A4
Acer Dr. Hasw DH6 121 F3
Acklam Ave. Sland SR2 111 A1
Acomb Ave. S Del NE25 23 D2
Acomb Ave. Walls NE28 49 D7
Acomb Cres. N-u-T NE3 39 A4
Acomb Ct. Gates NE9 89 B2
Acomb Ct. Kill NE12 29 D3
Acomb Ct. Sland SR2 110 C1
Acomb Dr. Wylam NE41 60 A7
Acomb Gdns. N-u-T NE5 43 C1
Acorn Ave. Bed NE22 15 F8
Acorn Ave. Gates NE8 88 C8
Acorn Rd. N-u-T NE2 46 B2
Acreford Ct. Chopp NE62 10 E6
Acton Dr. Tyne NE29 50 D8
Acton Pl. N-u-T NE7 47 B2
Acton Rd. N-u-T NE5 62 F8
Ada St. N-u-T NE6 68 B2
Ada St. S Shs NE33 51 D1
Adair Ave. N-u-T NE15 & NE4 63 C2
Adair Way. Hebb NE31 76 A5
Adams Terr. Medom DH8 95 A2
Adderlane Rd. Prud NE42 59 E3
Adderstone Ave. Cram NE23 22 B5
Adderstone Cres. N-u-T NE2 46 C2
Adderstone Gdns. Tyne NE29 31 B1
Addington Cres. N Shs NE29 50 E6
Addington Dr. Blyth NE24 17 E5
Addington Dr. Walls NE28 49 D7
Addison Cl. N-u-T NE6 67 B2
Addison Ct. Walls NE28 50 A3
Addison Gdns. Gates NE10 90 B8
Addison Rd. Boldon NE36 92 A7
Addison Rd. N-u-T NE15 62 D7
Addison Rd. N-u-T NE6 67 B2
Addison St. N Shs NE29 51 A4
Addison St. Sland SR2 106 C2
Addison Wlk. B Hall NE34 77 A3
Addycombe Terr. N-u-T NE6 47 C1
Adelaide Cl. Sland SR1 106 C3
Adelaide Ct. Gates NE8 72 B3
Adelaide Pl. Sland SR1 106 C3
Adelaide St. C le S DH3 112 C2
Adelaide Terr. N-u-T NE4 64 A1
Adelaide Terr. N-u-T NE4 70 B4
Adeline Gdns. N-u-T NE3 45 A3
Adelphi Cl. Tyne NE29 50 C8
Adelphi Pl. N-u-T NE6 68 B1
Aden Tower. Sland SR3 115 E8
Admirals House. 9 Tyne NE30 51 C8
Adolphus St. Whit SR6 78 F1
Affleck St. Gates NE8 72 B2
Afton Ct. S Shs NE34 77 C5
Afton Way. N-u-T NE3 38 B2
Agar Rd. Sland SR3 115 D8
Aged Miner's Cotts. M Sq NE43 82 F8
Aged Miner's Homes. Boldon NE35 76 D1
Aged Miner's Homes. Burnop NE16 97 A6
Aged Miner's Homes. E Rain DH5 118 C4
Aged Miner's Homes. H le H DH5 118 F6
Aged Miner's Homes. H le H DH5 119 A2
Aged Miner's Homes. 5 H-le-Sp DH4 118 C8
Aged Miner's Homes. 3 H-le-Sp DH5 118 F8
Aged Miner's Homes. Ryhope SR2 116 E7
Aged Miner's Homes. 2 Seaham SR7 116 F1
Aged Miners' Homes. Annit NE23 22 B1
Aged Miners' Homes. Ashgn NE63 6 A4
Aged Miners' Homes. B Vill NE13 28 A6
Aged Miners' Homes. Bourn DH4 113 E2
Aged Miners Homes. Cam NE24 12 D4
Aged Miners' Homes. Cram NE23 21 F7
Aged Miners' Homes. Dud NE23 29 A6
Aged Miners' Homes. E Cram NE25 23 E6
Aged Miners' Homes. Gr Lum DH3 113 B1
Aged Miners' Homes. H Spen NE39 85 A4
Aged Miners Homes. Kibble NE11 99 C6
Aged Miners' Homes. N Silk SR3 109 A1
Aged Miners Homes. N-b-t-S NE64 7 D3
Aged Miners Homes. N-u-T NE5 36 E3
Aged Miners Homes. Prud NE42 59 B1
Aged Miners' Homes. R Gill NE39 85 F1
Aged Miners' Homes. Ryton NE40 61 E4
Aged Miners' Homes. S Hill DH6 120 C1
Aged Miners' Homes. S Shs NE34 78 A7
Aged Miners' Homes. Sland SR5 92 E2
Aged Miners' Homes. Stake NE62 11 C8
Aged Miners' Homes. Sunn NE16 87 A1
Aged Miners'Homes. Shire NE27 30 F3
Aged Mineworkers Homes. Long NE61 5 B7
Aged Mineworkers Homes. Tley NE15 35 B2
Agincourt. Hebb NE31 75 D7
Agincourt. Kill NE12 29 D4
Agnes Maria St. N-u-T NE3 39 A1
Agricola Ct. 1 S Shs NE33 51 C4
Agricola Gdns. Walls NE28 49 D7
Agricola Rd. N-u-T NE4 64 C2
Aidan Ave. S Slu NE26 24 B6
Aidan Cl. B Vill NE13 28 A6
Aidan Cl. Lbtn NE7 41 C1
Aidan Gr. Elling NE61 1 E4
Aidan Wlk. N-u-T NE3 40 B1
Aiden Way. H le H DH5 119 A5
Ailesbury St. Sland SR4 105 A3
Ainderby Rd. Tley NE15 35 B2
Ainsdale Gdns. N-u-T NE5 36 C2
Ainslie Pl. N-u-T NE5 43 C2
Ainsworth Ave. B Hall NE34 77 A3
Ainthorpe Cl. N Silk SR3 116 B7
Ainthorpe Gdns. N-u-T NE7 47 C4
Aintree Cl. Wash NE37 101 D7
Aintree Gdns. Gates NE8 88 C7
Aintree Rd. Sland SR3 115 D8
Airedale. Walls NE28 42 C1
Airedale Gdns. H le H DH5 118 F2
Airey Terr. Gates NE8 72 A1
Airey Terr. N-u-T NE6 75 A5
Aireys Cl. H-le-Sp DH4 118 C8
Airport Freightway. Wools NE13 26 E2
Airport Ind Est. N-u-T NE3 37 C2
Airville Mount. Silk SR3 116 A4
Aisgill Cl. Cram NE23 22 B6
Aisgill Dr. N-u-T NE5 36 C1
Aiskell St. Sland SR4 105 A2
Akeld Cl. Cram NE23 22 B5
Akeld Ct. N-u-T NE3 46 B4
Akeman Way. S Shs NE34 77 B5
Akenside Hill. N-u-T NE1 72 B4
Akenside Terr. N-u-T NE2 66 C4
Akhurst Sch. N-u-T NE2 46 C2
Alamein Ave. H-le-Sp DH5 118 F8
Alanbrooke Row. Hebb NE31 75 C3
Albany Ave. Lbtn NE12 42 A3
Albany Ct. N-u-T NE4 71 A3
Albany Gdns. 1 W Bay NE26 32 B4
Albany Inf Sch. Wash NE37 101 B7
Albany Jun Sch. Wash NE37 101 C7
Albany Mews. N-u-T NE3 45 A2
Albany Rd. Gates NE8 73 A3
Albany St E. S Shs NE33 77 D8
Albany St W. S Shs NE33 77 D8
Albany Way. Wash NE37 101 C7
Albatross Way. Blyth NE24 17 E3
Albemarle Ave. N-u-T NE2 46 A3
Albemarle St. 5 S Shs NE33 51 C3
Albert Ave. Walls NE28 49 B2
Albert Dr. Gates NE9 88 F4
Albert Edward Terr. Boldon NE35 76 E2
Albert Pl. Gates NE9 88 F4
Albert Pl. Wash NE38 101 F4
Albert Rd. Bed NE22 11 E2
Albert Rd. Jarrow NE32 76 A6
Albert Rd. Jarrow NE32 76 B6
Albert Rd. S Slu NE26 24 D6
Albert Rd. Sland SR4 105 A3
Albert St. Blyth NE24 17 E8
Albert St. C le S DH3 112 C3
Albert St. Hebb NE31 75 D6
Albert St. N-u-T NE2 66 C2
Albert St. R Gill NE39 85 A1
Albert Terr. Lbtn NE12 29 C1
Albert Terr. 4 W Bay NE26 32 B4
Albion Ct. N-u-T NE6 67 B1
Albion Ct. 10 S Shs NE33 51 C4
Albion Gdns. Burnop NE16 96 F5
Albion House. 3 N Shs NE29 51 A5
Albion Pl. Sland SR1 105 C2
Albion Rd. N Shs NE29 & NE30 51 A6
Albion Rd W. N Shs NE29 51 A5
Albion Row. N-u-T NE6 67 B1
Albion Row. N-u-T NE6 67 B2
Albion St. Gates NE10 89 D6
Albion St. Sland SR4 103 A2
Albion Terr. Hexham NE46 54 A5
Albion Terr. Lmth NE61 2 A3
Albion Terr. 8 N Shs NE29 51 A6
Albion Way. Blyth NE24 17 C7
Albion Way. Cram NE23 16 D1
Albury Park Rd. Tyne NE30 51 C7
Albury Pl. Whick NE16 87 A5
Albury Rd. N-u-T NE2 46 A3
Albyn Gdns. Sland SR3 109 A3
Alcester Cl. Stake NE62 10 F7
Alconbury Cl. Blyth NE24 17 E5
Alcroft Cl. N-u-T NE5 36 B3
Aldborough St. Blyth NE24 17 E7
Aldbrough Cl. 11 Ryhope SR2 116 F6
Aldbrough St. S Shs NE34 77 A5
Aldeburgh Ave. N-u-T NE15 62 C8
Aldenham Gdns. Tyne NE30 32 C1
Aldenham Rd. Sland SR3 115 E8
Aldenham Tower. Sland SR3 115 E8
Alder Ave. N-u-T NE4 & NE5 64 A4
Alder Cl. H le H DH5 118 F3
Alder Cl. Mpeth NE61 9 A8
Alder Cres. Tant DH9 96 F2
Alder Gr. W Bay NE25 31 E6
Alder Rd. Shire NE29 50 B7
Alder Rd. Walls NE28 49 E6
Alder St. Gates NE11 88 C5
Alder St. Sland SR5 92 B1
Alder Way. Kill NE12 29 C4
Alderley Cl. Boldon NE35 76 E1
Alderley Dr. Kill NE12 29 F4
Alderley Rd. Gates NE9 88 E5
Alderley Way. Cram NE23 16 D1
Alderney Gdns. N-u-T NE5 36 C2
Aldershot Rd. Sland SR3 115 D7
Aldershot Sq. Sland SR3 115 D7
Alderwood. Ashgn NE63 6 C2
Alderwood. Wash NE38 113 B8
Alderwood Cres. N-u-T NE6 48 C1
Alderwyk. Gates NE10 90 B6
Aldwick Rd. N-u-T NE15 63 A1
Aldwych Dr. Tyne NE29 50 B7
Aldwych Rd. Sland SR3 115 D7
Aldwych Sq. Sland SR3 115 D6
Aldwych St. S Shs NE33 51 E2
Alemouth Rd. Hexham NE46 54 B5
Alexander Dr. H le H DH5 118 F3
Alexander Terr. Hazle NE13 28 A5
Alexander Terr. Sland SR6 93 D3
Alexandra Cres. Hexham NE46 53 F5
Alexandra Ct. Ashgn NE63 6 E4
Alexandra Dr. Whick NE16 87 C8
Alexandra Gdns. Ryton NE40 61 E4
Alexandra Pk. Sland SR2 109 C4
Alexandra Rd. Ashgn NE63 6 F3
Alexandra Rd. Gates NE8 72 B1
Alexandra Rd. Mpeth NE61 9 A8
Alexandra Rd. N-u-T NE6 47 B1
Alexandra Rd Inf Sch. Gates NE8 72 B1
Alexandra St. R Gill NE39 85 A1
Alexandra St. Walls NE28 49 C2
Alexandra Terr. Hasw DH6 121 F3
Alexandra Terr. Hexham NE46 53 F5
Alexandra Terr. N-u-T NE5 36 F3
Alexandra Terr. 3 Pens DH4 114 B8
Alexandra Terr. Stocks NE43 82 D7
Alexandra Terr. Sunn NE16 87 C2
Alexandra Terr. 3 W Bay NE26 32 B4
Alexandra Way. Cram NE23 22 B5
Alford. Ouston DH2 99 F2
Alford Gn. Lbtn NE12 41 C3
Alfred Ave. Bed NE22 11 B1
Alfred St. Blyth NE24 17 F6
Alfred St. Hebb NE31 75 D5
Alfred St. N-u-T NE6 68 B2
Algernon Ct. N-u-T NE6 67 C3
Algernon Ind Est. Shire NE27 30 F1
Algernon Pl. W Bay NE26 32 B4
Algernon Rd. N-u-T NE15 62 C6
Algernon Rd. N-u-T NE6 67 C3
Algernon Terr. Tyne NE30 51 C8
Algernon Terr. Wylam NE41 60 A6
Algiers Rd. Sland SR3 115 C7
Alice St. Blay NE21 62 B1
Alice St. S Shs NE33 77 C8
Alice St. Sland SR2 105 C1
Alice Well Villas. Pens DH4 102 B3
Aline St. N Silk SR3 116 B7
Alison Dr. Boldon NE36 92 D7
All Church. N-u-T NE15 63 B2
All Saints C of E Inf Sch. S Shs NE34 77 C5
All Saints C of E Jun Sch. S Shs NE34 77 B4
All Saints Dr. H le H DH5 119 A5
Allan Rd. N-b-t-S NE64 7 D5
Allandale Ave. Lbtn NE12 42 A3
Allanville. Kill NE12 29 C5
Allchurch Dr. Ashgn NE63 7 A3
Allen Ave. Gates NE11 88 D7
Allen Dr. Hexham NE46 54 B4
Allen St. C le S DH3 112 C2
Allendale Ave. Walls NE28 49 B4
Allendale Cres. Pens DH4 114 B8
Allendale Cres. Shire NE27 31 A3
Allendale Cres. Stake NE62 11 A6
Allendale Dr. S Shs NE34 78 A8
Allendale Pl. Tyne NE30 51 D7
Allendale Rd. Blyth NE24 17 F6
Allendale Rd. Hexham NE46 53 F4
Allendale Rd. N-u-T NE6 68 A1
Allendale Rd. Sland SR3 115 D8
Allendale Sq. Sland SR3 115 E8
Allendale St. H le H DH5 119 A2
Allendale Terr. Hasw DH6 121 F3
Allendale Terr. N-u-T NE6 68 C1
Allenhead. Wash NE38 101 E1
Allenheads. N-u-T NE5 36 E1
Allensgreen. Cram NE23 22 B6
Allerdean Cl. N-u-T NE15 62 B7
Allerdean Cl. S Del NE25 23 D2
Allerdene Wlk. Whick NE16 87 B6
Allerhope. Cram NE23 22 B5
Allerton Gdns. N-u-T NE6 48 A2
Allerton Pl. Whick NE16 86 F5
Allerwash. N-u-T NE5 36 E1
Allery Banks. Mpeth NE61 9 A8
Allgood Terr. Bed NE22 11 B1
Allhusen Terr. Gates NE8 73 B1
Alliance Pl. Sland SR4 105 B3
Alliance St. Sland SR4 105 B3
Allingham Ct. N-u-T NE7 48 B3
Allison Ct. Whick NE16 69 B1
Alloa Rd. Sland SR3 115 D8
Allonby Way. N-u-T NE5 63 B4
Alloy Terr. R Gill NE39 85 C1
Allwork Terr. Whick NE16 87 B7
Alma Pl. N Shs NE29 51 A6
Alma Pl. W Bay NE26 32 C4
Alma St. Sland SR4 103 A3
Alma Terr. Green NE40 61 C2
Almond Cl. Hasw DH6 121 F3
Almond Cres. Gates NE8 88 C8
Almond Dr. Sland SR5 103 A4
Almond Pl. N-u-T NE4 64 A3
Almshouses. Newb NE15 61 F7
Aln Ave. N-u-T NE3 39 A3
Aln Cres. N-u-T NE3 39 A3
Aln Ct. Elling NE61 1 E5
Aln Ct. N-u-T NE15 62 C6
Aln Gr. N-u-T NE15 62 C7
Aln St. Ashgn NE63 6 E4
Aln St. Hebb NE31 75 D6
Aln St. Hebb NE31 75 E5
Aln Wlk. N-u-T NE3 39 A2
Alnham Ct. N-u-T NE3 38 B3
Alnham Gr. N-u-T NE5 36 C2
Alnmouth Ave. N Shs NE29 50 D4
Alnmouth Dr. N-u-T NE3 46 B4
Alnmouth Terr. Acomb NE46 53 F8
Alnwick Ave. N Shs NE29 50 D4
Alnwick Ave. W Bay NE26 32 A5
Alnwick Cl. C le S DH2 112 A1
Alnwick Cl. Wash NE38 101 B5
Alnwick Cl. Whick NE16 87 A7
Alnwick Dr. Bed NE22 10 D1
Alnwick Gr. Jarrow NE32 76 B2
Alnwick Rd. S Shs NE33 & NE34 77 C6
Alnwick Rd. Sland SR3 115 E8
Alnwick Sq. Sland SR3 115 E8
Alnwick St. Newb NE15 61 F8
Alnwick St. Walls NE28 49 C2
Alnwick Terr. W Open NE13 28 C7
Alpine Gr. Boldon NE36 92 B7
Alpine Way. Sland SR3 109 A3
Alresford. Kill NE12 29 D4
Alston Ave. E Cram NE23 22 D5
Alston Ave. N-u-T NE6 68 B2
Alston Cl. Tyne NE29 50 C7
Alston Cl. Walls NE28 50 A4
Alston Cres. Sland SR6 93 C4
Alston Gdns. Tley NE15 35 D3
Alston Gr. S Slu NE26 24 B7
Alston Rd. E Cram NE25 23 D6
Alston Rd. Wash NE38 102 B6
Alston St. Gates NE8 72 A1
Alston Wlk. Sherb DH6 120 A1
Altan Pl. Lbtn NE12 41 B3
Altrincham Tower. Sland SR3 115 E8
Alum Well Rd. Gates NE9 88 E5
Alum Well Rd. 1 Gates NE9 88 F5
Alverston Cl. N-u-T NE15 62 C8
Alverstone Ave. Gates NE9 88 E4
Alverstone Rd. Sland SR3 115 D7
Alverthorpe St. S Shs NE33 77 D8
Alveston Cl. Stake NE62 10 F7
Alwin. Wash NE38 101 A1
Alwin Cl. Bourn DH4 113 E3
Alwinton Ave. Tyne NE29 50 D8
Alwinton Cl. Blyth NE24 17 C8
Alwinton Cl. N-u-T NE5 43 A4
Alwinton Dr. C le S DH2 112 A1
Alwinton Gdns. Duns NE11 88 A5
Alwinton Rd. Shire NE27 31 A3
Alwinton Terr. N-u-T NE3 40 A1
Amalfi Tower. Sland SR3 115 E8
Amara Sq. Sland SR3 115 E8
Ambassadors Way. Tyne NE29 50 B8
Amberley Chase. Kill NE12 29 E4
Amberley Cl. Walls NE28 50 A3
Amberley Ct. Gates NE8 71 C1
Amberley Cty Fst Sch. Kill NE12 29 E4
Amberley Gdns. N-u-T NE7 47 C2
Amberley St. Gates NE8 71 C1
Amberley St. Sland SR2 106 B1
Amberley St S. Sland SR2 106 B1
Amberley Way. Blyth NE24 17 E5
Amberley Wlk. Whick NE16 87 B5
Amberly Gr. Whick NE16 87 A5
Amble Ave. S Shs NE34 78 B8
Amble Ave. W Bay NE25 32 B4
Amble Cl. Blyth NE24 17 C5
Amble Gr. N-u-T NE2 67 A3
Amble Pl. Lbtn NE12 29 F1
Amble Tower. Sland SR3 115 E8
Amble Way. N-u-T NE3 39 B2
Ambleside. Tley NE15 35 E3
Ambleside Ave. S Shs NE34 77 E6
Ambleside Cl. S Del NE25 23 D3
Ambleside Gdns. Gates NE9 89 A4
Ambleside Gdns. N-u-T NE5 63 B4
Ambleside Terr. Sland SR6 93 C4
Ambridge Way. N-u-T NE3 38 C1
Ambrose Pl. N-u-T NE6 75 B6
Ambrose Rd. Sland SR3 115 D8
Amec Way. Walls NE28 49 E1
Amelia Cl. Duns NE4 70 B3
Amelia Gdns. Sland SR3 115 C7
Amelia Wlk. Duns NE4 70 B3
Amen Cnr. N-u-T NE1 72 A4
Amersham Pl. N-u-T NE5 43 B2
Amersham Rd. Blyth NE24 17 E4
Amersham Sq. Sland SR3 115 E8
Amesbury Cl. N-u-T NE5 36 B3
Amethyst Rd. N-u-T NE4 71 A2
Amethyst St. Sland SR4 104 C3
Amherst Rd. N-u-T NE3 38 B2
Amos Ayre Pl. Jarrow NE34 76 F5
Amsterdam Rd. Sland SR3 115 E8
Amy St. Sland SR5 93 B2
Ancaster Ave. Lbtn NE12 41 B2
Ancaster Rd. Whick NE16 86 F6
Anchorage The. C le S DH3 112 D3
Anchorage The. Pens DH4 114 B6
Ancona St. Sland SR4 104 C3
Ancroft Ave. Tyne NE29 50 F7
Ancroft Pl. Ashgn NE63 6 F1
Ancroft Pl. N-u-T NE5 63 B4
Ancroft Rd. S Del NE25 23 B3
Ancrum St. N-u-T NE2 65 B3
Ancrum Way. Whick NE16 86 F5
Anderson St. S Shs NE33 51 D3
Andover Pl. Walls NE28 49 E6
Andrew Rd. Sland SR3 115 D7
Anfield Ct. N-u-T NE3 38 B1
Anfield Rd. N-u-T NE3 38 B1
Angerton Ave. Shire NE27 30 F2
Angerton Ave. Tyne NE30 32 A1
Angerton Gdns. N-u-T NE5 64 A4
Angerton Terr. Dud NE23 28 F8
Angle Terr. Walls NE28 49 F2
Anglesey Gdns. N-u-T NE5 36 C2
Anglesey Pl. N-u-T NE4 65 B1
Anglesey Rd. Sland SR3 115 D7
Anglesey Sq. Sland SR3 115 D7
Angram Dr. Sland SR2 111 A1
Angram Wlk. N-u-T NE5 36 C1
Angrove Gdns. Sland SR4 104 C1
Angus. Ouston DH2 99 F2
Angus Cl. Kill NE12 29 C3
Angus House. N-u-T NE4 70 B4
Angus Rd. Gates NE8 88 C8
Angus Sq. Sland SR3 115 D7
Ann St. Blay NE21 62 C3
Ann St. Gates NE8 72 C2
Ann St. Hebb NE31 75 C7
Ann St. Shire NE27 30 E4
Ann Wlk. N-u-T NE6 75 A4
Ann's Row. Blyth NE24 12 E1
Anne Dr. Lbtn NE12 49 A8
Annfield Rd. Cram NE23 16 B2
Annie St. Sland SR6 93 E4
Annitsford Dr. Annit NE23 29 B8
Annitsford Fst Sch. Annit NE23 22 B1
Annville Cres. N-u-T NE6 75 A4
Anscomb Gdns. N-u-T NE7 47 A3
Anson Cl. S Shs NE33 77 B8
Anson Pl. N-u-T NE5 36 F3
Anson St. Gates NE8 73 B1
Anstead Cl. Cram NE23 22 B6
Anthony Rd. Sland SR3 115 D8
Anton Pl. Cram NE23 22 B5
Antonine Wlk. H-o-t-W NE15 34 F2
Antrim Cl. N-u-T NE5 43 C3
Antwerp Rd. Sland SR3 115 C7
Apperley. N-u-T NE5 36 E1
Apperley Ave. N-u-T NE5 43 C4
Apperley Rd. Stocks NE43 82 C6
Appian Pl. Gates NE9 89 B7
Appian Pl. Tley NE15 35 D2
Apple Cl. N-u-T NE15 62 C8
Apple Ct. E Cram NE25 23 D6
Appleby Ct. N Shs NE29 50 F5
Appleby Gdns. Gates NE9 89 A3
Appleby Gdns. Walls NE28 50 A4
Appleby Pk. N Shs NE29 50 F6
Appleby Rd. Sland SR3 115 D7
Appleby Sq. Sland SR3 115 D7
Appleby St. N Shs NE29 51 A4
Appledore Gdns. C le S DH3 112 D5
Appledore Gdns. 1 Gates NE9 88 F3
Appledore Rd. Blyth NE24 17 E5
Appleforth Ave. Sland SR2 111 A1
Appletree Gdns. W Bay NE25 31 E3
Appletree La. Crbdge NE45 56 A5
Appletree Rise. Crbdge NE45 56 A5
Applewood. Kill NE12 29 F3
Appley Terr. Sland SR6 93 E2
Apsley Cres. N-u-T NE3 38 B1
Aqua Terr. N-b-t-S NE64 7 D4
Aquila Dr. H-o-t-W NE15 34 E2
Arbroath. Ouston DH2 99 F1
Arbroath Rd. Sland SR3 115 D8
Arcade The. 2 Tyne NE30 51 D7
Arcadia. Ouston DH2 99 F1
Arcadia Ave. C le S DH3 112 C5
Arcadia Terr. Blyth NE24 17 E6
Archbishop Runcie C of E Aided Fst Sch. N-u-T NE3 40 A1
Archbold Terr. N-u-T NE2 66 B3
Archer Rd. Sland SR3 115 D8
Archer Sq. Sland SR3 115 D8
Archer St. Walls NE28 49 E3
Archibald Fst Sch. N-u-T NE3 39 C1
Archibald St. N-u-T NE3 39 C1
Arcot Ave. Cram NE23 21 E8
Arcot Ave. W Bay NE25 31 E3
Arcot Cty Fst Sch. Cram NE23 22 C5
Arcot Dr. N-u-T NE5 62 F8
Arcot Dr. W Bay NE25 31 E3
Arcot Hall Golf Course. Cram NE23 21 D4
Arcot Terr. Blyth NE24 17 D8
Arden Ave. N-u-T NE3 28 B1
Arden Cl. Walls NE28 49 D7
Arden Cres. N-u-T NE5 44 A1
Arden Sq. Sland SR3 115 E8
Ardrossan. Ouston DH2 99 F1
Ardrossan Rd. Sland SR3 115 D7
Arena Bsns Pk. H-le-Sp DH4 118 C7
Argus Cl. Gates NE11 88 B7
Argyle Ct. Tanf DH9 98 A1
Argyle Pl. S Hett DH6 121 F7
Argyle Pl. Tyne NE29 51 A8
Argyle Sq. Sland SR2 105 C1
Argyle St. Blyth NE24 12 E1
Argyle St. Hebb NE31 75 D7
Argyle St. N-u-T NE1 66 B1
Argyle St. Sland SR2 105 C1
Argyle St. Tyne NE30 51 D8
Argyle Terr. Hexham NE46 54 B4
Argyle Terr. N-b-t-S NE64 7 D4
Argyle Terr. Tyne NE30 51 A8
Argyll. Ouston DH2 99 F1
Ariel St. Ashgn NE63 6 E3
Arisaig. Ouston DH2 99 F1
Arkle Rd. Sland SR3 115 D7
Arkle St. Gates NE8 88 C8
Arkle St. Hazle NE13 28 A4
Arklecrag. Wash NE37 101 C6
Arkleside Pl. N-u-T NE5 36 D1
Arkwright St. Gates NE8 88 D7
Arlington Ave. N-u-T NE3 44 C3
Arlington Cl. Bourn DH4 113 E3
Arlington Gr. Cram NE23 16 B2
Arlington Gr. Whick NE16 87 A6
Arlington Rd. Hebb NE31 75 F4
Arlington St. Sland SR4 104 C2
Armitage Gdns. Gates NE9 89 C1
Armondside Rd. B Mill NE17 95 C6
Armstrong Ave. N-u-T NE6 47 B1
Armstrong Ave. S Shs NE34 77 E6
Armstrong Cl. Hexham NE46 53 F3
Armstrong Dr. Kill NE12 29 B2
Armstrong Ind Est. Wash NE37 101 A7
Armstrong Rd. N-u-T NE15 & NE4 63 B1
Armstrong Rd. Walls NE28 50 A1
Armstrong Rd. Wash NE37 101 A7
Armstrong St. Gates NE11 & NE8 88 D7
Armstrong St. Wools NE5 36 B7
Armstrong Terr. Mpeth NE61 9 A8
Armstrong Terr. S Shs NE33 77 C8
Arncliffe Ave. Sland SR4 108 B4
Arncliffe Gdns. N-u-T NE5 36 C2
Arndale Arc. 9 Jarrow NE32 76 B7
Arndale House. 11 Birt DH3 100 C4
Arndale House. Lbtn NE12 41 A2
Arndale House. 6 Wash NE37 101 D8
Arnold Rd. Sland SR3 115 D8
Arnold St. Boldon NE35 91 F8
Arnside Wlk. N-u-T NE5 36 C2
Arran Ct. Silk SR3 116 A6
Arran Dr. B Wh NE32 76 E3
Arran Gdns. Gates NE10 89 C7
Arran Pl. Tyne NE29 50 C8
Arras La. Sland SR1 106 B3
Arrol Pk. Sland SR4 105 B2
Arrow Cl. Kill NE12 29 B2
Arthur Ave. Ryhope SR2 117 A6
Arthur Cook Ave. Whick NE16 87 C6
Arthur St. Blyth NE24 17 E8
Arthur St. Gates NE8 72 C2
Arthur St. Jarrow NE32 76 B6
Arthur St. 11 Ryhope SR2 117 A6
Arthur St. Whit SR6 78 F4
Arthur Terr. Whit SR6 78 F3
Arundel Cl. B Vill NE13 28 A5
Arundel Cl. Bed NE22 11 C3
Arundel Ct. N-u-T NE3 37 C3
Arundel Dr. N-u-T NE15 62 E7
Arundel Dr. W Bay NE25 31 C4
Arundel Gdns. Gates NE9 89 A5
Arundel Gdns. Sland SR3 115 C7
Arundel Rd. Sland SR3 115 D8
Arundel Sq. Ashgn NE63 6 C3
Arundel Wlk. Whick NE16 87 A5
Asama Ct. N-u-T NE4 71 A3
Ascham House Mid Sch. N-u-T NE3 45 C4
Ascot Cl. Walls NE28 49 D6
Ascot Cres. Gates NE8 88 C7
Ascot Ct. N-u-T NE3 37 C3
Ascot Ct. Sland SR3 115 D7
Ascot Gdns. S Shs NE34 77 D7
Ascot Wlk. N-u-T NE3 37 C3
Ash Ave. Dgton NE13 27 C7
Ash Banks. Mpeth NE61 9 A7
Ash Cl. Hexham NE46 53 E3
Ash Ct. Tyne NE29 31 E1
Ash Gr. Duns NE11 70 B1
Ash Gr. Mpeth NE61 8 E7
Ash Gr. Ryton NE40 61 C6
Ash Gr. Walls NE28 49 D1
Ash Gr. Whit SR6 79 A1
Ash Meadows. C le S DH3 112 E7
Ash Sq. Wash NE38 101 E4
Ash St. Blay NE21 62 C1
Ash St. M Sq NE43 82 E8
Ash Terr. Tant DH9 97 B2
Ash Tree Dr. Bed NE22 10 F2
Ashberry Gr. Sland SR6 93 D1
Ashbourne Ave. N-u-T NE6 68 C2
Ashbourne Cl. Bworth NE27 30 C5
Ashbourne Cres. Ashgn NE63 6 C3
Ashbourne Rd. Jarrow NE32 76 C5
Ashbrooke. W Bay NE25 31 E5
Ashbrooke Cl. W Bay NE25 31 E5
Ashbrooke Cres. Sland SR2 110 A4
Ashbrooke Cross. Sland SR2 109 C3
Ashbrooke Ct. 4 Sland NE36 92 D7
Ashbrooke Dr. Pont NE20 25 E7
Ashbrooke Gdns. Walls NE28 49 E3
Ashbrooke Mt. Sland SR2 109 C4
Ashbrooke Range. Sland SR2 110 A3
Ashbrooke Rd. Sland SR2 109 C4
Ashbrooke St. N-u-T NE3 44 B3
Ashbrooke Terr. Sland SR2 110 A4
Ashburn Rd. Walls NE28 49 E6
Ashburne Ct. Sland SR2 110 A4
Ashburne House (Art Coll). Sland SR2 110 A4
Ashburton Rd. N-u-T NE3 45 A4
Ashbury. W Bay NE25 31 C6
Ashby St. Sland SR2 110 C3
Ashcroft Dr. Lbtn NE12 42 B3
Ashdale. Pens DH4 113 E8
Ashdale. Pont NE20 25 C3
Ashdale Cres. N-u-T NE5 36 D1
Ashdown Cl. Lbtn NE12 41 B3
Ashdown Rd. Sland SR3 115 D7
Ashdown Way. Lbtn NE12 41 B3
Asher St. Gates NE10 & NE8 73 B1
Ashfield. Hedw NE32 76 D2
Ashfield Ave. Whick NE16 87 C8
Ashfield Cl. N-u-T NE4 71 A4
Ashfield Ct. H Spen NE39 85 A4
Ashfield Gdns. Walls NE28 49 A3
Ashfield Gr. 6 N Shs NE29 51 A6
Ashfield Gr. W Bay NE26 32 A7
Ashfield Rd. N-u-T NE3 45 A4
Ashfield Rd. Whick NE16 87 B5
Ashfield Rise. Whick NE16 87 B5
Ashfield Terr. C le S DH3 112 D2

Compton Rd. N Shs NE29 50 F5
Concord House. N-u-T NE5 36 F2
Concorde Sq. 5 N Silk SR3 116 A7
Concorde Way. Jarrow NE32 76 B6
Condercum Ct. N-u-T NE15 63 C1
Condercum House Sch. N-u-T NE15 64 A2
Condercum Ind Est. N-u-T NE15 64 A1
Condercum Rd. N-u-T NE4 64 A1
Cone St. S Shs NE33 51 B2
Cone Terr. C le S DH3 112 D4
Conewood House. N-u-T NE3 38 C2
Conhope La. N-u-T NE15 & NE4 64 A1
Conifer Cl. Blay NE21 86 B8
Conifer Cl. Lbtn NE12 42 C4
Coniscliffe Ave. N-u-T NE3 44 C4
Conishead Terr. S Hett DH6 121 F8
Coniston. Birt DH3 100 D2
Coniston. Gates NE10 90 A8
Coniston Ave. E Lane DH5 121 C8
Coniston Ave. Hebb NE31 75 F4
Coniston Ave. N-b-t-S NE64 7 C3
Coniston Ave. N-u-T NE2 46 B2
Coniston Ave. Sland SR5 93 C4
Coniston Ave. Whick NE16 87 D7
Coniston Cl. C le S DH2 112 C2
Coniston Cl. Newb NE15 61 E7
Coniston Cres. Blay NE21 86 B8
Coniston Ct. N-u-T NE5 63 B4
Coniston Dr. Hedw NE32 76 D3
Coniston Gdns. Gates NE9 89 B5
Coniston Pl. Gates NE9 89 B5
Coniston Rd. Blyth NE24 12 A1
Coniston Rd. Tyne NE30 32 A2
Coniston Rd. Walls NE28 50 A4
Connaught Gdns. Lbtn NE12 42 A3
Connaught Terr. Jarrow NE32 76 B6
Conningsby Cl. N-u-T NE3 40 A4
Conniscliffe Ct. Hexham NE46 53 F3
Conniscliffe Rd. Hexham NE46 53 F3
Connolly Terr. B Mill NE17 95 C6
Consett Rd. Duns NE11 88 A5
Constable Cl. Ryton NE40 61 C4
Constable Gdns. White NE34 77 C3
Constables Garth. 6 Birt DH3 100 C4
Content St. Blay NE21 62 C1
Conway Dr. N-u-T NE7 47 A4
Conway Gdns. Sland SR3 115 C7
Conway Gdns. Walls NE28 49 A4
Conway Gr. S Slu NE26 24 B7
Conway Rd. Sland SR5 91 F2
Conway Sq. Gates NE9 89 A8
Conway Sq. Sland SR5 91 F2
Conyers Ave. C le S DH2 112 B5
Conyers Gdns. C le S DH2 112 B5
Conyers Pl. C le S DH2 112 B5
Conyers Rd. C le S DH2 112 C5
Conyers Rd. N-u-T NE6 67 C2
Cook Cl. S Shs NE33 77 B8
Cook Gdns. Gates NE10 90 B8
Cook Sq. Sland SR5 92 A2
Cooks Wood. Wash NE38 101 D3
Cookshold La. S Hill DH6 120 B2
Cookshold La. Sherb DH6 120 B2
Cookson Cl. Crbdge NE45 55 F6
Cookson Cl. N-u-T NE4 65 B1
Cookson House. 1 S Shs NE33 51 C3
Cookson St. N-u-T NE4 65 A1
Cookson Terr. C le S DH2 112 C3
Cookson's La. N-u-T NE1 72 A4
Coomassie Rd. Blyth NE24 17 E7
Coomside. Cram NE23 22 C4
Cooper St. Sland SR6 93 E1
Coopie's La. Mpeth NE61 9 B7
Coopie's La. Mpeth NE61 9 B8
Coopies Field. Mpeth NE61 9 B8
Coopies Haugh. Mpeth NE61 9 C7
Coopies Lane Ind Est. Mpeth NE61 9 C7
Coopies Way. Mpeth NE61 9 C7
Copland Terr. N-u-T NE2 66 C2
Copley Ave. White NE34 77 C2
Copley Dr. Sland SR3 109 B2
Copper Chare. Mpeth NE61 3 F1
Copperas La. N-u-T NE15 62 F7
Coppice The. S Slu NE26 24 C6
Coppice Way. N-u-T NE2 66 C2
Coppy La. Beam DH9 98 C4
Copse The. Blay NE21 62 F2
Copse The. Burnop NE16 96 F6
Copse The. N-u-T NE3 40 A4
Copse The. Wash NE37 90 B2
Coptleigh. H-le-Sp DH5 119 A7
Coquet. Wash NE38 100 F1
Coquet. Wash NE38 101 A1
Coquet Ave. Blyth NE24 17 E5
Coquet Ave. N-u-T NE3 39 B2
Coquet Ave. S Shs NE34 78 B8
Coquet Ave. W Bay NE26 32 A5
Coquet Bldgs. N-u-T NE15 36 B1
Coquet Dr. Elling NE61 1 E5
Coquet Gr. Tley NE15 35 C2
Coquet House. 16 Silk SR3 115 F6
Coquet Park Fst Sch. W Bay NE26 32 A6
Coquet St. Ashgn NE63 6 E4
Coquet St. Chopw NE17 84 C1
Coquet St. Hebb NE31 75 D6
Coquet St. Jarrow NE32 76 A5
Coquet St. N-u-T NE1 67 A2
Coquet Terr. Dud NE23 28 F8
Coquet Terr. N-u-T NE6 67 B4
Coquetdale Ave. N-u-T NE6 75 A6
Coquetdale Cl. Pegs NE61 4 E3
Coquetdale Pl. Bed NE22 11 C1
Coquetdale Villas. Sland SR6 93 E2
Coram Pl. N-u-T NE15 63 A1
Corbiere Cl. Silk SR3 115 E6
Corbitt St. Gates NE8 71 C1
Corbridge Ave. W Open NE13 28 B6
Corbridge C of E (Aided) Prim Sch. Crbdge NE45 56 A6
Corbridge Cl. Walls NE28 49 E6
Corbridge Cty Mid Sch. Crbdge NE45 55 F7
Corbridge Rd. N-u-T NE6 67 C2
Corbridge St. N-u-T NE6 67 B2
Corby Gate. Sland SR2 110 A4
Corby Gdns. N-u-T NE6 68 C2
Corby Hall Dr. Sland SR2 110 A4
Corchester La. Crbdge NE46 & NE45 55 C7
Corchester La. Oak NE46 55 C7
Corchester Rd. Bed NE22 10 F2
Corchester Towers. Crbdge NE45 55 E7
Corchester Wlk. N-u-T NE7 47 C4
Corfu Rd. Sland SR5 92 A2
Corinthian Sq. Sland SR5 92 A2
Cork St. Sland SR1 106 B3
Cormorant Cl. Ashgn NE63 6 E1
Cormorant Cl. Blyth NE24 17 F4
Cormorant Cl. 4 Wash NE38 100 F3
Corn Mill Dr. H-le-Sp DH5 118 D6
Cornbank Cl. Silk SR3 116 A5
Corndean. Pens NE38 102 A4
Cornel Rd. N-u-T NE7 47 C3
Cornelia Cl. 7 N Silk SR3 116 A7
Corney St. S Shs NE33 77 B7
Cornfields The. Hebb NE31 75 E6
Cornforth Cl. Ashgn NE63 6 B2
Cornforth Cl. Gates NE10 90 C6
Cornhill. Hedw NE32 76 C1
Cornhill. N-u-T NE5 36 F1
Cornhill Ave. N-u-T NE3 38 C3
Cornhill Cres. Tyne NE29 50 D7
Cornhill Rd. Cram NE23 22 C6
Cornhill Rd. Sland SR5 93 B2
Cornmoor Gdns. Whick NE16 87 B5
Cornmoor Rd. Whick NE16 87 B6
Cornsay. Ouston DH2 99 F2
Cornthwaite Dr. Whit SR6 93 E8
Cornwall Rd. Hebb NE31 75 F3
Cornwallis Sq. S Shs NE33 51 B1
Cornwallis St. 14 S Shs NE33 51 C3
Cornwell Cres. Bed NE22 16 B8
Cornwell Ct. N-u-T NE7 46 C4
Coronation Ave. 6 Ryhope SR2 116 F6
Coronation Ave. Sunn NE16 87 B2
Coronation Bglws. N-u-T NE3 40 A1
Coronation Cl. Sland SR1 106 B3
Coronation Cotts. Lmth NE61 2 A3
Coronation Cres. Burn DH4 114 C2
Coronation Cres. W Bay NE25 31 F4
Coronation Gn. E Lane DH5 121 D8
Coronation Rd. N-u-T NE5 36 B3
Coronation Rd. S Del NE25 23 C3
Coronation Rd. Sunn NE16 87 B2
Coronation St. Annit NE23 22 B1
Coronation St. Blyth NE24 17 E6
Coronation St. C le S DH3 112 D1
Coronation St. N Shs NE29 51 A4
Coronation St. N-b-t-S NE64 7 E5
Coronation St. Ryton NE40 61 E4
Coronation St. S Shs NE33 51 C2
Coronation St. Sland SR1 106 B3
Coronation St. Walls NE28 49 C2
Coronation Terr. Ashgn NE63 6 E1
Coronation Terr. 3 Boldon NE35 76 E1
Coronation Terr. C le S DH3 112 C2
Coronation Terr. H le H DH5 119 A2
Coronation Terr. Kibble NE11 99 C6
Coronation Terr. Sland SR4 103 B2
Coronation Terr. Tyne NE29 31 B1
Corporation Rd. Sland SR2 110 C4
Corporation St. N-u-T NE4 65 C1
Corporation Yd. Mpeth NE61 3 F1
Corpus Christie RC Prim Sch. Gates NE8 88 E8
Corrighan Terr. E Rain DH5 118 C4
Corrofield Gdns. Gates NE10 74 C1
Corry Ct. Sland SR4 108 B4
Corsair. Whick NE16 86 F6
Corsenside. N-u-T NE5 36 F1
Corstorphine Town. S Shs NE33 51 B1
Cortina Ave. Sland SR4 108 A4
Corvan Terr. Tant DH9 97 A2
Cosford Ct. N-u-T NE3 37 C3
Cossack Terr. Sland SR4 104 B3
Cosser St. Blyth NE24 17 E7
Cosserat Pl. Hebb NE31 75 D7
Coston Dr. S Shs NE33 51 C3
Cosyn St. N-u-T NE6 67 A1
Cotehill Dr. Pont NE20 25 B4
Cotehill Rd. N-u-T NE5 43 B1
Cotemede. Gates NE10 90 A5
Cotfield Wlk. Gates NE8 72 A1
Cotgarth The. Gates NE10 89 E7
Cotherstone Ct. Sland SR3 109 B2
Cotman Gdns. White NE34 77 D2
Cotswold Ave. C le S DH2 112 B1
Cotswold Ave. Lbtn NE12 29 B1
Cotswold Cl. Wash NE38 101 B4
Cotswold Dr. Ashgn NE63 6 F1
Cotswold Dr. W Bay NE25 31 F3
Cotswold Gdns. Duns NE11 88 A7
Cotswold Gdns. N-u-T NE7 47 A3
Cotswold La. Boldon NE35 76 F2
Cotswold Rd. Sland SR5 92 A2
Cotswold Rd. Tyne NE29 31 E2
Cotswold Sq. Sland SR5 92 A3
Cottage La. N-u-T NE5 44 A1
Cottenham Chare. N-u-T NE4 65 B1
Cottenham St. N-u-T NE4 65 B1
Cotter Riggs Pl. N-u-T NE5 36 B2
Cotter Riggs Wlk. N-u-T NE5 36 B2
Cotterdale. Walls NE28 42 C1
Cotterdale Ave. 1 Gates NE8 88 F8
Cottersdale Gdns. N-u-T NE5 36 B3
Cottinglea. Mpeth NE61 3 F2
Cottingvale. Mpeth NE61 3 F2
Cottingwood Ct. N-u-T NE4 65 B2
Cottingwood Gdns. N-u-T NE4 65 B2
Cottingwood Gn. Blyth NE24 17 C3
Cottingwood La. Mpeth NE61 3 F1
Coulson Park Cty Fst Sch. Ashgn NE63 6 F2
Coulthards La. Gates NE8 72 C3
Coulthards Pl. Gates NE8 73 A4
Coulton Dr. Boldon NE36 92 D7
Council Ave. Pens DH4 114 B6
Council Rd. Ashgn NE63 6 C4
Council Terr. Wash NE37 101 D7
Counden Rd. N-u-T NE5 36 E3
Countess Ave. W Bay NE26 32 A5
Countess Dr. N-u-T NE15 63 A3
Coupland Gr. Jarrow NE32 76 B3
Coupland Rd. Ashgn NE63 6 C3
Court Rd. Bed NE22 10 F1
Court The. Whick NE16 87 C6
Courtfield Rd. N-u-T NE6 68 C4
Courtney Ct. N-u-T NE3 37 C3
Courtney Dr. N Silk SR3 115 F8
Courtyard The. Elling NE61 1 C4
Cousin St. Sland SR1 106 C3
Coutts Rd. N-u-T NE6 68 B4
Cove The. Pens DH4 114 B6
Covent Gdn. Sland SR1 106 B3
Coventry Gdns. N Shs NE29 50 E4
Coventry Gdns. N-u-T NE4 70 B4
Coventry Way. Hedw NE32 76 B1
Coverdale. Gates NE10 90 A6
Coverdale. Walls NE28 42 C1
Coverdale Ave. Blyth NE24 17 A7
Coverdale Ave. Wash NE37 101 C8
Coverley Rd. Sland SR5 92 B2
Covers The. Lbtn NE12 42 B2
Covers The. Mpeth NE61 9 A7
Cow La. Crbdge NE45 55 F7
Cow La. Crbdge NE45 55 F8
Cowan Cl. Ryton NE21 62 A4
Cowan Terr. Sland SR2 106 A2
Cowans Ave. Kill NE12 29 C4
Cowdray Ct. N-u-T NE3 37 C3
Cowdray Rd. Sland SR5 92 B2
Cowen Gdns. Gates NE9 89 A1
Cowen Rd. Blay NE21 62 D3
Cowen St. Blay NE21 86 B8
Cowen St. N-u-T NE6 68 C2
Cowen Terr. R Gill NE39 85 F3
Cowgarth. Hexham NE46 54 A5
Cowgate. N-u-T NE1 66 B1
Cowgate L Ctr. N-u-T NE5 44 A3
Cowgate Prim Sch. N-u-T NE4 64 A4
Cowley Cres. E Rain DH5 118 C4
Cowley Pl. Blyth NE24 17 B8
Cowley Rd. Blyth NE24 12 B1
Cowpath Gdns. Gates NE10 75 B2
Cowpen Rd. Blyth NE24 17 C8
Cox Chare. N-u-T NE1 66 C1
Coxfoot Cl. S Shs NE34 77 C5
Coxgreen Rd. Pens DH4 102 B2
Coxlodge Rd. N-u-T NE3 39 A1
Coxlodge Terr. N-u-T NE3 39 A1
Coxon St. Gates NE10 75 B2
Coxon St. Sland SR2 106 B1
Coxon Terr. Gates NE8 73 C1
Crabtree Rd. Stocks NE43 82 C7
Cradock Ave. Hebb NE31 75 D4
Craggyknowe. Wash NE37 100 F6
Craghall Dene. N-u-T NE2 46 B4
Craghall Dene Ave. N-u-T NE2 46 B4
Cragleas. Burnop NE16 97 A4
Cragside. B Vill NE13 28 B6
Cragside. C le S DH2 112 A4
Cragside. Cram NE23 22 C4
Cragside. N-u-T NE7 47 B3
Cragside. S Shs NE34 78 B5
Cragside. W Bay NE26 31 E7
Cragside Ave. Tyne NE29 50 D8
Cragside Ct. Duns NE11 88 A6
Cragside Ct. 4 H-le-Sp DH5 118 F8
Cragside Cty Prim Sch. N-u-T NE7 47 A3
Cragside Gdns. Duns NE11 88 A5
Cragside Gdns. Walls NE28 49 F3
Cragside Rd. Wash NE37 101 A7
Cragston Ave. N-u-T NE5 43 C3
Cragston Cl. N-u-T NE5 43 C2
Cragton Gdns. Blyth NE24 17 B7
Craig Cres. Annit NE23 29 A8
Craig St. 1 Birt DH3 100 C4
Craigavon Rd. Sland SR5 92 B2
Craigend. Cram NE23 22 B5
Craighill. 1 S Row DH4 114 A6
Craiglands The. Sland SR3 109 C3
Craigmill Pk. Blyth NE24 17 A8
Craigmillar Ave. N-u-T NE5 43 C3
Craigmillar Cl. N-u-T NE5 43 C3
Craigmont Ct. Lbtn NE12 42 A2
Craigshaw Rd. Sland SR5 91 F3
Craigshaw Sq. Sland SR5 91 F3
Craigwell Dr. Silk SR3 116 A4
Craik Ave. S Shs NE34 77 B5
Crake Way. Wash NE38 100 F2
Cramer St. Gates NE8 72 C1
Cramlington Terr. Shire NE27 30 E1
Cramlington Beacon Hill Fst Sch. Cram NE23 21 E6
Cramlington Cragside Cty Fst Sch. Cram NE23 22 B4
Cramlington Cty High Sch. Cram NE23 22 A4
Cramlington Eastlea Cty Fst Sch. Cram NE23 22 C8
Cramlington Parkside Cty Mid Sch. Cram NE23 22 B7
Cramlington Rd. Sland SR5 91 F2
Cramlington Shanklea Cty Fst Sch. Cram NE23 22 B7
Cramlington Southlands Cty Mid Sch. Cram NE23 22 B3
Cramlington Sq. Sland SR5 91 F2
Cramlington St Peter's RC Mid Sch. Cram NE23 22 B4
Cramlington Sta. Cram NE23 21 F7
Cramlington Stonelaw Cty Mid Sch. Cram NE23 22 A4
Cramlington Terr. Blyth NE24 17 C4
Cramond Ct. Gates NE9 88 E3
Cramond Way. Cram NE23 22 B4
Cranberry Rd. Sland SR5 92 A2
Cranberry Sq. Sland SR5 92 A2
Cranborne. Sland SR3 115 C6
Cranbourne Gr. Tyne NE30 32 B3
Cranbrook Ave. N-u-T NE3 39 C3
Cranbrook Ct. N-u-T NE3 38 B3
Cranbrook Dr. Prud NE42 59 B2
Cranbrook Pl. N-u-T NE15 69 B4
Cranbrook Rd. N-u-T NE15 69 B4
Cranemarsh Cl. Ashgn NE63 6 C1
Craneshaugh Cl. Hexham NE46 54 E4
Cranesville. Gates NE9 89 C5
Craneswater Ave. W Bay NE26 24 F1
Cranfield Pl. N-u-T NE15 62 C7
Cranford Gdns. N-u-T NE15 62 E7
Cranford St. S Shs NE34 77 C6
Cranford Terr. Sland SR4 105 A1
Cranham Cl. Kill NE12 29 F4
Cranlea. N-u-T NE3 37 C2
Cranleigh Ave. N-u-T NE3 37 C3
Cranleigh Gr. Prud NE42 59 D3
Cranleigh Pl. W Bay NE25 31 D6
Cranleigh Rd. Sland SR5 92 A2
Cranshaw Pl. Cram NE23 22 C5
Cranston Pl. 9 Ryhope SR2 117 A6
Crantock Rd. N-u-T NE3 38 C1
Cranwell Ct. N-u-T NE3 37 C3
Cranwell Dr. W Open NE13 28 B6
Craster Ave. Lbtn NE12 29 F1
Craster Ave. S Shs NE34 78 B8
Craster Ave. Shire NE27 30 F3
Craster Cl. Blyth NE24 17 C7
Craster Cl. W Bay NE25 31 D7
Craster Gdns. Walls NE28 49 F3
Craster Rd. N Shs NE29 50 D5
Craster Sq. N-u-T NE3 39 A2
Craster Terr. N-u-T NE7 47 B2
Crathie. Birt DH3 100 C7
Crawcrook La. Craw NE40 & NE41 60 D5
Crawcrook Terr. Craw NE40 60 E3
Crawford Ct. Silk SR3 115 F6
Crawford Pl. W Bay NE25 31 E4
Crawford St. Blyth NE24 12 D1
Crawford Terr. Mpeth NE61 4 A1
Crawford Terr. N-u-T NE6 68 C1
Crawhall Cres. Mpeth NE61 8 E7
Crawhall Cty Fst Sch. Cram NE23 22 A5
Crawhall Rd. N-u-T NE1 66 C1
Crawley Ave. Hebb NE31 75 D3
Crawley Gdns. Whick NE16 87 C7
Crawley Rd. Walls NE28 49 B1
Crawley Sq. Hebb NE31 75 D3
Craythorne Gdns. N-u-T NE6 48 A2
Creeverlea. Wash NE38 101 C3
Creighton Ave. N-u-T NE3 44 B4
Creland Way. N-u-T NE5 43 C3
Crescent Ave. Hexham NE46 53 F5
Crescent The. C le S DH2 112 B3
Crescent The. Clea SR6 92 F8
Crescent The. Duns NE11 88 F7
Crescent The. H le H DH5 119 A3
Crescent The. H Spen NE39 84 F3
Crescent The. Jarrow NE32 76 A4
Crescent The. Kibble NE11 99 C6
Crescent The. Mpeth NE61 8 F6
Crescent The. N Silk SR3 109 A1
Crescent The. N-u-T NE13 37 B2
Crescent The. N-u-T NE7 41 B1
Crescent The. New DH4 114 D4
Crescent The. Pont NE20 25 A3
Crescent The. R Gill NE39 85 F2
Crescent The. Ryton NE40 61 D5
Crescent The. S Row DH4 114 A5
Crescent The. S Shs NE34 77 F5
Crescent The. Seg NE23 22 F1
Crescent The. Sunn NE16 87 B2
Crescent The. Tley NE15 35 D2
Crescent The. Tyne NE30 51 D7
Crescent The. W Bay NE26 32 B4
Crescent The. Walls NE28 49 B3
Crescent The. Whick NE16 87 C6
Crescent The. Wylam NE41 60 B5
Crescent Vale. W Bay NE26 32 A4
Crescent Way. Lbtn NE12 42 B4
Crescent Way N. Lbtn NE12 42 B4
Crescent Way S. Lbtn NE12 42 B4
Creslow. Gates NE10 89 F6
Creslow. Gates NE10 89 F7
Cressbourne Ave. Sland SR6 93 E4
Cresswell Ave. Lbtn NE12 29 F1
Cresswell Ave. S Slu NE26 24 C6
Cresswell Ave. Tyne NE29 50 F7
Cresswell Cl. Blay NE21 86 A8
Cresswell Cl. W Bay NE25 31 E3
Cresswell Dr. Blyth NE24 17 C5
Cresswell Dr. N-u-T NE3 38 B3
Cresswell Home Farm Cotts. Cress NE61 2 B4
Cresswell Rd. Elling NE61 1 D5
Cresswell Rd. Walls NE28 & NE6 49 A1
Cresswell St. N-u-T NE6 68 A1
Cresswell St. N-u-T NE6 68 A2
Cresswell Terr. Ashgn NE63 6 C4
Cresswell Terr. Sland SR2 105 C1
Crest The. Bed NE22 10 E1
Crest The. Dgton NE13 27 B7
Crest The. S Slu NE26 24 E4
Cresthaven. Gates NE10 89 E6
Crichton Ave. C le S DH3 112 D1
Cricket Terr. Burnop NE16 97 A6
Cricklewood Dr. Pens DH4 114 B6
Cricklewood Rd. Sland SR5 92 A1
Criddle St. Gates NE8 73 A4
Crieff Gr. B Wh NE32 76 D3
Crieff Sq. Sland SR5 91 F2
Crigdon Hill. N-u-T NE5 36 F1
Crighton. Wash NE38 101 A5
Crimdon Gr. H-le-Sp DH4 118 C7
Crindledykes. Wash NE38 101 E2
Cripps Ave. Gates NE10 90 B8
Crocus Cl. Blay NE21 62 A2
Croft Ave. Lbtn NE12 42 B3
Croft Ave. Sland SR4 105 A2
Croft Ave. Walls NE28 49 C2
Croft Cl. Ryton NE40 61 D4
Croft Cotts. Stocks NE43 82 D7
Croft House Sch. Hexham NE46 53 F5
Croft Rd. Blyth NE24 17 E7
Croft St. N-u-T NE1 66 B1
Croft Terr. Hexham NE46 54 A4
Croft Terr. Hors NE15 59 C8
Croft Terr. Jarrow NE32 76 B6
Croft The. N-u-T NE3 45 A4
Croft The. Ryton NE40 61 D4
Croft The. S Hill DH6 120 D1
Croft View. Craw NE40 60 E3
Croft Villas. 2 Craw NE40 60 E3
Croft's La. Hors NE15 59 C8
Croftdale Rd. Blay NE21 62 B2
Crofter Cl. Annit NE23 22 A1
Crofthead Dr. Cram NE23 22 B4
Crofton Cty Fst Sch. Blyth NE24 17 E6
Crofton Mill Ind Est. Blyth NE24 17 F7
Crofton St. Blyth NE24 17 E7
Crofton St. S Shs NE34 77 C6
Crofton Way. N-u-T NE15 62 B7
Crofts Ave. Crbdge NE45 56 B5
Crofts Cl. Crbdge NE45 56 B5
Crofts Pk. Heps NE61 9 E5
Crofts The. Pont NE20 25 F6
Crofts Way. Crbdge NE45 56 A6
Croftside. Birt DH3 100 C5
Croftside Ave. Whit SR6 93 F8
Croftside House. 4 Silk SR3 115 F5
Croftsway. N-u-T NE4 70 C4
Croftwell Cl. Blay NE21 62 D1
Cromarty St. Sland SR6 93 D2
Cromdale Pl. N-u-T NE5 43 B1
Cromer Ave. Gates NE9 88 F3
Cromer Ct. Gates NE9 89 A3
Cromer Gdns. N-u-T NE2 46 B3
Cromer Gdns. W Bay NE26 32 A6
Crompton Rd. N-u-T NE6 67 B4
Cromwell Ave. Blay NE21 62 B2
Cromwell Ct. Ryton NE21 62 A4
Cromwell Pl. Blay NE21 62 A1
Cromwell Rd. Gates NE10 75 B2
Cromwell Rd. Whick NE16 87 C8
Cromwell St. Gates NE8 73 A1
Cromwell St. Sland SR4 105 A3
Cromwell Terr. Gates NE8 72 A1
Cromwell Terr. Gates NE10 75 C3
Crondall St. S Shs NE33 77 D7
Cronin Ave. B Hall NE34 77 B4
Cronniewell. Hams NE17 95 B5
Crookham Way. Cram NE23 22 C4
Crookhill Prim Sch. Ryton NE40 61 E5
Crookhill Terr. Ryton NE40 61 E4
Cropthorne. Gates NE10 90 B6
Crosby Gdns. Gates NE9 89 B3
Cross Ave. Walls NE28 48 C4
Cross Camden La. N Shs NE29 & NE30 51 B5
Cross Carliol St. N-u-T NE1 66 B1
Cross Dr. Ryton NE40 61 C6
Cross Keys La. Gates NE9 88 F5
Cross La. Duns NE11 70 A2
Cross La. Kibble NE11 88 B4
Cross Morpeth St. N-u-T NE2 65 B4
Cross Par. N-u-T NE4 71 B4
Cross Pl. Sland SR1 106 B3
Cross Row. Gates NE8 73 B1
Cross Row. Ryton NE40 61 E3
Cross Sheraton St. N-u-T NE2 65 B4
Cross St. 8 Fence DH4 118 A8
Cross St. Gates NE8 72 C1
Cross St. H Pitt DH6 120 D3
Cross St. H-le-Sp DH4 114 D1
Cross St. N-u-T NE1 65 C1
Cross St. N-u-T NE6 67 A1
Cross Terr. R Gill NE39 85 D1
Cross Vale Rd. Sland SR2 109 C4
Cross Villa Place No 1. N-u-T NE1 & NE4 65 C1
Cross Villa Place No 2. N-u-T NE4 65 C1
Cross Villa Place No 3. N-u-T NE4 65 C1
Cross Villa Place No 4. N-u-T NE4 65 B1
Cross Villa Place No 5. N-u-T NE4 65 B1
Cross Way The. Mpeth NE61 8 F6
Cross Way The. N-u-T NE3 44 C4
Crossbank Rd. N-u-T NE5 44 A3
Crossbrook Rd. N-u-T NE5 44 A2
Crossby Ct. Sland SR2 106 C1
Crossfell. Pont NE20 25 C4
Crossfell Gdns. Stake NE62 11 A8
Crossfield Pk. Gates NE10 89 C6
Crossfield Terr. N-u-T NE6 75 A4
Crossgate. S Shs NE33 51 C2
Crossgate Rd. H le H DH5 119 A2
Crossgill. Wash NE37 101 B7
Crosshill Rd. N-u-T NE15 69 B4
Crosslaw. N-u-T NE5 36 F1
Crosslea Ave. Sland SR3 109 B3
Crossley Terr. Lbtn NE12 29 F1
Crossley Terr. N-u-T NE4 64 C2
Crossley Terr. N-u-T NE4 65 A2
Crossway. G Post NE62 10 F7
Crossway. Gates NE9 89 B6
Crossway. N-u-T NE2 46 B3
Crossway. S Shs NE34 78 A5
Crossway. Tyne NE30 51 C8
Crossway The. N-u-T NE15 62 D7
Crossways. Boldon NE36 92 E7
Crossways. Hedw NE32 76 C1
Crossways. N Silk SR3 115 F7
Crossways The. Hazle NE13 28 A4
Croudace Row. Gates NE10 89 D8
Crow Bank. Walls NE28 49 C2
Crow Hall La. Cram NE23 21 F7
Crow Hall Rd. Cram NE23 15 F1
Crow La. Sland SR3 115 B7
Crowhall La. Gates NE10 89 D8
Crowhall Towers. 4 Gates NE10 89 D8
Crowley Ave. Whick NE16 87 C8
Crowley Gdns. Blay NE21 62 C2
Crowley Rd. Whick NE16 69 A1
Crown And Anchor Cotts. Hors NE15 59 C8
Crown Rd. Sland SR5 93 A1
Crown St. Blyth NE24 17 F7
Crown St. Mpeth NE61 9 A8
Crowther Ind Est. Wash NE38 100 F5
Crowther Rd. Wash NE38 100 F5
Crowtree L Ctr. Sland SR1 105 C2
Crowtree Rd. Sland SR1 105 C2
Crowtree Terr. Sland SR1 105 C2
Croxdale Ct. S Shs NE34 77 A5
Croxdale Gdns. Gates NE10 75 B2
Croxdale Terr. Gates NE10 75 B2
Croxdale Terr. Green NE40 61 C1
Croydon Rd. N-u-T NE4 65 A2
Crozier St. Sland SR5 93 C1
Cruddas Pk. N-u-T NE4 71 A4
Cruddas Pk Sh Ctr. N-u-T NE4 71 A4
Crudwell Cl. Boldon NE35 76 E2
Crummock Ave. Sland SR6 93 C4
Crummock Rd. N-u-T NE5 63 B4
Crumstone Ct. Kill NE12 29 E4
Crusade Wlk. Jarrow NE32 76 A5
Cty Cricket Gd. N-u-T NE2 66 C4
Cuba St. Sland SR2 110 B4
Cuillin Cl. Wash NE38 101 B3
Culford Pl. Walls NE28 49 E6
Cullercoats Prim Sch. Tyne NE30 32 C3
Cullercoats Rd. Sland SR5 91 F1
Cullercoats Sq. Sland SR5 91 F1
Cullercoats St. N-u-T NE6 68 B1
Cullercoats St. N-u-T NE6 68 B2
Cullercoats Sta. Tyne NE30 32 C3
Culloden Wlk. Kill NE12 29 D4
Cumberland Ave. Bed NE22 10 E1
Cumberland Ave. N-b-t-S NE64 7 D4
Cumberland Pl. Birt DH3 100 D1
Cumberland Pl. S Shs NE34 78 B7
Cumberland Rd. N Silk SR3 116 A8
Cumberland Rd. Shire NE29 50 B7
Cumberland St. Sland SR1 106 A3
Cumberland St. Walls NE28 49 C2
Cumberland St. Walls NE28 50 B1
Cumberland Way. Wash NE37 90 D2
Cumberland Wlk. N-u-T NE7 47 B4
Cumbria Wlk. N-u-T NE4 65 A1
Cumbrian Ave. Sland SR6 93 C5
Cummings St. Blyth NE24 17 E8
Curlew Cl. Ashgn NE63 11 E8
Curlew Cl. Lbtn NE12 41 A3
Curlew Cl. Ryton NE40 61 E4
Curlew Cl. Wash NE38 101 A2
Curlew Hill. Mpeth NE61 3 D2
Curlew Rd. Jarrow NE32 76 C8
Curlew Rd. Jarrow NE32 76 D8
Curlew Way. Blyth NE24 17 E4
Curly Kews. Mpeth NE61 8 E8
Curran House. Jarrow NE32 76 C8
Curren Gdns. Gates NE10 73 C2
Curtis Rd. N-u-T NE4 64 C3
Curzon Pl. N-u-T NE5 43 B2
Curzon Rd W. Walls NE28 49 B1
Curzon St. Gates NE8 88 E8
Cushat Cl. N-u-T NE6 67 C1
Cushy Cow La. Ryton NE40 61 D4
Cut Bank. N-u-T NE1 67 A1
Cut Throat La. Medom NE17 95 C4
Cuthbert Ct. Jarrow NE32 76 C6
Cuthbert St. Gates NE8 72 A2
Cuthbert St. Hebb NE31 75 D7
Cuthbert St. Sunn NE16 87 A1
Cuthbert Wlk. N-u-T NE3 40 B1
Cuthbertson Cl. Sland SR6 93 E5
Cutting St. 3 Seaham SR7 116 F1
Cygnet Cl. Ashgn NE63 11 D8
Cygnet Cl. N-u-T NE5 36 D4
Cyncopa Way. N-u-T NE5 44 A2
Cypress Ave. N-u-T NE4 & NE5 & NE99 64 A4
Cypress Cres. Blyth NE24 17 E7
Cypress Cres. Duns NE11 88 A7
Cypress Dr. Blyth NE24 17 E7
Cypress Gdns. Blyth NE24 17 E7
Cypress Gdns. Kill NE12 29 C4
Cypress Gr. Ryton NE40 61 C6
Cypress Rd. Blay NE21 62 C2
Cypress Rd. Gates NE9 89 D2
Cypress Sq. N Silk SR3 116 A8
Cyprus Gdns. Gates NE9 89 A6

D'arcy Ct. Sland SR1 106 B2
D'arcy Sq. Sland SR1 106 B2
Dachet Rd. W Bay NE25 31 D7
Dacre Rd. Sland SR6 93 D4
Dacre St. Mpeth NE61 3 F1
Dacre St. S Shs NE33 77 C8
Daffodil Cl. Blay NE21 62 B2
Dahlia Ct. Sland SR4 105 B3
Dahlia Pl. N-u-T NE4 & NE5 64 A4
Dahlia Way. Hebb NE31 75 E4
Dairy La. H-le-Sp DH4 118 C8
Daisy Cotts. 9 Birt DH3 100 C4
Dale Rd. W Bay NE25 31 D4
Dale St. Cam NE24 12 E1
Dale St. Craw NE40 60 F4
Dale St. S Shs NE33 51 D3
Dale Terr. Sland SR6 93 E3
Dale Top. Holy NE25 23 F1
Dale View. Stocks NE43 82 D7
Dale View Gdns. Craw NE40 60 F3
Dalegarth. Wash NE37 & NE38 101 B6
Dalegarth Gr. Sland SR6 93 C5
Dales The. N-u-T NE5 44 B2
Dalla St. Sland SR4 103 A3
Dalmahoy. Wash NE37 90 D3
Dalmatia Terr. Blyth NE24 17 E6
Dalston Pl. Blyth NE24 17 E4
Dalton Ave. Lmth NE61 2 A3
Dalton Cl. Cram NE23 22 B6
Dalton Cres. N-u-T NE6 67 B2
Dalton Ct. Walls NE28 42 C1
Dalton Pl. N-u-T NE5 36 C3
Dalton St. N-u-T NE6 67 B1
Dalton St. N-u-T NE6 67 B2
Dalton Terr. Chopw NE17 95 B8
Dalton Way. Pens DH4 114 A7
Daltons La. S Shs NE33 51 B2
Dame Allan's Schs. N-u-T NE4 64 B3
Dame Dorothy Cres. Sland SR6 93 E1
Dame Dorothy Prim Sch. Sland SR6 106 B4
Dame Dorothy St. Sland SR6 106 A4
Dame Flora Robson Ave. S Shs NE34 76 F4
Damside. Mpeth NE61 9 A8
Danby Cl. N Silk SR3 116 B6
Danby Cl. Wash DH3 & NE38 112 F8
Danby Gdns. N-u-T NE6 48 A1
Danville Rd. Sland SR6 93 E4
Darden Cl. Kill NE12 29 F4
Darden Lough. N-u-T NE5 36 F1
Darden St. S Shs NE34 77 C6
Darien Ave. Sland SR6 93 D4
Dark La. Mpeth NE61 4 A1
Darley Ct. 15 Silk SR3 115 F6

Darley Pl. N-u-T NE15 63 A1
Darnell Pl. N-u-T NE4 65 B2
Darnley Rd. Ashgn NE63 6 C3
Darras Ct. S Shs NE33 51 D1
Darras Dr. Tyne NE29 50 C7
Darras Hall Cty Fst Sch. Pont NE 20 25 C3
Darras Mews. Pont NE 20 25 C4
Darras Rd. Pont NE20 25 D4
Darrell St. B Vill NE13 28 A6
Dartford Rd. S Shs NE33 51 F2
Dartford Rd. Sland SR6 93 D4
Dartmouth Ave. Gates NE9 88 F2
Darvall Cl. W Bay NE25 31 D7
Darwin Cres. N-u-T NE3 44 C3
Darwin St. Sland SR5 92 F2
Daryl Cl. Blay NE21 62 A1
Daryl Way. Gates NE10 90 D8
Davenport Dr. N-u-T NE3 28 B1
David Adams House. N-u-T NE15 64 A1
David Gdns. Sland SR6 93 F3
David St. Walls NE28 49 B2
David Terr. 7 Craw NE40 60 F3
Davidson Cotts. N-u-T NE2 46 B3
Davidson Rd. Gates NE10 75 B2
Davidson St. Gates NE10 89 D8
Davison Ave. N Silk SR3 116 B7
Davison Ave. W Bay NE26 31 F6
Davison St. Blyth NE24 17 E8
Davison St. Boldon NE35 76 E1
Davison St. Newb NE15 61 E8
Davison Terr. Sland SR5 93 A2
Davy Bank. Walls NE28 49 D1
Dawlish Cl. Tyne NE29 50 D8
Dawlish Gdns. Gates NE9 88 F3
Dawlish Pl. N-u-T NE5 36 C3
Dawson Pl. Mpeth NE61 3 F1
Dawson Sq. 4 Tyne NE30 51 D7
Dawson Terr. Sland SR4 103 A3
Daylesford Dr. N-u-T NE3 & NE7 46 C4
Daylesford Rd. Cram NE23 16 A2
Dayshield. N-u-T NE5 36 F1
De Merley Rd. Mpeth NE61 3 F1
De Mowbray Way. Mpeth NE61 3 D2
De Walden Sq. Pegs NE61 4 E3
Deacon Cl. N-u-T NE5 36 B2
Deaconsfield Cl. Silk SR3 115 F5
Deadridge La. Crbdge NE45 56 B7
Deal Cl. Blyth NE24 17 E4
Dean Cl. Whick NE16 87 B7
Dean House. N-u-T NE6 75 A8
Dean Rd. S Shs NE33 77 B7
Dean Rd. S Shs NE33 77 C8
Dean St. Gates NE9 89 A5
Dean St. Hexham NE46 54 C5
Dean St. N-u-T NE1 66 B1
Dean Terr. Ryton NE40 61 C5
Dean Terr. S Shs NE33 77 B7
Dean Terr. Sland SR5 93 A1
Dean View Dr. Blyth NE24 17 B8
Deanery St. Bed NE22 10 F1
Deanham Gdns. N-u-T NE5 64 A4
Deans Ave. N-b-t-S NE64 7 C5
Deans Hospl. S Shs NE33 77 C7
Deansfield Cl. Silk SR3 115 F5
Dearham Gr. Cram NE23 16 A2
Debdon Gdns. N-u-T NE6 48 A1
Debdon Pl. Cram NE23 22 B6
Debdon Rd. Ashgn NE63 6 F2
Debussy Ct. Jarrow NE32 76 C6
Deckham St. Gates NE8 89 A8
Deckham Terr. Gates NE8 & NE9 89 A8
Dee Rd. Hebb NE31 75 F3
Dee St. Jarrow NE32 76 C7
Deepbrook Rd. N-u-T NE5 43 C1
Deepdale. Walls NE28 42 C1
Deepdale. Wash NE38 101 A1
Deepdale Cl. Whick NE16 86 F4
Deepdale Cres. N-u-T NE5 44 B2
Deepdale Gn. N-u-T NE5 44 B2
Deepdale Rd. Tyne NE30 32 B2
Deepdale St. H le H DH5 119 A2
Deepdene Gr. Sland SR6 93 E5
Deepdene Rd. Sland SR6 93 D5
Deer Bush. N-u-T NE5 36 F1
Deer Park Way. Blay NE21 62 E1
Deerbolt Pl. Lbtn NE12 41 C3
Deerfell Cl. Ashgn NE63 6 B2
Deerness Rd. Sland SR2 106 B1
Dees Ave. Walls NE28 49 B3
Defender Ct. Sland SR5 103 C4
Defoe Ave. B Hall NE34 77 C3
Deighton Wlk. N-u-T NE5 36 F1
Delacour Rd. Blay NE21 62 C3
Delamere Cres. Cram NE23 16 A2
Delamere Ct. 7 Silk SR3 116 A6
Delamere Rd. N-u-T NE3 38 C1
Delaval. C le S DH2 112 A3
Delaval Ave. N Shs NE29 50 E6
Delaval Ave. S Del NE25 23 C3
Delaval Cres. Blyth NE24 17 B4
Delaval Ct. Bed NE22 11 C2
Delaval Ct. 15 S Shs NE33 51 D1
Delaval Cty Mid Sch. Blyth NE24 17 D5
Delaval Gdns. Blyth NE24 17 B4
Delaval Gdns. N-u-T NE15 69 B4
Delaval Prim Sch. Lbtn NE12 29 D1
Delaval Prim Sch. N-u-T NE15 63 B1
Delaval Rd. N-u-T NE15 63 B1
Delaval Rd. N-u-T NE15 69 B4
Delaval Rd. W Bay NE26 32 C4
Delaval St. Blyth NE24 17 B4
Delaval Terr. Blyth NE24 17 D7
Delaval Terr. N-u-T NE3 45 A4
Delaval Trad Est. E Cram NE25 23 C5
Delhi Cres. Craw NE40 61 A3
Delhi Gdns. Craw NE40 61 A3
Delhi View. Craw NE40 61 A3
Dell The. Mpeth NE61 3 E3
Dell The. New DH4 114 D3
Dellfield Dr. Sland SR4 107 A4
Demesne Dr. Bed NE22 15 F8
Demesne The. Ashgn NE63 7 B2
Dempsey Rd. Hazle NE13 28 B4
Denbeigh Pl. Lbtn NE12 41 C3
Denbigh Ave. Sland SR6 93 D4
Denbigh Ave. Walls NE28 50 A3
Denbigh Community Fst Sch. Walls NE28 50 A3
Denby Cl. Cram NE23 16 A2
Dene Ave. B Vill NE13 28 A5
Dene Ave. H-le-Sp DH5 119 A7
Dene Ave. Hexham NE46 54 C4
Dene Ave. Kill NE12 29 A2
Dene Ave. N-u-T NE3 46 B4
Dene Ave. N-u-T NE15 62 D7
Dene Ave. R Gill NE39 85 D1
Dene Bank View. N-u-T NE3 44 B3
Dene Cl. N-u-T NE7 47 A1
Dene Cl. Oham NE42 59 B5
Dene Cl. R Mill NE44 80 F8
Dene Cl. Ryton NE40 61 D5
Dene Cres. N-u-T NE3 46 B4
Dene Cres. R Gill NE39 85 D1
Dene Cres. Ryton NE40 61 D5
Dene Cres. W Bay NE26 31 F6
Dene Cres. Walls NE28 49 D2
Dene Ct. Birt DH3 100 C7
Dene Ct. Hams NE17 95 B6
Dene Ct. N-u-T NE7 47 B1
Dene Ct. Wash NE38 101 C6
Dene Garth. Oham NE42 59 A5
Dene Gdns. Gates NE10 75 B1
Dene Gdns. H-le-Sp DH5 118 F7
Dene Gdns. N-u-T NE15 62 D6
Dene Gdns. W Bay NE25 31 E5
Dene Gr. N-u-T NE3 46 B4
Dene Gr. Prud NE42 59 B3
Dene Gr. Seg NE23 23 B2
Dene Head Cotts. Walb NE15 35 E2
Dene La. Clea SR6 93 C7
Dene La. Sland SR6 93 D4
Dene Mews. Sland SR5 92 C1
Dene Pk. Hexham NE46 54 C4
Dene Pk. Pont NE20 25 B3
Dene Pk. Sland SR5 92 C1
Dene Rd. Blay NE21 62 D3
Dene Rd. G Post NE62 10 E7
Dene Rd. R Gill NE39 85 D1
Dene Rd. Sland SR5 92 C1
Dene Rd. Tyne NE30 51 C8
Dene Rd. Wylam NE41 60 B7
Dene Side. Blay NE21 62 D2
Dene St. H le H DH5 119 B6
Dene St. N Silk SR3 109 A1
Dene St. Prud NE42 59 E3
Dene St. Sland SR4 104 C3
Dene Terr. Blay NE21 62 B2
Dene Terr. Jarrow NE32 76 A4
Dene Terr. N-u-T NE3 46 B4
Dene Terr. Newb NE15 61 F8
Dene Terr. Oving NE42 58 D4
Dene The. Medom DH8 95 A2
Dene The. W Bay NE25 31 E5
Dene The. W Rain DH4 118 A2
Dene The. Wylam NE41 60 B6
Dene View. Ashgn NE63 6 B3
Dene View. Bed NE22 11 C1
Dene View. Burnop NE16 97 A6
Dene View. Elling NE61 1 E4
Dene View. H Spen NE39 85 A3
Dene View. N-u-T NE3 46 B4
Dene View. R Gill NE39 85 C2
Dene View Cres. Sland SR4 103 B2
Dene View Ct. Blyth NE24 17 B7
Dene View Dr. Blyth NE24 17 B8
Dene View E. Bed NE22 11 C1
Dene View W. Bed NE22 16 B8
Dene Villas. C le S DH3 112 D1
Denebank. W Bay NE25 31 E5
Deneburn. Gates NE10 90 A7
Denecrest. Medom DH8 95 A2
Denecroft. Wylam NE41 60 A6
Deneholm. W Bay NE25 31 E5
Deneholm. Walls NE28 49 D3
Denelands. Hexham NE46 54 C5
Deneside. Duns NE11 87 F7
Deneside. Hedw NE32 76 C1
Deneside. N-u-T NE5 36 F4
Deneside. N-u-T NE15 63 A3
Deneside. S Shs NE34 78 C6
Deneside. Seg NE23 23 A2
Deneside Ave. Gates NE9 88 F4
Deneside Ct. N-u-T NE1 67 A4
Denesyde. Medom DH8 95 A2
Deneway. R Gill NE39 86 A4
Denewell Ave. Gates NE9 88 F5
Denewell Ave. N-u-T NE7 47 A3
Denewood. Kill NE12 29 E2
Denewood Ct. Walls NE28 50 A2
Denham Ave. Sland SR6 93 D4
Denham Dr. S Del NE25 23 D2
Denham Gr. Blay NE21 85 F8
Denham Wlk. N-u-T NE5 36 C3
Denhill Pk. N-u-T NE15 & NE4 64 A2
Denholm Ave. Cram NE23 16 A2
Denholme Lodge. Duns NE11 71 A1
Denmark Ct. N-u-T NE6 67 C3
Denmark St. Gates NE8 72 C2
Denmark St. N-u-T NE6 67 C3
Dennison Cres. Birt DH3 100 C6
Denshaw Cl. Cram NE23 16 B2
Dent Cl. Hasw DH6 121 E3
Dent St. Blyth NE24 17 F6
Dent St. Sland SR6 93 D4
Dentdale. Pens DH4 113 E8
Denton Ave. N Shs NE29 50 C6
Denton Ave. N-u-T NE15 62 D6
Denton Chare. N-u-T NE1 72 A4
Denton Gate. N-u-T NE5 43 A3
Denton Gr. N-u-T NE5 43 A3
Denton Park Mid Sch. N-u-T NE5 36 F2
Denton Park Sh Ctr. N-u-T NE5 36 E2
Denton Rd. N-u-T NE15 62 F6
Denton Road Inf Sch. N-u-T NE15 62 F5
Denton Road Jun Sch. N-u-T NE15 62 F5
Denton View. Blay NE21 62 B2
Denver Gdns. N-u-T NE6 68 B1
Denway Gr. S Slu NE26 24 B7
Denwick Ave. N-u-T NE15 62 C6
Denwick Terr. Tyne NE30 51 C7
Depot Rd. N-u-T NE6 68 A3
Deptford Rd. Gates NE8 73 A4
Deptford Rd. Sland SR4 105 B3
Deptford Terr. Sland SR4 105 A4
Derby Cres. Hebb NE31 75 D5
Derby Ct. N-u-T NE4 65 B2
Derby Gdns. Walls NE28 49 A4
Derby St. Jarrow NE32 76 C7
Derby St. N-u-T NE2 & NE4 65 B2
Derby St. S Shs NE33 51 C2
Derby St. Sland SR2 105 C2
Derby Terr. S Shs NE33 51 D2
Dereham Cl. S Slu NE26 24 D5
Dereham Ct. N-u-T NE5 43 B4
Dereham Rd. S Slu NE26 24 D5
Dereham Terr. Stake NE62 11 C8
Dereham Way. Tyne NE29 50 B8
Derry Ave. Sland SR6 93 E4
Derwent Ave. Gates DH98 & NE11 88 D5
Derwent Ave. Hebb NE31 75 E3
Derwent Ave. Newb NE15 61 E7
Derwent Ave. R Gill NE39 85 E1
Derwent Cote. Hams NE17 95 B5
Derwent Cres. Hams NE17 95 B5
Derwent Cres. Whick NE16 87 B8
Derwent Crook Dr. Gates NE9 88 E5
Derwent Gdns. Gates NE9 89 A5
Derwent Gdns. Walls NE28 50 A4
Derwent Haven. Hams NE17 95 B5
Derwent Inf Sch. Gates NE8 71 C1
Derwent Rd. Hexham NE46 54 C4
Derwent Rd. S Slu NE26 24 C6
Derwent Rd. Tyne NE30 32 B2
Derwent St. B Mill NE17 95 C6
Derwent St. Chopw NE17 84 B1
Derwent St. H le H DH5 119 B2
Derwent St. N-u-T NE15 63 B1
Derwent St. Pens DH4 114 B6
Derwent St. Sland SR1 105 C2
Derwent Terr. Burnop NE16 97 B7
Derwent Terr. S Hett DH6 121 E8
Derwent Terr. Wash NE38 101 E4
Derwent Tower. Duns NE11 71 A1
Derwent Valley Villas. Hams NE17 95 A6
Derwent View. Blay NE21 62 B1
Derwent View. Burnop NE16 97 B6
Derwent View. Chopw NE17 84 C2
Derwent View Terr. Dipton DH9 96 D1
Derwent Way. Blay NE21 62 E1
Derwentdale Gdns. N-u-T NE7 47 B3
Derwenthaugh Marina. Whick NE21 69 A3
Derwenthaugh Rd. Whick NE21 69 A3
Derwentwater Ave. C le S DH2 112 B1
Derwentwater Ct. Gates NE8 72 A1
Derwentwater Gdns. Whick NE16 87 D7
Derwentwater Rd. Gates NE8 71 C1
Derwentwater Rd. N-b-t-S NE64 7 C3
Derwentwater Terr. S Shs NE33 77 C8
Deuchar House. N-u-T NE2 66 C3
Deuchar St. N-u-T NE2 66 C4
Devon Ave. Whick NE16 87 C7
Devon Cl. Ashgn NE63 5 F4
Devon Cres. Birt DH3 100 B6
Devon Dr. N Silk SR3 116 A8
Devon Gdns. Gates NE9 88 F7
Devon Gdns. S Shs NE34 78 B7
Devon Rd. Hebb NE31 75 F3
Devon Rd. Tyne NE29 31 D1
Devon St. H le H DH5 118 F4
Devon St. Pens DH4 114 C6
Devon Wlk. Wash NE37 90 D1
Devonshire Dr. Lbtn NE12 & NE27 30 C1
Devonshire Gdns. Walls NE28 49 A3
Devonshire Pl. N-u-T NE2 46 C1
Devonshire St. S Shs NE33 77 B7
Devonshire St. Sland SR5 93 C1
Devonshire Terr. N-u-T NE2 66 A3
Devonshire Terr. 6 W Bay NE26 32 B4
Devonshire Tower. Sland SR5 93 D1
Devonworth Pl. Blyth NE24 17 A7
Dewhurst Terr. Sunn NE16 87 B2
Dewley. Cram NE23 22 B5
Dewley Ct. Cram NE23 22 B5
Dewley Pl. N-u-T NE5 36 E3
Dewley Rd. N-u-T NE5 43 B1
Dewsgreen. Cram NE23 22 B6
Dexter Way. Gates NE10 89 C8
Deyncourt. Pont NE20 25 D2
Deyncourt Cl. Pont NE20 25 D1
Diamond Ct. N-u-T NE3 38 A1
Diamond Hall Jun & Inf Sch. Sland SR4 104 C3
Diamond St. Walls NE28 49 B2
Diana St. N-u-T NE4 65 B1
Dibley Sq. N-u-T NE6 67 B1
Dibley St. N-u-T NE6 67 B1
Dick St. 11 Craw NE40 60 F3
Dickens Ave. B Hall NE34 77 B3
Dickens Ave. Whick NE16 87 A8
Dickens St. H-le-Sp DH4 118 D8
Dickens St. Sland SR5 93 A1
Dickens Wlk. N-u-T NE5 36 C3
Dickson Dr. Hexham NE46 53 E3
Didcot Ave. N Shs NE29 50 E4
Didcot Way. Boldon NE36 91 E7
Dillon St. Jarrow NE32 76 A5
Dilston Ave. Hexham NE46 54 D4
Dilston Ave. W Bay NE25 32 B4
Dilston Cl. Pegs NE61 5 A3
Dilston Cl. Shire NE27 30 F2
Dilston Cl. Wash NE38 101 A4
Dilston Dr. Ashgn NE63 6 D2
Dilston Dr. N-u-T NE5 36 E3
Dilston Gdns. Sland SR4 104 C1
Dilston Haugh Cotts. Crbdge NE45 55 D4
Dilston Rd. N-u-T NE4 65 A2
Dilston Terr. Jarrow NE32 76 C3
Dilston Terr. N-u-T NE3 46 B4
Dimbula Gdns. N-u-T NE7 48 A2
Dinmont Pl. Cram NE23 22 B5
Dinnington Cty Fst Sch. Dgton NE13 27 C7
Dinsdale Ave. Walls NE28 49 C4
Dinsdale Cotts. 3 Ryhope SR2 116 F6
Dinsdale Pl. N-u-T NE2 66 C3
Dinsdale Rd. N-u-T NE2 66 C3
Dinsdale Rd. Sland SR6 93 E2
Dinsdale St. Ryhope SR2 116 F6
Dinsdale St S. 9 Ryhope SR2 116 F6
Dipe La. Boldon NE36 92 B7
Dipton Ave. N-u-T NE4 70 B4
Dipton Cl. Hexham NE46 54 E4
Dipton Gdns. Sland SR3 109 B2
Dipton Gr. Cram NE23 22 B6
Dipton Rd. W Bay NE25 31 D7
Dipwood Rd. R Gill NE39 85 E1
Dipwood Way. R Gill NE39 96 D8
Discovery Ct. Silk SR3 115 F7
Dishforth Gn. Gates NE9 89 B1
Dispensary La. N-u-T NE1 66 A1
Disraeli St. Blyth NE24 17 D8
Disraeli St. Blyth NE24 17 E8
Disraeli St. Fence DH4 118 B8
Disraeli Terr. Chopw NE17 84 B1
Dissington Pl. N-u-T NE5 63 C4
Dissington Pl. Whick NE16 87 A5
Ditchburn Terr. Sland SR4 104 C4
Dixon Ave. Ebch DH8 94 F4
Dixon Pl. Duns NE11 87 F8
Dixon Rd. H-le-Sp DH5 118 D6
Dixon St. Gates NE8 73 A3
Dixon St. S Shs NE33 51 C1
Dixon's Sq. Sland SR6 93 D1
Dobson Cl. N-u-T NE4 71 B3
Dobson Cres. N-u-T NE6 73 C4
Dock Rd. N Shs NE29 51 A4
Dock Rd S. N Shs NE29 51 A3
Dock St. S Shs NE33 77 B7
Dock St. Sland SR6 93 E1
Dockendale La. Whick NE16 87 C7
Dockwray Cl. N Shs NE30 51 C6
Dockwray Sq. N Shs NE30 51 B5
Doddington Cl. N-u-T NE15 62 B7
Doddington Dr. Cram NE23 22 B6
Doddington Villas. Gates NE10 89 C7
Dodds Ct. Sland SR5 92 A3
Dodds Terr. Birt DH3 100 C6
Dodsworth N. Green NE40 61 B1
Dodsworth Terr. Green NE40 61 B1
Dodsworth Villas. Green NE40 61 B1
Dog Bank. N-u-T NE1 72 B4
Dogger Bank. Mpeth NE61 3 E1
Dolphin Ct. N-u-T NE4 64 A1
Dolphin Quay. N Shs NE30 51 B5
Dolphin St. N-u-T NE4 64 A1
Dominies Cl. R Gill NE39 85 F3
Don Dixon Dr. Hedw NE32 76 B1
Don Gdns. Boldon NE36 91 F7
Don Gdns. Wash NE37 90 D1
Don Rd. Jarrow NE32 76 D7
Don St. Gates NE11 88 C4
Don View. Boldon NE36 92 A7
Donald Ave. S Hett DH6 121 F8
Donald St. N-u-T NE3 40 B1
Doncaster Rd. N-u-T NE2 66 C3
Doncrest Rd. Wash NE37 90 B1
Donkin Rd. Wash NE37 100 F7
Donkin Terr. N Shs NE30 51 C7
Donkins St. Boldon NE35 76 E1
Donnington Cl. Sland SR5 92 A1
Donnington Ct. N-u-T NE3 & NE7 46 C4
Donridge. Wash NE37 90 B1
Donside. Gates NE10 89 F4
Donvale Rd. Wash NE37 90 A1
Dorcas Ave. N-u-T NE15 62 E8
Dorcas Terr. 3 Wash NE37 101 D8
Dorchester Cl. N-u-T NE5 36 B3
Dorchester Ct. E Cram NE25 23 C6
Dorchester Gdns. Gates NE9 88 F2
Dorking Ave. N Shs NE29 50 E4
Dorking Cl. Blyth NE24 17 E4
Dorking Rd. Sland SR6 93 E4
Dornoch Cres. Gates NE10 89 E6
Dorrington Rd. N-u-T NE3 38 B3
Dorset Ave. Birt DH3 100 D1
Dorset Ave. Hebb NE31 75 F5
Dorset Ave. S Shs NE34 78 B7
Dorset Ave. Sland SR6 93 E4
Dorset Ave. Walls NE28 49 A3
Dorset Cl. Ashgn NE63 5 F4
Dorset Gr. Tyne NE29 31 D1
Dorset La. N Silk SR3 116 B7
Dorset Rd. Gates NE8 73 A4
Dorset Rd. N-u-T NE15 62 F6
Dorset St. E Lane DH5 121 C8
Dotland Cl. Hexham NE46 54 E4
Double Row. E Cram NE25 23 B5
Douglas Ave. N-u-T NE3 45 A4
Douglas Bader House. Blyth NE24 17 F6
Douglas Cl. White NE34 77 C4
Douglas Ct. Gates NE11 88 E2
Douglas Ct. Sland SR1 106 B3
Douglas Gdns. Duns NE11 88 A7
Douglas Par. Jarrow NE31 76 A2
Douglas Rd. Sland SR6 93 E4
Douglas St. Walls NE28 50 A1
Douglas Terr. N-u-T NE4 65 B1
Douglas Terr. Pens DH4 114 C8
Douglas Terr. Wash NE37 90 D1
Douglass St. Walls NE28 49 B2
Doulting Cl. Lbtn NE12 41 B2
Dove Ave. Hedw NE32 76 C3
Dove Ct. 8 Birt DH3 100 C5
Dove Ct. Tyne NE30 32 C3
Dove Row. Tyne NE30 32 C3
Dovecote Cl. W Bay NE25 31 C6
Dovecote Rd. Lbtn NE12 42 B3
Dovedale Ave. Blyth NE24 17 A8
Dovedale Ct. S Shs NE34 77 A5
Dovedale Gdns. Gates NE9 89 A4
Dovedale Gdns. N-u-T NE7 47 B3
Dovedale Rd. Sland SR6 93 C5
Dover Cl. N-u-T NE5 36 C3
Dovercourt Rd. N-u-T NE6 75 A4
Dowling Ave. W Bay NE25 31 F4
Downe Cl. Blyth NE24 17 E4
Downend Rd. N-u-T NE5 36 E3
Downfield. Wash NE37 90 D3
Downham. N-u-T NE5 36 F1
Downham Ct. S Shs NE33 51 C1
Downhill Cty Inf Sch. S Shs NE34 78 B7
Downhill La. Boldon NE37 91 F5
Downhill La. Hedw NE36 91 D4
Downhill Prim Sch. Sland SR5 92 B4
Downing Dr. Mpeth NE61 8 E7
Downs La. H le H DH5 119 B5
Downs Pit La. H le H DH5 119 C5
Downswood. Kill NE12 29 F3
Doxford Ave. H le H DH5 118 F6
Doxford Gdns. N-u-T NE5 44 A1
Doxford Park Way. Silk SR3 115 E6
Doxford Pk Sh Ctr. Silk SR3 115 F6
Doxford Pl. Cram NE23 22 B5
Doxford Terr. H le H DH5 118 F6
Dr Henry Russell Ct. N-u-T NE15 63 A1
Dr Pit Cotts. Bed NE22 10 F1
Drake Cl. S Shs NE33 77 B8
Drawback Cl. Prud NE42 59 D2
Dray The. Pont NE20 25 B3
Drayton Rd. N-u-T NE3 44 B4
Drayton Rd. Sland SR6 93 D4
Drive Prim Sch The. Gates NE10 89 E8
Drive The. Birt DH3 100 D1
Drive The. Gates NE9 88 F6
Drive The. Gates NE10 89 E8
Drive The. N-u-T NE3 45 C3
Drive The. N-u-T NE7 47 B4
Drive The. N-u-T NE5 63 A4
Drive The. Tyne NE30 51 D8
Drive The. Walls NE28 49 B2
Drive The. Wash NE37 90 C1
Drive The. Whick NE16 87 C6
Dronfield Cl. C le S DH2 112 A1
Drove Rd. Tley NE15 35 B3
Drum Ind Est. C le S DH2 112 B7
Drum Rd. C le S DH2 112 B7
Drum Rd. C le S DH2 & DH3 112 B8
Drummond Cres. S Shs NE34 76 F5
Drummond Rd. N-u-T NE3 44 C4
Drummond Terr. N Shs NE30 51 B6
Drumoyne Cl. Sland SR3 115 B6
Drumoyne Gdns. W Bay NE25 31 D3
Drumsheugh Pl. N-u-T NE5 43 B2
Druridge Ave. Sland SR6 93 E5
Druridge Cres. Blyth NE24 17 B5
Druridge Cres. S Shs NE34 78 B8
Druridge Dr. Blyth NE24 17 B5
Druridge Dr. N-u-T NE5 44 A2
Drury La. N-u-T NE1 66 A1
Drury La. Sland SR1 106 B3
Drury La. Tyne NE29 50 C7
Drybeck Ct. Cram NE23 22 D8
Drybeck Ct. N-u-T NE4 65 B1
Drybeck Sq. Silk SR3 116 B6
Drybeck Wlk. Cram NE23 22 D8
Dryburgh. Wash NE38 101 D5
Dryburgh Cl. Tyne NE29 50 E8
Dryden Cl. B Hall NE34 77 B2
Dryden Rd. Gates NE8 & NE9 88 F7
Dryden Road Hospl. Gates NE9 88 F8
Dryden St. Sland SR5 93 A2
Drysdale Cres. B Vill NE13 28 A6
Drysdale Ct. B Vill NE13 28 B6
Dubmire Cotts. Fence DH4 118 A8
Dubmire Ct. Fence DH4 118 A8
Dubmire Ind Est. Fence DH4 114 B1
Dubmire Jun & Inf Schs. Fence DH4 118 A8
Duchess Cres. Jarrow NE32 76 B3
Duchess Cres E. Jarrow NE32 76 B3
Duchess Dr. N-u-T NE15 63 A3
Duchess St. W Bay NE26 32 A5
Duckpool La. Whick NE16 87 C7
Duddon Pl. Gates NE9 89 B4
Dudley Ave. Sland SR6 93 D4
Dudley Bsns Ctr. Cram NE23 22 A2
Dudley Ct. Cram NE23 22 A6
Dudley Dr. Annit NE23 29 A8
Dudley Fst Sch. Dud NE23 29 A7
Dudley Gdns. Sland SR3 115 C7
Dudley House. N-u-T NE4 65 B2
Dudley La. Cram NE23 22 A4
Dudley La. S Burn NE13 & NE23 28 D8
Dudley Lane Cotts. S Burn NE13 28 C8
Dudley Mid Sch. Annit NE23 29 A8
Dugdale Rd. N-u-T NE3 38 A1
Duke of Northumberland Ct. Walls NE28 49 E5
Duke St. Ashgn NE63 6 C4
Duke St. Gates NE10 75 A1
Duke St. N Shs NE29 51 B4
Duke St. N-u-T NE1 & NE4 71 C4
Duke St. Sland SR4 105 A2
Duke St. W Bay NE26 32 A5
Duke St N. Sland SR6 93 D2
Duke Wlk. Gates NE8 71 C1
Duke's Ave. Hebb NE31 75 D4
Duke's Gdns. Blyth NE24 17 C8
Dukes Cott. Newb NE15 61 F7
Dukes Dr. N-u-T NE3 28 B1
Dukes Meadow. Wools NE13 36 E8
Dukes Rd. Hexham NE46 53 E5
Dukes Way. Prud NE42 59 E4
Dukesfield. Cram NE23 22 B6
Dukesway. Gates NE11 88 C4
Dukesway Ct. Gates NE11 88 C3
Dukesway W. Gates NE11 88 C2
Dulverton Ct. N-u-T NE5 36 C3
Dulverton Ave. S Shs NE33 & NE34 77 D7
Dulverton Ct. N-u-T NE2 46 C2
Dumas Wlk. N-u-T NE5 36 C3
Dumfries Cres. B Wh NE32 76 E3
Dun Cow St. Sland SR1 105 C3
Dunbar Cl. N-u-T NE5 36 C3
Dunbar Gdns. Walls NE28 49 F4
Dunbar St. Sland SR4 104 C1
Dunblane Cres. N-u-T NE5 36 F1
Dunblane Dr. Blyth NE24 17 E4
Dunblane Rd. Sland SR6 93 E4
Dunbreck Gr. Sland SR4 109 A4
Duncan Gdns. Mpeth NE61 8 F7
Duncan St. Gates NE8 73 B1
Duncan St. N-u-T NE6 75 A5
Duncan St. Sland SR4 104 C3
Dundas St. Sland SR6 106 A4
Dundas Way. Gates NE10 89 C8
Dundee Cl. N-u-T NE5 36 C3
Dundee Ct. B Wh NE32 76 E3
Dundrennan. Wash NE38 101 C3
Dunelm. Sland SR2 109 B4
Dunelm Cl. 5 Birt DH3 100 C4
Dunelm Dr. Boldon NE35 & NE36 92 B8
Dunelm Dr. H-le-Sp DH4 118 D7
Dunelm Rd. H le H DH5 118 F4
Dunelm S. Sland SR4 109 B4
Dunelm St. S Shs NE33 51 D2
Dunford Gdns. N-u-T NE5 36 D4
Dunholme Rd. N-u-T NE4 64 C1
Dunira Cl. N-u-T NE2 46 C2
Dunkeld Cl. Blyth NE24 17 E4
Dunkirk Ave. H-le-Sp DH5 118 F7
Dunlin Cl. Ryton NE40 61 E4
Dunlin Dr. Blyth NE24 17 E4
Dunlin Dr. Wash NE38 100 F3
Dunlop Cl. N-u-T NE7 47 C4
Dunlop Cres. S Shs NE34 78 A6
Dunmoor Cl. N-u-T NE3 45 A4
Dunmore Ave. Sland SR6 93 E4
Dunmorlie St. N-u-T NE6 68 A2
Dunn Ave. N Silk SR3 109 A1
Dunn St. N-u-T NE4 71 B3
Dunn St Cty Jun & Inf Sch. Jarrow NE32 76 C7
Dunn Terr. N-u-T NE6 67 B2
Dunn's Terr. N-u-T NE2 65 B4
Dunne Rd. Blay NE21 62 E4
Dunning St. Sland SR1 105 C3
Dunnlynn Cl. Silk SR3 115 E6
Dunnock Dr. Sunn NE16 87 A3
Dunnock Dr. Wash NE38 100 F2
Dunnock Lodge. N-u-T NE15 62 D6
Dunnykirk Ave. N-u-T NE3 38 A1
Dunsdale Dr. Cram NE23 22 D8
Dunsdale Rd. S Del NE25 23 E2
Dunsgreen. Pont NE20 25 E5
Dunsgreen Ct. Pont NE 20 25 E5
Dunsley Gdns. Dgton NE13 27 B7
Dunslow Croft. Hors NE15 33 C1
Dunsmuir Gr. Gates NE8 88 D8
Dunstable Pl. N-u-T NE5 36 B3
Dunstan Cl. C le S DH2 112 A1
Dunstan Wlk. N-u-T NE5 36 F1
Dunstanburgh. Bed NE22 10 D1
Dunstanburgh Cl. Bed NE22 10 D1
Dunstanburgh Cl. N-u-T NE6 68 A1
Dunstanburgh Cl. Wash NE38 101 B4
Dunstanburgh Ct. Gates NE10 90 B7
Dunstanburgh Rd. N-u-T NE6 68 A1
Dunston Bank. Duns NE11 87 F7
Dunston Enterprise Pk. Duns NE11 70 B2
Dunston Hill Hospl. Duns NE11 87 D7
Dunston Hill Jun & Inf Sch. Duns NE11 87 F8
Dunston Pl. Blyth NE24 17 B8
Dunston Rd. Duns NE11 70 C1
Dunston Rd. Duns NE11 70 C2
Dunston Riverside Prim Sch. Duns NE11 70 C1
Dunston Sta. Duns NE11 88 A8
Dunvegan. Birt DH3 100 E2
Dunvegan Ave. C le S DH2 112 B1
Dunwoodie Terr. Hexham NE46 54 A5
Durant Rd. N-u-T NE1 66 B2
Durban St. Blyth NE24 17 D8
Durham Ave. Wash NE37 101 B8
Durham Cl. Bed NE22 10 D2
Durham Ct. Hebb NE31 75 D5
Durham Cty Cricket Gnd. C le S DH3 112 E2
Durham Dr. Hedw NE32 76 B2
Durham Gr. Jarrow NE32 76 B2
Durham House. Sland SR5 91 F4
Durham La. Hasw DH6 121 C1
Durham La. Hasw DH6 121 E1
Durham La. 3 S Hill DH6 120 D1
Durham Pl. Birt DH3 100 D1
Durham Pl. Gates NE8 72 C1
Durham Rd. Birt DH3 100 C3
Durham Rd. C le S DH3 112 C1
Durham Rd. C le S DH3 112 C8
Durham Rd. Cram NE23 16 C1
Durham Rd. E Rain DH5 118 C4
Durham Rd. Gates NE8 & NE9 88 F6
Durham Rd. H-le-Sp DH5 114 F3
Durham Rd. H-le-Sp DH5 118 E7
Durham Rd. Sland SR3 108 B2
Durham St. Fence DH4 118 A8
Durham St. Gates NE10 74 C1
Durham St. N-u-T NE4 64 C1
Durham St. N-u-T NE4 70 C4
Durham St. Walls NE28 49 C2
Durham St W. Walls NE28 49 C2
Durham Terr. N Silk SR3 109 A1
Duxfield Rd. N-u-T NE7 47 B3
Dwyer Cres. Ryhope SR2 116 F6
Dyer Sq. Sland SR5 93 B2
Dyke Heads La. Green NE40 61 B1
Dykefield Ave. N-u-T NE3 38 B3
Dykelands Rd. Sland SR6 93 E5
Dykelands Way. B Wh NE34 76 F3
Dykenook Cl. Whick NE16 87 A4
Dykes Way. Gates NE10 89 D5
Dymock Ct. N-u-T NE5 37 B1
E D Morel Terr. Chopw NE17 95 C8
Eagle St. Gates NE11 88 B6
Eaglescliffe Dr. N-u-T NE7 48 A2
Eaglesdene. H le H DH5 119 A4
Ealing Ct. N-u-T NE13 37 B2
Ealing Dr. Tyne NE30 32 C1
Ealing Sq. Cram NE23 21 D6
Ealing Sq. Sland SR5 93 A3
Eardulph Ave. C le S DH3 112 D3
Earl Grey Way. N Shs NE29 50 F3
Earl St. Sland SR4 105 B2
Earl's Dr. N-u-T NE15 63 A3
Earl's Gdns. Blyth NE24 17 C8
Earlington Ct. Lbtn NE12 29 E1
Earls Ct. Prud NE42 59 E4
Earls Dene. 5 Gates NE9 88 F4
Earls Dr. Gates NE9 88 F4

Gainers Terr. Walls NE28 75 C8
Gainford. C le S DH2 112 A3
Gainford. Gates NE9 88 F2
Gainsborough Ave. Wash NE38 101 E4
Gainsborough Ave. White NE34 77 D2
Gainsborough Cl. W Bay NE25 31 C7
Gainsborough Cres. Gates NE9 89 B7
Gainsborough Cres. S Row DH4 114 A5
Gainsborough Pl. Cram NE23 22 B3
Gainsborough Rd. Slnd SR4 107 C2
Gainsborough Sq. Slnd SR4 107 C2
Gainsbro Gr. N-u-T NE4 64 C2
Gainsbro Gr. N-u-T NE4 64 C3
Gainsford Ave. Gates NE9 88 E4
Gairloch Dr. Wash NE38 101 A3
Gairloch Rd. Slnd SR4 107 C3
Gairsay Cl. 5 Slnd SR2 116 E8
Galashiels Gr. S Row DH4 114 B5
Galashiels Rd. Slnd SR4 107 C3
Galashiels Sq. Slnd SR4 107 C3
Gallalaw Terr. N-u-T NE3 & NE7 40 C1
Gallant Terr. N Shs NE28 50 C1
Galleries The. Wash NE38 101 C5
Galley's Gill Rd. Slnd SR1 105 C3
Galloping Green Cotts. Gates NE9 89 D2
Galloping Green Rd. Gates NE9 89 D2
Gallowgate. N-u-T NE1 65 C1
Gallowhill La. Hors NE15 59 B7
Gallowhill La. Oham NE42 59 B7
Gallows Bank. Hexham NE46 54 B3
Galsworthy Rd. B Hall NE34 77 B3
Galsworthy Rd. Slnd SR4 107 C3
Galsworthy Rd. White NE34 77 B3
Galway Rd. Slnd SR4 107 B3
Galway Sq. Slnd SR4 107 B3
Gambia Rd. Slnd SR4 107 B2
Gambia Sq. Slnd SR4 107 B2
Ganton Ave. Cram NE23 22 B4
Ganton Cl. Wash NE37 90 C2
Ganton Ct. S Shs NE34 77 F3
Gaprigg Ct. Hexham NE46 54 B4
Gaprigg La. Hexham NE46 54 A4
Garasdale Cl. Blyth NE24 17 D4
Garcia Terr. Slnd SR6 93 E4
Garden City Villas. Ashgn NE63 6 D3
Garden Cl. S Burn NE13 28 B8
Garden Cres. Ebch DH8 94 F4
Garden Croft. Lbtn NE12 42 B4
Garden Dr. Hebb NE31 75 D4
Garden Est. H le H DH5 119 B4
Garden House Est. Craw NE40 60 E4
Garden La. Clea SR6 92 F8
Garden La. S Shs NE33 51 C2
Garden Pl. Pens DH4 114 B7
Garden Pl. Slnd SR1 105 C3
Garden St. Blay NE21 62 C3
Garden St. N-u-T NE3 39 C1
Garden St. New DH4 114 D3
Garden Terr. 8 Blay NE21 62 B1
Garden Terr. Craw NE40 60 F4
Garden Terr. Craw NE40 61 A3
Garden Terr. Ears NE25 31 A5
Garden Terr. Hexham NE46 54 A5
Gardener St. N-u-T NE4 71 A3
Gardens The. C le S DH2 112 B3
Gardens The. W Bay NE25 31 F4
Gardens The. Wash NE38 101 E4
Gardiner Rd. Slnd SR4 107 B3
Gardiner Sq. Kibble NE11 99 C6
Gardiner Sq. Slnd SR4 107 B3
Gardner Pk. N Shs NE29 50 F5
Gardner Pl. N Shs NE29 51 B5
Garesfield Gdns. Burnop NE16 96 F6
Garesfield Gdns. R Gill NE39 85 E3
Garesfield Golf Course. Chopw NE17 84 D4
Garesfield La. Barlow NE21 & NE39 85 E6
Gareston Cl. Blyth NE24 17 B7
Garfield St. Slnd SR4 104 C3
Garforth Cl. Cram NE23 22 A4
Garland Terr. 6 Fence DH4 118 A8
Garleigh Cl. Kill NE12 & NE27 29 F3
Garmondsway. N-u-T NE6 67 C1
Garner Cl. N-u-T NE5 36 D3
Garnet St. Slnd SR4 104 C3
Garrick Cl. Tyne NE29 50 C7
Garrick St. S Shs NE33 77 C8
Garrigill. Wash NE38 101 F1
Garsdale. Birt DH3 100 E1
Garsdale Ave. Wash NE37 101 C8
Garsdale Rd. W Bay NE26 24 E1
Garside Ave. Birt DH3 100 C6
Garsin Cl. N-u-T NE7 48 B3
Garth Cotts. Hexham NE46 54 A4
Garth Cres. Blay NE21 62 B1
Garth Cres. S Shs NE34 52 A1
Garth Farm Rd. Blay NE21 62 B1
Garth Four. Kill NE12 29 C3
Garth Heads. N-u-T NE1 66 C1
Garth Nine. Kill NE12 29 C3
Garth Seven. Kill NE12 29 C3
Garth Six. Kill NE12 29 C3
Garth Sixteen. Kill NE12 29 D4
Garth The. 6 Blay NE21 62 B1
Garth The. Medom DH8 95 C2
Garth The. N-u-T NE5 36 E1
Garth The. N-u-T NE3 44 C4
Garth Thirteen. Kill NE12 29 C4
Garth Thirty Three. Kill NE12 29 D3
Garth Thirty Two. Kill NE12 29 E3
Garth Twelve. Kill NE12 29 C4
Garth Twenty. Kill NE12 29 E3
Garth Twenty Five. Kill NE12 29 F3
Garth Twenty Four. Kill NE12 29 F3
Garth Twenty One. Kill NE12 29 E4
Garth Twenty Seven. Kill NE12 29 F3
Garth Twenty Two. Kill NE12 29 E3
Garthfield Cl. N-u-T NE5 43 A3
Garthfield Cnr. N-u-T NE5 43 A3
Garthfield Cres. N-u-T NE5 43 A3
Gartland Rd. Slnd SR4 107 A3
Gartland Rd. Slnd SR4 107 B3
Garvey Villas. Gates NE10 & NE9 89 C6
Garwood St. S Shs NE33 77 B8
Gas House La. 1 H-le-Sp DH4 114 D1
Gas House La. Mpeth NE61 4 A1
Gas La. Blay NE21 62 C4
Gaskell Ave. B Hall NE34 77 B3
Gatacre St. Blyth NE24 17 E8
Gateley Ave. Blyth NE24 17 D4
Gatesgarth. Gates NE9 89 A5
Gatesgarth Gr. Slnd SR6 93 E5
Gateshead Highway. Gates NE8 72 C2
Gateshead International Stad (Athletics Gd). Gates NE6 73 C3
Gateshead Jewish Boarding Sch. Gates NE8 72 B1
Gateshead Jewish Prim Sch. Gates NE8 72 B1
Gateshead Jewish Teachers Training Coll. Gates NE8 72 B1
Gateshead Metro Centre Sta. Whick NE11 70 A2
Gateshead Rd. Whick NE16 87 C3
Gateshead Sta. Gates NE8 72 B3
Gateshead Stadium Sta. Gates NE8 73 A2
Gateshead Talmudical Coll. Gates NE8 72 B1
Gateshead Tech Coll. Gates NE9 88 F7
Gateshead Tech Coll. Gates NE9 89 A7
Gatwick Ct. N-u-T NE3 37 C3
Gatwick Rd. Slnd SR4 107 B3
Gaughan Cl. N-u-T NE6 74 C3
Gaweswell Terr. New DH4 114 D4
Gayhurst Cres. Silk SR3 116 B6
Gayton Rd. Wash NE37 90 E1
Geddes Rd. Slnd SR4 107 B3
Gellesfield Chare. Whick NE16 87 B4
Gelt Cres. H le H DH5 119 B2
General Graham St. Slnd SR4 105 A1
General Havelock Rd. Slnd SR4 104 B2
General's Wood The. Wash NE38 113 B8
Geneva Rd. Slnd SR4 107 B3
Genister Pl. N-u-T NE4 64 A4
Geoffrey St. Whit SR6 78 F1
Geoffrey St. White NE34 77 C3
George Pl. N-u-T NE1 66 A2
George Rd. Bed NE22 11 D2
George Rd. Walls NE28 75 B8
George Scott St. S Shs NE33 51 D4
George Smith Gdns. Gates NE10 73 C2
George St. Ashgn NE63 6 E4
George St. B Vill NE13 28 A6
George St. Birt DH3 100 B4
George St. Blay NE21 62 D3
George St. Blyth NE24 17 E6
George St. C le S DH3 112 D2
George St. 4 Craw NE40 60 F3
George St. Gates NE10 74 C1
George St. H le H DH5 119 A5
George St. Hasw DH6 121 F3
George St. N Shs NE30 51 B6
George St. N Silk SR3 116 A8
George St. N-u-T NE3 39 A1
George St. N-u-T NE1 & NE4 71 C4
George St. Ryhope SR2 117 A6
George St. Sherb DH6 120 A1
George St. Walb NE5 35 F2
George St. Walls NE28 50 B1
George St. Whick NE16 87 A7
George St N. Slnd SR6 106 A4
George St W. 10 N Silk SR3 116 A8
George Stephenson Cty High Sch. Kill NE12 29 D3
George Stephenson Way. N Shs NE29 51 A3
George's View. Dud NE23 29 A7
Georges Rd. N-u-T NE4 70 C3
Georges Rd. N-u-T NE4 70 C4
Georgian Ct. Lbtn NE12 29 D1
Georgian Ct. Slnd SR4 109 A4
Gerald St. N-u-T NE4 70 A4
Gerald St. White NE34 77 C3
Gerrard Cl. Cram NE23 22 B4
Gerrard Cl. W Bay NE26 24 E1
Gerrard Rd. Slnd SR4 107 B3
Gerrard Rd. W Bay NE26 24 F1
Gertrude St. New DH4 114 D2
Gibbon's Wlk. B Hall NE34 77 A2
Gibbs Ct. 2 C le S DH2 112 C2
Gibside. C le S DH2 112 A3
Gibside Cres. Byer NE16 97 D8
Gibside Ct. Duns NE11 87 F6
Gibside Gdns. N-u-T NE15 63 B7
Gibside Terr. Burnop NE16 97 B6
Gibside View. Blay NE21 86 B8
Gibside Way. Whick NE16 69 B2
Gibson Ct. Boldon NE35 91 F8
Gibson Pl. Hexham NE46 54 A5
Gibson St. N-b-t-S NE64 7 D4
Gibson St. N-u-T NE1 66 C1
Gibson St. Walls NE28 49 F5
Gifford Sq. Slnd SR4 107 C4
Gilberdyke. Gates NE10 90 A5
Gilbert Rd. Slnd SR4 107 B2
Gilbert Sq. Slnd SR4 107 B2
Gilbert St. S Shs NE33 77 C8
Gilderdale. Pens DH4 113 E8
Gilderdale Way. Cram NE23 22 A3
Gilesgate. Hexham NE46 54 A5
Gilesgate Rd. H le H DH5 119 B1
Gilhurst Grange. Slnd SR1 105 B2
Gill Bridge Ave. Slnd SR1 105 C3
Gill Crescent N. Gr Lum DH4 113 E1
Gill Crescent S. Gr Lum DH4 113 E1
Gill Rd. Slnd SR1 105 C3
Gill Side Gr. Slnd SR6 93 E2
Gill St. N-u-T NE4 64 B1
Gillas La. H-le-Sp DH5 119 A7
Gillas La E. H-le-Sp DH5 118 F7
Gillas La W. H-le-Sp DH5 118 E6
Gillas Lane Inf Sch. H-le-Sp DH5 118 F7
Gillhurst House. Slnd SR1 105 B3
Gillies St. N-u-T NE6 68 A2
Gilling Cres. Birt DH3 100 C6
Gillingham Rd. Slnd SR4 107 C3
Gillside Ct. S Shs NE34 77 A5
Gilmore Ct. Pens DH4 114 A6
Gilmore Cl. N-u-T NE5 36 D3
Gilpin St. H-le-Sp DH4 118 D8
Gilsland Ave. Walls NE28 49 F3
Gilsland Gr. Cram NE23 16 B1
Gilsland St. Slnd SR4 105 A2
Gilwell Way. N-u-T NE3 28 B1
Gingler La. Green NE40 61 A2
Girtin Rd. White NE34 77 D2
Girvan Terr. E Lane DH5 119 B1
Girvan Terr W. E Lane DH5 119 B1
Gishford Way. N-u-T NE5 43 B2
Givens St. Slnd SR6 93 E2
Glade The. Hedw NE32 91 B8
Glade The. Walb NE5 36 A2
Gladeley Way. Sunn NE16 87 B2
Gladewell Ct. G Post NE62 10 E7
Gladstonbury Pl. Lbtn NE12 41 C3
Gladstone Ave. W Bay NE26 31 F6
Gladstone Pl. N-u-T NE2 66 B3
Gladstone St. Blyth NE24 17 D8
Gladstone St. Fence DH4 118 B8
Gladstone St. Hebb NE31 & NE32 76 A6
Gladstone St. Mpeth NE61 9 B8
Gladstone St. N-u-T NE15 62 C6
Gladstone St. Slnd SR6 93 D1
Gladstone St. 3 Walls NE28 50 B1
Gladstone Terr. Bed NE22 11 A1
Gladstone Terr. Birt DH3 100 B4
Gladstone Terr. 2 Boldon NE35 76 E1
Gladstone Terr. Gates NE8 72 C1
Gladstone Terr. N-u-T NE2 66 B3
Gladstone Terr. Pens DH4 113 F8
Gladstone Terr. 7 W Bay NE26 32 B4
Gladstone Terr. Wash NE37 101 F8
Gladstone Terr W. Gates NE8 72 B1
Gladwyn Rd. Slnd SR4 107 B2
Gladwyn Sq. Slnd SR4 107 B2
Glaholm Rd. Slnd SR2 106 C2
Glaisdale Ct. S Shs NE34 77 A4
Glaisdale Dr. Slnd SR6 93 E6
Glaisdale Rd. N-u-T NE7 41 A1
Glamis Ave. N-u-T NE3 28 C1
Glamis Ave. Slnd SR4 107 C4
Glamis Cres. R Gill NE39 86 B4
Glamis Ct. S Shs NE34 77 F3
Glamis Terr. Sunn NE16 87 A1
Glamis Villas. Birt DH3 100 C6
Glanmore Rd. Slnd SR4 107 B3
Glantlees. N-u-T NE5 43 A2
Glanton Ave. S Del NE25 23 C3
Glanton Cl. C le S DH2 112 A2
Glanton Cl. N-u-T NE6 73 C4
Glanton Ct. Duns NE11 71 A1
Glanton House. Blyth NE24 17 B8
Glanton Rd. Hexham NE46 54 D4
Glanton Rd. Tyne NE29 50 D7
Glanton Sq. Slnd SR4 107 C3
Glanton Wynd. N-u-T NE3 39 B3
Glanville Cl. Gates NE11 88 B7
Glasbury Ave. Slnd SR4 107 C4
Glasgow Rd. B Wh NE32 76 E3
Glassey Terr. Beb NE22 11 D1
Glasshouse St. N-u-T NE6 73 C4
Glastonbury. Wash NE38 101 D4
Glastonbury Gr. N-u-T NE2 46 C2
Glebe Ave. Lbtn NE12 42 A3
Glebe Ave. Whick NE16 87 B7
Glebe Cl. N-u-T NE5 36 D3
Glebe Cl. Pont NE20 25 E7
Glebe Cres. Lbtn NE12 29 D1
Glebe Cres. Wash NE38 101 E6
Glebe Ct. Bed NE22 10 F1
Glebe Dr. Seaham SR7 116 F2
Glebe Est. Seaham SR7 116 F2
Glebe Farm. Bothal NE61 10 F8
Glebe Inf Sch. Wash NE38 101 D5
Glebe Jun Sch. Wash NE38 101 D5
Glebe Mews. Bed NE22 10 F1
Glebe Rd. Bed NE22 10 F1
Glebe Rd. Lbtn NE12 29 D1
Glebe Rise. Whick NE16 87 B7
Glebe Sch The. Kill NE12 29 D2
Glebe St. N-u-T NE4 64 B2
Glebe Terr. Chopp NE62 10 E5
Glebe Terr. Duns NE11 87 F8
Glebe Terr. 2 H-le-Sp DH4 114 D1
Glebe Terr. Lbtn NE12 29 D1
Glebe The. Stan NE61 14 C4
Glebe Villas. Lbtn NE12 29 C1
Glebe Wlk. Whick NE16 87 B7
Glebelands. Crbdge NE45 56 A6
Glen Ave. Stocks NE43 82 C7
Glen Barr. C le S DH2 112 B4
Glen Cl. R Gill NE39 85 E3
Glen Ct. Hebb NE31 75 D5
Glen Luce Dr. Slnd SR2 110 C2
Glen Path. Slnd SR2 110 A3
Glen St. Hebb NE31 75 D5
Glen Terr. C le S DH2 112 A4
Glen Terr. Hexham NE46 53 F5
Glen Terr. Wash NE38 101 E4
Glen The. Slnd SR2 110 A3
Glen Thorpe Ave. Slnd SR6 93 A2
Glen's Flats. H Pitt DH6 120 B5
Glenallen Gdns. Tyne NE30 32 C1
Glenavon Ave. C le S DH2 112 B4
Glenbrooke Terr. Gates NE9 88 F4
Glenburn Cl. Wash NE38 100 F3
Glencarron Cl. Wash NE38 101 A3
Glencoe. Kill NE12 29 D4
Glencoe Ave. C le S DH2 112 B4
Glencoe Ave. Cram NE23 22 B3
Glencoe Rd. Slnd SR4 107 B2
Glencoe Sq. Slnd SR4 107 B3
Glencoe Terr. R Gill NE39 85 C1
Glencourse. Boldon NE36 92 E7
Glendale Ave. Blyth NE24 16 E8
Glendale Ave. N Shs NE29 50 F6
Glendale Ave. N-u-T NE3 45 A4
Glendale Ave. Stake NE62 11 A8
Glendale Ave. W Bay NE26 32 A7
Glendale Ave. Walls NE28 49 B4
Glendale Ave. Wash NE37 101 C8
Glendale Ave. Whick NE16 87 A6
Glendale Cl. Blay NE21 85 F8
Glendale Cl. N-u-T NE5 36 D3
Glendale Cl. Slnd SR3 115 C6
Glendale Gdns. Gates NE9 89 B5
Glendale Gdns. Stake NE62 11 A8
Glendale Gr. N Shs NE29 50 F6
Glendale Rd. Ashgn NE63 7 A2
Glendale Rd. Shire NE27 31 A3
Glendale Terr. N-u-T NE6 67 C2
Glendford Pl. Blyth NE24 17 D4
Glendower Ave. N Shs NE29 50 D6
Glendyn Cl. N-u-T NE7 47 A1
Gleneagle Cl. N-u-T NE5 36 D3
Gleneagles. S Shs NE33 51 F1
Gleneagles. W Bay NE25 31 D6
Gleneagles Cl. Lbtn NE7 41 C1
Gleneagles Ct. W Bay NE25 31 D6
Gleneagles Dr. Wash NE37 90 C2
Gleneagles Rd. Gates NE9 88 E3
Gleneagles Rd. Slnd SR4 107 B2
Gleneagles Sq. Slnd SR4 107 B2
Glenesk Gdns. Slnd SR2 109 C2
Glenesk Rd. Slnd SR2 109 C3
Glenfield Ave. Cram NE23 16 B1
Glenfield Rd. Lbtn NE12 41 B3
Glenfield Rd. Lbtn NE12 41 C3
Glengarvan Cl. Wash NE38 101 A3
Glenholme Cl. Wash NE38 100 F3
Glenhurst Dr. N-u-T NE5 36 D3
Glenhurst Dr. Whick NE16 86 F4
Glenhurst Gr. S Shs NE34 77 F6
Glenkerry Cl. Wash NE38 101 A3
Glenleigh Dr. Slnd SR4 107 C4
Glenluce Dr. Cram NE23 22 B3
Glenmoor. Hebb NE31 75 D7
Glenmore Ave. C le S DH2 112 C4
Glenmuir Ave. Cram NE23 22 A3
Glenorrin Cl. Wash NE38 101 A3
Glenridge Ave. N-u-T NE6 47 B1
Glenroy Gdns. C le S DH2 112 B4
Glenshiel Cl. Wash NE38 101 A3
Glenside. Elling NE61 1 E5
Glenside. Hedw NE32 76 C2
Glenside Ct. Gates NE9 88 E4
Glenthorn Rd. N-u-T NE2 46 B2
Glenthorne Rd. Slnd SR6 93 E2
Glenuce. Birt DH3 100 E3
Glenwood. Ashgn NE63 6 C2
Glenwood Wlk. N-u-T NE5 36 D3
Gloria Ave. E Cram NE25 23 D6
Glossop St. H Spen NE39 84 F4
Gloucester Ave. Slnd SR6 93 E4
Gloucester Ct. N-u-T NE3 37 C4
Gloucester Pl. S Shs NE34 78 A5
Gloucester Rd. N-u-T NE4 65 A1
Gloucester Rd. Shire NE29 50 B7
Gloucester St. E Cram NE25 23 D6
Gloucester Terr. Hasw DH6 121 E1
Gloucester Terr. N-u-T NE4 71 A4
Gloucester Way. Hedw NE32 76 B2
Gloucester Way. N-u-T NE4 71 B4
Glover Ind Est. Wash NE37 101 E7
Glover Rd. Slnd SR4 107 B2
Glover Rd. Wash NE37 101 F8
Glover Sq. Slnd SR4 107 B2
Glynfellis. Gates NE10 89 F4
Glynfellis Ct. Gates NE10 89 F5
Glynn House. N-u-T NE4 70 B4
Glynwood Cl. Cram NE23 16 B1
Glynwood Gdns. Gates NE9 89 A5
Glynwood Prim Sch. Gates NE9 89 A5
Goathland Ave. Lbtn NE12 41 C2
Goathland Cl. N Silk SR3 116 A7
Goathland Dr. N Silk SR3 116 B6
Godfrey Rd. Slnd SR4 107 B3
Gofton Wlk. N-u-T NE5 43 A2
Goldcrest Rd. Wash NE38 100 F3
Goldfinch Cl. N-u-T NE4 70 C4
Goldlynn Dr. Silk SR3 115 E6
Goldsbrough Ct. N-u-T NE2 65 C3
Goldsmith Rd. Slnd SR4 107 B2
Goldspink La. N-u-T NE2 67 A3
Goldstone Ct. Kill NE12 29 E4
Golf Course Rd. S Row DH4 114 A4
Gompertz Gdns. S Shs NE33 77 B8
Gooch Ave. Bed NE22 11 A4
Goodrich Cl. S Row DH4 114 C5
Goodwood. Kill NE12 29 E3
Goodwood Ave. Gates NE8 88 D8
Goodwood Cl. N-u-T NE5 36 D3
Goodwood Rd. Slnd SR4 107 A3
Goodwood Sq. Slnd SR4 107 A3
Goole Rd. Slnd SR4 107 C3
Goose Hill. Mpeth NE61 9 A8
Gordon Ave. N-u-T NE3 45 C4
Gordon Ave. Slnd SR5 103 A4
Gordon Ct. Gates NE10 74 A1
Gordon Dr. Boldon NE36 92 D7
Gordon House. N-u-T NE6 67 B1
Gordon Rd. Blyth NE24 17 F6
Gordon Rd. N-u-T NE6 67 B1
Gordon Rd. S Shs NE34 77 C6
Gordon Rd. Slnd SR4 107 B2
Gordon Sq. N-u-T NE6 67 B1
Gordon Sq. W Bay NE26 32 C4
Gordon St. Gates NE8 72 A2
Gordon St. S Shs NE33 77 D8
Gordon Terr. Bed NE22 16 A8
Gordon Terr. Prud NE42 59 D2
Gordon Terr. 3 Ryhope SR2 117 A6
Gordon Terr. Slnd SR5 93 A2
Gordon Terr. Stake NE62 11 C7
Gordon Terr. W Bay NE26 32 C5
Gordon Terrace W. Stake NE62 11 C7
Gorleston Way. Silk SR3 116 A4
Gorse Ave. S Shs NE34 78 A5
Gorse Hill Way. N-u-T NE5 43 C3
Gorse Rd. Slnd SR2 106 A1
Gorsedene Ave. W Bay NE26 24 F1
Gorsedene Rd. W Bay NE26 24 F1
Gorsehill. Gates NE9 89 C5
Gorseway. Mpeth NE61 8 D7
Goschen St. Blyth NE24 12 E1
Goschen St. Blyth NE24 17 D8
Goschen St. Gates NE8 72 B1
Goschen St. Gates NE8 88 D8
Goschen St. Slnd SR5 93 A2
Gosforth Ave. White NE34 77 C3
Gosforth Cen Cty Mid Sch. N-u-T NE3 40 A2
Gosforth Ctr. N-u-T NE3 45 C4
Gosforth East Mid Sch. N-u-T NE3 40 A3
Gosforth Golf Course. N-u-T NE3 40 B3
Gosforth Grange Fst Sch. N-u-T NE3 39 B2
Gosforth High Sch. N-u-T NE3 39 C2
Gosforth Park Fst Sch. N-u-T NE3 40 A3
Gosforth Park Villas. W Open NE13 28 C4
Gosforth St. Gates NE10 74 A1
Gosforth St. N-u-T NE2 66 C2
Gosforth St. Slnd SR6 93 E1
Gosforth St Charles Prim Sch. N-u-T NE3 40 A1
Gosforth Terr. Gates NE10 74 C1
Gosforth Terr. N-u-T NE3 40 B1
Gosforth West Mid Sch. N-u-T NE3 39 B1
Gosport Way. Blyth NE24 17 D4
Gossington. Wash NE38 102 A5
Goswick Ave. N-u-T NE7 47 B3
Goswick Dr. N-u-T NE3 38 C4
Goundry Ave. Ryhope SR2 117 A6
Gourock Sq. Slnd SR4 107 A3
Govt Bldgs (Dept of Health & Social Security). N-u-T NE98 47 B4
Gowan Terr. N-u-T NE2 46 C1
Gowanburn. Cram NE23 22 A3
Gowanburn. Wash NE38 101 F2
Gower Rd. Slnd SR5 93 A2
Gower St. N-u-T NE6 75 A4
Gower Wlk. Gates NE10 89 C8
Gowland Ave. N-u-T NE4 64 B2
Grace Gdns. Walls NE28 49 A4
Grace St. Duns NE11 87 F8
Grace St. N-u-T NE6 67 C2
Grace St. N-u-T NE6 68 A2
Gracefield Cl. N-u-T NE5 36 D3
Grafton Cl. N-u-T NE6 67 B2
Grafton House. N-u-T NE6 67 B2
Grafton Rd. W Bay NE26 32 C4
Grafton St. N-u-T NE6 67 B2
Graham Ave. Whick NE16 87 B8
Graham Park Rd. N-u-T NE3 45 C3
Graham Rd. Hebb NE31 75 D5
Graham St. S Shs NE33 51 D2
Graham Terr. H Pitt DH6 120 B5
Grahamsley St. Gates NE8 72 C2
Grainger Mkt. N-u-T NE1 66 A1
Grainger Park Rd. N-u-T NE4 64 C1
Grainger St. N-u-T NE1 66 A1
Graingerville N. N-u-T NE4 65 A1
Graingerville S. N-u-T NE4 65 A1
Grampian Ave. C le S DH2 112 B2
Grampian Cl. Tyne NE29 31 F1
Grampian Gdns. Duns NE11 88 B6
Grampian Gr. Boldon NE36 92 B7
Grampian Pl. Lbtn NE12 29 B1
Granaries The. Fence DH4 118 B8
Granaries The. Pens SR4 102 F3
Granby Cl. Slnd SR3 109 B3
Granby St. Sunn NE16 87 B3
Granby St. Sunn NE16 87 B2
Grand Par. Tyne NE30 32 D1
Grandstand Rd. N-u-T NE2 45 B2
Grange Ave. Bed NE22 11 E3
Grange Ave. Fence DH4 114 A1
Grange Ave. Lbtn NE12 42 B2
Grange Ave. Shire NE27 30 F4
Grange Cl. Blyth NE24 17 D4
Grange Cl. Tyne NE30 32 B2
Grange Cl. W Bay NE25 31 D4
Grange Cl. Walls NE28 49 C2
Grange Cres. Gates NE10 90 A7
Grange Cres. Ryton NE40 61 C4
Grange Cres. Slnd SR2 106 A1
Grange Ct. Gates NE10 90 A7
Grange Ct. 6 Jarrow NE32 76 B7
Grange Ct. Prud NE42 59 D2
Grange Ct. Ryton NE40 61 C4
Grange Dr. Ryton NE40 61 C4
Grange Est. Kibble NE11 99 C6
Grange Farm Dr. Whick NE16 87 A5
Grange La. Whick NE16 87 B5
Grange Lonnen. Ryton NE40 61 B5
Grange Nook. Whick NE16 87 A5
Grange Park Ave. Bed NE22 11 E3
Grange Park Ave. Slnd SR5 93 C3
Grange Park Prim Sch. Slnd SR5 93 C2
Grange Pk. W Bay NE25 31 D4
Grange Pl. Jarrow NE32 76 B7
Grange Rd. Gates NE10 90 A7
Grange Rd. Jarrow NE32 76 B7
Grange Rd. Mpeth NE61 9 A6
Grange Rd. N-u-T NE3 39 C3
Grange Rd. N-u-T NE4 64 A3
Grange Rd. Newb NE15 61 E8
Grange Rd. Pont NE20 25 F7
Grange Rd. Ryton NE40 61 C5
Grange Rd. Slnd SR5 103 A4
Grange Rd W. Jarrow NE32 76 B7
Grange St S. Slnd SR2 110 C2
Grange Terr. Boldon NE36 92 D7
Grange Terr. Gates NE9 89 A8
Grange Terr. Kibble NE11 99 C6
Grange Terr. Medom DH8 95 B1
Grange Terr. Slnd SR5 93 B2
Grange Terr. Slnd SR2 106 A1
Grange The. Boldon NE36 92 D7
Grange View. E Rain DH5 118 D5
Grange View. New DH4 114 D3
Grange View. Ryton NE40 61 C4
Grange View. Slnd SR5 93 C3
Grange Villas. Walls NE28 49 C2
Grange Wlk. Whick NE16 87 A5
Grangemere Cl. Slnd SR2 110 C1
Grangetown Prim Sch. Slnd SR2 110 C3
Grangeway. Tyne NE29 31 F1
Grangewood Cl. S Row DH4 114 A5
Grant St. Jarrow NE32 76 A7
Grantham Dr. Gates NE9 88 E4
Grantham Pl. Cram NE23 22 A4
Grantham Rd. N-u-T NE2 66 C3
Grantham Rd. Slnd SR6 93 E2
Grantham St. Blyth NE24 17 F6
Granville Ave. Lbtn NE12 29 E1
Granville Ave. S Slu NE26 24 D5
Granville Cres. Lbtn NE12 42 B3
Granville Ct. N-u-T NE2 66 C4
Granville Dr. Lbtn NE12 42 B3
Granville Dr. N-u-T NE5 36 D3
Granville Dr. S Row DH4 114 C5
Granville Gdns. N-u-T NE2 67 A4
Granville Gdns. Stake NE62 11 A8
Granville Lodge. Lbtn NE12 42 B4
Granville Rd. N-u-T NE3 40 A3
Granville Rd. N-u-T NE2 66 C4
Granville St. Gates NE8 72 C1
Granville St. Slnd SR4 105 B3
Grasmere. Birt DH3 100 E2
Grasmere. Clea SR6 78 A1
Grasmere Ave. E Lane DH5 121 C8
Grasmere Ave. Gates NE10 89 F8
Grasmere Ave. Hedw NE32 76 D3
Grasmere Ave. N-u-T NE6 68 C1
Grasmere Ave. Newb NE15 61 E7
Grasmere Cres. Blay NE21 86 B8
Grasmere Cres. 3 Pens DH4 114 B6
Grasmere Cres. Slnd SR5 93 C2
Grasmere Cres. Slnd SR5 93 C3
Grasmere Cres. W Bay NE26 31 F7
Grasmere Ct. Newb NE15 61 E7
Grasmere Gdns. S Shs NE34 77 E6
Grasmere Gdns. Wash NE38 101 E4
Grasmere House. N-u-T NE6 68 B1
Grasmere Pl. N-u-T NE3 39 C3
Grasmere Rd. C le S DH2 112 B1
Grasmere Rd. Hebb NE31 75 F4
Grasmere Rd. Walls NE28 & NE6 49 A1
Grasmere Rd. Whick NE16 87 C7
Grasmere St. Gates NE8 72 B1
Grasmere St W. Gates NE8 72 B1
Grasmere Terr. N-b-t-S NE64 7 D4
Grasmere Terr. Wash NE38 101 E5
Grasmere Way. Blyth NE24 17 A8
Grasmoor Pl. N-u-T NE15 62 B7
Grassbanks. Gates NE10 90 A6
Grassholm Pl. Lbtn NE12 41 A3
Grassholme Meadows. Slnd SR3 109 B2
Grassington Dr. Cram NE23 22 A4
Grasslees. Wash NE38 112 F8
Grasswell Dr. N-u-T NE5 44 A3
Gravel Wlks. H-le-Sp DH5 114 F1
Gravesend Rd. Slnd SR4 107 B2
Gravesend Sq. Slnd SR4 107 C2
Gray Ave. C le S DH2 112 B2
Gray Ave. W Open NE13 28 C7
Gray Ct. Slnd SR2 110 A4
Gray Rd. Slnd SR2 106 C2
Gray St. Cam NE24 12 E1
Gray's Wlk. B Hall NE34 77 A2
Graylands. Wash NE38 112 E8
Grayling Ct. Silk SR3 115 C5
Grays Terr. 7 Boldon NE35 76 E1
Graystones. Gates NE10 90 B6
Great Lime Rd. Kill NE12 & NE3 29 A3
Great Lime Rd. Kill NE12 29 D1
Great Lime Rd. W Open NE12 & NE13 & NE23 29 A5
Great North Rd. N-u-T NE3 39 C3
Great North Rd. N-u-T NE2 46 A2
Great North Rd. Stann NE61 9 A1
Greathead St. S Shs NE33 77 B7
Grebe Cl. Ashgn NE63 6 E1
Grebe Cl. Blyth NE24 17 E5
Grebe Ct. N-u-T NE2 46 C1
Greely Rd. N-u-T NE5 36 F2
Green Acres. Mpeth NE61 8 E7
Green Acres. Pont NE20 25 C1
Green Ave. New DH4 114 D4
Green Bank. Hexham NE46 54 C4
Green Cl. Stan NE61 14 C4
Green Cl. Tyne NE30 32 B1
Green Cl. W Bay NE25 31 D4
Green Cres. Dud NE23 28 F8
Green Gr. Green NE40 61 B3
Green Hill Wlk. S Shs NE34 78 C6
Green La. Ashgn NE63 6 C3
Green La. Boldon NE36 92 E6
Green La. Dud NE23 28 F8
Green La. Gates NE10 73 C1
Green La. Gates NE10 74 A2
Green La. Gates NE10 75 A1
Green La. Hasw DH6 121 B3
Green La. Kill NE12 29 E2
Green La. Mpeth NE61 4 B1
Green La. S Shs NE34 77 B4
Green La. Seaton DH5 & SR7 119 F6
Green La. Stann NE61 & NE13 13 D2
Green La. Stann NE61 13 D5
Green La. Wools NE13 36 F8
Green Lane Gdns. Gates NE10 73 C2
Green Pk. Walls NE28 48 B3
Green Sq. W Bay NE25 31 D4
Green St. Slnd SR1 106 A3
Green Terr. Slnd SR1 105 C2
Green The. C le S DH2 112 B3
Green The. Chopw NE17 95 B8
Green The. Gates NE10 89 E8
Green The. H-le-Sp DH5 114 F1
Green The. Oving NE42 58 C4
Green The. Pont NE20 25 F7
Green The. R Gill NE39 85 C2
Green The. Slnd SR5 93 A1
Green The. Slnd SR1 105 C2
Green The. W Bay NE25 31 E6
Green The. Walb NE15 35 F1
Green Way. W Bay NE25 31 D4
Green's Pl. S Shs NE33 51 C4
Green-Fields. Ryton NE40 61 B5
Greenacre Pk. Gates NE9 88 E3
Greenacres Cl. Craw NE40 61 A3
Greenbank. Blay NE21 62 C2
Greenbank. Jarrow NE32 76 B7
Greenbank Dr. Slnd SR4 103 A1
Greenbank St. C le S DH3 112 D4
Greenbourne Gdns. Gates NE10 89 C7
Greencroft. Ashgn NE63 6 C2

Heather Terr. Burnop NE16 97 B6
Heatherdale Terr. Gates NE9 89 B3
Heatherlaw. Gates NE9 89 C5
Heatherlaw. Wash NE37 100 F6
Heatherlea Gdns. Sland SR3 109 B3
Heatherlee Gdns. Stake NE62 11 A8
Heatherslaw Rd. N-u-T NE5 63 C4
Heatherwell Gn. Gates NE10 89 C7
Heathery La. Lbtn NE3 40 B3
Heatheryhill. Hexham NE46 53 A4
Heathfield. Mpeth NE61 9 B6
Heathfield. Sland SR2 109 C2
Heathfield Cres. N-u-T NE5 44 A3
Heathfield Gdns. Green NE40 61 A1
Heathfield Pl. N-u-T NE3 28 D1
Heathfield Rd. Gates NE9 88 F6
Heathfield Sen High Sch. Gates NE9 88 F6
Heathway. Hedw NE32 76 C2
Heathwell Gdns. Whick NE16 87 B8
Heathwell Rd. N-u-T NE15 62 F7
Heathwood Ave. Whick NE16 87 A7
Heaton Cl. N-u-T NE6 67 B3
Heaton Gdns. B Hall NE34 77 C2
Heaton Gr. N-u-T NE6 67 B3
Heaton Hall Rd. N-u-T NE6 67 B3
Heaton Manor Sch. N-u-T NE7 47 C4
Heaton Park Ct. N-u-T NE6 67 B3
Heaton Park Rd. N-u-T NE6 67 B3
Heaton Park View. N-u-T NE6 67 B3
Heaton Pl. N-u-T NE6 67 B2
Heaton Rd. N-u-T NE6 67 B3
Heaton Sch. N-u-T NE7 47 A2
Heaton Terr. N Shs NE29 50 E6
Heaton Terr. N-u-T NE6 67 A2
Heaton Wlk. N-u-T NE6 67 B2
Hebburn (C of E Controlled) Jun Mix Inf Sch. Hebb NE32 75 F7
Hebburn Clegwell Comp Sch. Hebb NE31 75 F6
Hebburn Comp Sch. Hebb NE31 75 E4
Hebburn Hospl. Hebb NE31 75 D4
Hebburn Quay Cty Inf Sch. Hebb NE31 75 E7
Hebburn St Aloysius RC Inf Sch. Hebb NE31 75 E7
Hebburn Sta. Hebb NE31 75 D6
Heber St. N-u-T NE1 65 C1
Hebron Ave. Pegs NE61 4 E4
Hebron Pl. Ashgn NE63 6 F3
Hebron Way. Cram NE23 22 A5
Hector St. Shire NE27 30 F4
Heddon Ave. Hazle NE13 28 A4
Heddon Banks. H-o-t-W NE15 34 E1
Heddon C of E Prim Sch. H-o-t-W NE15 34 E2
Heddon Cl. N-u-T NE3 39 A2
Heddon View. Blay NE21 62 B2
Heddon View. Ryton NE40 61 D5
Heddon Way. S Shs NE34 77 B6
Hedgefield Ave. Ryton NE21 61 F5
Hedgefield Cotts. Ryton NE21 61 F5
Hedgefield Gr. Blyth NE24 17 C3
Hedgefield View. Dud NE23 22 A1
Hedgehope Rd. N-u-T NE5 43 A4
Hedgelea. Ryton NE40 61 B5
Hedgelea Rd. E Rain DH5 118 C3
Hedgeley Rd. Hebb NE31 75 E6
Hedgeley Rd. N-u-T NE5 62 E8
Hedgeley Rd. Tyne NE29 50 D7
Hedgeley Terr. N-u-T NE6 68 C2
Hedgerow Mews. Ashgn NE63 6 B2
Hedley Ave. Blyth NE24 17 F6
Hedley Cl. S Shs NE33 51 C4
Hedley Ct. Blyth NE24 17 F6
Hedley La. Kibble NE11 & NE16 98 C6
Hedley Pl. Walls NE28 49 B1
Hedley Rd. N Shs NE29 50 F3
Hedley Rd. S Del NE25 23 E2
Hedley Rd. Wylam NE41 60 B6
Hedley St. Gates NE8 88 D8
Hedley St. N-u-T NE3 39 C1
Hedley St. 5 S Shs NE33 51 C4
Hedley Terr. N-u-T NE3 39 C1
Hedley Terr. Ryhope SR2 117 A6
Hedworth Ave. S Shs NE34 77 A4
Hedworth Ct. Sland SR1 106 B2
Hedworth La. Boldon NE35 76 E1
Hedworth La. Hedw NE32 & NE35 76 D2
Hedworth Lane Jun Sch. Boldon NE35 76 D1
Hedworth Pl. Gates NE9 89 C3
Hedworth Sq. Sland SR1 106 B2
Hedworth St. C le S DH3 112 C3
Hedworth Terr. S Row DH4 114 B6
Hedworth Terr. Sland SR1 106 B2
Hedworthfield Comp Sch. Hedw NE32 76 B1
Hedworthfield Prim Sch. Hedw NE32 76 D1
Heighley St. N-u-T NE15 62 F5
Helen St. Blay NE21 62 A2
Helen St. Sland SR6 93 E4
Helena Ave. W Bay NE26 32 B5
Hellpool La. Hexham NE46 53 F5
Helmdon. Wash NE37 101 E8
Helmsdale Ave. Gates NE10 74 A1
Helmsdale Rd. Sland SR4 104 A1
Helmsley Cl. Pens DH4 114 A6
Helmsley Ct. Sland SR5 92 E3
Helmsley Dr. Walls NE28 49 F2
Helmsley Gn. Gates NE9 89 B2
Helmsley Rd. N-u-T NE2 66 C3
Helston Ct. N-u-T NE15 62 B7
Helvellyn Ave. Wash NE38 101 A3
Helvellyn Rd. Sland SR2 110 A2
Hemel St. C le S DH3 112 C2
Hemlington Cl. 12 Ryhope SR2 116 F6
Hemming St. Sland SR2 110 C2
Hemsley Rd. S Shs NE34 52 A1
Hencotes. Hexham NE46 54 A4
Henderson Ave. Whick NE16 87 A8
Henderson Cl. Hexham NE46 53 F3
Henderson Ct. N Shs NE29 50 F3
Henderson Gdns. Gates NE10 90 B8
Henderson Rd. S Shs NE34 76 F4
Henderson Rd. Sland SR4 104 C2
Henderson Rd. Walls NE28 49 B3
Henderson Rd. Walls NE28 49 B4
Hendon Burn Ave. Sland SR2 106 B1
Hendon Burn Ave W. Sland SR2 110 B4
Hendon Cl. Sland SR1 106 B2
Hendon Gdns. Hedw NE32 76 D2
Hendon Rd. Gates NE8 & NE9 89 B8
Hendon Rd. Sland SR1 & SR2 106 B2
Hendon Rd. Sland SR1 106 B3
Hendon Rd E. Sland SR1 106 C2
Hendon Sq. Sland SR1 106 B2
Hendon St. Sland SR1 106 C2
Hendon Valley Ct. Sland SR2 110 B4
Hendon Valley Rd. Sland SR2 106 B1
Henley Cl. Cram NE23 22 D7
Henley Gdns. Walls NE28 50 B4
Henley Rd. Sland SR4 104 A1
Henley Rd. Tyne NE30 32 C1
Henley Sq. Lmth NE61 2 A3
Henley Way. Boldon NE35 91 E8
Henlow Rd. N-u-T NE15 62 C7
Henry Nelson St. S Shs NE33 51 D4
Henry Sq. N-u-T NE2 66 C2
Henry St. H le H DH5 119 A5
Henry St. H-le-Sp DH5 114 E1
Henry St. N Shs NE29 51 A4
Henry St. N-u-T NE3 39 C1
Henry St. S Row DH4 114 B6
Henry St. S Shs NE33 51 B6
Henry St E. Sland SR2 106 C2
Henry Terr. Gr Lum DH4 113 F2
Hensby Ct. N-u-T NE5 43 B4
Henshaw Gr. S Del NE25 23 F2
Henshaw Pl. N-u-T NE5 63 B3
Henshelwood Terr. N-u-T NE2 46 B1
Henson Cl. Wash NE38 101 D4
Hepburn Gdns. Gates NE10 73 C1
Hepple Ct. Blyth NE24 17 C6
Hepple Rd. N-b-t-S NE64 7 C3
Hepple Way. N-u-T NE3 39 A2
Hepscott Dr. W Bay NE25 31 D6
Hepscott Terr. S Shs NE34 77 D8
Hepscott Wlk. Pegs NE61 4 E3
Hepworth View. Hedw NE32 76 D3
Herbert St. Gates NE8 73 A1
Herbert Terr. Sland SR5 93 B5
Herd Cl. Blay NE21 62 A1
Herd House La. Blay NE21 61 F2
Herdinghill. Wash NE37 100 F6
Herdlaw. Cram NE23 22 A6
Hereford Ct. N-u-T NE13 38 A4
Hereford Rd. Sland SR2 110 A1
Hereford Sq. Sland SR2 110 A1
Hereford Way. Hedw NE32 76 B2
Hermiston. W Bay NE25 31 E5
Hermitage Pk. C le S DH3 112 C1
Heron Cl. Ashgn NE63 6 E1
Heron Cl. Blyth NE24 17 E4
Heron Cl. Wash NE38 101 A2
Heron Dr. S Shs NE33 51 C4
Heron Pl. Lbtn NE12 41 A3
Herrick St. N-u-T NE5 43 A3
Herring Gull Cl. Blyth NE24 17 E3
Herrington Mews. N Herr DH4 114 E6
Herrington Rd. Sland SR3 115 B6
Hersham Cl. N-u-T NE13 38 A4
Hertburn Gdns. Wash NE37 101 D7
Hertburn Ind Est. Wash NE37 101 E7
Hertford. Gates NE9 88 F2
Hertford Ave. S Shs NE34 78 C7
Hertford Cl. W Bay NE25 31 D6
Hertford Cres. H le H DH5 118 F4
Hertford Gr. Cram NE23 22 C7
Hesket Ct. N-u-T NE3 38 B3
Hesleyside. Ashgn NE63 6 F1
Hesleyside Dr. N-u-T NE5 63 C4
Hesleyside Rd. Ears NE25 31 B5
Hessewelle Cres. Hasw DH6 121 E1
Hester Ave. E Cram NE25 23 D6
Hester Bungalows. E Cram NE25 23 D6
Hester Gdns. E Cram NE25 23 E6
Heswall Rd. Cram NE23 16 A2
Hetton Lyons Ind Est. H le H DH5 119 B3
Hetton Lyons Inf Sch. H le H DH5 119 A2
Hetton Lyons Jun Sch. H le H DH5 119 A2
Hetton Prim Sch. H le H DH5 118 F3
Hetton Rd. H-le-Sp DH5 118 E7
Hetton Sch. H le H DH5 118 F3
Heugh Hill. Spring NE9 90 A2
Hewitson Terr. Gates NE10 89 C8
Hewitt Ave. Sland SR2 116 E8
Hewley Cres. Tley NE15 35 D1
Heworth Burn Cres. Gates NE10 89 E8
Heworth Cres. 1 Wash NE37 101 D8
Heworth Ct. S Shs NE34 77 A5
Heworth Dene Gdns. Gates NE6 74 B1
Heworth Golf Course. Gates NE10 90 C6
Heworth Gr. Wash NE37 101 C8
Heworth Grange Comp Sch. Gates NE10 89 F8
Heworth Rd. Wash NE37 90 D1
Heworth Sta (British Rail & Metro). Gates NE10 89 F8
Heworth Way. Gates NE10 90 A8
Hewson Pl. Gates NE9 89 B6
Hexham. Wash NE38 100 F4
Hexham Ave. Cram NE23 22 D7
Hexham Ave. Hebb NE31 75 E3
Hexham Ave. N-u-T NE6 68 C1
Hexham Cl. Tyne NE29 50 C7
Hexham Ct. Duns NE11 87 F6
Hexham Cty Mid Sch. Hexham NE46 54 B4
Hexham East Cty Fst Sch. Hexham NE46 54 C4
Hexham General Hospl. Hexham NE46 54 C4
Hexham Old Rd. Ryton NE21 & NE40 61 E5
Hexham Priory Sch. Hexham NE46 54 C4
Hexham Race Course. Hexham NE46 53 D1
Hexham Rd. H-o-t-W NE15 34 E2
Hexham Rd. Sland SR4 104 A1
Hexham Rd. Tley NE15 35 C2
Hexham Rd. Whick NE16 69 A1
Hexham Sta. Hexham NE46 54 C5
Hexham Wlk. Gates NE8 72 A3
Hextol Cres. Hexham NE46 54 A4
Hextol Gdns. N-u-T NE15 62 F7
Hextol Terr. Hexham NE46 53 F4
Heybrook Ave. Tyne NE29 50 F8
Heyburn Gdns. N-u-T NE15 64 A2
Hi-Tec Village. Boldon NE36 91 D7
Hibernia Rd. N-u-T NE6 75 A4
Hibernian Rd. Jarrow NE32 76 B7
Hickling Ct. N-u-T NE5 43 C4
Hickstead Cl. Walls NE28 49 E7
Hickstead Gr. Cram NE23 22 D7
Hiddleston Ave. N-u-T NE7 41 B1
Higgins Terr. N Silk SR3 116 B7
High Axwell. Blay NE21 62 D2
High Back Cl. Hebb NE32 76 A4
High Barnes Terr. Sland SR4 105 A1
High Bridge. N-u-T NE1 & NE99 66 A1
High Burswell. Hexham NE46 53 F5
High Chare. C le S DH3 112 D3
High Cl. Prud NE42 59 F3
High Croft. Wash NE37 90 C1
High Croft Cl. Hebb NE31 75 D4
High Dene. N-u-T NE7 47 B1
High Downs Sq. H le H DH5 119 A5
High Farm Mid Sch. Walls NE28 49 B5
High Fell Sch. Gates NE9 89 A7
High Flatworth. N Shs NE29 50 B4
High Friar La. N-u-T NE1 66 A1
High Garth. Sland SR1 106 B3
High Gate The. N-u-T NE3 44 B4
High Gr. Ryton NE40 61 D4
High Hamsterley Rd. H Mill NE39 96 A5
High Hedgefield Terr. Ryton NE40 61 E5
High Heworth La. Gates NE10 89 E7
High Horse Cl. R Gill NE39 86 A4
High Horse Close Wood. R Gill NE39 86 A4
High House Gdns. Gates NE10 74 B1
High Lane Row. Hebb NE31 75 F7
High Lanes. Gates NE10 89 F7
High Laws. N-u-T NE3 & NE7 46 C4
High Level Rd. Gates NE8 72 B3
High Market. Ashgn NE63 6 A4
High Meadow. S Shs NE34 77 F8
High Meadows. N-u-T NE3 44 B3
High Mill Rd. H Mill NE39 96 A5
High Moor. Mpeth NE61 8 D7
High Moor Ct. N-u-T NE5 44 B2
High Moor Pl. S Shs NE34 77 C5
High Pasture. Wash NE38 101 E1
High Pk. Mpeth NE61 9 A7
High Primrose Hill. Bourn DH4 113 D3
High Quay. Blyth NE24 17 F8
High Rd The. S Shs NE34 78 A6
High Reach. Gates NE10 75 A2
High Ridge. Hazle NE13 28 B4
High Row. Gr Lum DH4 113 E1
High Row. N-u-T NE15 62 C6
High Row. Ryton NE40 61 E4
High Row. Wash NE37 90 D1
High Sandgrove. Clea SR6 78 A1
High Shaw. Prud NE42 59 B1
High Spen Ct. H Spen NE39 85 A4
High Spen Prim Jun & Inf Sch. H Spen NE39 84 F3
High St. Blyth NE24 17 D7
High St. Blyth NE24 17 E7
High St. Chopp NE62 10 E6
High St. E Lane DH5 119 C1
High St. G Post NE62 10 E7
High St. Gates NE8 72 C3
High St. Gates NE9 89 C3
High St. 2 Gates NE10 89 D8
High St. H Pitt DH6 120 B6
High St. Jarrow NE32 76 C7
High St. Jarrow NE32 76 D7
High St. N-b-t-S NE64 7 F5
High St. N-u-T NE3 45 C4
High St. Newb NE15 61 F7
High St. Sland SR4 103 A2
High St E. Sland SR1 106 B3
High St E. Walls NE28 49 C1
High St W. N-u-T NE28 & NE6 49 A1
High St W. Sland SR1 105 C3
High St W. Sland SR1 106 A3
High St W. Walls NE28 & NE6 49 A1
High Stobhill. Mpeth NE61 9 A6
High Swinburne Pl. N-u-T NE4 65 B1
High Usworth Cty Inf Sch. Wash NE37 90 C1
High Usworth Cty Jun Sch. Wash NE37 90 C1
High View. H o t H NE43 82 F3
High View. Pont NE20 25 D2
High View. Walls NE28 49 B3
High View N. Walls NE28 49 B4
High Well Gdns. Gates NE6 74 B1
High West St. Gates NE8 72 C2
Higham Pl. N-u-T NE1 66 B2
Highburn. Cram NE23 22 A5
Highbury. Gates NE10 89 E8
Highbury. N-u-T NE2 46 A2
Highbury. W Bay NE25 31 E5
Highbury Ave. Spring NE9 90 A2
Highbury Cl. Spring NE9 90 A2
Highbury Pl. N Shs NE29 50 F6
Highcliffe Gdns. Gates NE8 89 A8
Highcroft Dr. Whit SR6 78 E1
Highcroft Pk. Whit SR6 78 F1
Highcross Rd. Tyne NE25 & NE30 32 A3
Highfield. Birt DH3 100 C6
Highfield. Prud NE42 59 D2
Highfield. Sunn NE16 87 B3
Highfield Ave. Lbtn NE12 42 A4
Highfield Cl. N-u-T NE5 36 F3
Highfield Cres. C le S DH3 112 C5
Highfield Ct. Gates NE10 89 E7
Highfield Cty Inf Sch. S Shs NE34 52 A1
Highfield Day Hospl. C le S DH3 112 C5
Highfield Dr. Ashgn NE63 7 A2
Highfield Dr. Fence DH4 118 B7
Highfield Dr. S Shs NE34 77 F8
Highfield Gdns. C le S DH3 112 C5
Highfield Grange. Fence DH4 118 B7
Highfield Jun & Inf Schs. R Gill NE39 85 C2
Highfield La. Prud NE42 59 C1
Highfield Pl. B Vill NE13 28 A5
Highfield Rd. Gates NE8 73 A1
Highfield Rd. N-u-T NE5 36 F3
Highfield Rd. R Gill NE39 85 C1
Highfield Rd. S Row DH4 114 A6
Highfield Rd. S Shs NE33 & NE34 77 F8
Highfield Rise. C le S DH3 112 C5
Highfield Terr. N-u-T NE6 75 A4
Highfield Terr. Prud NE42 59 B2
Highford Gdns. Mpeth NE61 8 E7
Highford La. Hexham NE46 53 E4
Highgate Gdns. Hedw NE32 76 D2
Highgate Rd. Sland SR4 104 A1
Highgreen Chase. Whick NE16 87 A4
Highgrove. N-u-T NE5 36 D2
Highheath. Wash NE37 101 A6
Highland Rd. N-u-T NE5 44 A3
Highlaws Gdns. Gates NE9 89 B2
Highridge. Birt DH3 100 C5
Highside Dr. Sland SR3 109 A3
Highstead Ave. Cram NE23 16 A1
Hightree Cl. Silk SR3 115 F5
Highwell La. N-u-T NE5 36 E1
Highwood Rd. N-u-T NE15 62 F7
Highworth Dr. N-u-T NE7 48 A3
Highworth Dr. Spring NE9 89 F1
Hilda Pk. C le S DH2 112 B5
Hilda St. Gates NE8 72 A1
Hilda St. Sland SR6 93 D3
Hilda Terr. C le S DH2 112 B4
Hilda Terr. Tley NE15 35 D2
Hilden Bldgs. N-u-T NE7 47 C2
Hilden Gdns. N-u-T NE7 47 C2
Hill Ave. Seg NE23 23 A2
Hill Brow. N Silk SR3 116 B6
Hill Crest. Burnop NE16 97 B6
Hill Crest. Gates NE10 89 E6
Hill Crest Gdns. N-u-T NE2 46 B4
Hill Croft. Hors NE15 33 C1
Hill Dyke. Gates NE9 89 C2
Hill Gate. Mpeth NE61 9 A8
Hill Head Dr. N-u-T NE5 36 D1
Hill Head Rd. N-u-T NE5 36 D2
Hill House Rd. Tley NE15 35 C2
Hill La. Pens DH4 102 C1
Hill Park Rd. Jarrow NE32 76 C5
Hill Pk. Pont NE20 25 D2
Hill Rise. Craw NE40 60 F3
Hill Rise. Wash NE38 101 E6
Hill Sq. Sland SR1 106 B2
Hill St. Crbdge NE45 55 F5
Hill St. Jarrow NE32 76 A7
Hill St. N Silk SR3 116 A7
Hill St. S Shs NE33 51 B1
Hill Terr. N Herr DH4 114 E6
Hill The. Oham NE42 59 B4
Hill Top. Birt DH3 100 D4
Hill Top. Blay NE21 62 B1
Hill Top Ave. Gates NE9 89 B5
Hill Top Cl. Stake NE62 10 F8
Hill Top Gdns. Gates NE9 89 A5
Hill View Gdns. Sland SR3 109 B3
Hill View Inf Sch. Sland SR2 110 A2
Hill View Jun Sch. Sland SR2 110 A2
Hill View Rd. Sland SR2 110 A2
Hill View Sq. Sland SR2 110 A2
Hillary Ave. Lbtn NE12 42 B4
Hillary Pl. N-u-T NE5 43 A3
Hillcrest. Ashgn NE63 7 A2
Hillcrest. Hedw NE32 76 D2
Hillcrest. Prud NE42 59 D2
Hillcrest. S Shs NE34 78 B5
Hillcrest. Sland SR3 115 B8
Hillcrest. W Bay NE25 31 E5
Hillcrest Ave. G Post NE62 10 F8
Hillcrest Ct. Prud NE42 59 D2
Hillcrest Dr. Duns NE11 87 E7
Hillcrest Dr. Hexham NE46 54 C4
Hillcrest Sch. Cram NE23 22 B6
Hillcroft. 4 Birt DH3 100 C5
Hillcroft. Gates NE9 89 A6
Hillcroft. R Gill NE39 85 C2
Hillfield. W Bay NE25 31 D5
Hillfield Gdns. Sland SR3 109 B3
Hillfield St. Gates NE8 72 B2
Hillford Terr. Chopw NE17 84 B1
Hillgate. Gates NE8 72 B4
Hillhead Gdns. Duns NE11 88 A6
Hillhead La. Byer NE16 86 D2
Hillhead Parkway. N-u-T NE5 36 C2
Hillhead Way. N-u-T NE5 36 E3
Hillheads Rd. W Bay NE25 32 A4
Hillingdon Gr. Sland SR4 107 A2
Hillrise Cres. Seaton SR7 116 D1
Hills St. Gates NE8 72 B3
Hillsden Rd. W Bay NE25 31 D7
Hillside. Blay NE21 62 B1
Hillside. Boldon NE36 92 A7
Hillside. C le S DH3 112 C4
Hillside. Duns NE11 87 F7
Hillside. Kill NE12 29 E2
Hillside. Mpeth NE61 8 F7
Hillside. Pont NE20 25 C1
Hillside. S Shs NE34 78 B4
Hillside. Sland SR3 109 C3
Hillside Ave. N-u-T NE15 62 F8
Hillside Cl. R Gill NE39 85 E3
Hillside Cres. N-u-T NE15 69 A4
Hillside Dr. Whit SR6 78 E1
Hillside Gdns. Sland SR3 109 C3
Hillside Grove. H Pitt DH6 120 B5
Hillside Pl. Gates NE9 89 A6
Hillside Rd. Hexham NE46 54 D4
Hillside Way. H-le-Sp DH4 & DH5 114 E1
Hillsleigh Rd. N-u-T NE5 44 A2
Hillsview Ave. N-u-T NE3 38 B1
Hillsview Prim Sch. N-u-T NE3 38 A2
Hillthorne Cl. Wash NE38 101 E4
Hilltop Gdns. N Silk SR3 116 C7
Hillview. Sland SR3 115 B7
Hillview Cres. New DH4 114 D3
Hillview Gr. New DH4 114 D3
Hillview Rd. New DH4 114 D3
Hilton Ave. N-u-T NE5 43 B2
Hilton Cl. Cram NE23 16 A2
Hind St. Sland SR1 105 C2
Hindley Cl. Craw NE40 60 E3
Hindley Gdns. N-u-T NE4 64 A3
Hindmarch Dr. Boldon NE35 & NE36 92 B7
Hindson's Cres N. S Row DH4 114 A5
Hindson's Cres S. S Row DH4 114 A5
Hinkley Cl. Silk SR3 116 B6
Hippingstones La. Crbdge NE45 55 F6
Hipsburn Dr. Sland SR3 109 A3
Hiram Dr. Boldon NE36 92 D7
Hirst Cty High Sch. Ashgn NE63 6 F2
Hirst Head. Bed NE22 11 A1
Hirst Park Cty Mid Sch. Ashgn NE63 6 F3
Hirst Terr N. Bed NE22 11 A1
Hirst Villas. Bed NE22 11 B1
Histon Ct. N-u-T NE5 43 B3
Histon Way. N-u-T NE5 43 B3
Hither Gn. Hedw NE32 76 D2
Hobart. W Bay NE26 31 F7
Hobart Ave. B Wh NE34 76 F3
Hodgkin Park Cres. N-u-T NE15 63 C1
Hodgkin Park Rd. N-u-T NE15 63 C1
Hodgson Terr. 6 Wash NE37 101 F8
Hodgson's Rd. Blyth NE24 12 D1
Hodkin Gdns. Gates NE9 89 B6
Hogarth Cotts. Bed NE22 16 A8
Hogarth Dr. Wash NE38 101 E3
Hogarth Rd. White NE34 77 C2
Holbein Rd. White NE34 77 C3
Holborn Pl. N-u-T NE5 36 E1
Holborn Rd. Sland SR4 104 A1
Holborn Sq. Sland SR4 108 A4
Holburn Cl. Ryton NE40 61 D5
Holburn Cres. Ryton NE40 61 E5
Holburn Gdns. Ryton NE40 61 E5
Holburn La. Ryton NE40 61 D6
Holburn Lane Ct. Ryton NE40 61 D6
Holburn Terr. Ryton NE40 61 E5
Holburn Way. Ryton NE40 61 D5
Holburn Wlk. Gates NE8 72 A3
Holburn Wlk. Ryton NE40 61 E5
Holden Pl. N-u-T NE5 44 A2
Holder House La. White NE34 77 E3
Holder House Way. White NE34 77 E2
Holderness Rd. N-u-T NE6 47 B1
Holderness Rd. Walls NE28 50 B3
Hole La. Sunn NE16 87 B3
Holeyn Hall Rd. Wylam NE41 60 A7
Holeyn Rd. Tley NE15 35 C1
Holland Dr. N-u-T NE2 & NE4 65 B3
Holland Park Dr. Hedw NE32 76 D2
Holland Pk. Walls NE28 48 B3
Holley Park Prim Sch. Wash NE38 101 A3
Hollinghill Rd. S Del NE25 23 E2
Hollings Cres. Walls NE28 49 B4
Hollings Terr. Chopw NE17 84 A1
Hollingside Way. S Shs NE34 77 D5
Hollington Ave. Lbtn NE12 41 B2
Hollington Cl. Lbtn NE12 41 B2
Hollinhill. R Gill NE39 86 A5
Hollinhill La. R Gill NE39 85 F4
Hollinhill Rd. Wash NE37 101 E7
Hollinside Cl. Whick NE16 87 A5
Hollinside Gdns. N-u-T NE15 63 B2
Hollinside Rd. Sland SR4 108 A4
Hollinside Rd. Whick NE16 69 B2
Hollinside Sq. Sland SR4 103 C1
Hollinside Terr. R Gill NE39 85 D2
Hollon St. Mpeth NE61 3 E1
Hollow The. Hedw NE32 76 B2
Hollowdene. H le H DH5 119 A3
Hollows The. Ashgn NE63 7 B2
Holly Ave. Duns NE11 87 F7
Holly Ave. Ears NE25 31 B5
Holly Ave. H-le-Sp DH5 118 F8
Holly Ave. Lbtn NE12 29 D1
Holly Ave. Mpeth NE61 8 E7
Holly Ave. N Silk SR3 116 B8
Holly Ave. N-b-t-S NE64 7 C5
Holly Ave. N-u-T NE3 38 C2
Holly Ave. N-u-T NE2 46 C1
Holly Ave. Ryton NE40 61 C6
Holly Ave. S Shs NE34 78 A5
Holly Ave. W Bay NE26 32 A5
Holly Ave. Walls NE28 49 C1
Holly Ave. Whit SR6 93 F8
Holly Ave. Win M NE21 86 C6
Holly Ave W. N-u-T NE2 46 B1
Holly Cl. Kill NE12 29 C4
Holly Cres. Wash NE38 101 C1
Holly Ct. N-u-T NE5 43 B2
Holly Ct. Sland SR4 105 A2
Holly Gdns. Gates NE9 88 F6
Holly Gr. Prud NE42 59 B3
Holly Haven. E Rain DH5 118 D4
Holly Hill. Gates NE10 89 D8
Holly House. Blyth NE24 17 B5
Holly Mews. W Bay NE26 32 A5
Holly Park View. Gates NE10 89 D8
Holly Rd. Tyne NE29 50 F7
Holly St. Ashgn NE63 6 D3
Holly St. Jarrow NE32 76 A7
Holly Terr. Burnop NE16 97 C5
Holly View. Gates NE10 89 C8
Hollycarrside Rd. Sland SR2 116 E8
Hollycrest. C le S DH2 112 B5
Hollydene. Kibble NE11 99 D6
Hollydene. R Gill NE39 85 F2
Hollyhock. Hebb NE31 75 E3
Hollymount Sq. Bed NE22 16 A8
Hollymount Terr. Bed NE22 16 A8
Hollys The. Birt DH3 100 B7
Hollystone Ct. Gates NE8 72 A1
Hollywell Gr. Wools NE13 36 F8
Hollywell Rd. N Shs NE29 50 D6
Hollywood Ave. N-u-T NE3 40 A2
Hollywood Ave. N-u-T NE6 49 A1
Hollywood Ave. Sland SR5 92 F2
Hollywood Cres. N-u-T NE3 40 A2
Hollywood Gdns. Duns NE11 88 B5
Holm Gn. W Bay NE25 31 D4
Holmcroft. N-b-t-S NE64 7 E5
Holmdale. Ashgn NE63 6 C2
Holme Ave. N-u-T NE6 48 C1
Holme Ave. Whick NE16 87 B7
Holme Gdns. Sland SR3 109 B3
Holme Gdns. Walls NE28 50 A2
Holme Rise. Whick NE16 87 B7
Holmesdale Rd. N-u-T NE5 44 A1
Holmeside. Sland SR1 106 A2
Holmewood Dr. R Gill NE39 96 D8
Holmfield Ave. S Shs NE34 77 E7
Holmland. N-u-T NE15 69 C4
Holmlands. W Bay NE25 31 E5
Holmlands Cl. W Bay NE25 31 E5
Holmlands Pk. C le S DH3 112 D2
Holmlands Pk N. Sland SR2 109 C4
Holmlands Pk S. Sland SR3 109 C4
Holmside Ave. Duns NE11 88 A8
Holmwood Ave. N-b-t-S NE64 7 D5
Holmwood Ave. W Bay NE25 31 D4
Holmwood Gr. N-u-T NE2 46 A2
Holwick Cl. Wash NE38 101 A2
Holy Cross RC Prim Sch. Walls NE28 49 F4
Holy Island. Hexham NE46 54 A5
Holylake Sq. Sland SR4 104 A1
Holyoake Gdns. Birt DH3 100 C4
Holyoake Gdns. Gates NE9 88 F8
Holyoake St. Prud NE42 59 D3
Holyoake Terr. 8 Wash NE37 101 D8
Holyrood Rd. Sland SR2 110 C2
Holystone Ave. Blyth NE24 17 C5
Holystone Ave. N-u-T NE3 39 B2
Holystone Ave. W Bay NE25 & NE30 32 B4
Holystone Cl. Blyth NE24 17 B5
Holystone Cl. Burn DH4 114 B2
Holystone Cres. N-u-T NE7 47 B2
Holystone Cty Prim Sch. Lbtn NE27 30 C2
Holystone Dr. Lbtn NE27 30 C2
Holystone Gdns. Tyne NE29 50 D8
Holystone St. Hebb NE31 75 D6
Holywell Ave. Holy NE25 23 F2
Holywell Ave. N-u-T NE6 74 B3
Holywell Ave. W Bay NE26 31 F6
Holywell Cl. Blay NE21 62 D1
Holywell Cl. Holy NE25 23 F2
Holywell Cl. N-u-T NE2 & NE4 65 B2
Holywell Cty Fst Sch. Holy NE25 23 F2
Holywell Dene Rd. Holy NE25 23 F2
Holywell Mews. W Bay NE26 31 F6
Holywell Terr. Shire NE27 30 D1
Home Ave. 2 Gates NE9 88 F4
Home Farm Cl. Ashgn NE63 5 F4
Home Pk. Walls NE28 48 B3
Homedale. Hexham NE46 54 C4
Homedale. Prud NE42 59 E2
Homedale Pl. Prud NE42 59 E1
Homedowne House. N-u-T NE3 39 C1
Homeforth House. N-u-T NE3 39 C1
Homeside Pl. N-u-T NE6 67 B3
Homestall Cl. S Shs NE34 77 D5
Honeycomb Cl. 7 Silk SR3 115 F5
Honeysuckle Ave. S Shs NE34 77 B5
Honeysuckle Cl. Silk SR3 116 A5
Honister Ave. N-u-T NE2 46 B3
Honister Cl. N-u-T NE15 62 D7
Honister Dr. Sland SR5 93 C3
Honister Pl. N-u-T NE15 62 D7
Honister Rd. Tyne NE30 32 B2
Honister Way. Blyth NE24 17 C3
Honiton Ct. N-u-T NE3 37 B2
Honiton Way. Tyne NE29 50 B8
Hood Cl. Sland SR5 93 C1
Hood St. Mpeth NE61 3 F1
Hood St. N-u-T NE1 66 A1
Hood St. Whick NE16 69 A1
Hookergate Comp Sch. H Spen NE39 85 B3
Hookergate La. H Spen NE39 85 A2
Hope Shield. Wash NE38 100 F1
Hope St. Jarrow NE32 76 C7
Hope St. S Shs NE34 77 B5
Hope St. Sland SR1 105 C2
Hope View. Sland SR2 116 F7
Hopedene. Gates NE10 90 A5
Hopgarth Ct. C le S DH3 112 D4
Hopgarth Gdns. C le S DH3 112 D4
Hopkins Wlk. B Hall NE34 77 A2
Hopper Pl. Gates NE8 72 C3
Hopper Rd. Gates NE10 89 C7
Hopper St. Gates NE8 72 C3
Hopper St. 5 N Shs NE29 50 F5
Hopper St. Walls NE28 49 B2
Horatio St. N-u-T NE1 67 A1
Horatio St. Sland SR6 93 E1
Hornbeam Pl. N-u-T NE4 71 B3
Horncliffe Gdns. Whick NE16 87 C8
Horncliffe Pl. Tley NE15 35 B2
Horncliffe Wlk. N-u-T NE15 62 A7
Horning Ct. N-u-T NE5 43 B4
Hornsea Cl. B Vill NE13 28 B5
Hornsey Cres. H le H DH5 119 B1
Hornsey Terr. H le H DH5 119 B1
Horse Crofts. Blay NE21 62 C3
Horsegate Bank. H Spen NE17 84 D5
Horsham Gdns. Sland SR3 109 A3
Horsham Gr. N Shs NE29 50 E4
Horsley Ave. Craw NE40 60 E3
Horsley Ave. Shire NE27 30 F2
Horsley Cl. Stake NE62 10 F8
Horsley Ct. N-u-T NE3 38 B2
Horsley Gdns. Duns NE11 88 A8
Horsley Gdns. S Del NE25 23 F2
Horsley Gr. Sland SR3 109 A3
Horsley Hill Rd. S Shs NE33 51 E1
Horsley Hill Sq. S Shs NE34 78 B7

Horsley Rd. N-u-T NE7 47 B2
Horsley Rd. Oham NE42 59 A5
Horsley Rd. Wash NE38 101 F5
Horsley Rd. Wash NE38 102 A5
Horsley Terr. N-u-T NE6 68 C1
Horsley Terr. 12 Tyne NE30 51 D7
Horsley Vale. S Shs NE34 78 A8
Horsley View. Prud NE42 59 F3
Horsley Wood Cotts. Hors NE15 59 D7
Horton Ave. Bed NE22 15 F8
Horton Ave. Shire NE27 30 F2
Horton Ave. White NE34 77 D3
Horton Cres. Dgton NE13 27 B7
Horton Dr. Cram NE23 16 B2
Horton Pl. Blyth NE24 17 B4
Horton Rd. Beb NE24 16 C5
Horton St. Blyth NE24 17 F7
Hortondale Gr. Blyth NE24 17 B7
Horwood Ave. N-u-T NE5 36 E2
Hospital Dr. Hebb NE31 75 D4
Hospital La. N-u-T NE15 62 B8
Hospital La. Newb NE15 62 B8
Hospital of King James The. Gates NE8 73 B1
Hospl of St Mary the Virgin The. N-u-T NE4 71 B4
Hospl of The Holy Jesus. N-u-T NE2 65 B4
Hotch Pudding Pl. N-u-T NE5 36 F1
Hotspur Ave. Bed NE22 15 F8
Hotspur Ave. S Shs NE34 77 F7
Hotspur Ave. W Bay NE25 32 A4
Hotspur Prim Sch. N-u-T NE2 67 A2
Hotspur Rd. Walls NE28 49 A5
Hotspur St. N-u-T NE6 67 A3
Hotspur St. Tyne NE30 51 D8
Houghton Ave. N-u-T NE5 44 A3
Houghton Ave. Tyne NE30 32 B3
Houghton Cut. H-le-Sp DH5 114 E1
Houghton Enterprise Ctr. H-le-Sp DH5 118 E8
Houghton Gate. Bourn DH3 113 B3
Houghton Infant Sch. H-le-Sp DH4 114 D1
Houghton Junior Sch. H-le-Sp DH4 114 D1
Houghton Kepier Sch. H-le-Sp DH4 118 D8
Houghton Prim Sch. H-le-Sp DH5 118 E8
Houghton Rd. H le H DH5 119 A4
Houghton Rd. New DH4 114 D3
Houghton Rd W. H le H DH5 119 A4
Houghton St. Sland SR4 105 A2
Houghton-le-Spring Golf Course. H-le-Sp DH5 119 B7
Houghton-Le-Spring Sch. H-le-Sp DH5 118 D7
Houghtonside. H-le-Sp DH4 114 E1
Houlet Garth. N-u-T NE6 67 C1
Houlskye Cl. N Silk SR3 116 C7
Houndelee Pl. N-u-T NE5 43 C1
Houndslow Dr. Ashgn NE63 6 B2
Hounslow Gdns. Hedw NE32 76 D2
House Terr. Wash NE37 101 D8
Housing La. Medom DH8 & DH9 95 D1
Houston Ct. N-u-T NE4 71 B4
Houston St. N-u-T NE4 71 B4
Houxty Rd. Ears NE25 31 B5
Hovingham Gdns. Sland SR3 109 A3
Howard Gr. Pegs NE61 4 E3
Howard Pl. N-u-T NE3 39 C1
Howard Rd. Mpeth NE61 4 A1
Howard St. Gates NE8 73 B1
Howard St. Gates NE10 89 C6
Howard St. Jarrow NE32 76 C6
Howard St. N Shs NE30 51 B5
Howard St. N-u-T NE1 66 C1
Howard St. Sland SR5 93 D1
Howard Terr. H Spen NE39 84 F4
Howard Terr. Mpeth NE61 3 F1
Howardian Cl. Wash NE38 101 B3
Howarth St. Sland SR4 105 A2
Howarth Terr. Hasw DH6 121 F3
Howat Ave. N-u-T NE5 44 B1
Howburn Cres. Pegs NE61 4 E3
Howdene Rd. N-u-T NE15 62 F6
Howdon Green Ind Est. Walls NE28 50 B2
Howdon La. Walls NE28 50 A2
Howdon Rd. N Shs NE28 & NE29 50 E3
Howdon Sta. Walls NE28 50 A2
Howe Sq. Sland SR4 103 C1
Howe St. Gates NE8 73 A1
Howe St. Hebb NE31 76 A6
Howick Ave. N-u-T NE3 39 A3
Howick Pk. Sland SR6 106 A4
Howlett Hall Rd. N-u-T NE15 62 F6
Howley Ave. Sland SR5 92 C2
Hownam Cl. N-u-T NE3 45 A4
Hoy Cres. Seaham SR7 116 F1
Hoylake Ave. Lbtn NE7 41 C1
Hoyle Ave. N-u-T NE4 64 B2
Hoyle Fold. Silk SR3 116 A4
Hubert St. Boldon NE35 91 F8
Hucklow Gdns. S Shs NE34 77 D5
Huddart Terr. 2 Birt DH3 100 C5
Huddleston Rd. N-u-T NE6 68 A3
Huddlestone Rise. Sland SR6 106 B4
Hudleston. W Bay NE26 32 C4
Hudshaw Gdns. Hexham NE46 54 D4
Hudson Ave. Annit NE23 29 B8
Hudson Ave. Bed NE22 11 B1
Hudson Rd. Sland SR1 106 B2
Hudson Road Prim Sch. Sland SR1 106 B2
Hudson St. Gates NE8 72 B3
Hudson St. N Shs NE30 51 C6
Hudson St. S Shs NE34 77 B6
Hugar Rd. H Spen NE39 85 A3
Hugh Ave. Shire NE27 30 F4
Hugh Gdns. N-u-T NE4 70 A4
Hugh St. Sland SR6 93 E4
Hugh St. Walls NE28 49 B1
Hugh St. Wash NE38 101 F4
Hull St. N-u-T NE4 64 C1
Hulne Ave. Tyne NE30 51 D7
Humber Ct. 11 Silk SR3 115 F6
Humber Gdns. Gates NE8 73 B1
Humber St. Chopw NE17 84 C1
Humbert St. Jarrow NE32 76 B6
Humbledon Sch. Sland SR3 108 C3
Humbledon View. Sland SR2 109 C4
Hume St. N-u-T NE6 67 A1
Hume St. Sland SR4 105 A2
Humford Gn. Blyth NE24 16 F7
Humford Way. Bed NE22 16 A7
Humsford Gr. Cram NE23 22 C8
Humshaugh Cl. Lbtn NE12 49 A8
Humshaugh Rd. N Shs NE29 50 C6
Hunstanton Ct. Gates NE9 88 E3
Hunt Lea. Whick NE16 86 E5
Huntcliffe Ave. Sland SR6 93 E6
Huntcliffe Gdns. N-u-T NE6 48 A1
Hunter Ave. Blyth NE24 17 F6
Hunter Cl. Boldon NE36 92 D6
Hunter House. N-u-T NE6 75 A4
Hunter St. S Row DH4 114 A5
Hunter St. S Shs NE33 51 D1
Hunter Terr. Sland SR2 110 B3
Hunter's Moor Cl. N-u-T NE2 65 B4
Hunter's Moor Hospl. N-u-T NE2 65 B4
Hunter's Pl. N-u-T NE2 65 B4
Hunter's Rd. N-u-T NE3 40 C1
Hunter's Rd. N-u-T NE2 & NE4 & NE99 65 B3
Hunters Cl. N Shs NE29 50 D3
Hunters Ct. N-u-T NE3 40 B1
Hunters Hall Rd. Sland SR4 105 B1
Huntingdon Cl. N-u-T NE13 38 A4
Huntingdon Gdns. Sland SR3 109 A3
Huntingdon Pl. Tyne NE30 51 D7
Huntington Dr. Cram NE23 22 D7
Huntley Cres. Blay NE21 86 A8
Huntley Sq. Sland SR4 104 A1
Huntley Terr. 4 Ryhope SR2 116 F6
Huntly Rd. W Bay NE25 31 D7
Hurst Terr. N-u-T NE6 68 B2
Hurstwood Rd. Sland SR4 109 A4
Hurworth Ave. S Shs NE34 78 B7
Hurworth Pl. Jarrow NE32 76 B6
Hutton Cl. H-le-Sp DH4 118 C8
Hutton Cl. Wash NE38 100 F5
Hutton St. Boldon NE35 76 F1
Hutton St. N-u-T NE3 39 A1
Hutton St. Sland SR4 105 B1
Hutton Terr. Gates NE9 88 F4
Hutton Terr. N-u-T NE2 66 C3
Huxley Cl. B Hall NE34 77 B2
Huxley Cres. Gates NE8 88 D7
Hyacinth Ct. Sland SR4 105 B3
Hyde Pk. Walls NE28 48 C3
Hyde St. S Shs NE33 51 D2
Hyde St. Sland SR2 110 C4
Hyde Terr. N-u-T NE3 40 A1
Hydepark St. Gates NE8 88 D8
Hylton Ave. S Shs NE34 78 B7
Hylton Bank. Sland SR4 103 B2
Hylton Castle Inf Sch. Sland SR5 92 A2
Hylton Castle Jun Sch. Sland SR5 92 A2
Hylton Castle Rd. Sland SR5 92 B1
Hylton Cl. Bed NE22 10 D1
Hylton Ct. Wash NE38 101 B5
Hylton La. Boldon NE36 & SR5 92 A5
Hylton Park. Sland SR5 92 E1
Hylton Rd. Jarrow NE32 76 B4
Hylton Rd. Sland SR4 104 B2
Hylton Red House Prim Sch. Sland SR5 92 D2
Hylton Red House Sch. Sland SR5 92 E4
Hylton St. Gates NE8 73 B1
Hylton St. N Shs NE29 51 A5
Hylton St. New DH4 114 D2
Hylton St. Sland SR4 105 A2
Hylton Terr. 6 N Shs NE29 51 A5
Hylton Terr. Ryhope SR2 116 E6
Hylton Wlk. Sland SR4 103 A1
Hymers Ave. S Shs NE34 76 F4
Hyperion Ave. S Shs NE34 77 A5

Ilderton Pl. N-u-T NE5 62 E8
Ilex St. Gates NE11 88 C6
Ilford Ave. Cram NE23 16 A1
Ilford Pl. Gates NE8 & NE9 89 A8
Ilford Rd. N-u-T NE2 46 A3
Ilford Rd. Walls NE28 49 F3
Ilford Road Sta. N-u-T NE2 46 B3
Ilfracombe Ave. N-u-T NE4 64 B1
Ilfracombe Gdns. Gates NE9 88 F3
Ilfracombe Gdns. W Bay NE26 31 F6
Ilminster Ct. N-u-T NE3 37 C2
Imeary Gr. 9 S Shs NE33 51 D1
Imeary St. S Shs NE33 51 D1
Imperial Bldgs. 9 H-le-Sp DH4 118 E8
Inchberry Cl. N-u-T NE4 70 B4
Inchcliffe Cres. N-u-T NE5 43 C2
Indigo St. Gates NE11 88 C6
Industrial Mus. Wash NE37 101 C7
Industrial Rd. Wash NE37 101 E7
Industry Rd. N-u-T NE6 48 A2
Ingham Gr. Cram NE23 16 A1
Ingham Grange. S Shs NE33 51 E1
Ingham Pl. N-u-T NE2 66 C2
Ingham Row. Wylam NE41 60 B6
Ingleborough Dr. Ryton NE40 61 D4
Ingleby Terr. Lmth NE61 2 A3
Ingleby Terr. Sland SR4 105 A1
Inglemere Pl. N-u-T NE15 63 A2
Ingleside. S Shs NE34 78 B6
Ingleside. Whick NE16 86 F6
Ingleton Ct. Sland SR4 105 B1
Ingleton Dr. Tley NE15 35 B2
Inglewood Cl. Blyth NE24 16 F7
Inglewood Pl. N-u-T NE3 28 C1
Ingoe Ave. N-u-T NE3 38 C3
Ingoe Cl. Blyth NE24 17 C7
Ingoe St. N Shs NE28 50 C2
Ingoe St. N-u-T NE15 62 C6
Ingoldsby Ct. Sland SR4 108 B4
Ingram Ave. N-u-T NE3 38 C4
Ingram Cl. C le S DH2 112 A1
Ingram Cl. Walls NE28 49 F5
Ingram Dr. Blyth NE24 17 B7
Ingram Dr. N-u-T NE5 36 D4
Ingram Terr. N-u-T NE6 75 A6
Inkerman Rd. Wash NE37 90 D1
Inkerman St. Sland SR5 93 A1
Innesmoor. Hebb NE31 75 D7
Inskip Terr. Gates NE8 & NE9 88 F8
Inst for Higher Rabbinical Studies. Gates NE8 72 B1
Institute Rd. Ashgn NE63 6 B4
Inverness Rd. Boldon NE32 & NE34 76 E2
Inverness St. Sland SR6 93 D2
Invincible Dr. N-u-T NE4 71 A3
Iolanthe Cres. N-u-T NE6 68 B3
Iolanthe Terr. S Shs NE33 51 E1
Iona Pl. N-u-T NE6 75 A6
Iona Rd. B Wh NE32 & NE34 76 E3
Iona Rd. Gates NE10 & NE9 89 B7
Irene Ave. Sland SR2 110 C1
Iris Cl. Blay NE21 62 A2
Iris Cres. Ouston DH2 99 F2
Iris Pl. N-u-T NE4 64 A3
Iris St. Gates NE11 88 C6
Iris Steedman House. N-u-T NE4 65 A2
Iris Terr. Bourn DH4 113 E3
Iris Terr. Craw NE40 60 F3
Iroko St. Gates NE11 88 C6
Ironside St. H-le-Sp DH5 114 E1
Irthing. Elling NE61 1 E5
Irthing Ave. N-u-T NE6 74 A4
Irton St. N-u-T NE3 39 C1
Irwin Ave. Walls NE28 49 C3
Isabella Cl. N-u-T NE4 70 B3
Isabella Rd. Blyth NE24 17 C6
Ivanhoe. W Bay NE25 31 E5
Ivanhoe Cres. Sland SR2 109 B4
Ivanhoe Terr. C le S DH3 112 C2
Ivanhoe Terr. Dipton DH9 96 E1
Ivanhoe View. Gates NE9 89 B2
Iveagh Cl. N-u-T NE4 70 A4
Iveson Rd. Hexham NE46 53 E3
Ivor St. Sland SR2 111 A2
Ivy Ave. N-b-t-S NE64 7 C5
Ivy Ave. Ryton NE40 61 C6
Ivy Cl. N-u-T NE4 71 B3
Ivy La. Gates NE9 89 A3
Ivy Pl. Tant DH9 97 C3
Ivy Rd. Lbtn NE12 42 B4
Ivy Rd. N-u-T NE3 45 C4
Ivy Rd. N-u-T NE6 68 C4
Ivy St. Gates NE11 88 C6
Ivy St. S Burn NE13 28 C8
Ivy Terr. Pens DH4 114 B6
Ivymount Rd. N-u-T NE6 47 B1
Ixia St. Gates NE11 88 C6

Jack's Terr. S Shs NE34 77 C5
Jackson Ave. Pont NE20 25 F7
Jackson Rd. Wylam NE41 60 B6
Jackson St. Gates NE8 72 C3
Jackson St. N-u-T NE6 68 C2
Jackson St. Sland SR4 105 A1
Jackson St W. N Shs NE30 51 B6
Jackson Terr. Mpeth NE61 9 A8
Jacques St. Sland SR4 104 C4
Jacques Terr. C le S DH2 112 B4
Jade Cl. N-u-T NE15 62 C8
James Armitage St. Sland SR5 93 B2
James Ave. Shire NE27 30 F4
James Mather St. S Shs NE33 51 D3
James St. N-u-T NE5 36 F2
James St. N-u-T NE4 70 C4
James St. Sland SR5 93 A2
James St. Tanf L DH9 97 F1
James St. Whick NE16 87 A7
James Terr. E Lane DH5 121 B8
James Terr. Fence DH4 118 A8
James Terr. N Silk SR3 116 B7
James Terr. Walls NE28 49 B1
James Williams St. Sland SR1 106 B3
Jameson Dr. Crbdge NE45 56 B7
Jane Eyre Terr. Gates NE8 73 B1
Jane St. H le H DH5 119 A6
Jane St. N-u-T NE6 67 C2
Jane Terr. N-u-T NE6 75 A4
Janet Sq. N-u-T NE6 73 C4
Janet St. N-u-T NE6 67 C1
Janet St. N-u-T NE6 73 C4
Janus Cl. N-u-T NE5 36 C4
Jarrow Bede Burn Jun & Inf Sch. Hebb NE32 76 A4
Jarrow Ellison (C of E) Controlled Jun & Inf Sch. Jarrow NE32 76 B6
Jarrow Epinay Sch. Jarrow NE32 76 C6
Jarrow Hall (Mus). Jarrow NE32 76 D7
Jarrow Hedworthfield St Joseph's RC Jun & Inf Sch. Hedw NE32 76 B1
Jarrow Rd. Jarrow NE32 & NE34 76 F6
Jarrow St Mary RC Jun & Inf Sch. B Wh NE32 76 D3
Jarrow St Peter's C of E Prim Sch. Jarrow NE32 76 C7
Jarrow Sta. Jarrow NE32 76 B7
Jarrow Valley View Cty Jun Mix Sch. Jarrow NE32 76 B4
Jasmin Ave. N-u-T NE5 36 C4
Jasmine Cl. N-u-T NE6 48 B1
Jasmine Ct. Ashgn NE63 6 C1
Jasmine Ct. Sland SR4 105 B3
Jasmine Terr. Birt DH3 100 D4
Jasper Ave. Green NE40 61 B1
Jedburgh Cl. Gates NE8 72 C1
Jedburgh Cl. N-u-T NE5 36 C4
Jedburgh Cl. Tyne NE29 50 E8
Jedburgh Ct. Gates NE11 88 E2
Jedburgh Gdns. N-u-T NE15 63 B2
Jedburgh Rd. S Row DH4 114 B6
Jedmoor. Hebb NE31 75 D7
Jefferson Pl. N-u-T NE4 65 B2
Jellicoe Rd. N-u-T NE6 74 B3
Jenifer Gr. N-u-T NE7 47 A4
Jenison Ave. N-u-T NE15 63 C1
Jennifer Ave. Sland SR5 92 B1
Jersey Sq. Lmth NE61 2 A3
Jervis St. Hebb NE31 75 F6
Jesmond Dene Rd. N-u-T NE2 46 B3
Jesmond Gdns. B Hall NE34 77 C3
Jesmond Gdns. N-u-T NE2 46 C1
Jesmond Park Ct. N-u-T NE7 47 B1
Jesmond Pk E. N-u-T NE7 47 B1
Jesmond Pk W. N-u-T NE7 47 A2
Jesmond Pl. N-u-T NE2 46 B1
Jesmond Rd. N-u-T NE2 66 B3
Jesmond Rd. N-u-T NE2 66 C4
Jesmond Sta. N-u-T NE2 66 C3
Jesmond Terr. W Bay NE26 32 B4
Jesmond Vale. N-u-T NE2 67 A3
Jesmond Vale La. N-u-T NE6 67 B4
Jesmond Vale Terr. N-u-T NE6 67 B4
Jessel St. Gates NE9 88 F4
Jesus' Hospl John George Joicey Mus. N-u-T NE1 66 B1
Jetty The. Gates NE10 75 A2
Joan Ave. Sland SR2 110 C1
Joan St. N-u-T NE4 70 A4
Joannah St. Sland SR5 93 C3
Jobling Ave. Blay NE21 62 B2
Jobling Cres. Mpeth NE61 9 B6
Joel Terr. Gates NE10 75 B2
John & Margaret Common Homes for Aged Miners. Blyth NE24 16 F8
John Ave. Green NE40 61 B1
John Brown Ct. Bed NE22 10 F1
John Candlish Rd. Sland SR4 105 A3
John Clay St. 3 S Shs NE33 51 D1
John Dobson St. N-u-T NE1 & NE99 66 B2
John F Kennedy Est. Wash NE38 101 E5
John F Kennedy Prim Sch. Wash NE38 101 E5
John Reid Rd. S Shs NE34 77 C4
John Spence Community High Sch. Tyne NE30 51 A8
John St. Ashgn NE63 6 C4
John St. Blyth NE24 17 B8
John St. Boldon NE35 91 F8
John St. Ears NE25 31 A5
John St. Fence DH4 118 A8
John St. Gates NE8 73 B1
John St. Gates NE10 74 C1
John St. H le H DH5 119 A3
John St. H-le-Sp DH5 118 F8
John St. N-u-T NE3 39 A1
John St. Pegs NE61 4 F3
John St. 13 Ryhope SR2 117 A6
John St. Sland SR4 103 A3
John St. Sland SR1 106 A3
John St. Tyne NE26 & NE30 32 C3
John St. Walls NE28 49 B2
John Wesley Ct. Prud NE42 59 D2
John Williamson St. S Shs NE33 77 C7
Johnson St. Duns NE11 70 C1
Johnson St. Gates NE8 71 B1
Johnson St. N-u-T NE15 62 C6
Johnson St. S Shs NE33 77 C7
Johnson Terr. H Spen NE39 84 F4
Johnson Terr. 5 Wash NE37 101 F8
Johnsons Villas. G Post NE62 10 B7
Johnston Ave. Hebb NE31 75 D3
Joicey Aged Miners Homes. 6 S Row DH4 114 B6
Joicey Rd. Gates NE9 88 F6
Joicey Road Open Air Sch. Gates NE9 88 F6
Joicey St. Gates NE10 75 A1
Jolliffe St. C le S DH3 112 D1
Jonadab Rd. Gates NE10 75 A2
Jonadab St. Gates NE10 75 A1
Jones St. 3 Birt DH3 100 C4
Jonquil Cl. N-u-T NE5 36 C4
Joseph Cl. N-u-T NE4 70 B4
Joseph Hopper Aged Miners Homes. Birt DH3 100 C7
Joseph Hopper Meml Homes. Gates NE9 89 C6
Joseph Terr. Chopw NE17 84 B1
Jowett Sq. Sland SR5 93 A2
Joyce Cl. Gates NE10 90 D8
Joyce Terr. Sland SR5 92 B1
Jubilee Ave. Gates NE9 89 C1
Jubilee Cotts. Green NE40 84 D7
Jubilee Cotts. H-le-Sp DH4 118 D8
Jubilee Cotts. Lmth NE61 2 A3
Jubilee Cres. N-u-T NE3 39 A1
Jubilee Cres. S Hill DH6 120 D1
Jubilee Ct. Annit NE23 22 B1
Jubilee Ct. Blyth NE24 17 D6
Jubilee Ct. Hebb NE31 76 A6
Jubilee Est. Ashgn NE63 6 D1
Jubilee House. E Lane DH5 119 C1
Jubilee IndEst. Ashgn NE63 6 D1
Jubilee Rd. Blyth NE24 17 E6
Jubilee Rd. N-u-T NE3 39 B1
Jubilee Rd. N-u-T NE1 66 C1
Jubilee Rd. Oving NE42 58 C4
Jubilee Sq. E Lane DH5 119 C1
Jubilee Sq. S Hett DH6 121 F7
Jubilee St. Walls NE28 49 B2
Jubilee Terr. Bed NE22 11 D2
Jubilee Terr. Craw NE40 60 E3
Jubilee Terr. N-b-t-S NE64 7 E4
Jubilee Terr. N-u-T NE6 68 A2
Jubilee Terr. S Burn NE13 28 B8
Jubilee Terr. Tant DH9 97 A2
Jubilee Terr. Wash NE38 102 A2
Jubilee Terr. Whick NE16 69 A1
Julian Ave. N-u-T NE6 68 B3
Julian Ave. S Shs NE33 51 D4
Julian Rd. Gates NE10 90 D8
Julian St. S Shs NE33 51 D4
Juliet Ave. N Shs NE29 50 D6
Juliet St. Ashgn NE63 6 E4
Julius Caesar St. Sland SR5 93 A2
Julius Ct. S Shs NE33 51 C4
June Ave. Win M NE21 86 C6
Juniper Cl. N-u-T NE3 28 D1
Juniper Cl. Sland SR2 110 B4
Juniper Ct. Blay NE21 62 C3
Juniper Wlk. N-u-T NE5 36 D4
Jutland Ave. Hebb NE31 75 E6
Kalmia St. Gates NE11 88 C5
Kane Gdns. Gates NE10 89 C6
Kateregina. Birt DH3 100 D4
Katherine St. Ashgn NE63 6 E4
Katrine Cl. C le S DH2 112 B1
Katrine Ct. Silk SR3 116 A5
Kay's Cotts. Gates NE10 89 C7
Kayll Rd. Sland SR4 104 C2
Kearsley Cl. S Del NE25 23 D3
Kearton Ave. N-u-T NE5 36 C3
Keats Ave. Blyth NE24 17 C5
Keats Ave. Boldon NE35 & NE36 92 B8
Keats Ave. Sland SR5 93 A2
Keats Gr. Ashgn NE63 6 F3
Keats Rd. Newb NE15 62 A6
Keats Wlk. B Hall NE34 77 A3
Keats Wlk. Gates NE8 73 A2
Keeble Ct. Ashgn NE63 7 B3
Keebledale Ave. N-u-T NE6 68 C3
Keele Dr. Cram NE23 21 D6
Keelman's La. Sland SR4 103 B3
Keelman's Rd. Sland SR4 103 B3
Keelmans Terr. Blyth NE24 17 E8
Keelmen's Hospl. N-u-T NE1 66 C1
Keighley Ave. Sland SR5 92 B4
Keighley Sq. Sland SR5 92 A4
Keir Hardie Ave. Gates NE10 90 A8
Keir Hardie Ct. N-b-t-S NE64 7 E5
Keir Hardie St. Fence DH4 118 B8
Keir Hardy Terr. Birt DH3 100 B6
Keith Cl. N-u-T NE4 70 B4
Keith Sq. Sland SR5 92 B4
Keldane Gdns. N-u-T NE4 64 B2
Kelham Sq. Sland SR5 92 A4
Kell Cres. S Hill DH6 120 C1
Kell's Way. R Gill NE39 85 E1
Kellfield Ave. Gates NE9 89 A6
Kellfield Rd. Gates NE9 89 A5
Kells Gdns. Gates NE9 89 A5
Kells La. Gates NE9 88 F5
Kellsway. Gates NE10 89 F5
Kellsway Ct. Gates NE10 89 F5
Kelly Rd. Hebb NE31 75 E3
Kelso Cl. N-u-T NE5 36 C4
Kelso Dr. Tyne NE29 50 E8
Kelso Gdns. Bed NE22 11 C1
Kelso Gdns. N-u-T NE15 63 B2
Kelso Gdns. Walls NE28 50 A4
Kelso Gr. S Row DH4 114 A6
Kelso Pl. Gates NE8 71 B1
Kelson Way. N-u-T NE5 36 C4
Kelston Way. N-u-T NE5 43 C2
Kelvin Close Prim Sch. Gates NE8 88 E8
Kelvin Gdns. Duns NE11 70 C1
Kelvin Gr. Clea SR6 77 E1
Kelvin Gr. Gates NE8 88 D8
Kelvin Gr. N-u-T NE2 66 C3
Kelvin Gr. S Shs NE33 & NE34 51 F1
Kelvin Gr. Sland SR6 93 E2
Kelvin Gr. Tyne NE29 & NE30 51 A8
Kelvin Pl. Lbtn NE12 30 A1
Kemble Sq. Sland SR5 92 B4
Kempton Gdns. Gates NE8 88 C7
Kendal. Birt DH3 100 E2
Kendal Ave. Blyth NE24 17 D6
Kendal Ave. Tyne NE30 32 B2
Kendal Cres. Gates NE9 89 B5
Kendal Dr. Boldon NE36 92 C8
Kendal Dr. Cram NE23 22 C8
Kendal Gdns. Walls NE28 50 A4
Kendal Gn. N-u-T NE6 67 B2
Kendal House. N-u-T NE6 67 B2
Kendal Pl. N-u-T NE6 67 B2
Kendal St. N-u-T NE6 67 B1
Kendale Wlk. N-u-T NE5 36 E3
Kendor Gr. Mpeth NE61 8 F6
Kenilworth. Kill NE12 29 D4
Kenilworth Ct. N-u-T NE4 71 A4
Kenilworth Ct. 4 Wash NE37 101 F8
Kenilworth Rd. Ashgn NE63 6 C3
Kenilworth Rd. N-u-T NE4 71 A4
Kenilworth Rd. W Bay NE25 31 F4
Kenilworth Sq. Sland SR5 92 C4
Kenilworth View. 7 Gates NE9 89 A2
Kenilworth Wlk. Wash NE37 101 F8
Kenley Rd. N-u-T NE5 63 A4
Kenmoor Way. N-u-T NE5 36 C3
Kenmore Cres. Green NE40 61 B2
Kennersdene. Tyne NE30 51 C8
Kennet Ave. Hedw NE32 76 C3
Kennet Sq. Sland SR5 92 B4
Kennford. Gates NE9 89 A2
Kennington Gr. N-u-T NE6 68 B1
Kensington Ave. N-u-T NE3 39 C3
Kensington Cl. W Bay NE25 31 F5
Kensington Cotts. Mpeth NE61 9 B8
Kensington Ct. S Shs NE33 77 E8
Kensington Gdns. 1 N Shs NE30 51 B6
Kensington Gdns. W Bay NE25 31 F6
Kensington Gdns. Walls NE28 48 B3
Kensington Gr. N Shs NE30 51 B7
Kensington Terr. Duns NE11 87 F8
Kensington Terr. N-u-T NE2 66 A3
Kensington Villas. N-u-T NE5 36 E3
Kent Ave. 3 Duns NE11 88 A8
Kent Ave. Hebb NE31 75 D5
Kent Ave. Walls NE28 49 F2
Kent Cl. Ashgn NE63 6 A4
Kent Ct. N-u-T NE13 38 A4
Kent Gdns. H le H DH5 118 F4
Kent Pl. S Shs NE34 78 A6
Kent St. Jarrow NE32 76 A6
Kent Terr. Hasw DH6 121 E1
Kentchester Rd. Sland SR5 92 C4
Kentmere. Birt DH3 100 E1
Kentmere Ave. N-u-T NE6 68 C3
Kentmere Ave. Sland SR6 93 C5
Kentmere Cl. Seg NE23 23 A2
Kenton Ave. N-u-T NE3 45 A3
Kenton Bank. N-u-T NE5 37 C1
Kenton Bar Prim Sch. N-u-T NE5 44 A4
Kenton Cres. N-u-T NE3 44 C4
Kenton Ct. S Shs NE33 51 D1
Kenton Gr. Sland SR6 93 D1
Kenton La. N-u-T NE3 44 B4
Kenton Lodge (Residential Special Sch). N-u-T NE3 45 B2
Kenton Park Sh Ctr. N-u-T NE3 45 A4
Kenton Rd. N-u-T NE3 45 A3
Kenton Rd. Tyne NE29 50 C7
Kenton Sch. N-u-T NE5 44 B4
Kentucky Rd. Sland SR5 92 A4
Kenwood Gdns. Gates NE9 89 A2
Kenya Rd. Sland SR5 92 C4
Kepier Chare Prim Sch. Craw NE40 60 F3
Kepier Gdns. Sland SR4 103 A2
Keppel St. Duns NE11 70 C1
Keppel St. 4 S Shs NE33 51 C3
Kepwell Bank Top. Prud NE42 59 C3
Kepwell Bk. Prud NE42 59 D3
Kepwell Ct. Prud NE42 59 D3
Kepwell Rd. Prud NE42 59 C2
Kerby Cl. S Shs NE34 76 F4
Kerry Cl. Blyth NE24 17 E8
Kerry Sq. Sland SR5 92 A4
Kesteven Sq. Sland SR5 92 B4
Kestrel Cl. Wash NE38 101 A2
Kestrel Ct. 13 Birt DH3 100 C4
Kestrel Dr. Ashgn NE63 6 B1
Kestrel Lodge Flats. 6 S Shs NE33 51 D3
Kestrel Pl. Lbtn NE12 41 A3
Kestrel Sq. Sland SR5 92 B4
Kestrel St. Gates NE11 88 C6
Kestrel Way. N Shs NE29 51 A3
Kestrel Way. S Shs NE34 77 B4
Keswick Ave. Sland SR6 93 D4
Keswick Dr. Tyne NE30 32 B2
Keswick Gdns. Walls NE28 50 A3
Keswick Gr. N-u-T NE5 63 A4
Keswick St. Gates NE8 72 B1
Keswick Terr. S Hett DH6 121 E8
Kettering Pl. Cram NE23 22 C8
Kettering Sq. Sland SR5 92 B4
Kettlewell Terr. N Shs NE30 51 B6
Ketton Cl. Lbtn NE12 41 B2
Kew Gdns. W Bay NE26 31 F6
Keyes Gdns. N-u-T NE2 46 B3
Kibblesworth Bank. Kibble NE11 99 B6
Kibblesworth Cty Jun & Inf Sch. Kibble NE11 99 D6
Kidd Sq. Sland SR5 92 B4
Kidderminster Dr. N-u-T NE5 36 C3
Kidderminster Rd. Sland SR5 92 B3
Kidderminster Sq. Sland SR5 92 B3
Kidlandlee Gn. N-u-T NE5 43 A4
Kidlandlee Pl. N-u-T NE5 43 A4
Kidsgrove Sq. Sland SR5 92 B3
Kielder. Wash NE38 100 F4
Kielder Ave. Cram NE23 21 D6
Kielder Cl. Blyth NE24 17 B5
Kielder Cl. Kill NE12 29 C4
Kielder Cl. N-u-T NE5 43 A4
Kielder Dr. Ashgn NE63 6 C3
Kielder Gdns. Jarrow NE32 76 B3
Kielder Gdns. Stake NE62 6 A1
Kielder Pl. Ears NE25 31 B5
Kielder Rd. Ears NE25 31 B5
Kielder Rd. N-u-T NE15 62 C7
Kielder Terr. N Shs NE30 51 B6
Kielder Way. N-u-T NE3 39 B3
Kier Hardie St. R Gill NE39 85 B2
Kilburn Cl. 4 Ryhope SR2 117 A6
Kilburn Gn. Gates NE9 89 B1
Kilburne Cl. N-u-T NE7 48 B3
Kildale. Pens DH4 113 E8
Kildare Sq. Sland SR5 92 B4
Killarney Ave. Sland SR5 92 B4
Killarney Sq. Sland SR5 92 B4
Killiebrigs. H-o-t-W NE15 34 E2
Killin Cl. N-u-T NE5 36 C4
Killingworth Ave. Bworth NE27 30 B4
Killingworth Dr. Kill NE12 29 B2
Killingworth Dr. Sland SR3 & SR4 108 B4
Killingworth La. Bworth NE27 30 A5
Killingworth Mid Sch. Kill NE12 29 D2
Killingworth Pl. N-u-T NE1 66 A2
Killingworth Rd. Kill NE12 29 E2
Killingworth Rd. N-u-T NE3 & NE7 40 C1
Killingworth Way. Kill NE12 & NE23 & NE27 29 D4
Killowen St. Gates NE9 88 E4
Kiln Rise. Whick NE16 87 A4
Kilnshaw Pl. N-u-T NE3 28 D1
Kilsyth Ave. Tyne NE29 31 E2
Kilsyth Sq. Sland SR5 92 B4
Kimberley. Wash NE38 102 A5
Kimberley Ave. N Shs NE29 50 E6
Kimberley Gdns. N-u-T NE2 67 A4
Kimberley Gdns. Stocks NE43 82 C7
Kimberley St. Blyth NE24 17 D8
Kimberley St. Sland SR4 104 C2
Kinfauns Terr. 5 Gates NE9 89 A5
King Charles Ct. Sland SR5 92 A4
King Charles Tower. N-u-T NE2 66 C2
King Edward Inf Sch. Tyne NE30 51 B7
King Edward Jun Sch. Tyne NE30 51 B7
King Edward Pl. Gates NE8 73 B1
King Edward Rd. N-u-T NE6 47 B1
King Edward Rd. Ryton NE40 61 E4
King Edward Rd. Sland SR4 103 B3
King Edward Rd. Tyne NE30 51 C7
King Edward St. Gates NE8 73 B1
King Edward St. Tanf L DH9 97 C1
King Edward VI Sch. Mpeth NE61 3 F2
King George Ave. Duns NE11 87 F8
King George Comp Sch. White NE34 77 E3
King George Rd. N-u-T NE3 38 B2
King George Rd. S Shs NE34 77 E5
King George's Rd. N-b-t-S NE64 7 D5
King Henry Ct. Sland SR5 92 A4
King James Ct. Sland SR5 92 A4
King John St. N-u-T NE6 67 B4
King John Terr. N-u-T NE6 67 B4
King John's Ct. Pont NE20 25 A4
King St. Birt DH3 100 B4

Marquisway. Gates NE11 .... 88 D2
Marr Rd. Hebb NE31 .... 75 F5
Marsden Ave. Whit SR6 .... 78 F3
Marsden Cl. H-le-Sp DH4 ...... 118 C8
Marsden Cty Prim Sch.
Whit SR6 .... 78 F3
Marsden Gr. Gates NE9 .... 89 D3
Marsden La. N-u-T NE5 .... 43 A3
Marsden La. S Shs NE34 .... 78 C7
Marsden Rd. Clea SR6 .... 92 F8
Marsden Rd. S Shs NE34 .... 78 A7
Marsden View. Whit SR6 .... 78 F3
Marsh Ct. Gates NE11 .... 88 B7
Marshall St. Sland SR6 .... 93 D4
Marshall Wallis Rd.
S Shs NE33 .... 77 C8
Marshall's Ct. N-u-T NE1 .... 66 A1
Marsham Cl. Clea SR6 .... 78 A2
Marsham Cl. N-u-T NE15 .... 62 E7
Marsham Rd. N-u-T NE5 .... 36 E3
Marshes' Houses. W Sle NE62 11 D7
Marshmont Ave. Tyne NE30 ... 32 C1
Marske Terr. N-u-T NE6 .... 68 B2
Marston. Kill NE12 .... 29 D4
Marston Wlk. Whick NE16 ...... 86 F5
Martello Gdns. N-u-T NE7 ...... 48 A2
Martha St. Tant DH9 .... 97 B2
Martin Ct. Wash NE38 .... 100 F2
Martin Rd. Walls NE28 .... 50 A2
Martin Terr. Sland SR4 .... 104 C3
Martindale Ave. Sland SR6 ..... 93 C5
Martindale Pk. H-le-Sp DH5 118 E8
Martindale Pl. S Del NE25 ...... 23 E3
Marwell Dr. Wash NE37 .... 90 E2
Marwood Ct. W Bay NE25 .... 31 D6
Marx Terr. Chopw NE17 .... 95 C8
Mary Agnes St. N-u-T NE3 ...... 39 A1
Mary Ave. Birt DH3 .... 100 B6
Mary St. Blay NE21 .... 62 A2
Mary St. Blay NE21 .... 62 C3
Mary St. N Silk SR3 .... 116 A8
Mary St. Sland SR1 .... 105 C2
Mary Terr. N-u-T NE5 .... 43 A3
Mary Trevelyan Prim Sch.
N-u-T NE4 .... 71 A3
Mary's Pl. N-u-T NE6 .... 75 B6
Maryhill Cl. N-u-T NE4 .... 70 B4
Maryside Pl. Craw NE40 .... 60 F7
Masefield Ave. Whick NE16 ..... 69 B1
Masefield Dr. B Hall NE34 ...... 77 A2
Masefield Pl. Gates NE8 .... 72 C2
Mason Ave. W Bay NE26 .... 32 B5
Mason Rd. Walls NE28 .... 49 A4
Mason St. B Vill NE13 .... 28 A6
Mason St. N-u-T NE6 .... 67 C1
Massingham Way. S Shs NE34 77 B5
Mast La. Tyne NE30 .... 32 B3
Master Mariners' Homes.
Tyne NE30 .... 51 C7
Master's Cres. Prud NE42 .... 59 B2
Matamba Terr. Sland SR4 ...... 105 B2
Matanzas St. Sland SR2 .... 110 B3
Matfen Ave. Hazle NE13 .... 28 A4
Matfen Ave. Shire NE27 .... 31 A2
Matfen Cl. Blyth NE24 .... 17 C7
Matfen Cl. N-u-T NE15 .... 62 E6
Matfen Ct. C le S DH2 .... 112 A3
Matfen Dr. Silk SR3 .... 115 D6
Matfen Gdns. Walls NE28 .... 49 F5
Matfen Pl. N-u-T NE3 .... 39 A2
Matfen Pl. N-u-T NE4 .... 64 C3
Matfen Terr. N-b-t-S NE64 .... 7 D3
Mather Rd. N-u-T NE4 .... 71 B4
Mathesons Gdns. Mpeth NE61 . 8 F8
Matlock Gdns. N-u-T NE5 .... 36 F3
Matlock Rd. Jarrow NE32 .... 76 C5
Matlock Sq. Lmth NE61 .... 2 A2
Matlock St. Sland SR1 .... 106 A3
Matthew Bank. N-u-T NE2 .... 46 B3
Matthew Rd. Blyth NE24 .... 17 F5
Matthew St. N-u-T NE6 .... 67 B2
Maud St. N-u-T NE15 .... 62 C6
Maud St. Sland SR6 .... 93 E4
Maud Terr. Shire NE27 .... 30 E1
Maud Terr. Tanf DH9 .... 97 D3
Maud's Terr. N-b-t-S NE64 .... 7 E5
Maude Gdns. Walls NE28 .... 49 B1
Maudlin Pl. N-u-T NE5 .... 44 A1
Maudlin St. H le H DH5 .... 119 B6
Mauds La. Sland SR1 .... 106 B3
Maughan St. Blyth NE24 .... 17 F7
Maurice Rd. Walls NE28 .... 75 B8
Maurice Road Ind Est.
Walls NE28 .... 75 B8
Mautland St. H-le-Sp DH4 ...... 114 E1
Maxstoke Pl. Lbtn NE12 .... 41 A2
Maxton Cl. Silk SR3 .... 115 D5
Maxwell. S Shs NE33 .... 51 C2
Maxwell St. Gates NE8 .... 88 D7
Maxwell St. S Shs NE33 .... 51 C2
Maxwell St. Sland SR4 .... 104 C3
Maxwell St Ind Est.
S Shs NE33 .... 51 C2
May Ave. N-b-t-S NE64 .... 7 C5
May Ave. Ryton NE40 .... 61 C6
May Ave. Win M NE21 .... 86 C7
May Gr. Whit SR6 .... 78 F3
May St. Birt DH3 .... 100 C4
May St. Blay NE21 .... 62 B1
May St. S Shs NE33 .... 51 D1
May St. Sland SR4 .... 105 B3
Maydown Cl. Sland SR5 .... 102 F8
Mayfair Bldgs. Sland SR2 .... 105 B1
Mayfair Ct. Hebb NE31 .... 75 D5
Mayfair Gdns. Gates NE8 .... 89 A8
Mayfair Gdns. Pont NE20 .... 25 F6
Mayfair Gdns. S Shs NE34 .... 77 E7
Mayfair Rd. N-u-T NE2 .... 46 A2
Mayfield. Mpeth NE61 .... 8 E7
Mayfield. Whick NE16 .... 87 B5
Mayfield Ave. Cram NE23 .... 22 C6
Mayfield Ave. Tley NE15 .... 35 E1
Mayfield Ct. Sland SR6 .... 93 D3
Mayfield Dr. Clea SR6 .... 93 B8
Mayfield Gdns. Jarrow NE32 .... 76 A6
Mayfield Gdns. Tley NE15 .... 35 E1
Mayfield Gdns. Walls NE28 .... 49 A3
Mayfield Gr. Sland SR4 .... 107 A2
Mayfield Pl. B Vill NE13 .... 28 A5
Mayfield Rd. N-u-T NE3 .... 45 C4
Mayfield Rd. Sland SR4 .... 103 A2
Mayfield Terr. N-u-T NE5 .... 44 B1
Mayo Dr. Silk SR3 .... 115 E5
Mayoral Way. Gates NE11 .... 88 D3
Mayswood Rd. Sland SR6 .... 93 D3
Maytree House. N-u-T NE4 .... 71 A4
Maywood Cl. N-u-T NE3 .... 44 B4
Mazine Terr. Hasw DH6 .... 121 E8
McAnany Ave. S Shs NE34 .... 77 D5
McAteer Ct. Hasw DH6 .... 121 E1
McClaren Way. N Herr DH4 . 114 F7
McCracken Cl. N-u-T NE3 .... 39 C4
McCracken Dr. W Open NE13 28 C7
McCutcheon Ct. N-u-T NE10 .. 74 B3
McCutcheon St. 7
Seaham SR2 .... 116 E1
McErlane Sq. Gates NE10 .... 75 B2
McEwan Gdns. N-u-T NE4 .... 64 C1
McGowen Ct. N-u-T NE6 .... 67 C1
McIlvenna Gdns. Walls NE28 49 B4
McKendrick Villas. N-u-T NE5 44 A1
McLennan Ct. Wash NE38 ...... 101 D6
McNamara Rd. Walls NE28 .... 49 F3
Meaburn Terr. Sland SR1 ...... 106 B2
Meacham Way. Whick NE16 .. 87 A5
Mead Ave. Lbtn NE12 .... 42 B4
Mead Cres. Lbtn NE12 .... 42 C4
Mead Way. Lbtn NE12 .... 42 C4
Mead Wlk. N-u-T NE6 .... 68 C2
Meadow Bank Dr.
Chopp NE62 .... 10 E6
Meadow Brook Dr.
Chopw NE17 .... 84 C2
Meadow Cl. Blay NE21 .... 61 F1
Meadow Cl. Duns NE11 .... 70 B1
Meadow Cl. H-le-Sp DH5 .... 118 F7
Meadow Cl. Lbtn NE12 .... 41 A3
Meadow Cl. Ryton NE40 .... 61 D5
Meadow Cl. Seg NE23 .... 22 F2
Meadow Ct. Bed NE22 .... 10 E1
Meadow Ct. Pont NE20 .... 25 E5
Meadow Dr. S Burn NE13 .... 28 C8
Meadow Dr. Sland SR4 .... 103 A1
Meadow Dr. Sland SR3 .... 115 B6
Meadow Gdns. Sland SR3 ...... 109 B3
Meadow Gr. Sland SR4 .... 103 B1
Meadow Grange. Bourn DH4 113 E2
Meadow La. Craw NE40 .... 61 A4
Meadow La. Duns NE11 .... 70 B1
Meadow La. Sland SR3 .... 115 B6
Meadow Laws. S Shs NE34 .... 78 A4
Meadow Pk. R Mill NE44 .... 80 F7
Meadow Rd. N-u-T NE15 .... 62 D8
Meadow Rd. S Slu NE26 .... 24 B6
Meadow Rd. W Bay NE25 .... 31 D4
Meadow Rd. Walls NE28 .... 49 F1
Meadow Rise. N-u-T NE5 .... 43 B4
Meadow St. E Rain DH5 .... 118 C3
Meadow Terr. Pens DH4 .... 114 C6
Meadow Vale. Sland SR2 .... 109 C4
Meadow View. Dipton DH9 ...... 96 E1
Meadow View. E Cram NE25 .. 23 D6
Meadow View. Sland SR3 ...... 115 B5
Meadow Well Sch.
N Shs NE29 .... 50 D4
Meadow Well Sta.
N Shs NE29 .... 50 E4
Meadow Wlk. Ryton NE40 .... 61 D5
Meadowbrook Dr.
Gates NE10 .... 90 C7
Meadowcroft Mews.
Gates NE8 .... 72 A1
Meadowdale Cres. Bed NE22 10 D1
Meadowdale Cres. N-u-T NE5 44 A3
Meadowfield. Ashgn NE63 .... 7 A2
Meadowfield. Pont NE20 .... 25 E7
Meadowfield. W Bay NE25 .... 31 D5
Meadowfield Ave. N-u-T NE3 39 A2
Meadowfield Cres. Craw NE40 61 A4
Meadowfield Dr. Clea SR6 .... 78 B1
Meadowfield Est. Spring NE9 89 F1
Meadowfield Gdns. N-u-T NE6 49 A1
Meadowfield Pk S.
Stocks NE43 .... 82 C5
Meadowfield Rd. N-u-T NE3 .. 45 B4
Meadowfield Rd. Stocks NE43 82 C5
Meadowfield Terr. Kill NE12 . 29 F1
Meadowfield Terr.
Stocks NE43 .... 82 D7
Meadows La.
W Rain DH4 & DH5 .... 118 B3
Meadows The. Bourn DH4 .. 113 D3
Meadows The. N-u-T NE3 .... 38 C2
Meadows The. Ryton NE40 ...... 61 D5
Meadows The. W Rain DH4 . 118 A3
Meadowside. Sland SR2 .... 109 B4
Meadowvale. Pont NE20 .... 25 A2
Meadway Dr. Lbtn NE12 .... 42 C4
Meal Market. Hexham NE46 .... 54 B5
Means Dr. Kill NE23 .... 29 B5
Medburn Ave. Tyne NE30 .... 32 C2
Medburn Rd. N-u-T NE15 .... 62 C7
Medburn Rd. S Del NE25 .... 23 E2
Medham Cl. Gates NE10 .... 89 E6
Medina Cl. Silk SR3 .... 115 E5
Medlar. Gates NE9 .... 89 D4
Medomsley Gdns. Gates NE9 89 E4
Medomsly St. Sland SR4 .... 105 A3
Medway. Hedw NE32 .... 76 C2
Medway Ave. Hebb NE31 .... 75 E3
Medway Cres. Gates NE8 .... 89 B8
Medway Gdns. Sland SR4 ...... 108 A4
Medway Gdns.
Tyne NE29 & NE30 .... 51 A7
Medway Pl. Cram NE23 .... 16 D1
Medwyn Cl. Bourn DH4 .... 113 E3
Megstone Ave. Cram NE23 ...... 22 A5
Megstone Ct. Kill NE12 .... 29 E4
Melbeck Dr. Urpeth DH2 .... 99 E2
Melbourne Cres. W Bay NE25 31 E3
Melbourne Ct. Gates NE8 .... 72 B3
Melbourne Ct. N-u-T NE1 .... 66 C1
Melbourne Gdns. B Wh NE34 76 F3
Melbourne Pl. Sland SR4 ...... 108 B4
Melbourne St. N-u-T NE1 .... 66 B1
Melbury. W Bay NE25 .... 31 D6
Melbury Ct. Slard SR6 .... 93 D3
Melbury Rd. N-u-T NE7 .... 47 A1
Meldon Ave. N-u-T NE3 .... 38 C3
Meldon Ave. S Shs NE34 .... 77 E6
Meldon Ave. Sherb DH6 .... 120 A1
Meldon Cl. Walls NE28 .... 49 E3
Meldon Ct. Craw NE40 .... 60 E3
Meldon Gdns. Duns NE11 .... 88 A5
Meldon Gdns. Stake NE62 .... 10 F8
Meldon House. Blyth NE24 ...... 17 B8
Meldon Rd. Sland SR4 .... 104 C3
Meldon St. N Shs NE28 .... 50 C1
Meldon Terr. Green NE40 .... 60 F1
Meldon Terr. N-b-t-S NE64 .... 7 D3
Meldon Terr. N-u-T NE6 .... 67 B4
Meldon Way. Blay NE21 .... 85 F8
Melgarve Dr. Silk SR3 .... 115 E5
Melkington Ct. N-u-T NE5 .... 43 B3
Melkridge Pl. Cram NE23 .... 22 A5
Melmerby Cl. N-u-T NE3 .... 40 A3
Melness Rd. Hazle NE13 .... 28 A5
Melock Ct. Hazle NE13 .... 28 A5
Melrose. Wash NE38 .... 101 D3
Melrose Ave. Beb NE22 .... 11 D1
Melrose Ave. Bworth NE27 ...... 30 C5
Melrose Ave. Gates NE9 .... 89 A5
Melrose Ave. Hebb NE31 .... 75 E3
Melrose Ave. S Del NE25 .... 23 D2
Melrose Ave. Tyne NE30 .... 32 A2
Melrose Cl. Hazle NE3 .... 28 B2
Melrose Cl. N-u-T NE15 .... 62 E6
Melrose Ct. Bed NE22 .... 11 D2
Melrose Gdns. New DH4 .... 114 C3
Melrose Gdns. Sland SR6 .... 93 E3
Melrose Gdns. Walls NE28 .... 50 A4
Melrose Gr. Jarrow NE32 .... 76 E4
Melrose Terr. Bed NE22 .... 11 D2
Melrose Terr. N-b-t-S NE64 .... 7 D3
Melrose Villas. Bed NE22 .... 11 D2
Melsonby Cl. Silk SR3 .... 115 D6
Meltham Ct. N-u-T NE5 .... 36 B2
Meltham Dr. Silk SR3 .... 115 E5
Melton Ave. N-u-T NE6 .... 68 C1
Melton Cres. S Slu NE26 .... 24 D5
Melton Dr. E Cram NE25 .... 23 D6
Melvaig Cl. Silk SR3 .... 115 E5
Melville Gdns. W Bay NE25 ...... 31 C4
Melville Gr. N-u-T NE7 .... 47 A4
Melville St. C le S DH3 .... 112 C2
Melvin Pl. N-u-T NE5 .... 43 B2
Melvyn Gdns. Slard SR6 .... 93 E3
Membury Cl. Silk SR3 .... 115 E5
Memorial Sq. N-b-t-S NE64 .... 7 D5
Menai Ct. 9 Silk SR3 .... 115 F6
Mendip Ave. C le S DH2 .... 112 C2
Mendip Cl. Ashgn NE63 .... 6 E1
Mendip Cl. Tyne NE29 .... 31 F1
Mendip Dr. Wash NE38 .... 101 B3
Mendip Gdns. Duns NE11 .... 88 B6
Mendip Way. Lbtn NE12 .... 40 C2
Mentieth Cl. Wash NE38 .... 101 B3
Mercantile Rd. H-le-Sp DH4 118 C7
Merchants Wharf. N-u-T NE6 73 C4
Mercia Way. N-u-T NE15 .... 62 E5
Mere Knolls Rd. Slard SR6 ...... 93 E4
Meredith Gdns. Gates NE8 .... 72 C1
Meresyde. Gates NE10 .... 90 A7
Meresyde Ct. Gates NE10 .... 90 A7
Merevale Cl. Wash NE37 .... 90 E2
Merganser Lodge. 7
Gates NE10 .... 89 D8
Meridan Way. N-u-T NE7 .... 48 A3
Merlay Dr. Dgton NE13 .... 27 B6
Merlay Hall. N-u-T NE6 .... 75 A4
Merle Gdns. Mpeth NE61 .... 3 D2
Merle Gdns. N-u-T NE6 .... 67 C1
Merle Terr. Slard SR4 .... 104 C3
Merle Terr. Slard SR4 .... 104 C4
Merley Gate. Mpeth NE61 .... 9 A6
Merlin Cres. Walls NE28 .... 49 F3
Merlin Ct. Gates NE10 .... 74 A1
Merlin Dr. C le S DH3 .... 112 D7
Merlin Pl. Lbtn NE12 .... 41 A3
Merrick House. 21 Silk SR3 .. 115 F6
Merrington Cl. E Cram NE25 .. 23 D7
Merrington Cl. Silk SR3 .... 115 D6
Merrion Cl. Silk SR3 .... 115 D6
Merryfield Gdns. Slard SR6 .. 93 E3
Merryshields Terr.
Stocks NE43 .... 82 C8
Mersey Ct. 17 Silk SR3 .... 115 F6
Mersey Pl. Gates NE8 .... 89 B8
Mersey Rd. Gates NE8 .... 89 B8
Mersey Rd. Hebb NE31 .... 75 F3
Mersey St. Chopw NE17 .... 84 C1
Merton Ct. N-u-T NE4 .... 70 A4
Merton Rd. Pont NE20 .... 25 E6
Merton Sq. Blyth NE24 .... 17 E8
Merton Way. Pont NE 20 .... 25 E6
Methuen St. Gates NE9 .... 89 A8
Mews The. Blay NE21 .... 62 E2
Mews The. Fence DH4 .... 118 A7
Mews The. N Shs NE30 .... 51 A6
Mews The. N-u-T NE1 .... 66 A2
Mews The. Slard SR3 .... 115 B7
Michaelgate. N-u-T NE6 .... 67 C2
Mickleton Gdns. Slard SR3 109 B2
Micklewood Cl. Long NE61 .... 4 E6
Mickley Cty Fst Sch.
M Sq NE43 .... 58 E1
Middle Chare. C le S DH3 .... 112 D3
Middle Cl. Wash NE38 .... 101 B1
Middle Dr. Pont NE20 .... 25 C3
Middle Dr. Wools NE13 .... 26 F1
Middle Engine La.
Shire NE27 & NE28 & NE29 ..... 50 A7
Middle Engine La. Walls NE28 49 F5
Middle Gate. Mpeth NE61 .... 8 F6
Middle Gate. N-u-T NE5 .... 36 D1
Middle Gn. W Bay NE25 .... 31 C4
Middle Row. Blay NE40 .... 61 E3
Middle St. Blyth NE24 .... 17 B4
Middle St. Crbdge NE45 .... 55 F5
Middle St. N-u-T NE6 .... 68 C2
Middle St. Slard SR1 .... 105 C3
Middle St. Slard SR1 .... 106 A3
Middle St. Tyne NE30 .... 51 E7
Middle St E. N-u-T NE6 .... 75 A6
Middlebrook. Pont NE20 .... 25 B3
Middlefields Ind Est.
S Shs NE34 .... 77 B6
Middlegarth. N-u-T NE5 .... 44 A2
Middleham Cl. Urpeth DH2 ...... 99 E1
Middleham Ct. Slard SR5 .... 92 E3
Middleton Ave. N-u-T NE4 .... 64 B2
Middleton Ave. R Gill NE39 ..... 85 F1
Middleton Cl. Seaham SR7 .. 116 E1
Middleton St. Blyth NE24 .... 17 E7
Middlewood Pk. N-u-T NE4 ...... 64 B3
Midgley Dr. Silk SR3 .... 115 E5
Midhurst Ave. S Shs NE34 .... 78 A8
Midhurst Cl. Silk SR3 .... 115 D6
Midhurst Rd. Lbtn NE12 .... 42 A3
Midmoor Rd. Slard SR4 .... 104 B3
Midsomer Cl. Silk SR3 .... 115 D5
Midway. N-u-T NE6 .... 75 A6
Milbanke Cl. Ouston DH2 .... 99 F1
Milbanke St. Ouston DH2 .... 99 F1
Milbur Cl. Hexham NE46 .... 53 F2
Milburn Cl. C le S DH3 .... 112 E2
Milburn Dr. N-u-T NE15 .... 63 B2
Milburn Rd. Ashgn NE63 .... 6 D2
Milburn Terr. S Row DH4 114
Milburn Terr. Stake NE62 .... 11 E6
Milcombe Cl. Silk SR3 .... 115 D6
Mildmay Rd. N-u-T NE2 .... 46 A2
Mildred St. H-le-Sp DH5 .... 114 E1
Mile End Rd. S Shs NE33 .... 51 C4
Milecastle Ct. N-u-T NE5 .... 36 D2
Milecastle Fst Sch. N-u-T NE5 36 C2
Milfield Ave. Shire NE27 .... 31 A3
Milfield Ave. Walls NE28 .... 49 C4
Milford Ct. Gates NE10 .... 90 B6
Milford Gdns. N-u-T NE3 .... 28 B1
Milford Rd. N-u-T NE15 .... 63 C1
Military Rd. H-o-t-W NE15 .... 34 C3
Military Rd. N Shs NE30 .... 51 B6
Milk Market. N-u-T NE1 .... 66 C1
Milkwell. Crbdge NE45 .... 56 A6
Milkwell La. Crbdge NE45 .... 56 A7
Mill Bank. Slard SR5 .... 93 C4
Mill Cl. N Shs NE29 .... 50 E5
Mill Cl. R Mill NE44 .... 80 F7
Mill Cres. Hebb NE31 .... 75 C2
Mill Cres. Pens DH4 .... 114 B6
Mill Ct. Bourn DH4 .... 113 E2
Mill Dam. S Shs NE33 .... 51 B2
Mill Dyke Cl. W Bay NE25 .... 31 C6
Mill Farm. Linton NE61 .... 1 C4
Mill Farm Cl. N-u-T NE4 .... 65 B1
Mill Farm Rd. H Mill NE39 .... 96 A5
Mill Gr. S Shs NE34 .... 78 B4
Mill Gr. Tyne NE30 .... 51 C8
Mill Grange. R Mill NE44 .... 81 A8
Mill Hill. H-le-Sp DH5 .... 118 D6
Mill Hill Prim Sch. Silk SR3 116 A5
Mill Hill Rd. N-u-T NE5 .... 62 F8
Mill Hill Rd. Silk SR3 .... 116 A6
Mill House. N-u-T NE2 .... 65 B4
Mill La. Ebch DH8 .... 94 E4
Mill La. H-o-t-W NE15 .... 34 F3
Mill La. Hebb NE10 & NE31 ...... 75 E2
Mill La. Jarrow NE10 & NE31 ... 75 E2
Mill La. N Shs NE29 .... 51 B4
Mill La. N-u-T NE4 .... 71 A4
Mill La. Seg NE23 .... 22 D1
Mill La. Sherb DH6 .... 120 A1
Mill La. Slal NE47 .... 80 A1
Mill La. Urpeth DH2 & DH9 .... 99 D1
Mill La. Whit SR6 .... 78 F2
Mill La. Win M NE21 .... 86 B7
Mill Pit. Pens DH4 .... 114 B6
Mill Race Cl. B Mill NE17 .... 95 B6
Mill Rd. B Mill NE17 .... 95 B8
Mill Rd. Chopw NE17 .... 84 B1
Mill Rd. Chopw NE17 .... 95 B8
Mill Rd. Gates NE8 .... 72 C4
Mill Rise. N-u-T NE3 .... 46 B4
Mill St. Slard SR4 .... 105 B3
Mill Terr. H-le-Sp DH5 .... 118 D6
Mill View. Boldon NE36 .... 92 A7
Mill View. Gates NE10 .... 89 C7
Mill View Ave. Slard SR6 .... 93 D3
Mill Way. Hors NE15 & NE42 .. 59 D7
Millais Gdns. White NE34 .... 77 C2
Millbank Cres. Bed NE22 .... 11 A1
Millbank Ind Est. S Shs NE33 51 C2
Millbank Pl. Bed NE22 .... 16 B8
Millbank Rd. Bed NE22 .... 11 B1
Millbank Rd. N-u-T NE6 .... 75 A4
Millbank Terr. Bed NE22 .... 11 A1
Millbeck Gr. H-le-Sp DH5 ...... 118 D6
Millbrook. Gates NE10 .... 89 E7
Millbrook Rd. Cram NE23 .... 16 D1
Millburn St. Slard SR4 .... 105 B3
Milldale Ave. Blyth NE24 .... 17 A7
Milldene Ave. Tyne NE30 .... 51 C8
Miller St. Gates NE8 .... 88 D8
Miller Terr. N Silk SR3 .... 116 A8
Miller's La. Whick NE16 .... 69 B1
Millers Hill. Pens DH4 .... 114 C6
Millers Rd. N-u-T NE6 .... 67 C3
Millfield. Bed NE22 .... 16 A7
Millfield. S Slu NE26 .... 24 D5
Millfield Ave. N-u-T NE3 .... 44 B3
Millfield Cl. C le S DH2 .... 112 A1
Millfield Cl. Newb NE15 .... 61 F7
Millfield Ct. Bed NE22 .... 16 A8
Millfield Ct. Hexham NE46 .... 53 F5
Millfield Ct. S Slu NE26 .... 24 D5
Millfield Ct. Whick NE16 .... 87 C7
Millfield E. Bed NE22 .... 16 A7
Millfield Gdns. Blyth NE24 .... 12 D1
Millfield Gdns. Gates NE10 ...... 89 C8
Millfield Gdns. Hexham NE46 ... 53 F5
Millfield Gdns. Tyne NE30 .... 51 C8
Millfield Gr. Tyne NE30 .... 51 C8
Millfield La. Newb NE15 .... 61 F8
Millfield N. Bed NE22 .... 16 A8
Millfield Rd. R Mill NE44 .... 80 F7
Millfield Rd. Whick NE16 .... 87 B6
Millfield S. Bed NE22 .... 16 A7
Millfield Terr. Hexham NE46 .. 53 F5
Millfield Terr. Whit SR6 .... 78 F2
Millfield W. Bed NE22 .... 16 A8
Millford. Gates NE10 .... 90 B6
Millgrove View. N-u-T NE3 .... 44 C3
Milling Ct. Gates NE8 .... 71 C2
Millom Pl. Gates NE9 .... 89 B4
Mills Gdns. Walls NE28 .... 49 B3
Millthorp Cl. Slard SR2 .... 111 A1
Millview Dr. Tyne NE30 .... 51 C8
Millway. Gates NE9 .... 89 A7
Millway. S Slu NE26 .... 24 D5
Millway Gr. S Slu NE26 .... 24 D5
Milne Ct. Bed NE22 .... 10 F1
Milne Way. N-u-T NE3 .... 38 C2
Milner Cres. Blay NE21 .... 62 A1
Milner St. S Shs NE33 .... 51 E2
Milrig Cl. Silk SR3 .... 115 E5
Milsted Cl. Silk SR3 .... 115 D5
Milsted Ct. N-u-T NE5 .... 36 B2
Milton Ave. H-le-Sp DH5 .... 118 F7
Milton Ave. Hebb NE31 .... 75 E6
Milton Cl. N-u-T NE2 .... 66 C3
Milton Gn. N-u-T NE2 .... 66 C3
Milton Gr. Ashgn NE63 .... 6 F3
Milton Gr. N Shs NE29 .... 50 F6
Milton Gr. Prud NE42 .... 59 B2
Milton Pl. N Shs NE29 .... 50 F6
Milton Pl. N-u-T NE2 .... 66 C3
Milton Pl. Spring NE9 .... 89 E1
Milton Rd. Whick NE16 .... 87 B8
Milton Sq. Gates NE8 .... 73 A2
Milton St. Green NE40 .... 60 E1
Milton St. Jarrow NE32 .... 76 B8
Milton St. S Shs NE33 .... 77 D8
Milton St. Slard SR4 .... 105 A3
Milton Terr. N Shs NE29 .... 50 F6
Milvain Ave. N-u-T NE4 .... 64 B2
Milvain Cl. Gates NE8 .... 72 C1
Milvain St. Gates NE8 .... 72 C1
Milverton Ct. N-u-T NE3 .... 37 C2
Mimosa Dr. Hebb NE31 .... 75 E3
Mimosa Pl. N-u-T NE4 .... 64 A4
Minden St. N-u-T NE1 .... 66 B1
Mindrum Terr. N Shs NE29 .... 50 D4
Mindrum Terr. N-u-T NE6 .... 68 C1
Mindrum Way. S Del NE25 .... 23 D3
Minehead Gdns. 9
N Silk SR3 .... 116 A8
Miners Cotts. N-u-T NE15 .... 63 A3
Minerva Cl. N-u-T NE5 .... 36 C4
Mingarry. Birt DH3 .... 100 E2
Mingary Cl. E Rain DH5 .... 118 C4
Minorca Cl. Slard SR1 .... 106 C2
Minorca Pl. N-u-T NE3 .... 44 C3
Minskip Cl. Silk SR3 .... 115 E5
Minster Ct. Gates NE8 .... 72 C3
Minster Par. Jarrow NE32 .... 76 C7
Minton Ct. N Shs NE29 .... 50 F4
Minton La. N Shs NE29 .... 50 F4
Minton Sq. Slard SR4 .... 104 B3
Mirk La. Gates NE8 .... 72 B4
Mirlaw Rd. Cram NE23 .... 21 F5
Mistletoe Rd. N-u-T NE2 .... 46 B1
Mitcham Cres. N-u-T NE7 .... 47 B4
Mitchell Ave. N-u-T NE2 .... 46 B2
Mitchell Ave. W Bay NE25 .... 31 D4
Mitchell Dr. Ashgn NE63 .... 7 B3
Mitchell Gdns. S Shs NE34 .... 77 F7
Mitchell St. Birt DH3 .... 100 C4
Mitchell St. Craw NE40 .... 60 E3
Mitchell St. N-u-T NE6 .... 75 B5
Mitchell Terr. Tant DH9 .... 97 B2
Mitchell's Bldgs. Spring NE9 . 90 A1
Mitford Ave. Blyth NE24 .... 17 C6
Mitford Ave. Pegs NE61 .... 4 E4
Mitford Ave. S Del NE25 .... 23 C3
Mitford Cl. C le S DH3 .... 112 D8
Mitford Cl. Wash NE38 .... 101 B4
Mitford Dr. Ashgn NE63 .... 6 D2
Mitford Dr. N-u-T NE5 .... 36 E3
Mitford Dr. Sherb DH6 .... 120 A2
Mitford Gdns. Duns NE11 .... 88 A5
Mitford Gdns. Stake NE62 .... 10 F8
Mitford Gdns. W Open NE13 .. 28 C6
Mitford Gdns. Walls NE28 .... 49 F5
Mitford Pl. N-u-T NE3 .... 39 A2
Mitford Rd. Mpeth NE61 .... 3 E1
Mitford Rd. S Shs NE34 .... 77 E6
Mitford St. N Shs NE28 .... 50 C2
Mitford St. Slard SR6 .... 93 E4
Mitford Terr. Hedw NE32 .... 76 B2
Mitford Way. Dgton NE13 .... 27 B7
Mithras Gdns. H-o-t-W NE15 .. 34 E2
Mitre Ind Est. S Shs NE33 .... 77 B7
Mitre Pl. S Shs NE33 .... 77 B7
Moat Gdns. Gates NE10 .... 90 C8
Modder St. N-u-T NE6 .... 74 C3
Model Dwellings.
Wash NE38 .... 101 E4
Model Terr. Pens DH4 .... 114 A8
Modigars La. H o t H NE43 ...... 82 F4
Moffat Ave. Jarrow NE32 .... 76 E4
Moffat Cl. Tyne NE29 .... 50 C8
Moine Gdns. Slard SR6 .... 93 E3
Molesdon Cl. Tyne NE30 .... 32 A1
Molineux Cl. N-u-T NE6 .... 67 B2
Molineux Ct. N-u-T NE6 .... 67 B2
Molineux St. N-u-T NE6 .... 67 B2
Mollyfair Cl. Craw NE40 .... 61 A4
Monarch Rd. N-u-T NE4 .... 71 A2
Monarch Terr. Blay NE21 .... 62 C2
Monday Cres. N-u-T NE4 .... 65 B2
Monday Pl. N-u-T NE4 .... 65 B2
Monk Ct. Gates NE8 .... 72 C2
Monk St. N-u-T NE1 .... 65 C1
Monk St. Slard SR6 .... 93 D1
Monk's Terr. Hexham NE46 ...... 54 D4
Monkchester Gn. N-u-T NE6 . 68 B1
Monkchester Rd. N-u-T NE6 .. 74 B4
Monkdale Ave. Blyth NE24 .... 17 A6
Monkhouse Ave. Tyne NE30 .. 32 A1
Monkhouse Prim Sch.
Tyne NE30 .... 32 B1
Monkridge. N-u-T NE5 .... 36 B2
Monkridge. W Bay NE26 .... 31 E7
Monkridge Ct. N-u-T NE3 .... 46 B4
Monkridge Gdns. Duns NE11 88 A7
Monks Ave. W Bay NE25 .... 31 D3
Monks Meadows.
Hexham NE46 .... 54 D4
Monks Park Way. Lbtn NE12 . 41 A2
Monks Rd. W Bay NE25 .... 31 C3
Monks Ridge. Mpeth NE61 .... 8 D7
Monks Way. Tyne NE30 .... 32 C1
Monks Wood. Tyne NE29 .... 50 F8
Monkseaton Dr.
W Bay NE25 & NE26 .... 31 E6
Monkseaton High Sch.
Tyne NE29 .... 31 E2
Monkseaton Mid Sch.
W Bay NE25 .... 31 E4
Monkseaton Rd. Ears NE25 ..... 31 B5
Monkseaton Sta. W Bay NE25 31 F5
Monkseaton Village Fst Sch.
W Bay NE25 .... 31 E4
Monkseaton West Fst Sch.
W Bay NE25 .... 31 E4
Monksfeld. Gates NE10 .... 89 E7
Monksfield Cl. 5 Silk SR3 .... 115 F5
Monkside. Cram NE23 .... 21 F5
Monkside Cl. Wash NE38 .... 101 A2
Monkstone Ave. Tyne NE30 ... 51 C8
Monkstone Cl. Tyne NE30 .... 51 C8
Monkstone Cres. Tyne NE30 .. 32 C1
Monkstone Grange.
Tyne NE30 .... 32 B1
Monksway. Jarrow NE32 .... 76 E6
Monkswood Sq. Silk SR3 ...... 116 B6
Monkton. Gates NE10 .... 89 F6
Monkton Ave. S Shs NE34 .... 77 A4
Monkton Cty Inf Sch.
S Shs NE34 .... 77 A3
Monkton Cty Jun Sch.
S Shs NE34 .... 76 F4
Monkton Hall. Hebb NE31 .... 75 F4
Monkton La.
Hebb NE31 & NE32 .... 75 F4
Monkton La.
Jarrow NE31 & NE32 .... 75 F2
Monkton Rd. Jarrow NE32 .... 76 B7
Monkton Terr. Jarrow NE32 .. 76 C6
Monkwearmouth Coll of F Ed.
Slard SR5 .... 93 C2
Monkwearmouth Coll Shiney
Row Ctr. S Row DH4 .... 114 B5
Monkwearmouth Hospl.
Slard SR5 .... 93 C3
Monkwearmouth Sch.
Slard SR6 .... 93 D5
Monmouth Gdns. Walls NE28 50 A4
Monroe Pl. N-u-T NE5 .... 44 A2
Mons Ave. Hebb NE31 .... 75 E6
Montagu Ave. N-u-T NE3 .... 45 A2
Montagu Ct. N-u-T NE3 .... 45 A2
Montagu Prim Schs.
N-u-T NE5 .... 44 B2
Montague St. N-u-T NE15 .... 62 D6
Montague St. Slard SR6 .... 93 D3
Monterey. Wash NE37 .... 90 D1
Montford Cl. Silk SR3 .... 115 D5
Montpellier Pl. N-u-T NE3 .... 44 C3
Montpellier Terr. Slard SR2 110 B3
Montrose Cl. E Cram NE25 ...... 23 D6
Montrose Cres. Gates NE9 ...... 89 B7
Montrose Dr. Gates NE10 .... 90 C7
Montrose Gdns. Mpeth NE61 .... 8 F7
Montrose Gdns. Slard SR3 . 109 A3
Monument Mall Sh Ctr.
N-u-T NE1 .... 66 A1
Monument Sta. N-u-T NE1 ...... 66 A1
Monument Terr. 10 Birt DH3 100 C4
Monument Terr. Pens DH4 . 114 A8
Monument View. Pens DH4 114 B8
Moonfield. Hexham NE46 .... 54 B4
Moor Cl. Slard SR1 .... 106 C3
Moor Cl. Tyne NE29 .... 50 C8
Moor Cottages. H Pitt DH6 . 120 D4
Moor Cres. N-u-T NE3 .... 45 C3
Moor Crest Terr. 2
Tyne NE29 .... 50 F8
Moor Croft. N-b-t-S NE64 .... 7 E5
Moor Ct. N-u-T NE3 .... 45 B2
Moor Ct. Whit SR6 .... 93 E8
Moor Edge Fst Sch. Kill NE12 29 C3
Moor Edge Rd. Bworth NE27 . 30 E4
Moor Gdns. Tyne NE29 .... 50 C8
Moor Grange. Prud NE42 .... 59 D1
Moor La. N-u-T NE5 .... 44 A4
Moor La. Pont NE20 .... 25 C4
Moor La. S Shs NE34 .... 77 E6
Moor La. Stan NE61 .... 14 C6
Moor La. Whit SR6 .... 93 D8
Moor La E. S Shs NE34 .... 77 F7
Moor Park Ct. Tyne NE29 .... 50 C7
Moor Park Rd. Tyne NE29 .... 50 C7
Moor Pl. N-u-T NE3 .... 45 C3
Moor Rd. Prud NE42 .... 83 E7
Moor Rd N. N-u-T NE3 .... 46 A4
Moor Rd S. N-u-T NE2 & NE3 .. 46 A3
Moor St. Slard SR1 .... 106 B3
Moor Terr. Slard SR1 .... 106 C3
Moor View. Kill NE12 .... 29 C4
Moor View. N-b-t-S NE64 .... 7 E5
Moor View. Whit SR6 .... 93 E8
Moor View Cl. Pegs NE61 .... 4 E3
Moor View Wlk. Kill NE12 .... 29 C4
Moorcroft Cl. N-u-T NE15 .... 62 D7
Moorcroft Rd. N-u-T NE15 .... 62 E6
Moordale Ave. Blyth NE24 .... 17 A6
Moore Ave. Duns NE11 .... 87 F8
Moore Ave. S Shs NE34 .... 77 F6
Moore Cres. Birt DH3 .... 100 C6
Moore Cres N. H-le-Sp DH5 118 E7
Moore Cres S. H-le-Sp DH5 . 118 E7
Moore Ct. Tley NE15 61
Moore St. Gates NE8 .... 73 A1
Moorfield. N-u-T NE2 .... 46 A3
Moorfield Gdns. Clea SR6 .... 93 A8
Moorfields. Mpeth NE61 .... 9 A6
Moorfoot Ave. C le S DH2 ..... 112 C2
Moorfoot Gdns. Duns NE11 ...... 88 A7
Moorhead. N-u-T NE5 .... 44 B1
Moorhead Mews. N-u-T NE5 .. 44 B1
Moorhouse Cl. S Shs NE34 ..... 77 D5
Moorhouse Est. Ashgn NE63 ...... 6 F4
Moorhouse Gdns.
H le H DH5 .... 119 B2
Moorhouse La. Ashgn NE63 ..... 6 F3
Moorhouses Prim Sch.
Tyne NE29 .... 50 C8
Moorhouses Rd. Tyne NE29 .. 50 C8
Moorings The. N-u-T NE6 .... 73 C4
Moorland Ave. Bed NE22 .... 11 E3
Moorland Cotts. Bed NE22 .... 11 D3
Moorland Cres. Bed NE22 .... 11 E3
Moorland Cres. N-u-T NE6 .... 68 B3
Moorland Ct. Bed NE22 .... 11 E3
Moorland Dr. Bed NE22 .... 11 E3
Moorland View. Chopw NE17 .. 95 B8
Moorland Villas. Bed NE22 ...... 11 E3
Moorlands. Hedw NE32 .... 76 D1
Moorlands. Prud NE42 .... 59 E1
Moorlands The. Dipton DH9 .... 96 E1
Moormill. Kibble NE11 .... 99 D6
Moormill La. Kibble NE11 .... 99 E6
Moors Cl. Fence DH4 .... 118 B8
Moorsburn Dr. Burn DH4 ...... 114 C1
Moorsfield. Fence DH4 .... 118 B8
Moorside. Lbtn NE12 .... 29 B2
Moorside. Wash NE37 .... 101 B7

Moorside Community Prim Sch. N-u-T NE4 65 A2
Moorside Ct. N-u-T NE5 44 B1
Moorside Cty Fst Sch. N-b-t-S NE64 7 D5
Moorside N. N-u-T NE4 64 C4
Moorside Pl. N-u-T NE4 64 C4
Moorside Rd. Silk SR3 115 D5
Moorside S. N-u-T NE4 64 C3
Moorsley Rd. H le H DH5 118 F2
Moorvale La. N-u-T NE5 44 B2
Moorview Cres. N-u-T NE5 44 B2
Moorway. Wash NE37 & NE38 101 B6
Moorway Dr. N-u-T NE15 62 E7
Moraine Cres. B Mill NE17 95 B6
Moran St. Sland SR6 93 D4
Moray Cl. Birt DH3 100 D1
Moray St. Sland SR6 93 D3
Morcott Gdns. N Shs NE29 50 F4
Morden St. N-u-T NE1 66 A2
Mordey Cl. Sland SR2 106 B1
Morecambe Par. Jarrow NE31 76 A2
Moreland Rd. White NE34 77 D3
Moreland St. Sland SR6 93 D2
Morgan St. Sland SR5 93 B2
Morgy Hill E. 2 Craw NE40 60 F3
Morgy Hill W. 1 Craw NE40 60 F3
Morland Ave. Wash NE38 101 E4
Morland Gdns. Gates NE9 89 B7
Morley Ave. Gates NE10 75 B2
Morley Hill Rd. N-u-T NE5 62 F8
Morley Pl. Shire NE27 30 F4
Morley Terr. Fence DH4 114 A1
Morley Terr. 3 Gates NE10 89 D8
Morningside. Wash NE38 112 E8
Morningside Ct. C le S DH3 112 C4
Mornington Ave. N-u-T NE3 44 C3
Morpeth Ave. Jarrow NE32 76 B3
Morpeth Ave. Pegs NE61 4 E3
Morpeth Ave. S Shs NE34 77 E7
Morpeth Ave. W Open NE13 28 C7
Morpeth Chantry Mid Sch. Mpeth NE61 3 E1
Morpeth Cl. G Post NE62 10 E7
Morpeth Cl. Wash NE38 101 A4
Morpeth Cottage Hospl. Mpeth NE61 8 F6
Morpeth Cty Fst Sch. Mpeth NE61 9 A8
Morpeth Dr. Silk SR3 115 D6
Morpeth Newminster Mid Sch. Mpeth NE61 3 E1
Morpeth Rd. Ashgn NE61 & NE63 5 F4
Morpeth Rd. G Post NE62 10 E7
Morpeth St. N-u-T NE2 65 B4
Morpeth Sta. Mpeth NE61 9 A7
Morpeth Terr. N Shs NE29 50 D4
Morris Ave. B Hall NE34 77 B3
Morris Cres. Boldon NE35 92 A8
Morris Ct. Annit NE23 29 B8
Morris Gdns. Gates NE10 90 B8
Morris Rd. Whick NE16 87 B8
Morris St. Birt DH3 100 C4
Morris St. Gates NE8 88 C8
Morris St. Wash NE37 101 C8
Morrison Rd. Mpeth NE61 4 A1
Morrison St. Gates NE8 71 C2
Morriss Terr. H-le-Sp DH5 118 F7
Morrit Ct. Lbtn NE7 41 C1
Morston Dr. N-u-T NE15 62 E6
Mortimer Ave. N Shs NE29 50 D6
Mortimer Ave. N-u-T NE5 36 F3
Mortimer Chase. E Hart NE23 16 C3
Mortimer Comp Sch. S Shs NE34 77 D7
Mortimer Prim Sch. S Shs NE34 77 D7
Mortimer Rd. S Shs NE33 & NE34 77 D7
Mortimer St. Sland SR4 104 C3
Mortimer Terr. S Del NE25 23 E2
Morton Cl. Wash NE38 101 D4
Morton Cres. Gr Lum DH4 113 F1
Morton Cres. Wools NE5 36 B6
Morton Grange Terr. Gr Lum DH4 113 E1
Morton St. N-u-T NE6 68 A2
Morton St. 1 S Shs NE33 51 D4
Morton Wlk. 6 S Shs NE33 51 C4
Morval Cl. Silk SR3 115 D5
Morven Dr. Gates NE10 75 B1
Morven Lea. Blay NE21 62 B2
Morven Terr. Ashgn NE63 6 B4
Morwick Cl. Cram NE23 22 A5
Morwick Pl. N-u-T NE5 44 A1
Morwick Rd. Tyne NE29 50 D8
Mosley St. N-u-T NE1 66 B1
Moss Bank. Gates NE9 89 B3
Moss Cl. N-u-T NE15 62 C8
Moss Cres. Craw NE40 61 A4
Moss Side. Gates NE9 89 C3
Mosspool. Blay NE21 62 A2
Mostyn Gn. N-u-T NE3 38 C1
Moulton Ct. N-u-T NE5 43 C2
Moulton Pl. N-u-T NE5 43 C2
Mount Cl. Kill NE12 29 D4
Mount Cl. Sland SR4 103 B2
Mount Cl. W Bay NE25 31 D3
Mount Gr. Duns NE11 87 F7
Mount Gr. Sland SR4 109 A4
Mount La. Spring NE9 100 E8
Mount Lonnen. Spring NE9 100 E8
Mount Pleasant. Birt DH3 100 C5
Mount Pleasant. 4 Blay NE21 62 B1
Mount Pleasant. Dipton DH9 96 E1
Mount Pleasant. H-le-Sp DH5 118 F8
Mount Pleasant. N-u-T NE6 67 C2
Mount Pleasant. Sland SR5 93 A1
Mount Pleasant Bglws. 5 Birt DH3 100 C5
Mount Pleasant Ct. Tley NE15 35 D2
Mount Rd. Birt DH3 100 D5
Mount Rd. Gates NE9 100 E8
Mount Rd. Sland SR4 108 C4
Mount Terr. S Shs NE33 51 C2
Mount The. Ryton NE40 61 C5
Mount The. Tley NE15 35 C2
Mount View. 16 Craw NE40 60 F3
Mount View. Whick NE16 87 B8
Mount View Terr. Stocks NE43 82 A7
Mountbatten Ave. Hebb NE31 75 E4
Mountfield Gdns. N-u-T NE3 38 C1
Mountfield Prim Sch. N-u-T NE3 38 B1
Mountford Rd. E Cram NE25 23 D7
Mountside Gdns. Duns NE11 87 F7
Mourne Gdns. Duns NE11 88 A6
Mowbray Cl. Sland SR2 106 A1
Mowbray Cty Jun Mix Sch. S Shs NE33 51 F1
Mowbray Rd. Lbtn NE12 42 B4
Mowbray Rd. N Shs NE29 50 D6
Mowbray Rd. S Shs NE33 51 E1
Mowbray Rd. Sland SR2 106 B1
Mowbray St. N-u-T NE6 67 A3
Mowbray Terr. G Post NE62 10 F7
Mowden Hall (Prep Sch). Newt NE43 57 E7
Moyle Terr. Burnop NE16 97 A4
Mozart St. S Shs NE33 51 D2
Muirfield. S Shs NE33 51 F1
Muirfield. W Bay NE25 31 D5
Muirfield Dr. Gates NE10 89 E6
Muirfield Dr. Wash NE37 90 C2
Muirfield Rd. Lbtn NE7 41 C1
Mulben Cl. N-u-T NE4 70 B4
Mulberry Gdns. Gates NE10 73 C2
Mulberry Pl. N-u-T NE4 71 B3
Mulberry St. Gates NE10 74 A1
Mulcaster Gdns. Walls NE28 49 A3
Mulgrave Dr. Sland SR6 93 E1
Mulgrave Terr. Gates NE8 72 B3
Mulgrave Villas. Gates NE8 72 B2
Mull Gr. B Wh NE32 76 E3
Mullen Dr. Ryton NE40 61 D4
Mullen Gdns. Walls NE28 49 A4
Mullen Rd. Walls NE28 49 B4
Mundella Terr. N-u-T NE6 67 B3
Mundle Ave. Win M NE21 86 C6
Mundles La. Boldon NE36 92 D6
Municipal Terr. Wash NE38 101 D6
Munslow Rd. Sland SR3 115 D8
Murphy Gr. Ryhope SR2 116 E7
Murray Ave. Fence DH4 114 A1
Murray Gdns. 1 Duns NE11 88 A7
Murray Pl. C le S DH2 112 B3
Murray Rd. C le S DH2 & DH3 112 C3
Murray Rd. Walls NE28 49 F3
Murray St. Blay NE21 62 C3
Murrayfield. Seg NE23 22 F2
Murrayfield Rd. N-u-T NE5 44 A3
Murton La. E Lane DH5 119 D1
Murton La. Tyne NE27 & NE29 31 B2
Murton St. Sland SR1 106 B2
Mus of Science & Engineering. N-u-T NE99 71 C4
Muscott Gr. N-u-T NE15 63 A2
Musgrave Rd. Gates NE9 88 F6
Musgrave Sch. Gates NE9 88 F6
Musgrave Terr. Gates NE10 75 B2
Musgrave Terr. N-u-T NE6 68 B2
Musgrave Terr. Wash NE38 101 D6
Muswell Hill. N-u-T NE15 63 A1
Mutual St. Walls NE28 49 B1
Mylord Cres. Kill NE12 29 B5
Myre Hall. 8 H-le-Sp DH5 118 E8
Myrella Cres. Sland SR2 109 C2
Myreside Pl. Lbtn NE12 41 B3
Myrtle Ave. Duns NE11 87 F8
Myrtle Ave. Whit SR6 78 F1
Myrtle Cres. Lbtn NE12 29 D1
Myrtle Gr. Burnop NE16 96 F6
Myrtle Gr. Gates NE11 88 F5
Myrtle Gr. N Silk SR3 116 B7
Myrtle Gr. N-u-T NE2 46 B2
Myrtle Gr. S Shs NE34 77 F4
Myrtle Gr. Walls NE28 49 D1
Myrtle Rd. Blay NE21 62 C1
Myrtle Terr. Ashgn NE63 6 C4
Myrtles. C le S DH2 112 B5
Nafferton Pl. N-u-T NE5 63 C4
Nailsworth Cl. Boldon NE35 76 E2
Nairn Cl. Birt DH3 100 D2
Nairn Cl. Wash NE37 90 C2
Nairn Rd. Cram NE23 22 B7
Nairn St. B Wh NE32 76 E3
Nansen Cl. N-u-T NE5 36 F2
Napier Cl. C le S DH3 112 D8
Napier Ct. Whick NE16 87 B4
Napier Rd. Whick NE16 69 A1
Napier St. Jarrow NE32 76 B7
Napier St. N-u-T NE2 66 C2
Napier St. S Shs NE33 & NE34 77 B6
Napier Way. Blay NE21 62 E2
Narvik Way. N Shs NE29 50 B4
Nash Ave. White NE34 77 D3
Naters St. W Bay NE26 32 C4
Natley Ave. Boldon NE36 92 E7
Navenby Cl. N-u-T NE3 40 A4
Navenby Cl. Seaham SR7 117 A1
Naworth Ave. Tyne NE30 32 A1
Naworth Dr. N-u-T NE5 36 E3
Naworth Terr. Jarrow NE32 76 D4
Nawton Ave. Sland SR5 93 C2
Nayland Rd. Cram NE23 22 A7
Naylor Ave. Win M NE21 86 C6
Naylor Bldgs. Win M NE21 86 C6
Naylor Ct. Blay NE21 62 E4
Naylor Pl. S Slu NE26 24 B7
Neale St. Prud NE42 59 D3
Neale St. Sland SR6 93 E3
Neale St. Tant DH9 97 B2
Nearlane Cl. S Burn NE13 28 C8
Neasdon Cres. Tyne NE30 32 B1
Neasham Rd. Seaham SR7 117 A1
Nedderton Cl. N-u-T NE5 36 B4
Needham Pl. Cram NE23 22 B7
Neighbourhood Ctr The. N-u-T NE5 37 A1
Neil St. E Lane DH5 119 C1
Neill Dr. Sunn NE16 87 B2
Neilson Rd. Gates NE10 73 B3
Nell Terr. R Gill NE39 85 C1
Nellie Gormley House. Kill NE12 29 B2
Nelson Ave. Cram NE23 21 F8
Nelson Ave. N-u-T NE3 39 A1
Nelson Ave. S Shs NE33 51 E3
Nelson Cl. Ashgn NE63 6 E2
Nelson Cl. Sland SR2 106 B1
Nelson Cres. N Shs NE29 50 D2
Nelson Dr. Cram NE23 15 F1
Nelson House. 14 Tyne NE30 51 D7
Nelson Ind Est. Cram NE23 15 F2
Nelson Park Ind Est. Cram NE23 15 E1
Nelson Park West. Cram NE23 15 D1
Nelson Rd. Cram NE23 15 D1
Nelson Rd. Ears NE25 31 B5
Nelson Rd. N-u-T NE6 75 B4
Nelson Rd. Stake NE62 11 A7
Nelson St. C le S DH3 112 C2
Nelson St. Duns NE11 70 C2
Nelson St. Gates NE8 72 C3
Nelson St. Green NE40 60 F1
Nelson St. H le H DH5 119 A3
Nelson St. N-u-T NE1 66 A1
Nelson St. Ryhope SR2 116 F7
Nelson St. 12 S Shs NE33 51 C3
Nelson St. Wash NE38 101 E4
Nelson Terr. Chopw NE17 84 B1
Nelson Terr. N Shs NE29 50 D3
Nelson Terr. Sherb DH6 120 A1
Nelson Way. Cram NE23 15 E2
Nene Ct. 11 Wash NE37 101 E8
Nent Gr. Hexham NE46 54 C4
Neptune Rd. N-u-T NE15 62 D6
Neptune Rd. N-u-T NE15 62 E7
Neptune Rd. Walls NE28 75 B8
Nesburn Rd. Sland SR4 105 A1
Nesham Pl. H-le-Sp DH5 118 F8
Nesham Terr. Sland SR1 106 C3
Nest Rd. Gates NE10 74 A2
Nether Farm Rd. Gates NE10 74 C1
Nether Riggs. Bed NE22 15 F8
Netherburn Rd. Sland SR5 93 C2
Netherby Dr. N-u-T NE5 63 C4
Netherdale. Bed NE22 10 D1
Netherton Ave. Tyne NE29 50 D7
Netherton Gdns. W Open NE13 28 B6
Netherton Gr. Tyne NE29 50 D7
Netherton La. Bed NE22 10 C1
Netherton Park Assessment Ctr. Stan NE61 14 D6
Nettleham Rd. Sland SR5 93 C2
Nettles La. Burdon SR3 116 B6
Nettles La. N Silk SR3 116 B6
Nevill Rd. Stocks NE43 82 D7
Neville Cres. Birt DH3 100 C6
Neville Ct. 3 Wash NE37 101 F8
Neville Rd. N-u-T NE15 62 E7
Neville Rd. Sland SR4 104 C3
Neville Sq. Lmth NE61 2 A2
Neville St. N-u-T NE1 72 A4
Neville's Cross Rd. Hebb NE31 75 F5
Nevinson Ave. White NE34 77 E3
Nevis Cl. W Bay NE26 31 E8
Nevis Ct. W Bay NE26 31 E8
Nevis Gr. Boldon NE36 92 B7
Nevis Way. W Bay NE26 31 E7
New Bridge St. N-u-T NE1 66 C1
New Bridge St W. N-u-T NE1 & NE99 66 B2
New Durham Rd. Sland SR2 105 C2
New Front St. Tanf L DH9 97 D1
New George St. S Shs NE33 51 C1
New Green St. S Shs NE33 51 C1
New Hartley Cty Fst Sch. E Cram NE25 23 D6
New Herrington Ind Est. Pens DH4 114 D6
New King St. N-b-t-S NE64 7 F5
New Mills. N-u-T NE2 & NE4 65 B2
New Penshaw Inf Sch. Pens DH4 114 B8
New Phoenix Yd. Mpeth NE61 9 A8
New Quay. N Shs NE29 51 B4
New Queen St. N-b-t-S NE64 7 E5
New Rd. Boldon NE35 & NE36 92 B8
New Rd. Burnop NE16 97 B7
New Rd. Gates NE11 88 B6
New Rd. Gates NE10 90 C5
New Rd. Seaham SR7 117 B1
New Rd. Wash NE38 113 C8
New Ridley Rd. Stocks NE43 82 D5
New Seaham Byron Terrace Cty Sch. Seaham SR7 116 F1
New Silksworth Inf Sch. N Silk SR3 116 B7
New Silksworth Jun Sch. N Silk SR3 116 B7
New South Terr. Birt DH3 100 D4
New St. Sherb DH6 120 A1
New St. Sland SR4 103 A2
New York Rd. Shire NE27 30 E2
New York Rd. Tyne NE29 31 B1
New York Way. Shire NE29 31 A1
New York Way. Shire NE27 & NE29 50 A8
Newark Cres. Seaham SR7 117 A1
Newark Dr. Whit SR6 93 F8
Newark Sq. N Shs NE29 50 F4
Newarth Cl. N-u-T NE15 62 E7
Newbank Wlk. Blay NE21 62 A1
Newbiggin Hall Simonside Cty Mid Sch. N-u-T NE5 36 F5
Newbiggin La. N-u-T NE5 36 F4
Newbiggin Rd. Ashgn NE63 6 E1
Newbiggin-by-the-Sea Cty Mid Sch. N-b-t-S NE64 7 C4
Newbold Ave. Sland SR5 93 C2
Newbold St. N-u-T NE6 68 A1
Newbolt Ct. Gates NE8 73 A2
Newbottle Grange. New DH4 114 D4
Newbottle Prim Sch. New DH4 114 D3
Newbottle St. H-le-Sp DH4 114 E1
Newbridge Ave. Sland SR5 93 C2
Newbridge Bank. Bourn DH3 112 F5
Newbrough Cres. N-u-T NE2 46 B2
Newburgh Ave. S Del NE25 23 D2
Newburn Ave. Sland SR5 93 C2
Newburn Bridge Rd. Ryton NE15 & NE21 61 E6
Newburn Cres. Burn DH4 114 D1
Newburn Ct. S Shs NE33 51 D1
Newburn Haugh Ind Est. N-u-T NE15 62 C6
Newburn Ind Est. Newb NE21 62 A6
Newburn Lane End. Tley NE15 35 D2
Newburn Manor Fst Sch. Newb NE15 61 F8
Newburn Rd. Newb NE15 61 F8
Newburn Rd. Tley NE15 35 E1
Newbury. Kill NE12 29 D4
Newbury Ave. Gates NE8 88 D8
Newbury Cl. N-u-T NE15 62 D7
Newbury St. S Shs NE33 77 D7
Newbury St. Sland SR5 93 D3
Newby La. H Pitt DH6 120 C5
Newby Pl. Gates NE9 89 B4
Newcastle Airport. Wools NE20 26 D3
Newcastle Bank. Birt NE9 100 B7
Newcastle Bsns Pk. N-u-T NE4 70 C3
Newcastle Church High Sch The. N-u-T NE2 66 B4
Newcastle Coll Trevelyan Bldg. N-u-T NE4 71 B4
Newcastle General Hospl. N-u-T NE4 64 C2
Newcastle Nuffield Hospl The. N-u-T NE2 66 B4
Newcastle Rd. Birt DH3 100 C6
Newcastle Rd. Blyth NE24 17 C4
Newcastle Rd. Boldon NE36 91 E6
Newcastle Rd. C le S DH3 112 C5
Newcastle Rd. Hedw NE10 & NE36 91 C7
Newcastle Rd. Jarrow NE34 76 F5
Newcastle Rd. Sland SR5 93 C3
Newcastle Royal Gram Sch. N-u-T NE2 66 C3
Newcastle St. N Shs NE29 51 A5
Newcastle Terr. 6 Tyne NE30 51 D7
Newcastle-upon-Tyne Polytechnic. N-u-T NE1 66 B2
Newdene Wlk. N-u-T NE15 62 D7
Newfield Wlk. Whick NE16 87 A6
Newgate Sh Ctr. N-u-T NE1 66 A1
Newgate St. Mpeth NE61 3 F1
Newgate St. N-u-T NE1 66 A1
Newham Ave. Hazle NE13 28 A4
Newhaven Ave. Sland SR5 93 C2
Newington Ct. Sland SR5 93 C1
Newington Ct. Wash NE37 101 C8
Newington Rd. N-u-T NE6 67 A2
Newker Cty Inf Sch. C le S DH2 112 B2
Newland Ct. S Shs NE34 77 C5
Newlands. Tyne NE30 32 A2
Newlands Ave. Blyth NE24 17 D5
Newlands Ave. N-u-T NE3 28 D1
Newlands Ave. Sland SR3 109 B3
Newlands Ave. W Bay NE25 31 D3
Newlands Pl. Blyth NE24 17 D5
Newlands Prep Sch. N-u-T NE3 46 A4
Newlands Rd. Blyth NE24 17 D5
Newlands Rd. N-u-T NE2 46 A3
Newlands Rd W. Seaham SR7 117 B1
Newlyn Cres. N Shs NE29 50 E5
Newlyn Dr. Cram NE23 22 B8
Newlyn Dr. Jarrow NE32 76 D6
Newlyn Rd. N-u-T NE3 38 B1
Newman Terr. Gates NE8 89 A8
Newmarch St. Jarrow NE32 76 A7
Newmarket Wlk. 1 S Shs NE33 51 D1
Newmin Way. Whick NE16 86 F5
Newminster Cl. Burn DH4 114 B2
Newminster Rd. N-u-T NE4 64 A3
Newport Gr. 6 N Silk SR3 116 A8
Newquay Gdns. 4 Gates NE9 89 A2
Newriggs. Wash NE38 101 E2
Newsham Cl. N-u-T NE5 36 B4
Newsham Cty Fst Sch. Blyth NE24 17 C5
Newsham Rd. Blyth NE24 17 C6
Newstead Cl. Wash NE38 101 C5
Newstead Rd. Burn DH4 114 C2
Newstead Sq. Silk SR3 116 A6
Newsteads Cl. W Bay NE25 31 D5
Newsteads Dr. W Bay NE25 31 D5
Newton Ave. Tyne NE30 32 B3
Newton Ave. Walls NE28 49 F3
Newton Cl. N-u-T NE15 62 E7
Newton Gr. S Shs NE34 77 A5
Newton House. N-u-T NE4 65 B2
Newton Pl. N-u-T NE7 47 B2
Newton Rd. N-u-T NE7 47 B2
Newton St. Duns NE11 70 C2
Newton St. Gates NE8 88 D8
Newton Terr. M Sq NE43 58 E1
Nichol Ct. N-u-T NE4 64 A1
Nichol St. N-u-T NE4 64 A1
Nicholas Ave. Whit SR6 93 F8
Nicholas St. H le H DH5 119 B5
Nicholson Cl. Sland SR1 106 B2
Nicholson Terr. Kill NE12 29 E1
Nidderdale Ave. H le H DH5 118 F2
Nidderdale Cl. Blyth NE24 17 A8
Nidsdale Ave. N-u-T NE6 75 A7
Nightingale Cl. Sland SR4 107 B4
Nile Cl. N-u-T NE15 62 C8
Nile Ct. Gates NE8 73 A1
Nile St. N Shs NE29 51 A5
Nile St. S Shs NE33 51 B2
Nile St. Sland SR1 106 B3
Nilverton Ave. Sland SR2 110 A3
Nimbus Ct. 10 Silk SR3 116 A6
Nine Lands. H-le-Sp DH4 118 C8
Ninth Ave. Blyth NE24 17 D6
Ninth Ave. C le S DH2 112 B3
Ninth Ave. Gates NE11 88 D3
Ninth Ave. Mpeth NE61 9 B7
Ninth Ave. N-u-T NE6 67 C4
Ninth Ave E. Gates NE11 88 D3
Ninth Row. Ashgn NE63 6 B4
Nissan Way. Wash NE37 102 C7
Nithdale Cl. N-u-T NE6 75 B8
Nixon St. Gates NE8 73 A4
Nixon Terr. Blyth NE24 17 F6
Noble Gdns. S Shs NE34 76 F4
Noble St. Gates NE10 74 A1
Noble St. N-u-T NE4 70 C3
Noble St. Sland SR2 106 C1
Noble Terr. Mpeth NE61 9 A8
Noble Terr. Sland SR2 106 C1
Noble's Bank Rd. Sland SR2 106 C1
Noel Ave. Win M NE21 86 C6
Noel Terr. Win M NE21 86 D7
Noirmont Way. Silk SR3 115 E6
Nook The. N Shs NE29 50 F5
Nook The. W Bay NE25 31 F4
Nookside. Sland SR4 107 C4
Nookside Ct. Sland SR4 107 C4
Nora St. S Shs NE34 77 C5
Nora St. Sland SR4 108 C4
Norbury Gr. N-u-T NE6 68 A1
Nordale Way. Blyth NE24 17 A8
Norfolk Ave. Birt DH3 100 D1
Norfolk Ave. N Silk SR3 115 F8
Norfolk Cl. Ashgn NE63 6 A4
Norfolk Cl. Seaham SR7 117 A1
Norfolk Dr. Wash NE37 90 D2
Norfolk Gdns. Walls NE28 49 E4
Norfolk Pl. Birt DH3 100 D1
Norfolk Rd. Gates NE8 73 A4
Norfolk Rd. S Shs NE34 78 C7
Norfolk Sq. N-u-T NE6 67 B2
Norfolk St. H le H DH5 118 F4
Norfolk St. N Shs NE30 51 B5
Norfolk St. Sland SR1 106 A3
Norfolk Way. N-u-T NE15 62 E7
Norham Ave N. S Shs NE34 78 A8
Norham Ave S. S Shs NE34 78 A8
Norham Cl. B Vill NE13 28 A5
Norham Cl. Blyth NE24 17 C7
Norham Ct. Wash NE38 101 B4
Norham Dr. N-u-T NE5 36 E3
Norham Gdns. Stake NE62 6 A1
Norham High Sch. N Shs NE29 50 D5
Norham Pl. N-u-T NE2 46 B1
Norham Rd. Ashgn NE63 6 D2
Norham Rd. N Shs NE29 50 C5
Norham Rd. N-u-T NE3 39 B2
Norham Rd. W Bay NE26 31 F5
Norham Rd N. Shire NE29 50 B7
Norham Terr. Jarrow NE32 76 B3
Norhurst. Whick NE16 86 E5
Norland Rd. N-u-T NE15 62 F6
Norley Ave. Sland SR5 93 C2
Norma Cres. Tyne NE26 32 C4
Norman Ave. N Silk SR3 116 B7
Norman Rd. R Gill NE39 85 F1
Norman Terr. H Pitt DH6 120 C5
Norman Terr. Mpeth NE61 9 A8
Norman Terr. Walls NE28 50 B2
Normanby Cl. Seaham SR7 117 A1
Normandy Cres. H-le-Sp DH5 118 F8
Normanton Terr. N-u-T NE4 65 A1
Normount Ave. N-u-T NE4 64 B1
Normount Gdns. N-u-T NE4 64 B2
Normount Rd. N-u-T NE4 64 B1
North App. C le S DH2 112 B4
North Ave. G Post NE62 10 E7
North Ave. Lbtn NE12 42 A2
North Ave. N-u-T NE5 36 F3
North Ave. N-u-T NE3 45 C4
North Ave. S Shs NE34 77 F6
North Ave. Wash NE37 90 C1
North Balkwell Farm Ind Est. Shire NE29 50 B7
North Bank Ct. Sland SR5 93 B2
North Bridge St. Sland SR5 106 A4
North Burns. C le S DH3 112 C4
North Church St. 2 N Shs NE30 51 B6
North Cl. N-u-T NE6 67 C3
North Cl. Ryton NE40 61 C5
North Cl. S Shs NE34 77 F6
North Cres. Wash NE38 101 B1
North Croft. Lbtn NE12 42 B3
North Cross St. N-u-T NE3 39 C1
North Ct. 5 Jarrow NE32 76 B7
North Dr. C le S DH3 112 E7
North Dr. Clea SR6 77 F1
North Dr. Hebb NE31 75 C4
North Durham St. Sland SR1 106 B3
North East Aircraft Mus. Wash SR5 91 E2
North Eastern Ct. Duns NE16 87 E8
North Farm. Nedder NE22 15 A8
North Farm Ave. Sland SR4 107 B2
North Farm Rd. Hebb NE31 75 D5
North Fawdon Prim Sch. N-u-T NE3 38 C3
North Gr. Ryton NE40 61 D5
North Gr. Sland SR6 93 E3
North Grange. Pont NE20 25 E8
North Guards. Whit SR6 93 F8
North Hall Rd. Sland SR4 108 A4
North Hylton Rd. Sland SR5 92 E2
North Hylton Road Ind Est. Sland SR5 92 D2
North Jesmond Ave. N-u-T NE2 46 B2
North King St. N Shs NE30 51 B6
North La. Boldon NE36 92 D7
North La. H le H DH5 119 E5
North Leech. Mpeth NE61 3 D2
North Leigh. Tanf L DH9 97 D1
North Lodge. C le S DH3 112 D7
North Magdalene. Medom DH8 95 B1
North Meadows. Oham NE42 59 B5
North Milburn St. Sland SR4 105 B3
North Moor Ct. Sland SR3 108 B1
North Moor La. Sland SR3 115 E8
North Moor Rd. Sland SR3 108 B1
North Par. Chopp NE62 10 E6
North Par. W Bay NE26 32 B5
North Pl. Mpeth NE61 3 E1
North Ravensworth St. Sland SR4 105 B3
North Rd. Boldon NE35 & NE36 76 E1
North Rd. Boldon NE35 & NE36 91 F7
North Rd. Boldon NE36 92 C7
North Rd. C le S DH3 112 C7
North Rd. H le H DH5 118 E4
North Rd. H-le-Sp DH5 118 E4
North Rd. Pont NE20 25 E8
North Rd. Seaham SR7 117 C1
North Rd. Slal NE47 80 A4
North Rd. Tyne NE29 50 F8
North Rd. Tyne NE29 & NE30 51 A8
North Rd. Walls NE28 49 B2
North Ridge. Bed NE22 10 D1
North Ridge. Bed NE22 10 E1
North Ridge. W Bay NE25 31 C6
North Row. Prud NE42 59 A2
North Sands Bsns Ctr. Sland SR6 106 B4
North Seaton Ind Est. Ashgn NE63 6 F1
North Seaton Rd. Ashgn NE63 6 D2
North Seaton Rd. N-b-t-S NE64 7 D3
North Shields Sta. N Shs NE29 51 A5
North St. Birt DH3 100 E3
North St. Blay NE21 62 A2
North St. Clea SR6 78 A1
North St. E Rain DH5 118 D4
North St. Jarrow NE32 76 B7
North St. N Silk SR3 116 A8
North St. N-u-T NE1 66 A2
North St. New DH4 114 D4
North St. S Shs NE33 51 C3
North St. Sland SR5 93 C1
North St. W Rain DH4 118 A2
North St E. N-u-T NE1 66 B2
North Terr. Chopw NE17 84 B2
North Terr. Hexham NE46 54 B4
North Terr. 11 N Silk SR3 116 A8
North Terr. N-u-T NE2 65 C3
North Terr. Shire NE27 30 E1
North Terr. Walls NE28 49 D2
North Terr. Walls NE28 49 E2
North Tyne Ind Est. Lbtn NE12 49 A8
North Tyneside Coll. Walls NE28 49 E5
North Tyneside Coll of F Ed. W Bay NE26 32 C4
North Tyneside General Hospl. Tyne NE29 31 E1
North View. Ashgn NE63 6 C4
North View. Bed NE22 11 D3
North View. Bourn DH4 113 E2
North View. Cam NE62 12 C6
North View. Craw NE40 60 E7
North View. Dgton NE13 27 B7
North View. E Lane DH5 119 C1
North View. Gates NE9 89 B3
North View. H Spen NE39 84 F3
North View. Hasw DH6 121 E1
North View. Hazle NE13 28 A4
North View. Jarrow NE32 76 A6
North View. Lbtn NE12 42 A4
North View. M Sq NE43 58 E1
North View. Medom DH8 95 B1
North View. N-b-t-S NE64 7 D3
North View. N-u-T NE6 67 B3
North View. N-u-T NE6 67 C3
North View. Ouston DH2 99 F1
North View. R Gill NE39 85 C2
North View. Ryton NE40 61 A5
North View. S Hill DH6 120 D1
North View. S Shs NE34 77 F8
North View. Sland SR5 92 C1
North View. Sland SR6 93 D3
North View. Sland SR4 103 B1
North View. Stake NE62 11 C8
North View. Tyne NE26 & NE30 32 C4
North View. Tyne NE29 50 F8
North View. Walls NE28 49 C2
North View. Whick NE11 87 A7
North View Terr. Fence DH4 118 B8
North View Terr. Gates NE8 73 C1
North View Terr. Prud NE42 59 B2
North View Terr. Stocks NE43 82 C7
North View W. R Gill NE39 85 C2
North Villas. Dud NE23 22 A1
North Walbottle Rd. N-u-T NE5 36 B4
North Walbottle Rd. Walb NE5 36 A2
Northbourne. Gates NE9 88 F5
Northbourne Ave. Mpeth NE61 3 F2
Northbourne Rd. Hebb NE31 & NE32 76 A6
Northbourne St. Gates NE8 88 F8
Northbourne St. N-u-T NE4 70 C4
Northburn Wood. Cram NE23 16 A1
Northcote. Whick NE16 87 A5
Northcote Ave. N-u-T NE5 36 C1
Northcote Ave. Sland SR1 106 B2
Northcote Ave. W Bay NE25 31 D4
Northcote St. N-u-T NE4 65 A1
Northcote St. S Shs NE33 77 D8
Northcott Gdns. Seg NE23 22 E1
Northdene. Birt DH3 100 C7
Northern Counties Sch for the Deaf. N-u-T NE2 46 A1
Northern Terr. Dud NE23 22 A1
Northern Way. Sland SR5 93 A2
Northfield. Cam NE22 12 B4
Northfield Cl. Whick NE16 86 F5
Northfield Dr. Kill NE12 29 B2
Northfield Dr. Sland SR4 107 B2
Northfield Gdns. S Shs NE34 77 F8
Northfield Rd. N-u-T NE3 45 B4
Northfield Rd. S Shs NE33 & NE34 51 F1
Northgate. Kill NE12 29 D4
Northgate & District Hospl. Hebron NE61 3 D4
Northland Cl. Sland SR4 107 B2
Northlands. Blay NE21 62 B1
Northlands. C le S DH3 112 C5
Northlands. Tyne NE30 32 B1
Northlands Rd. Mpeth NE61 3 F2
Northlea. N-u-T NE15 62 E8
Northmoor Rd. N-u-T NE6 68 B4
Northolt Ave. Cram NE23 22 B7
Northside Pl. S Del NE25 23 E2
Northumberland Aged Mineworkers Homes. Cram NE23 22 D5
Northumberland Ave. Bed NE22 10 E1
Northumberland Ave. Lbtn NE12 42 A3
Northumberland Ave. N-b-t-S NE64 7 D4
Northumberland Ave. N-u-T NE3 45 A3

Nor – Pea 141

Northumberland Ave. Walls NE28 49 F2
Northumberland Cl. Ashgn NE63 6 A4
Northumberland Ct. Hebb NE31 75 D5
Northumberland Cty Tech Coll. Ashgn NE63 6 E2
Northumberland Dock Rd. N Shs NE28 50 C1
Northumberland Gdns. N-u-T NE5 36 B3
Northumberland Gdns. N-u-T NE2 67 A4
Northumberland Golf Course. N-u-T NE3 28 E2
Northumberland Pl. Birt DH3 100 D1
Northumberland Pl. 9 N Shs NE30 51 A6
Northumberland Pl. N-u-T NE1 66 A2
Northumberland Rd. N-u-T NE15 62 C6
Northumberland Rd. N-u-T NE1 & NE99 66 B2
Northumberland Rd. Ryton NE40 61 C6
Northumberland Sq. 4 N Shs NE30 51 A6
Northumberland Sq. W Bay NE26 32 A5
Northumberland St. Gates NE8 71 C1
Northumberland St. N Shs NE30 51 C6
Northumberland St. N-u-T NE1 66 A2
Northumberland St. Walls NE28 49 C2
Northumberland Terr. N-u-T NE6 67 B2
Northumberland Terr. Tyne NE30 51 D7
Northumberland Terr. Walls NE28 49 F2
Northumberland Villas. Walls NE28 49 E2
Northumberland Way. Wash NE10 & NE37 90 D3
Northumberland Way. Wash NE37 & NE38 101 F4
Northumbria Ct. N-u-T NE5 43 A2
Northumbria Lodge. N-u-T NE5 44 B1
Northumbria Police Headquarters. Pont NE 20 25 D8
Northumbria Wlk. N-u-T NE5 36 F1
Northumbrian Rd. Cram NE23 22 B6
Northumbrian Way. Kill NE12 29 C2
Northumbrian Way. N Shs NE29 51 A3
Northway. G Post NE62 10 F7
Northway. Gates NE9 89 B7
Northway. Tley NE15 35 E2
Northwood Ct. Sland SR5 93 C2
Norton Ave. Seaham SR7 117 A1
Norton Cl. C le S DH2 112 A1
Norton Rd. Sland SR5 93 A3
Norton Way. N-u-T NE15 62 E6
Norway Ave. Sland SR4 108 B4
Norwich Ave. W Open NE13 28 B5
Norwich Cl. Ashgn NE63 7 A2
Norwich Way. Cram NE23 22 A7
Norwich Way. Hedw NE32 76 B1
Norwood Ave. N-u-T NE3 28 C1
Norwood Ave. N-u-T NE6 47 B1
Norwood Cres. R Gill NE39 85 F2
Norwood Ct. Gates NE9 89 A8
Norwood Gdns. 4 Gates NE9 89 A8
Norwood Rd. Gates NE11 88 D7
Norwood Rd. N-u-T NE15 62 D8
Nun St. N-u-T NE1 66 A1
Nuneaton Way. N-u-T NE5 36 B4
Nunn St. S Row DH4 114 A5
Nunnykirk Cl. Oham NE42 59 A4
Nuns La. Gates NE8 72 C3
Nuns La. N-u-T NE1 66 A1
Nuns Moor Cres. N-u-T NE4 64 B3
Nuns Moor Rd. N-u-T NE4 64 B3
Nunthorpe Ave. Sland SR2 110 C1
Nunwick Gdns. N Shs NE29 50 C6
Nursery Cl. Sland SR3 109 A2
Nursery Ct. B Mill NE17 95 B6
Nursery La. Clea SR6 78 A1
Nursery La. Gates NE10 89 C7
Nursery Pk. Ashgn NE63 6 E1
Nursery Rd. Sland SR3 109 B2
Nutley Pl. N-u-T NE15 63 A1
Nye Dene. Sland SR5 92 B1

O'Hanlon Cres. Walls NE28 49 A4
Oak Ave. Dgton NE13 27 C7
Oak Ave. Duns NE11 87 F7
Oak Ave. 5 H-le-Sp DH4 118 D8
Oak Ave. S Shs NE34 78 A5
Oak Cl. Hexham NE46 53 D6
Oak Cres. Whit SR6 79 A1
Oak Gr. Lbtn NE12 42 A4
Oak Gr. Walls NE28 49 D1
Oak Rd. Shire NE29 50 B7
Oak Sq. Gates NE8 71 C1
Oak St. Gr Lum DH4 113 E1
Oak St. Jarrow NE32 76 A7
Oak St. M Sq NE43 82 E8
Oak St. S Burn NE13 28 C8
Oak St. Sland SR1 106 C2
Oak St. Tley NE15 35 D2
Oak St. Wash NE38 101 F4
Oak Terr. Blay NE21 62 C1
Oak Terr. Burnop NE16 97 C6
Oak Terr. Tant DH9 97 B2
Oakapple Cl. Bed NE22 10 F1
Oakdale Cl. N-u-T NE15 62 D6
Oakdale Terr. C le S DH3 112 C2
Oakenshaw. N-u-T NE15 62 E6
Oakes Pl. N-u-T NE4 65 B1
Oakeys Rd. Tanf L DH9 97 F1
Oakfield Ave. Whick NE16 87 B6
Oakfield Cl. Sland SR3 115 C6
Oakfield Cl. Whick NE16 87 B6
Oakfield Ct. Sland SR3 115 C6
Oakfield Dr. Kill NE12 29 F3
Oakfield Dr. Whick NE16 87 B6
Oakfield Gdns. N-u-T NE15 64 A1
Oakfield Gdns. Walls NE28 48 C3
Oakfield Inf Sch. Gates NE9 88 F3
Oakfield Jun Sch. Gates NE9 88 F3
Oakfield N. Ryton NE40 61 B5
Oakfield Pk. Prud NE42 59 D2
Oakfield Rd. Duns NE11 88 A6
Oakfield Rd. N-u-T NE3 45 B3
Oakfield Rd. Whick NE16 87 A5
Oakfield Terr. Gates NE10 75 B2
Oakfield Terr. Kill NE12 29 E1
Oakfield Terr. N-u-T NE3 45 B4
Oakfield Way. Seg NE23 22 F1
Oakfields. Burnop NE16 97 B7
Oakham Ave. Whick NE16 86 F6
Oakham Gdns. N Shs NE29 50 E5
Oakhurst Dr. N-u-T NE3 45 A3
Oakhurst Terr. Lbtn NE12 42 A3
Oakland Rd. N-u-T NE2 46 A2
Oakland Rd. W Bay NE25 31 D4
Oakland Terr. Ashgn NE63 6 C3
Oakland Terr. Lmth NE61 2 A2
Oaklands. N-u-T NE3 45 C3
Oaklands. Pont NE20 25 D4
Oaklands. R Mill NE44 80 F7
Oaklands. Stake NE62 11 A7
Oaklands. Whick NE16 69 B1
Oaklands. Whick NE16 87 C8
Oaklands Ave. N-u-T NE3 45 C3
Oaklands Ct. Pont NE20 25 D4
Oaklands Rise. R Mill NE44 80 F7
Oaklands Terr. Sland SR4 105 A1
Oaklea. C le S DH2 112 A5
Oakleigh Gdns. Clea SR6 78 A2
Oakley Cl. Annit NE23 29 B8
Oakley Dr. Cram NE23 22 D7
Oakley Gardens Special Sch. Clea SR6 78 B2
Oakridge. Whick NE16 86 F6
Oaks The. E Lane DH5 119 D1
Oaks The. Green NE40 61 B1
Oaks The. H Spen NE39 85 A3
Oaks The. Hexham NE46 53 F3
Oaks The. Pens DH4 114 B8
Oaks The. Sland SR2 106 B1
Oaks W The. Sland SR2 106 A1
Oaktree Ave. N-u-T NE28 & NE6 49 A1
Oaktree Gdns. W Bay NE25 31 E3
Oaktree Terr. Prud NE42 59 D2
Oakville. Ashgn NE63 7 A2
Oakwellgate. Gates NE8 72 C4
Oakwood. Gates NE10 89 E5
Oakwood. Hebb NE31 75 C7
Oakwood. Oak NE46 54 E8
Oakwood Ave. Gates NE9 89 A3
Oakwood Ave. N-b-t-S NE64 7 D5
Oakwood Ave. W Open NE13 28 C5
Oakwood Bank. Oak NE46 54 C7
Oakwood Cl. Spring NE9 89 F1
Oakwood Gdns. Duns NE11 88 B5
Oakwood Pl. N-u-T NE5 43 C1
Oakwood St. Sland SR2 105 B1
Oatens Bank. Hors NE15 33 A2
Oates St. Sland SR4 105 A2
Oatfield Cl. Ashgn NE63 6 B2
Oatlands Rd. Sland SR4 108 B4
Oban Ave. Walls NE28 49 F4
Oban Ct. N-u-T NE6 67 C1
Oban Gdns. N-u-T NE6 67 C1
Oban St. B Wh NE32 76 E3
Oban St. Gates NE10 & NE8 73 C1
Ocean Rd. S Shs NE33 51 D3
Ocean Rd. Sland SR2 110 C2
Ocean Rd N. Sland SR2 110 C2
Ocean Rd S. Sland SR2 110 C2
Ocean View. N-b-t-S NE64 7 E4
Ocean View. Sland SR2 116 F8
Ocean View. W Bay NE26 32 B5
Ochiltree Ct. S Slu NE26 24 D6
Octavia Cl. Bed NE22 10 E2
Octavia Ct. Walls NE28 49 F4
Octavian Way. Gates NE11 88 C3
Offerton Cl. Sland SR4 103 A2
Offerton La. Pens SR4 102 F4
Offerton La. Sland SR4 103 A1
Offerton St. Sland SR4 105 B2
Office Pl. H le H DH5 119 A3
Office Row. N Herr DH4 114 E7
Office Row. Wash NE38 101 A1
Ogden St. Sland SR4 105 B2
Ogle Ave. Hazle NE13 28 A4
Ogle Ave. Mpeth NE61 8 E8
Ogle Dr. Blyth NE24 17 C7
Ogle Gr. Jarrow NE32 76 A3
Oil Mill Rd. N-u-T NE6 75 B7
Okehampton Ct. 2 Gates NE9 89 A2
Okehampton Sq. Sland SR5 93 A3
Old Brewery Sq. Oving NE42 58 C4
Old Coronation St. S Shs NE33 51 C2
Old Course Rd. Clea SR6 93 A8
Old Durham Rd. Gates NE8 & NE9 89 B6
Old Farm Ct. Sunn NE16 87 B2
Old Fold Rd. Gates NE10 & NE8 73 B2
Old Forge The. Newt NE43 57 C5
Old Main St. Craw NE40 60 E3
Old Mill Rd. Sland SR5 93 A3
Old Mill Rd. Sland SR2 106 C1
Old Sawmill. Mford NE61 8 A8
Old Station Ct. Pont NE20 25 C3
Old Vicarage Wlk. N-u-T NE6 67 C2
Old Well La. Blay NE21 62 B1
Oldfield Rd. N-u-T NE6 74 C3
Oldgate. Mpeth NE61 8 F8
Oldgate Ct. Mpeth NE61 8 F8
Oldstead Gdns. Sland SR4 108 B4
Olga Terr. R Gill NE39 85 C1
Olive Gdns. Gates NE9 89 A6
Olive Pl. N-u-T NE4 64 A3
Olive St. S Shs NE33 77 B6
Olive St. Sland SR1 105 C2
Oliver Ave. N-u-T NE4 64 B2
Oliver Cres. Birt DH3 100 C6
Oliver St. N-u-T NE15 63 B1
Oliver St. Wash NE38 101 E4
Ollerton Dr. Tley NE15 35 B2
Ollerton Gdns. Gates NE10 89 C6
Olney Cl. Cram NE23 22 D7
Olympia Ave. G Post NE62 10 F7
Olympia Gdns. Mpeth NE61 4 A1
Olympia Hill. Mpeth NE61 3 F2
Ongar Way. Lbtn NE12 41 B3
Onslow Gdns. Gates NE9 88 F5
Onslow St. Sland SR4 104 B3
Open The. N-u-T NE1 66 A2
Oram Cl. Mpeth NE61 9 B8
Orange Gr. Annit NE23 22 B1
Orange Gr. Whick NE16 87 C8
Orchard Ave. R Gill NE39 85 D1
Orchard Cl. Ashgn NE63 6 C2
Orchard Cl. Kill NE12 29 F2
Orchard Cl. Mpeth NE61 9 B8
Orchard Cl. Prud NE42 59 D1
Orchard Cl. R Gill NE39 96 D8
Orchard Cl. S Shs NE34 77 B5
Orchard Cres. Crbdge NE45 56 A5
Orchard Ct. Green NE40 & NE41 60 F1
Orchard Ct. Ryton NE40 61 C5
Orchard Dene. R Gill NE39 85 D1
Orchard Gdns. C le S DH3 112 C1
Orchard Gdns. Gates NE9 89 A4
Orchard Gdns. Walls NE28 49 A4
Orchard Gdns. Whit SR6 93 E8
Orchard Gn. N-u-T NE5 44 A4
Orchard Pk. 7 Birt DH3 100 C4
Orchard Pl. N-u-T NE2 46 C1
Orchard Rd. R Gill NE39 85 D1
Orchard Rd. Whick NE16 87 C7
Orchard St. Birt DH3 100 C4
Orchard St. N-u-T NE1 72 A4
Orchard St. Sland SR4 104 C3
Orchard Terr. C le S DH3 112 C1
Orchard Terr. N-u-T NE15 62 C6
Orchard Terr. R Gill NE39 96 D8
Orchard Terr. Tley NE15 35 D2
Orchard The. Boldon NE36 92 C7
Orchard The. C le S DH3 112 D4
Orchard The. Heps NE61 9 E5
Orchard The. 4 N Shs NE29 51 A6
Orchard The. N-u-T NE15 62 D6
Orchard The. Whick NE16 87 C7
Orchard The. Wylam NE41 60 A6
Orchard-Leigh. N-u-T NE15 62 E5
Orchards The. Blyth NE24 17 B8
Orchid Cres. Gates NE10 73 C2
Ord Ct. N-u-T NE4 64 A3
Ord St. N-u-T NE4 71 C3
Ord Terr. Stake NE62 11 B8
Orde Ave. Walls NE28 49 E3
Ordley Cl. N-u-T NE15 62 E6
Oriel Cl. Sland SR6 93 D1
Oriole House. Lbtn NE12 42 A3
Orkney Dr. Sland SR2 116 D8
Orlando Rd. N Shs NE29 50 E6
Ormesby Rd. Sland SR6 93 D3
Ormiscraig. N-u-T NE15 62 E5
Ormiston. N-u-T NE15 62 E6
Ormonde Ave. N-u-T NE15 63 A2
Ormonde St. Jarrow NE32 76 B7
Ormonde St. Sland SR4 105 A1
Ormsby Gn. N-u-T NE5 63 A4
Ormskirk Cl. N-u-T NE15 62 D6
Ormskirk Gr. Cram NE23 22 C7
Ormston St. E Hart NE23 16 B3
Orpen Ave. White NE34 77 C3
Orpine Ct. Ashgn NE63 6 C2
Orpington Ave. N-u-T NE6 68 B2
Orpington Rd. Cram NE23 22 C7
Orr Ave. N Silk SR3 116 B6
Orton Cl. N-u-T NE4 70 B4
Orwell Cl. B Hall NE34 77 B2
Osbaldeston Gdns. N-u-T NE3 45 B3
Osborne Ave. Hexham NE46 53 F5
Osborne Ave. N-u-T NE2 66 C4
Osborne Ave. S Shs NE33 51 E1
Osborne Cl. Bed NE22 11 C2
Osborne Ct. N-u-T NE2 66 C4
Osborne Gdns. Tyne NE29 51 A7
Osborne Gdns. W Bay NE26 31 F5
Osborne House. Walls NE28 49 A4
Osborne Rd. C le S DH3 112 C3
Osborne Rd. N-u-T NE2 46 B2
Osborne Rd. Sland SR5 103 A3
Osborne St. S Shs NE33 51 E2
Osborne St. Sland SR6 93 D2
Osborne Terr. Cram NE23 22 A7
Osborne Terr. Gates NE8 72 A1
Osborne Terr. N-u-T NE2 66 B3
Osborne Villas. N-u-T NE2 66 B4
Osier Ct. Stake NE62 11 C7
Oslo Cl. N Shs NE29 50 B4
Osman Cl. Sland SR2 106 B1
Osprey Dr. Blyth NE24 17 F5
Osprey House. N-u-T NE2 46 B1
Osprey Way. S Shs NE34 77 B4
Oswald Rd. H le H DH5 119 A5
Oswald Rd. Mpeth NE61 4 A2
Oswald Rd. N-b-t-S NE64 7 D5
Oswald St. Sland SR4 105 A3
Oswald St. White NE34 77 C3
Oswald Terr. Gates NE8 72 A1
Oswald Terr. Sland SR5 92 C1
Oswald Terr. Sland SR2 110 C2
Oswald Terr S. Sland SR5 92 C1
Oswald Wlk. N-u-T NE3 40 B1
Oswestry Pl. Cram NE23 22 C7
Oswin Ave. Lbtn NE12 42 A4
Oswin Ct. Lbtn NE12 29 E1
Oswin Rd. Lbtn NE12 29 E1
Oswin Terr. N Shs NE29 50 D5
Otley Cl. Cram NE23 22 D7
Otter Burn Way. Prud NE42 59 B1
Otterburn Ave. Ears NE25 31 B4
Otterburn Ave. N-u-T NE3 45 A4
Otterburn Cl. Lbtn NE12 42 C4
Otterburn Cres. Burn DH4 114 C1
Otterburn Ct. Gates NE8 72 A1
Otterburn Ct. W Bay NE25 31 B4
Otterburn Dr. Ashgn NE63 6 B1
Otterburn Gdns. Duns NE11 88 A7
Otterburn Gdns. Gates NE9 88 E5
Otterburn Gdns. S Shs NE34 77 E6
Otterburn Gdns. Whick NE16 87 B7
Otterburn Gr. Blyth NE24 17 D6
Otterburn Rd. Tyne NE29 50 F7
Otterburn Terr. N-u-T NE2 46 B1
Ottercap Cl. N-u-T NE15 62 D6
Ottercops. Prud NE42 59 B1
Otterington. Pens NE38 102 B4
Ottershaw. N-u-T NE15 62 E6
Otto Terr. Sland SR2 105 B1
Ottovale Cres. Blay NE21 62 A1
Ottringham Cl. N-u-T NE15 62 D6
Oulton Cl. Cram NE23 22 C7
Oulton Cl. N-u-T NE5 43 B4
Our Lady Queen of Peace RC Prim Sch. Pens DH4 114 A7
Ousby Ct. N-u-T NE13 38 A4
Ouse St. N-u-T NE1 67 A1
Ouseburn Cl. Sland SR2 110 C1
Ouseburn Cl. Sland SR2 116 F8
Ouseburn Rd. N-u-T NE1 & NE2 67 A2
Ouseburn Rd. N-u-T NE6 67 A4
Ouselaw. Kibble NE11 99 D6
Ouslaw La. Kibble NE11 99 B6
Ouston Cl. Gates NE10 90 C7
Ouston Cty Jun Sch. Ouston DH2 99 F1
Ouston St. N-u-T NE15 62 F5
Outram St. H-le-Sp DH5 114 E1
Oval Park View. Gates NE10 89 D7
Oval The. Bed NE22 11 C1
Oval The. Blyth NE24 17 B3
Oval The. H-le-Sp DH4 118 D8
Oval The. Lbtn NE12 42 B2
Oval The. N-u-T NE6 74 A4
Oval The. Ouston DH2 99 F2
Oval The. Sland SR5 93 B2
Oval The. Wash NE37 101 D8
Oval The. Wools NE13 36 F8
Overdene. N-u-T NE15 62 F7
Overfield Rd. N-u-T NE3 38 C1
Overhill Terr. Gates NE8 72 A1
Overton Cl. N-u-T NE15 62 D6
Overton Rd. Tyne NE29 50 E8
Ovingham C of E Fst Sch. Oving NE42 59 A3
Ovingham Cl. Wash NE38 101 F5
Ovingham Cty Mid Sch. Oving NE42 59 A3
Ovingham Gdns. W Open NE13 28 B6
Ovingham Rd. Wylam NE41 60 A6
Ovington Gr. N-u-T NE5 64 A4
Ovington View. Prud NE42 59 B1
Owen Brannigan Dr. Dud NE23 29 B7
Owen Ct. N-u-T NE2 65 C3
Owen Dr. Boldon NE35 & NE36 92 B8
Owen Terr. Chopw NE17 95 C8
Owen Terr. Tant DH9 97 B2
Owlet Cl. Blay NE21 62 A1
Oxberry Gdns. Gates NE10 89 C7
Oxclose Inf Sch. Wash NE38 101 A4
Oxclose Jun Sch. Wash NE38 101 A5
Oxclose Rd. Wash NE38 101 E4
Oxclose Sch. Wash NE38 101 A5
Oxford Ave. Cram NE23 22 C7
Oxford Ave. Lbtn NE12 29 C1
Oxford Ave. S Shs NE33 77 D8
Oxford Ave. Walls NE28 49 A3
Oxford Ave. Wash NE37 101 B8
Oxford Cl. N Silk SR3 115 F8
Oxford Cres. H le H DH5 118 F4
Oxford Cres. Hebb NE31 75 F6
Oxford Pl. Birt DH3 100 C1
Oxford Rd. Stake NE62 11 A7
Oxford Sq. Sland SR4 104 B3
Oxford St. Blyth NE24 17 F7
Oxford St. N-u-T NE1 66 B2
Oxford St. S Shs NE33 77 D8
Oxford St. Sland SR4 104 B3
Oxford St. Sland SR2 106 C1
Oxford St. Tyne NE30 51 D7
Oxford St. W Bay NE26 32 B5
Oxford Terr. Gates NE8 72 B1
Oxford Terr. S Row DH4 114 A6
Oxford Way. Hedw NE32 76 B1
Oxnam Cres. N-u-T NE2 65 B3
Oxted Cl. Cram NE23 22 D7
Oxted Pl. N-u-T NE6 74 B3
Oyston St. S Shs NE33 51 C2
Ozanan Cl. Dud NE23 29 B7

Packham Rd. Sland SR4 103 C1
Paddock Cl. Clea SR6 77 E1
Paddock Cl. Prud NE42 59 E2
Paddock Cl. S Row DH4 113 F5
Paddock Hill. Pont NE20 25 F7
Paddock La. N Silk SR3 116 C7
Paddock Rise. Ashgn NE63 6 B2
Paddock The. Blyth NE24 17 C7
Paddock The. E Cram NE23 22 D5
Paddock The. Gates NE10 89 F6
Paddock The. N Herr DH4 114 F7
Paddock The. Stocks NE43 82 C5
Paddock The. Walb NE15 35 F1
Paddock The. Wools NE13 36 F8
Paddock Wood. Prud NE42 59 E2
Pader Cl. Hazle NE13 28 B5
Padgate Rd. Sland SR4 103 C2
Padonhill. Silk SR3 115 E5
Padstow Cl. 2 Sland SR2 116 F8
Padstow Ct. Gates NE9 88 F2
Padstow Rd. N Shs NE29 50 E4
Page Ave. S Shs NE34 77 E7
Page St. Hebb NE31 75 F7
Page's Bldgs. Boldon NE35 91 E8
Paignton Ave. N-u-T NE4 64 C1
Paignton Ave. W Bay NE25 31 E4
Paignton Sq. Sland SR3 108 B2
Painshawfield Rd. Stocks NE43 82 C6
Paisley Sq. Sland SR3 108 B2
Palace Rd. Bed NE22 11 D2
Palace St. N-u-T NE4 71 B4
Palermo St. Sland SR4 104 C4
Paley St. Sland SR1 105 C3
Palgrove Rd. Sland SR4 103 C1
Palgrove Sq. Sland SR4 103 C1
Pallinsburn Ct. N-u-T NE5 43 B3
Pallion Ind Est. Sland SR4 104 A3
Pallion New Rd. Sland SR4 104 C4
Pallion Pk. Sland SR4 104 C3
Pallion Prim Sch. Sland SR4 104 B4
Pallion Rd. Sland SR4 104 C2
Pallion Ret Pk. Sland SR4 104 B4
Pallion Subway. Sland SR4 104 C4
Pallion West Ind Est. Sland SR4 104 A3
Palm Ave. N-u-T NE4 64 A3
Palm Ave. S Shs NE34 78 A5
Palm Ct. Kill NE12 29 F1
Palm Terr. Tant DH9 97 C3
Palmer Community Hospl. Jarrow NE32 76 B7
Palmer Cres. Hebb NE31 75 F6
Palmer Gdns. Gates NE10 90 C8
Palmer Rd. Dipton DH9 96 E1
Palmer St. Jarrow NE32 76 A7
Palmer's Hill Rd. Sland SR6 106 A4
Palmers Gn. Kill NE12 29 F1
Palmerston Ave. N-u-T NE6 68 B3
Palmerston Rd. Sland SR4 107 B3
Palmerston Wlk. Gates NE8 72 A2
Palmersville. Kill NE12 29 F1
Palmersville Sta. Lbtn NE12 30 A1
Palmstead Rd. Sland SR4 103 C1
Palmstead Sq. Sland SR4 103 C1
Pancras Rd. Sland SR3 108 B2
Pandon. N-u-T NE1 66 B1
Pandon Bank. N-u-T NE1 66 B1
Pandon Ct. N-u-T NE2 66 C2
Pandon Quays. N-u-T NE1 66 C1
Panfield Terr. Bourn DH4 113 E2
Pangbourne Cl. N-u-T NE15 62 C8
Pankhurst Gdns. Gates NE10 90 A8
Pann La. Sland SR1 106 A3
Panns Bank. Sland SR1 106 A3
Pantiles The. Wash NE37 90 D2
Parade Cl. N-u-T NE6 75 A5
Parade The. C le S DH3 112 C1
Parade The. N-u-T NE6 75 A5
Parade The. Sland SR2 106 C1
Parade The. Walls NE28 49 D5
Parade The. Wash NE38 101 E4
Paradise Row. Cram NE23 22 B6
Park Ave. Bed NE22 11 E3
Park Ave. Blay NE21 62 C2
Park Ave. Duns NE11 87 E7
Park Ave. Hexham NE46 53 F5
Park Ave. N Shs NE30 51 C7
Park Ave. N Silk SR3 116 B7
Park Ave. N-u-T NE3 38 C3
Park Ave. N-u-T NE3 39 B2
Park Ave. Prud NE42 59 E1
Park Ave. S Shs NE34 77 F4
Park Ave. Shire NE27 31 A3
Park Ave. Sland SR6 93 E4
Park Ave. W Bay NE26 32 A5
Park Ave. Walls NE28 49 B2
Park Ave. Wash NE37 101 D8
Park Chare. Wash NE38 101 D5
Park Cl. N-u-T NE4 71 A4
Park Cotts. B Mill NE17 95 B6
Park Cres. N Shs NE30 51 B7
Park Cres. Shire NE27 30 F3
Park Cres E. N Shs NE30 51 C7
Park Ct. Gates NE8 72 C3
Park Ct. N-u-T NE6 49 A1
Park Dr. Blyth NE24 17 B4
Park Dr. Lbtn NE12 42 B4
Park Dr. Mpeth NE61 8 F7
Park Dr. N-u-T NE3 28 C1
Park Dr. Stann NE61 9 E1
Park Dr. Whick NE16 87 C8
Park Field. Ryton NE40 61 C5
Park Field Terr. S Slu NE26 24 C6
Park Gate. Sland SR6 93 E3
Park Gdns. W Bay NE26 32 A5
Park Gr. Shire NE27 30 F3
Park Gr. Shire NE27 31 A3
Park Gr. Wash NE37 90 D1
Park Head Rd. N-u-T NE7 47 A2
Park La. Blay NE21 86 B8
Park La. Gates NE8 73 A3
Park La. Prud NE42 59 D1
Park La. Shire NE27 30 F2
Park La. Sland SR1 106 A2
Park Lea. Sland DH4 & SR3 115 B6
Park Lea Rd. Sland SR6 93 E3
Park Par. Sland SR6 93 E2
Park Par. W Bay NE26 32 A5
Park Pl. C le S DH3 112 D5
Park Pl E. Sland SR2 106 A1
Park Pl W. Sland SR2 106 A1
Park Rd. Ashgn NE63 6 B3
Park Rd. Bed NE22 16 A8
Park Rd. Blyth NE24 17 F7
Park Rd. Gates NE10 & NE8 73 B2
Park Rd. Hebb NE31 75 E5
Park Rd. Jarrow NE32 76 A6
Park Rd. Lmth NE61 & NE63 2 A2
Park Rd. N-u-T NE4 71 A3
Park Rd. Newb NE15 61 F8
Park Rd. R Gill NE39 85 D2
Park Rd. S Del NE25 23 C3
Park Rd. Shire NE27 30 F3
Park Rd. Sland SR2 106 A1
Park Rd. W Bay NE26 32 A6
Park Rd. Walls NE28 49 C1
Park Rd N. C le S DH3 112 D4
Park Rd S. C le S DH3 112 D1
Park Rise. N-u-T NE15 62 C7
Park Road Central. C le S DH3 112 D3
Park Road East. Ashgn NE63 6 C4
Park Row. Gates NE10 89 D8
Park Row. Sland SR5 93 A1
Park Site. Heps NE61 9 F5
Park St S. Sland SR5 92 C1
Park Terr. Bed NE22 11 D3
Park Terr. Blay NE21 62 D2
Park Terr. Burnop NE16 97 A6
Park Terr. Duns NE11 87 F8
Park Terr. Kill NE12 29 B2
Park Terr. N Shs NE30 51 C7
Park Terr. N-u-T NE1 & NE2 66 A3
Park Terr. Sland SR5 93 A2
Park Terr. W Bay NE26 32 A6
Park Terr. Walls NE28 49 B2
Park Terr. Whick NE16 69 A1
Park View. Ashgn NE63 6 B4
Park View. Blay NE21 86 C8
Park View. Blyth NE24 17 F7
Park View. Bourn DH3 113 D4
Park View. Burnop NE16 97 B6
Park View. C le S DH2 112 B5
Park View. H le H DH5 119 A3
Park View. Jarrow NE32 76 B4
Park View. Lbtn NE12 29 B2
Park View. Lbtn NE12 42 A4
Park View. N-u-T NE6 75 A5
Park View. S Del NE25 23 D3
Park View. S Row DH4 114 B6
Park View. W Bay NE26 32 A5
Park View. W Open NE13 28 C6
Park View. Walls NE28 49 B2
Park View Cl. Ryton NE40 61 D5
Park View Comp Sch (North Lodge Premises). C le S DH3 112 D7
Park View Ct. W Bay NE26 32 A5
Park View Gdns. Ryton NE40 61 D5
Park Villas. Ashgn NE63 6 B4
Park Wall Cnr. Sland SR3 115 B6
Parkdale Rise. Whick NE16 87 A7
Parker Ave. N-u-T NE3 45 B3
Parkfield. Hedw NE32 76 C1
Parkgate La. Blay NE21 86 B8
Parkham Cl. Cram NE23 16 B1
Parkhead Gdns. Blay NE21 86 B8
Parkhead Sq. Blay NE21 62 C1
Parkhouse Ave. Sland SR5 103 B4
Parkhurst Rd. Sland SR4 107 B4
Parkin Gdns. Gates NE10 89 E7
Parkinson's Cotts. Ryton NE40 61 E4
Parkland. Lbtn NE12 42 A2
Parkland. Ryton NE21 62 A4
Parkland Ave. Blay NE21 86 B8
Parklands. Gates NE10 90 C8
Parklands. H Mill NE39 95 F5
Parklands. Pont NE20 25 B2
Parklands Ct. Gates NE10 75 C1
Parklands Way. Gates NE10 90 C8
Parklea. S Slu NE26 24 C6
Parkmore Rd. Sland SR4 107 A3
Parkshiel. S Shs NE34 78 A4
Parkside. Bed NE22 11 E3
Parkside. Duns NE11 87 F8
Parkside. Hebb NE31 75 D4
Parkside. Sland SR3 115 B6
Parkside. Tanf L DH9 97 C1
Parkside. Tley NE15 35 E1
Parkside. Tyne NE30 32 D1
Parkside. Walls NE28 49 D3
Parkside Ave. Blay NE21 62 C1
Parkside Ave. N-u-T NE7 41 B1
Parkside Cotts. Tanf L DH9 97 C1
Parkside Cres. Tyne NE30 51 D8
Parkside Ct. W Bay NE26 31 F5
Parkside S. Sland SR3 115 B6
Parkside Sch. Walls NE28 49 A5
Parkside Special Sch. Walls NE28 49 B2
Parkside Terr. Walls NE28 49 A4
Parkstone Cl. Sland SR4 107 A2
Parkville. N-u-T NE6 67 A3
Parkway. G Post NE62 10 F8
Parkway. Wash NE38 101 C4
Parkway. Wash NE38 101 D5
Parkway. Whick NE16 86 E6
Parkwood Ave. Prud NE42 59 F3
Parliament St. Hebb NE31 75 C7
Parmontley St. N-u-T NE15 62 F5
Parnell St. Fence DH4 118 B8
Parry Dr. Whit SR6 78 E1
Parson Rd. Wylam NE41 60 B6
Parson's Ave. N-u-T NE6 68 C1
Parsons Gdns. Duns NE11 70 C1
Parsons Ind Est. Wash NE37 101 B8
Parsons Rd. Wash NE37 101 B7
Partick Rd. Sland SR4 107 B4
Partick Sq. Sland SR4 107 C4
Partridge Cl. Wash NE38 100 F4
Pasteur Rd. S Hett DH6 121 F7
Paston Rd. S Del NE25 23 D2
Pastures The. Blyth NE24 17 D4
Pastures The. Mpeth NE61 8 D7
Pastures The. Stocks NE43 82 B8
Pathside. Hedw NE32 76 C2
Patience Ave. S Burn NE13 28 C8
Patina Cl. N-u-T NE15 62 C8
Paton Rd. Sland SR3 108 C2
Paton Sq. Sland SR3 108 C2
Patrick Cain House. S Shs NE33 77 B8
Patrick Cres. S Hett DH6 121 E8
Patrick Terr. Dud NE23 29 B7
Patterdale Cl. Boldon NE36 92 C7
Patterdale Gdns. N-u-T NE7 47 B4
Patterdale Gr. Sland SR5 93 C4
Patterdale Rd. Blyth NE24 17 A8
Patterdale St. H le H DH5 119 A2
Patterdale Terr. Gates NE8 88 F8
Patterson Cl. Hexham NE46 53 E3
Patterson St. Blay NE21 62 E4
Pattinson Gdns. Gates NE10 73 C2
Pattinson Gdns. Gates NE9 89 B7
Pattinson Ind Est. Wash NE38 101 F3
Pattinson Ind Est. Wash NE38 102 B6
Pattinson Rd. Wash NE38 102 B4
Patton Way. Pegs NE61 4 E3
Pauline Ave. Sland SR6 93 D3
Pauline Gdns. N-u-T NE15 63 A3
Pauls Gn. H le H DH5 119 A6
Paulsway. Jarrow NE32 76 E6
Pavilion Ct. N-u-T NE2 66 C4
Pawston Rd. H Spen NE21 & NE39 85 B5
Paxford Cl. N-u-T NE7 41 A1
Paxton Terr. Sland SR4 105 A3
Peacehaven Ct. Wash NE37 90 C2
Peacock Ct. Gates NE11 88 B7
Peacock St W. Sland SR4 104 C2
Pear Tree Terr. Chopw NE17 95 B8
Peareth Ct. Gates NE8 72 C3
Peareth Gr. Sland SR6 93 F3
Peareth Hall Rd. Spring NE37 & NE9 90 A2
Peareth Rd. Sland SR6 93 F4
Pearl Rd. Sland SR3 108 C2
Pearson Ct. 5 N Shs NE30 51 B6
Pearson Pl. Jarrow NE32 76 C8
Pearson Pl. N Shs NE30 51 B6
Pearson St. S Shs NE33 51 D4
Pearson's Terr. Hexham NE46 54 A5

Peart Cl. Sherb DH6 120 A1
Peartree Bglws. B Mill NE17 95 C6
Peartree Ct. B Mill NE17 95 C6
Peartree Gdns. N-u-T NE28 & NE6 49 A1
Peary Cl. N-u-T NE5 36 F2
Pease Ave. N-u-T NE15 & NE4 63 C2
Peasemoor Rd. Sland SR4 103 B1
Pebble Beach. Sland SR6 93 F7
Pecket Cl. Blyth NE24 17 A5
Peddars Way. S Shs NE34 77 B5
Peebles Cl. Tyne NE29 50 C8
Peebles Rd. Sland SR3 108 B2
Peel Ctr The. Wash NE37 101 F7
Peel Gdns. S Shs NE34 76 E4
Peel La. N-u-T NE1 71 C4
Peel St. N-u-T NE1 71 C4
Peel St. Sland SR2 106 B1
Peepy Cotts. Byw NE43 57 D2
Pegswood Cty Fst Sch. Pegs NE61 4 F4
Pegswood House. N-u-T NE4 65 B2
Pegswood Ind Est. Pegs NE61 4 F4
Pegswood Sta. Pegs NE61 4 F3
Pegwood Rd. Sland SR4 103 C1
Pelaw Ave. C le S DH2 112 C5
Pelaw Ave. N-b-t-S NE64 7 D5
Pelaw Bank. C le S DH3 112 C4
Pelaw Cres. C le S DH2 112 C5
Pelaw Grange Ct. C le S DH3 112 C8
Pelaw Ind Est. Gates NE10 90 A8
Pelaw Pl. C le S DH2 112 C5
Pelaw Rd. C le S DH2 112 C5
Pelaw Sq. C le S DH2 112 B5
Pelaw Sq. Sland SR4 103 C3
Pelaw Sta. Gates NE10 75 A1
Pelaw Way. Gates NE10 75 A1
Peldon Cl. N-u-T NE7 40 C1
Pelham Ct. N-u-T NE3 38 A3
Pelton Fell Rd. C le S DH2 112 B4
Pelton La. C le S DH2 & DH3 112 B5
Pelton Rd. Sland SR4 107 C4
Peltondale Ave. Blyth NE24 17 A6
Pemberton Bank. E Lane DH5 119 C1
Pemberton Cl. Sland SR5 93 B1
Pemberton Gdns. Sland SR3 109 B3
Pemberton St. H le H DH5 119 A4
Pembridge. Wash NE38 101 A5
Pembroke Ave. Birt DH3 100 D1
Pembroke Ave. N Silk SR3 116 B6
Pembroke Ave. N-u-T NE6 68 B3
Pembroke Ct. N-b-t-S NE64 7 E5
Pembroke Ct. N-u-T NE3 38 A3
Pembroke Dr. Pont NE20 25 B4
Pembroke Gdns. Ashgn NE63 7 A1
Pembroke Gdns. Walls NE28 50 A4
Pembroke Terr. S Shs NE33 77 C7
Pendeford. Pens NE38 102 A4
Pendle Cl. Wash NE38 101 B3
Pendle Gn. Sland SR4 105 A1
Pendleton Dr. Cram NE23 16 B1
Pendower Hall Sch. N-u-T NE15 63 C2
Pendower Way. N-u-T NE15 63 C1
Penfold Cl. N-u-T NE7 47 C4
Penhale Dr. Sland SR2 116 F7
Penhill Cl. Urpeth DH2 99 F1
Penistone Rd. Sland SR4 107 A4
Penman Pl. N Shs NE29 51 A4
Penman Sq. Sland SR4 107 C4
Penman St. N Shs NE29 51 A4
Penn Sq. Sland SR4 103 C2
Penn St. N-u-T NE4 71 B3
Pennant Sq. Sland SR4 103 C2
Pennine Ave. C le S DH2 112 B2
Pennine Ct. 23 Silk SR3 115 F6
Pennine Dr. Ashgn NE63 6 E1
Pennine Gdns. Duns NE11 88 A6
Pennine Gr. Boldon NE36 92 B7
Pennine View. Chopw NE17 95 B8
Pennine Way. Lbtn NE12 41 A2
Pennycross Rd. Sland SR4 107 A4
Pennycross Sq. Sland SR4 103 A1
Pennyfine Cl. Tyne NE29 51 A8
Pennyfine Rd. Sunn NE16 87 C2
Pennygate Sq. Sland SR4 103 A1
Pennygreen Sq. Sland SR4 103 A1
Pennymore Sq. Sland SR4 107 A4
Pennywell Comp Sch. Sland SR4 107 B4
Pennywell Ind Est. Sland SR4 107 A3
Pennywell Rd. Sland SR4 107 C4
Penrith Ave. Tyne NE30 32 A2
Penrith Gdns. Gates NE9 89 B4
Penrith Gr. Gates NE9 89 B4
Penrith Rd. Hebb NE31 & NE32 75 F4
Penrith Rd. Sland SR5 93 C4
Penrose Gn. N-u-T NE3 38 C1
Penrose Rd. Sland SR4 107 B4
Pensford Ct. N-u-T NE3 37 C2
Penshaw Gn. N-u-T NE5 44 A3
Penshaw La. Pens DH4 114 B8
Penshaw View. Birt DH3 100 E3
Penshaw View. Gates NE10 90 C8
Penshaw View. Hebb NE31 75 E4
Penshaw View. Jarrow NE32 76 B4
Penshaw Way. Birt DH3 100 E4
Pensher St. Gates NE10 73 C1
Pensher St. Sland SR4 105 B2
Pensher St E. Gates NE10 73 C1
Pentland Cl. Ashgn NE63 6 E1
Pentland Cl. Cram NE23 16 B1
Pentland Cl. Tyne NE29 31 F1
Pentland Cl. Wash NE38 101 B3
Pentland Ct. 3 C le S DH2 112 C2
Pentland Gdns. Duns NE11 88 A7
Pentland Gr. Lbtn NE12 29 B1
Pentridge Cl. Cram NE23 22 C7
Penwood Rd. Sland SR4 103 C1
Penzance Par. Jarrow NE31 76 A2
Penzance Rd. Sland SR4 107 B4
Peplow Sq. Sland SR4 103 C3
Peppercorn Ct. N-u-T NE1 72 B4
Percival St. Sland SR4 104 C3
Percy Ave. Tyne NE30 32 C3
Percy Ave. W Bay NE26 32 A5
Percy Cl. Hexham NE46 53 F3
Percy Cotts. S Del NE25 23 E2
Percy Cres. N Shs NE29 50 D3
Percy Ct. N Shs NE29 50 D3
Percy Gdns. Duns NE11 88 A7
Percy Gdns. Lbtn NE12 42 A4
Percy Gdns. Stake NE62 11 A8
Percy Gdns. Tyne NE30 51 E8
Percy Gdns. W Bay NE25 32 A4
Percy Main Prim Sch. N Shs NE29 50 D2
Percy Main Sta. N Shs NE29 50 D3
Percy Park Rd. Tyne NE30 51 D8
Percy Pk. Tyne NE30 51 D8
Percy Rd. W Bay NE26 32 B5
Percy Scott St. White NE34 77 C3
Percy St. Ashgn NE63 6 E4
Percy St. Blyth NE24 17 F8
Percy St. Cram NE23 22 C5
Percy St. H le H DH5 119 B4
Percy St. Jarrow NE32 76 C7
Percy St. Lbtn NE12 29 F1
Percy St. N-u-T NE15 62 C6
Percy St. N-u-T NE1 66 A2
Percy St. S Shs NE33 51 D2
Percy St. 5 Tyne NE30 51 E7
Percy St. Walls NE28 49 C2
Percy St John's C of E Prim Sch. N Shs NE29 50 E3
Percy St S. Blyth NE24 17 F7
Percy Terr. N-u-T NE3 40 B1
Percy Terr. Newb NE15 61 F7
Percy Terr. Pens DH4 114 A8
Percy Terr. Sland SR2 110 B4
Percy Terr. W Bay NE25 31 E5
Percy Terr. Whit SR6 78 F1
Percy Terr S. Sland SR2 110 C3
Percy Way. Walb NE15 36 A1
Peregrine Pl. Lbtn NE12 41 A3
Perivale Rd. Sland SR4 107 B4
Perry St. Gates NE8 & NE9 88 F8
Perrycrofts. Silk SR3 116 A4
Perth Ave. B Wh NE32 & NE34 76 E3
Perth Cl. Tyne NE29 50 C8
Perth Cl. Walls NE28 49 F4
Perth Ct. Gates NE9 88 E3
Perth Ct. Sland SR3 108 B1
Perth Gdns. Walls NE28 49 F4
Perth Rd. Sland SR3 108 C2
Perth Sq. Sland SR3 108 C2
Pescott Cl. Hexham NE46 54 B4
Pesspool Ave. Hasw DH6 121 F3
Pesspool Bglws. Hasw DH6 121 F3
Pesspool La. Hasw DH6 121 F3
Pesspool Terr. Hasw DH6 121 F3
Peterborough Cl. Gates NE8 72 B2
Peterborough Way. Hedw NE32 76 B1
Petersfield Rd. Sland SR4 107 B4
Petersham Rd. Sland SR4 103 C2
Peth Gn. H le H DH5 119 B1
Peth Head. Hexham NE46 54 C5
Peth La. Ryton NE40 61 D6
Petherton Ct. N-u-T NE3 37 C2
Petrel Cl. 12 S Shs NE33 51 C4
Petrel Way. Blyth NE24 17 F4
Petteril. Wash NE38 101 A1
Petworth Cl. S Shs NE33 51 D3
Pevensey Cl. Tyne NE29 31 F1
Pexton Way. N-u-T NE5 63 A4
Philadelphia Aged Miners Homes. 2 Pens DH4 114 B6
Philadelphia Complex. N Herr DH4 114 D6
Philadelphia La. New DH4 114 C4
Philip Pl. N-u-T NE4 65 A2
Philip Sq. Sland SR3 108 B2
Philip St. N-u-T NE4 65 A2
Philiphaugh. Walls NE28 75 B8
Philipson St. N-u-T NE6 68 C2
Phillips Ave. Whick NE16 87 A8
Phillips Cl. Hasw DH6 121 E3
Phoenix Chase. Tyne NE29 50 C8
Phoenix Ct. Mpeth NE61 8 F8
Phoenix Ct. Tyne NE29 50 C8
Phoenix Rd. Sland SR4 103 C2
Phoenix Rd. Wash NE38 100 E6
Phoenix St. Blyth NE24 17 B4
Phoenix Way. H-le-Sp DH4 118 C7
Piccadilly. Sland SR3 115 E8
Picherwell. Gates NE10 89 D7
Pickard St. Sland SR4 105 A3
Pickering Ct. Jarrow NE32 76 A7
Pickering Gn. Gates NE9 89 B2
Pickering Rd. Sland SR4 107 B3
Pickering Sq. Sland SR4 107 B4
Pickersgill House. Sland SR5 92 C3
Pickhurst Rd. Sland SR4 107 B3
Pickhurst Sq. Sland SR4 107 B3
Picktree Cotts. C le S DH3 112 D4
Picktree Cotts E. C le S DH3 112 D4
Picktree Farm Cotts. C le S DH3 112 E7
Picktree La. Birt NE38 100 E1
Picktree La. C le S DH3 112 D4
Picktree La. C le S DH3 & NE38 112 E7
Picktree La. Wash DH3 112 E7
Picktree Lodge. C le S DH3 112 D8
Picktree Terr. C le S DH3 112 D4
Pier Par. S Shs NE33 51 E4
Pier Rd. Tyne NE30 51 E7
Pier View. Sland SR6 93 F2
Pikestone Cl. Wash NE38 101 A3
Pilgrim Cl. Sland SR5 93 C1
Pilgrim St. N-u-T NE1 66 A1
Pilgrim St. N-u-T NE1 72 B4
Pilgrims Way. Mpeth NE61 8 D7
Pilgrimsway. Gates NE9 89 B7
Pilgrimsway. Jarrow NE32 76 E6
Pilton Rd. N-u-T NE5 36 F3
Pilton Wlk. N-u-T NE5 36 F3
Pimlico Ct. Gates NE9 88 F4
Pimlico Rd. H le H DH5 119 B1
Pimlico Rd. Sland SR4 107 B4
Pinders Way. S Hill DH6 120 D1
Pine Ave. Dgton NE13 27 C7
Pine Ave. G Post NE62 10 D7
Pine Ave. 3 H-le-Sp DH4 118 D8
Pine Ave. N-u-T NE3 38 C3
Pine Ave. S Shs NE34 78 A5
Pine Rd. Blay NE21 62 C2
Pine St. Birt DH3 100 C5
Pine St. C le S DH3 112 C3
Pine St. Green NE40 61 B1
Pine St. Jarrow NE32 76 A6
Pine St. S Burn NE13 28 C8
Pine St. Sland SR4 104 C3
Pine St. Tley NE15 35 D3
Pinedale Dr. S Hett DH6 121 F7
Pinegarth. Pont NE20 25 C2
Pines The. Green NE40 61 B1
Pines The. N-u-T NE4 71 A3
Pinesway. Sland SR3 109 B3
Pinetree Gdns. W Bay NE25 31 E3
Pinetree Way. Whick NE16 69 B2
Pinewood. Hebb NE31 75 C7
Pinewood Ave. Cram NE23 16 B1
Pinewood Ave. W Open NE13 & NE3 28 C5
Pinewood Ave. Wash NE38 101 C1
Pinewood Cl. N-u-T NE13 37 B3
Pinewood Cl. N-u-T NE6 48 C1
Pinewood Dr. Mpeth NE61 3 D2
Pinewood Gdns. Duns NE11 88 A5
Pinewood Rd. Sland SR5 92 F2
Pinewood Sq. Sland SR5 92 F2
Pinewood St. Gr Lum DH4 113 E1
Pinewood Villas. S Shs NE34 78 A6
Pinner Pl. N-u-T NE6 74 B4
Pinner Rd. Sland SR4 103 C1
Pioneer Terr. Bed NE22 11 C2
Pipe Ave. Burnop NE16 96 F6
Pipe Track La. N-u-T NE4 70 A4
Piper Rd. Oham NE42 59 B5
Pipershaw. Wash NE37 100 F6
Pipewellgate. Gates NE8 72 B3
Pit Row. N Silk SR3 115 F8
Pitcairn Rd. Sland SR4 103 C1
Pitt St. N-u-T NE1, NE4 & NE99 65 C2
Pittington Cty Jun & Inf Sch. H Pitt DH6 120 B5
Pittington La. H Pitt DH6 120 A6
Pittington Rd. W Rain DH5, DH6 & DH4 120 A7
Plains Farm Prim Sch. Sland SR3 108 C2
Plains Rd. Sland SR3 108 C2
Plaistow Sq. Sland SR4 103 C3
Plaistow Way. Cram NE23 16 B1
Plane Tree Ct. Silk SR3 115 E6
Planesway. Gates NE10 89 E5
Planet Pl. Kill NE12 29 C2
Planetree Ave. N-u-T NE4 64 A4
Plantagenet Ave. C le S DH3 112 D2
Plantation Ave. H Pitt DH6 120 E3
Plantation Ave. Whick NE16 87 A8
Plantation Gr. Gates NE10 75 C2
Plantation Rd. Sland SR4 104 B3
Plantation Sq. Sland SR4 104 B3
Plantation St. Walls NE28 75 B8
Plantation The. Gates NE9 89 A4
Plantation Wlk. S Hett DH6 121 F7
Plawsworth Gdns. Gates NE9 89 C3
Pleasant Pl. 6 Birt DH3 100 C5
Plenmeller Pl. Sunn NE16 87 A3
Plessey Ave. Blyth NE24 17 F6
Plessey Cres. W Bay NE25 & NE30 32 B4
Plessey Ct. Blyth NE24 17 B4
Plessey Gdns. N Shs NE29 50 D5
Plessey Rd. Blyth NE24 17 D5
Plessey Rd Cty Fst Sch. Blyth NE24 17 F7
Plessey St. E Hart NE23 16 B3
Plessey Terr. N-u-T NE7 47 B2
Plessey Woods Ctry Pk. Stann NE22 15 B4
Plough Rd. Silk SR3 115 F5
Plover Cl. Blyth NE24 17 E4
Plover Cl. 5 Wash NE38 100 F3
Plover Dr. Burnop NE16 97 C5
Ploverfield Cl. Ashgn NE63 6 C2
Plummer St. N-u-T NE4 71 C3
Plummer Tower Mus. N-u-T NE1 66 B1
Plumtree Ave. Sland SR5 92 C2
Plunkett Rd. Dipton DH9 96 E1
Plymouth Sq. Sland SR3 108 B2
Point Pleasant Ind Est. Walls NE28 49 F1
Point Pleasant Terr. Walls NE28 49 E1
Polden Cres. Tyne NE29 31 F1
Polebrook Rd. Sland SR4 103 C2
Pollard St. S Shs NE33 51 D3
Polmaise St. Blay NE21 62 C2
Polmuir Rd. Sland SR3 108 C2
Polmuir Sq. Sland SR3 108 B2
Polperro Cl. Birt DH3 100 D3
Polton Sq. Sland SR4 103 C2
Polwarth Cres. N-u-T NE3 39 C4
Polwarth Dr. N-u-T NE3 28 C1
Polwarth Rd. N-u-T NE3 28 C1
Polworth Sq. Sland SR3 108 C2
Polytechnic Prec. Sland SR2 105 B2
Pont Haugh. Pont NE20 25 F7
Pont St. Ashgn NE63 6 D3
Pont View. Pont NE20 25 F7
Pontdyke. Gates NE10 89 F4
Pontefract Rd. Sland SR4 107 B3
Ponteland Cl. Tyne NE29 50 C7
Ponteland Cl. Wash NE38 100 F4
Ponteland Coates Endowed Mid Sch. Pont NE 20 25 E7
Ponteland Cty Fst Sch. Pont NE 20 25 F7
Ponteland Cty High Sch. Pont NE 5 25 F5
Ponteland Golf Course. Pont NE20 26 B7
Ponteland Hospl. Pont NE 20 25 F7
Ponteland Rd. H-o-t-W NE15 35 D5
Ponteland Rd. N-u-T NE4 64 C4
Ponteland Rd. Pont NE20 26 A5
Ponteland Rd. Wools NE13 37 A3
Ponthaugh. R Gill NE39 85 F3
Pontop Sq. Sland SR4 103 C3
Pontop St. E Rain DH5 118 C4
Pontop View. R Gill NE39 85 D2
Poole Cl. Cram NE23 22 C7
Poole Rd. Sland SR4 103 C2
Pooley Cl. N-u-T NE5 43 B1
Pooley Rd. N-u-T NE5 43 B1
Poplar Ave. Blyth NE24 12 D1
Poplar Ave. Burnop NE16 96 F6
Poplar Ave. Dgton NE13 27 C7
Poplar Ave. 1 H-le-Sp DH4 118 D8
Poplar Ave. N-u-T NE6 48 C1
Poplar Cl. Hebb NE31 75 E3
Poplar Cres. Birt DH3 100 B5
Poplar Cres. Duns NE11 87 F7
Poplar Cres. Gates NE8 72 B2
Poplar Dr. Whit SR6 78 F1
Poplar Gr. Bed NE22 11 C1
Poplar Gr. S Shs NE34 77 F5
Poplar Gr. 6 Sland SR2 116 E8
Poplar Pl. N-u-T NE3 39 C1
Poplar Rd. Blay NE21 62 C1
Poplar St. Ashgn NE63 6 D4
Poplar St. C le S DH3 112 C3
Poplar St. Tley NE15 35 D3
Poplar Terr. C le S DH3 112 D4
Poplars The. E Lane DH5 119 C1
Poplars The. N-u-T NE3 45 C3
Poplars The. N-u-T NE4 71 A3
Poplars The. Pens DH4 114 B8
Poplars The. Sland SR5 92 F2
Poplars The. Sland SR4 103 A2
Poplars The. Wash NE38 101 D4
Popplewell Gdns. Gates NE9 89 A4
Popplewell Terr. Tyne NE29 51 A8
Popular Ct. C le S DH3 112 C3
Porchester Dr. Cram NE23 22 C7
Porlock Ct. Cram NE23 16 A1
Porlock Rd. Jarrow NE32 76 D5
Portadown Rd. Sland SR4 107 B3
Portberry St. S Shs NE33 51 B1
Portberry Way. S Shs NE33 51 B1
Portchester Gr. Boldon NE35 91 E8
Portchester Rd. Sland SR4 103 C1
Portchester Sq. Sland SR4 107 C4
Porthcawl Dr. Wash NE37 90 C2
Portia St. Ashgn NE63 6 E4
Portland Cl. C le S DH2 112 A1
Portland Gdns. Cram NE23 22 C7
Portland Gdns. 1 Gates NE9 88 F2
Portland Gdns. Tyne NE30 51 A7
Portland Mews. N-u-T NE2 66 C3
Portland Rd. N-u-T NE2 66 C2
Portland Rd. Sland SR3 108 C3
Portland Rd. Walb NE15 35 E2
Portland Sq. Sland SR3 108 C3
Portland St. Blyth NE24 17 D8
Portland St. Gates NE10 75 A1
Portland St. N-u-T NE4 70 C4
Portland Terr. Ashgn NE63 5 F5
Portland Terr. Hexham NE46 53 F5
Portland Terr. N-u-T NE2 66 C3
Portman Pl. N-u-T NE6 74 B3
Portman Sq. Sland SR4 103 C1
Portmarnock. Wash NE37 90 B2
Portmeads Rise. Birt DH3 100 D4
Portobello La. Sland SR5 & SR6 93 D1
Portobello Terr. Birt DH3 100 E2
Portobello Way. Birt DH3 100 D4
Portree Cl. Birt DH3 100 D1
Portree Sq. Sland SR3 108 B2
Portrush Cl. Wash NE37 90 C2
Portrush Rd. Sland SR4 103 C2
Portrush Way. Lbtn NE7 41 C1
Portslade Rd. Sland SR4 107 B4
Portsmouth Rd. N Shs NE29 50 C5
Portsmouth Rd. Sland SR4 103 B1
Portsmouth Sq. Sland SR4 103 B1
Portugal Pl. Walls NE28 49 B1
Post Office La. Tyne NE29 51 A8
Post Office St. Blyth NE24 17 F8
Postern Cres. Mpeth NE61 8 F7
Potland View. Linton NE61 1 A3
Potter Sq. Sland SR3 108 C2
Potter St. Jarrow NE32 76 A7
Potter St. Walls NE28 50 A1
Potteries The. S Shs NE33 51 E1
Pottersway. Gates NE9 89 B7
Pottery Bank. Mpeth NE61 3 E2
Pottery Bank. N-u-T NE6 74 C3
Pottery Bank Ct. Mpeth NE61 3 E2
Pottery La. N-u-T NE1 71 C3
Pottery La. Sland SR4 103 A3
Pottery Rd. Sland SR5 93 A1
Pottery Yd. 3 H-le-Sp DH4 118 E8
Potts St. N-u-T NE6 67 C2
Powburn Cl. C le S DH2 112 A1
Powburn Gdns. N-u-T NE4 64 B4
Powis Rd. Sland SR3 108 C2
Powis Sq. Sland SR3 108 C2
Powys Pl. N-u-T NE4 65 A2
Poynings Cl. N-u-T NE5 37 C1
Precinct The. Blay NE21 62 D3
Precinct The. Sland SR2 109 C2
Prefect Pl. Gates NE9 89 A7
Premier Rd. Sland SR3 108 C2
Prendwick Ave. Hebb NE31 75 D3
Prendwick Ct. Hebb NE31 75 D3
Prengarth Ave. Sland SR6 93 D3
Prensgarth Way. B Wh NE34 76 F3
Prescot Rd. Sland SR4 103 C2
Press La. Sland SR1 106 A3
Prestbury Ave. Cram NE23 16 A1
Prestbury Rd. N Shs NE29 50 E5
Prestbury Rd. Sland SR4 107 A3
Prestdale Ave. Blyth NE24 17 A7
Presthope Rd. Sland SR4 107 B4
Prestmede. Gates NE10 89 E7
Preston Ave. Tyne NE29 & NE30 51 B7
Preston Crem. Tyne NE29 50 F7
Preston Ct. Tyne NE29 51 A8
Preston Gate. Tyne NE30 31 F1
Preston Grange Cty Prim Sch. Tyne NE29 31 E1
Preston North Rd. Tyne NE29 31 F1
Preston Pk. Tyne NE29 51 A7
Preston Rd. Sland SR2 110 C4
Preston Rd. Tyne NE29 & NE30 51 A7
Preston Terr. Shire NE27 30 E1
Preston Terr. 1 Tyne NE29 50 F8
Preston Wood. Tyne NE30 32 A1
Prestonhill. Silk SR3 115 E5
Prestwick. Gates NE10 89 E5
Prestwick Ave. Tyne NE29 50 C6
Prestwick Cl. Wash NE37 90 C2
Prestwick Dr. Gates NE10 90 C7
Prestwick Gdns. N-u-T NE3 44 C4
Prestwick House. N-u-T NE4 65 B2
Prestwick Rd. Sland SR4 103 C2
Prestwick Terr. Pont NE20 26 C3
Pretoria Ave. Mpeth NE61 8 F8
Pretoria Sq. Sland SR3 108 B2
Pretoria St. N-u-T NE15 63 A1
Price St. Hebb NE31 75 C7
Price St. Mpeth NE61 3 E1
Priestclose Cotts. Prud NE42 59 F2
Priestclose Rd. Prud NE42 59 D2
Priestfield Cl. Silk SR3 115 F5
Priestfield Gdns. Burnop NE16 96 F6
Priestlands Ave. Hexham NE46 54 A4
Priestlands Cl. Hexham NE46 54 A3
Priestlands Cres. Hexham NE46 54 A4
Priestlands Dr. Hexham NE46 54 A4
Priestlands La. Hexham NE46 54 A4
Priestlands Rd. Hexham NE46 54 A4
Priestley Ct. B Hall NE34 77 A3
Priestley Gdns. Gates NE10 90 B7
Priestly Cres. Sland SR4 105 B4
Priestman Ct. Sland SR4 104 A2
Priestpopple. Hexham NE46 54 B4
Primary Gdns. Sland SR2 106 C1
Primate Rd. Sland SR3 108 B2
Primrose Cl. Annit NE23 29 A8
Primrose Cres. Bourn DH4 113 E3
Primrose Cres. Sland SR6 93 D3
Primrose Ct. Ashgn NE63 6 B1
Primrose Gdns. Ouston DH2 99 F2
Primrose Gdns. Walls NE28 49 A4
Primrose Hill. Gates NE9 89 A5
Primrose Hill Hospl. Jarrow NE32 76 C4
Primrose Hill Terr. Jarrow NE32 76 C3
Primrose Prec. Sland SR6 93 D3
Primrose St. Sland SR4 103 A2
Primrose Terr. Birt DH3 100 D4
Primrose Terr. Jarrow NE32 76 C4
Prince Albert Terr. N-u-T NE2 66 C2
Prince Consort Ind Est. Hebb NE31 75 C7
Prince Consort La. Hebb NE31 75 D6
Prince Consort Rd. Gates NE8 72 B1
Prince Consort Rd. Hebb NE31 75 C6
Prince Consort Rd. Hebb NE31 75 D6
Prince Consort Rd. Jarrow NE32 76 C6
Prince Edward Gr. S Shs NE34 78 C6
Prince Edward Rd. S Shs NE34 78 A5
Prince Edward Rd E. S Shs NE34 78 C6
Prince George Ave. Sland SR6 93 D3
Prince Of Wales Cl. S Shs NE34 77 E5
Prince Philip Cl. N-u-T NE15 63 C1
Prince Rd. Walls NE28 49 B3
Prince St. Chopw NE17 84 B1
Prince St. Sland SR1 106 A3
Prince's Gdns. Blyth NE24 17 C8
Prince's Meadow. N-u-T NE3 39 A1
Princes Ave. N-u-T NE3 39 B3
Princes Ave. Sland SR6 93 E5
Princes Cl. N-u-T NE3 39 B4
Princes Gdns. Sland SR6 93 E5
Princes Gdns. W Bay NE25 31 E5
Princes Rd. N-u-T NE3 28 B1
Princes St. Crbdge NE45 56 A5
Princes St. S Row DH4 114 A5
Princes St. Tyne NE30 51 B7
Princess Ct. Prud NE42 59 D4
Princess Dr. Duns NE8 71 A1
Princess Gdns. H le H DH5 119 A5
Princess Louise Cty Fst Sch. Blyth NE24 17 D7
Princess Louise Rd. Blyth NE24 17 E7
Princess Mary Maternity Hospl. N-u-T NE2 66 A4
Princess Sq. N-u-T NE1 66 B2
Princess St. Gates NE10 75 A1
Princess St. Sland SR2 105 C1
Princess St. Sunn NE16 87 B2
Princess Way. Prud NE42 59 C4
Princesway. Gates NE11 88 C5
Princesway Central. Gates NE11 88 C4
Princesway S. Gates NE11 88 C3
Princesway S. Gates NE11 88 C4
Princetown Terr. Sland SR3 108 B2
Princeway. Tyne NE30 51 D8
Prinn Pl. Sunn NE16 87 B2
Prior Terr. Crbdge NE45 55 F6
Prior Terr. Hexham NE46 54 A6
Prior's Terr. Tyne NE30 51 D7
Priors Grange. H Pitt DH6 120 B5
Priors Wlk. Mpeth NE61 8 E7
Priory Ave. W Bay NE25 31 F4
Priory Ct. Gates NE8 72 C3
Priory Ct. Tyne NE30 51 E8
Priory Gdns. Crbdge NE45 55 F7
Priory Gn. N-u-T NE6 67 B2
Priory Gr. Sland SR4 104 C1
Priory Grange. Blyth NE24 17 C8
Priory Mews. 7 Tyne NE30 51 D7
Priory Pl. B Vill NE13 28 A5
Priory Pl. Stake NE62 11 A8
Priory Rd. Jarrow NE32 76 C8
Priory Sch. Tyne NE30 51 D8
Priory Way. N-u-T NE5 36 F4
Proctor Ct. N-u-T NE6 75 A5
Proctor Sq. Sland SR3 108 C2
Proctor St. N-u-T NE6 75 A5
Promenade. N-b-t-S NE64 7 E4
Promenade. S Shs NE33 51 F3
Promenade. Seaham SR7 117 D1
Promenade. Sland SR2 111 A3
Promenade. W Bay NE26 32 B5
Promontory Terr. W Bay NE26 32 C4
Prospect Ave. S Del NE25 23 C3
Prospect Ave. Walls NE28 49 B3
Prospect Ave N. Walls NE28 49 B4
Prospect Cotts. Stake NE62 11 C5
Prospect Cres. E Lane DH5 121 C8
Prospect Gdns. Boldon NE36 92 A7
Prospect Pl. N-u-T NE4 65 A1
Prospect Row. Sland SR1 106 C3
Prospect St. C le S DH3 112 C4
Prospect St. N-b-t-S NE64 7 F5
Prospect Terr. Boldon NE36 92 C7
Prospect Terr. Burnop NE16 97 A4
Prospect Terr. C le S DH3 112 C4
Prospect Terr. Gates NE9 89 D1
Prospect Terr. Kibble NE11 99 C6
Prospect Terr. N Shs NE30 51 C6
Prospect Terr. Prud NE42 59 B2
Providence Pl. Gates NE10 74 A1
Provident Terr. Walls NE28 49 A2
Provost Gdns. N-u-T NE4 70 A4
Prudhoe Adderlane Fst Sch. Prud NE42 59 E3
Prudhoe Castle Cty Fst Sch. Prud NE42 59 B2
Prudhoe Chare. N-u-T NE1 66 A2
Prudhoe Ct. N-u-T NE3 38 B3
Prudhoe Cty High Sch. Prud NE42 59 D1
Prudhoe Gr. Jarrow NE32 76 A5
Prudhoe Highfields Cty Mid Sch. Prud NE42 59 C2
Prudhoe Hospl. Prud NE42 59 E1
Prudhoe Pl. N-u-T NE1 66 A2
Prudhoe St. N Shs NE29 51 A5
Prudhoe St. N-u-T NE1 66 A2
Prudhoe St. Sland SR4 104 C3
Prudhoe Sta. Prud NE42 59 B4
Prudhoe Terr. 16 N Shs NE29 51 A5
Prudhoe Terr. Tyne NE30 51 D8
Prudhoe West Cty Fst Sch. Prud NE42 59 C2
Pudding Chare. N-u-T NE1 66 A1
Pudding Mews. Hexham NE46 54 B5
Puffin Cl. Blyth NE24 17 F3
Pullman Ct. Gates NE9 88 E5
Purbeck Cl. Tyne NE29 31 F2
Purbeck Gdns. Cram NE23 22 C7
Purbeck Rd. Lbtn NE12 41 B2
Purley. Pens NE38 102 A4
Purley Cl. Walls NE28 49 F4
Purley Gdns. N-u-T NE3 44 C4
Purley Rd. Sland SR3 108 B2
Purley Sq. Sland SR3 108 B2
Putney Sq. Sland SR4 107 B4
Pykerley Mews. W Bay NE25 31 E4
Pykerley Rd. W Bay NE25 31 E5

Quadrant The. N Shs NE29 50 E5
Quadrant The. Sland SR1 106 C3
Quality Row. N-u-T NE6 67 A1
Quality Row Rd. Whick NE16 69 A1
Quantock Ave. C le S DH2 112 A2
Quantock Cl. Lbtn NE12 41 A2
Quantock Cl. Tyne NE29 31 F2
Quarry Edge. Hexham NE46 54 C3
Quarry House Gdns. E Rain DH5 118 C4
Quarry House La. E Rain DH5 118 D4
Quarry La. S Shs NE34 78 B5
Quarry La. S Shs NE34 78 D6
Quarry Rd. Hebb NE31 75 E5
Quarry Rd. N Silk SR3 116 B6
Quarry Rd. N-u-T NE15 62 C6
Quarry Row. Gates NE10 74 A1
Quarry St. N Silk SR3 116 A7
Quarryfield Rd. Gates NE8 72 C4
Quatre Bras. Hexham NE46 53 F5
Quay Rd. Blyth NE24 18 A7
Quay The. H le H DH5 119 A3
Quay View. Walls NE28 50 A2
Quayside. Blyth NE24 17 F8
Quayside. N-u-T NE1 & NE6 67 A1
Quayside. N-u-T NE1 72 B4
Quayside Ct. N Shs NE30 51 B5
Queen Alexandra Rd. Sland SR2 110 B2
Queen Alexandra Rd. Tyne NE29 51 A7
Queen Alexandra Rd W. Tyne NE29 50 E7
Queen Ann Ct. N-u-T NE6 67 C3
Queen Elizabeth Ave. Gates NE9 89 B6
Queen Elizabeth Dr. E Lane DH5 121 D8
Queen Elizabeth High Sch. Hexham NE46 53 E4
Queen Elizabeth Hospl. Gates NE9 89 B6
Queen Elizabeth II Ctry Pk. Ashgn NE63 6 E6
Queen St. Ashgn NE63 6 E4
Queen St. Birt DH3 100 B4
Queen St. Gates NE8 88 C8
Queen St. H le H DH5 119 A5
Queen St. Lmth NE61 2 A2
Queen St. Mpeth NE61 9 A8
Queen St. N Shs NE30 51 B6
Queen St. N-b-t-S NE64 7 E5
Queen St. N-u-T NE1 72 B4
Queen St. 2 S Shs NE33 51 C3
Queen St. Sland SR1 105 C3
Queen St. Sland SR1 106 A3
Queen St. Sland SR2 116 F8
Queen St E. Sland SR1 106 B3
Queen Victoria Rd. N-u-T NE1 & NE2 66 A3
Queen Victoria St. Gates NE10 75 A1
Queen's Cres. Hebb NE31 75 D4
Queen's Cres. Sland SR4 105 A1
Queen's Cres. Walls NE28 49 B3
Queen's Dr. W Bay NE26 32 A5
Queen's Gdns. Blyth NE24 17 C8
Queen's Gdns. Mpeth NE61 8 E7
Queen's Pk. C le S DH3 112 D2
Queen's Rd. Bed NE22 11 D2
Queen's Rd. N-u-T NE2 46 C1
Queen's Rd. Sland SR5 93 B1
Queen's Rd. W Bay NE26 31 F6
Queen's Terr. N-u-T NE2 46 C1
Queens Ave. Sland SR6 93 E5
Queens Ct. Gates NE8 71 C1
Queens Ct. N-u-T NE3 28 C2
Queens Ct. N-u-T NE4 65 B2
Queens Ct. Walb NE15 36 A1
Queens Dr. Sunn NE16 87 B2

Queens Dr. Whick NE16 87 C5
Queens Gdns. Annit NE23 22 B1
Queens Gdns. Lbtn NE12 42 A2
Queens La. N-u-T NE1 72 A4
Queens Pl. N-b-t-S NE64 7 E5
Queens Rd. Annit NE23 22 B1
Queens Rd. N-u-T NE5 43 A3
Queens Rd. S Slu NE26 24 D6
Queens Rd. Walb NE15 36 A1
Queens Terr. Walls NE28 49 C3
Queens Way. Hexham NE46 53 E5
Queensberry St. Sland SR4 105 B3
Queensbridge. Lbtn NE12 40 C3
Queensbury Dr. N-u-T NE5 36 B2
Queensland Ave. S Shs NE34 76 F4
Queensmere. C le S DH3 112 C7
Queensway. H-le-Sp DH5 118 F8
Queensway. Mpeth NE61 8 D7
Queensway. N-u-T NE3 28 B1
Queensway. N-u-T NE4 & NE99 64 A4
Queensway. Pont NE20 25 D2
Queensway. Tyne NE30 51 D8
Queensway N. Gates NE11 88 C5
Queensway S. Gates NE11 88 D4
Quentin Ave. N-u-T NE3 38 A1
Quigley Terr. Birt DH3 100 B6

Rabbit Banks Rd. Gates NE8 72 A3
Raby Cl. Fence DH4 114 A1
Raby Cres. N-u-T NE6 67 C2
Raby Cross. N-u-T NE6 67 C1
Raby Dr. Sland SR3 115 C7
Raby Gdns. Burnop NE16 96 E6
Raby Gdns. Jarrow NE32 76 B4
Raby Rd. Wash NE38 101 A5
Raby St. Gates NE8 88 F8
Raby St. N-u-T NE6 67 B2
Raby St. N-u-T NE6 67 C1
Raby St. Sland SR4 105 B2
Raby Street Schs. N-u-T NE6 67 B1
Raby Way. N-u-T NE6 67 C1
Rabygate. N-u-T NE6 67 C2
Rachel Cl. Ryhope SR2 & SR3 116 C7
Rackly Way. Whit SR6 93 F8
Radcliffe Cotts. Tley NE15 35 D2
Radcliffe Pl. N-u-T NE5 44 A2
Radcliffe Rd. Hexham NE46 54 C4
Radcliffe Rd. Sland SR5 92 E2
Radcliffe St. Birt DH3 100 C3
Radlett Rd. Sland SR5 92 D2
Radnor Gdns. Walls NE28 50 A3
Radnor St. N-u-T NE1 66 B2
Radstock Pl. Lbtn NE12 41 C3
Rae Ave. Walls NE28 49 B4
Raeburn Ave. Wash NE38 101 E4
Raeburn Gdns. Gates NE9 89 B7
Raeburn Rd. Sland SR5 92 C3
Raeburn Rd. White NE34 77 D2
Raglan. Wash NE38 101 A5
Raglan Ave. Sland SR2 110 B3
Raglan Pl. Burnop NE16 97 B6
Raglan Row. S Row DH4 114 C5
Raglan St. Jarrow NE32 76 C7
Railway Arches. N-u-T NE1 66 B1
Railway Cotts. Beb NE24 16 E8
Railway Cotts. Clea NE36 77 D1
Railway Cotts. Pens DH4 114 A8
Railway Cotts. Wylam NE41 59 F5
Railway Row. Sland SR1 105 B3
Railway St. Duns NE11 70 C2
Railway St. Duns NE11 71 A1
Railway St. H le H DH5 119 A4
Railway St. Hebb NE31 75 F7
Railway St. Jarrow NE32 76 A7
Railway St. 10 N Shs NE29 51 A5
Railway St. N-u-T NE4 71 C3
Railway St. New DH4 114 D2
Railway St. Sland SR1 106 C2
Railway Terr. Blyth NE24 17 C2
Railway Terr. Blyth NE24 17 D7
Railway Terr. N Shs NE29 51 A5
Railway Terr. N-u-T NE4 71 B3
Railway Terr. Pens DH4 114 A8
Railway Terr. Sland SR4 103 A2
Railway Terr. Walls NE28 49 D1
Railway Terr. Wash NE38 101 F4
Railway Terr N. Pens DH4 114 D6
Rainford Ave. Sland SR2 110 B3
Rainhill Cl. Wash NE37 90 F1
Rainhill Rd. Wash NE37 90 F1
Rainton Bridge Ind Est. H-le-Sp DH4 118 C7
Rainton Cl. Gates NE10 90 C6
Rainton Gr. H-le-Sp DH5 118 E6
Rainton St. Pens DH4 114 B8
Rainton St. Sland SR4 105 A2
Rake La. Tyne NE29 & NE30 31 E1
Raleigh Cl. S Shs NE33 77 B8
Raleigh Rd. Sland SR5 92 E2
Raleigh Sq. Sland SR5 92 D2
Ralph Ave. Sland SR2 116 E8
Ralph St. Hebb NE31 75 F7
Ramilies. Ryhope SR2 116 D6
Ramillies Rd. Sland SR5 92 C3
Ramillies Sq. Sland SR5 92 C3
Ramparts The. N-u-T NE15 62 F8
Ramsay Rd. Chopw NE17 84 B2
Ramsay Sq. Sland SR5 92 E3
Ramsay St. Blay NE21 62 B1
Ramsay St. H Spen NE39 85 A5
Ramsey St. C le S DH3 112 C2
Ramsgate Rd. Sland SR5 92 E3
Randolph St. Jarrow NE32 76 C7
Rangoon Rd. Sland SR5 92 C3
Ranmere Rd. N-u-T NE15 63 A1
Ranmore Cl. Cram NE23 22 B7
Rannoch Ave. C le S DH2 112 B1
Rannoch Rd. Sland SR5 92 C3
Ranson Cres. S Shs NE34 77 B6
Ranson St. Sland SR4 & SR2 109 B4
Raphael Ave. White NE34 77 C2
Rathmore Gdns. Tyne NE30 51 A7
Ratho Ct. Gates NE10 89 E6
Ravel Ct. Jarrow NE32 76 C6
Ravenburn Gdns. N-u-T NE15 62 F6
Ravenburn Walk. Tley NE15 35 D2
Ravenna Rd. Sland SR5 92 B3
Ravens Hill Dr. Ashgn NE63 6 B2
Ravensbourne Ave. Boldon NE36 92 D8
Ravenscar Cl. Whick NE16 86 F5
Ravenscourt Pl. Gates NE8 72 A1
Ravenscourt Rd. Sland SR5 92 C3
Ravensdale Cres. Gates NE9 89 A6
Ravensdale Gr. Blyth NE24 17 A7
Ravenshill Rd. N-u-T NE5 36 E1
Ravenside Rd. N-u-T NE4 64 B4
Ravenside Terr. Chopw NE17 84 A1
Ravenstone. Wash NE37 101 B7
Ravenswood Cl. Lbtn NE12 42 B4
Ravenswood Gdns. Gates NE9 88 F3
Ravenswood Inf Sch. N-u-T NE6 47 C1
Ravenswood Jnr Sch. N-u-T NE6 47 C1
Ravenswood Rd. N-u-T NE6 47 C1
Ravenswood Rd. Sland SR5 92 B3
Ravenswood Sq. Sland SR5 92 B3
Ravensworh St. Sland SR4 105 B3
Ravensworth. Birt DH3 100 D5
Ravensworth. Ryhope SR2 116 D7
Ravensworth Ave. Fence DH4 114 A1
Ravensworth Ave. Gates NE9 89 C2
Ravensworth Cres. Byer NE16 97 D8
Ravensworth Ct. Duns NE11 71 A1
Ravensworth Ct. N-u-T NE3 38 A3
Ravensworth Ct. S Hett DH6 121 F7
Ravensworth Gdns. Elling NE61 1 D4
Ravensworth Golf Course. Gates NE9 89 B3
Ravensworth Rd. Birt DH3 100 B5
Ravensworth Rd. Duns NE11 71 A1
Ravensworth St. Bed NE22 11 D3
Ravensworth Terr. Bed NE22 11 D3
Ravensworth Terr. Duns NE11 88 A8
Ravensworth Terr. Jarrow NE32 76 B3
Ravensworth Terr. N-u-T NE4 65 B1
Ravensworth Terr. S Shs NE33 77 C8
Ravine Terr. Sland SR6 93 F3
Rawdon Ct. Walls NE28 75 B8
Rawdon Rd. Sland SR5 92 E3
Rawling Rd. Gates NE8 88 D8
Rawlston Way. N-u-T NE5 43 C3
Rawmarsh Rd. Sland SR5 92 C3
Raydale Ave. Wash NE37 101 B8
Raylees Gdns. Duns NE11 88 A7
Rayleigh Dr. W Open NE13 28 B7
Rayleigh Gr. Gates NE8 88 D8
Raynes Cl. Mpeth NE61 8 D7
Raynham Cl. Cram NE23 21 F3
Raynham Ct. S Shs NE33 51 C2
Rea Pl. N-u-T NE3 39 A1
Readhead Ave. S Shs NE33 51 E1
Readhead Bldgs. S Shs NE33 51 C2
Readhead Dr. N-u-T NE6 74 C4
Readhead Rd. S Shs NE34 77 F8
Reading Rd. S Shs NE34 77 D7
Reading Rd. Sland SR5 92 D3
Reading Sq. Sland SR5 92 D3
Reasby Gdns. Ryton NE40 61 B5
Reasby Villas. Ryton NE40 61 B5
Reavley Ave. Bed NE22 11 E3
Reay Cres. Boldon NE35 92 B8
Reay Ct. 1 C le S DH2 112 C2
Reay Gdns. N-u-T NE5 43 A3
Reay Pl. S Shs NE34 77 B5
Reay St. Gates NE10 75 B2
Rectory Ave. N-u-T NE3 46 B4
Rectory Bank. Boldon NE36 92 A7
Rectory Dene. Mpeth NE61 8 F7
Rectory Dr. N-u-T NE3 46 B4
Rectory Gn. Boldon NE36 91 F7
Rectory Gr. N-u-T NE3 40 A1
Rectory La. Blay NE21 86 B8
Rectory La. Whick NE16 87 B7
Rectory Pk. Mpeth NE61 8 F7
Rectory Pl. Gates NE8 72 A1
Rectory Rd. Gates NE8 & NE9 88 E8
Rectory Rd. Gates NE10 89 C7
Rectory Rd. H le H DH5 119 A3
Rectory Rd. N-u-T NE3 46 A4
Rectory Rd E. Gates NE10 89 D7
Rectory Terr. N-u-T NE3 46 B4
Red Admiral Ct. Gates NE11 88 B7
Red Barnes. N-u-T NE1 66 C1
Red Berry Way. S Shs NE34 77 B4
Red Bglws. Spring NE9 89 E1
Red Hall Dr. N-u-T NE7 48 A3
Red House Dr. W Bay NE25 31 C6
Red House Farm. Bed NE22 15 D8
Red House Rd. Hebb NE31 76 A6
Red House Special Sch. Sland SR5 92 E3
Red Lion La. Wash NE37 90 C2
Red Rose Terr. C le S DH3 112 D2
Red Wlk. N-u-T NE7 47 A1
Redburn Cl. H-le-Sp DH4 118 C8
Redburn Rd. N-u-T NE5 36 F4
Redby Sch. Sland SR6 93 D2
Redcar Rd. N-u-T NE6 48 A1
Redcar Rd. Sland SR5 92 E2
Redcar Rd. Walls NE28 50 A3
Redcar Sq. Sland SR5 92 E2
Redcliffe Way. N-u-T NE5 43 B3
Redcroft Gn. N-u-T NE5 43 B3
Redditch Sq. Sland SR5 92 D3
Rede Ave. Hebb NE31 75 E6
Rede Ave. Hexham NE46 54 C4
Rede Ct. Elling NE61 1 E5
Rede St. Gates NE11 88 C5
Rede St. Jarrow NE32 76 A5
Redemarsh. Gates NE10 89 F6
Redesdale Ave. Blay NE21 85 F8
Redesdale Ave. N-u-T NE3 39 A2
Redesdale Cl. Lbtn NE12 41 C4
Redesdale Cl. N-u-T NE15 62 E7
Redesdale Fst Sch. Walls NE28 48 C4
Redesdale Gdns. Duns NE11 87 F7
Redesdale Gr. N Shs NE29 50 D6
Redesdale Pl. Blyth NE24 17 B7
Redesdale Rd. C le S DH2 112 A1
Redesdale Rd. N Shs NE29 50 D6
Redesdale Rd. Sland SR5 92 C3
Redewater Gdns. Whick NE16 87 A6
Redewater Rd. N-u-T NE4 64 B4
Redewood Lower Sch. N-u-T NE5 43 A1
Redford Pl. Kill NE12 & NE23 29 C5
Redheugh Bridge Rd. N-u-T NE1 & NE4 71 C3
Redheugh Ct. Gates NE8 88 B8
Redheugh Rd. Ears NE25 31 B5
Redhill. Whit SR6 93 E8
Redhill Dr. Whick NE16 86 E4
Redhill Rd. Sland SR5 92 D3
Redhill Sq. Sland SR5 92 D3
Redhill Wlk. Cram NE23 22 B7
Redhills Way. H le H DH5 119 A2
Redland Ave. N-u-T NE3 38 B2
Redlands. Pens DH4 114 A7
Redmayne Ct. 1 Gates NE10 89 D8
Redmires Cl. Urpeth DH2 99 E1
Redmond Rd. Sland SR5 92 E3
Redmond Sq. Sland SR5 92 E3
Rednam Pl. N-u-T NE5 43 B2
Redruth Gdns. Gates NE9 88 F2
Redruth Sq. Sland SR5 92 D3
Redshank Cl. Wash NE38 100 F2
Redshank Dr. Blyth NE24 17 E4
Redwell Ct. Prud NE42 59 D2
Redwell Ct. S Shs NE34 78 A7
Redwell La. S Shs NE34 78 D7
Redwell Rd. Prud NE42 59 E2
Redwing Cl. Wash NE38 100 F3
Redwing Ct. N-u-T NE6 68 B3
Redwood Cl. H le H DH5 118 F4
Redwood Cl. Kill NE12 29 C4
Reed Ave. Kill NE12 29 C4
Reed St. N Shs NE30 51 B6
Reed St. S Shs NE33 77 C8
Reedham Ct. N-u-T NE5 43 B4
Reedside. Ryton NE40 61 D5
Reedsmouth Pl. N-u-T NE5 63 B4
Reedswood Cres. E Cram NE23 22 E5
Reestones Pl. N-u-T NE3 38 A1
Reeth Rd. Sland SR5 92 D2
Reeth Sq. Sland SR5 92 D2
Reeth Way. Tley NE15 35 C1
Regal Rd. Sland SR4 105 A3
Regency Dr. N Silk SR3 116 B8
Regency Dr. Whick NE16 86 F6
Regency Gdns. N Shs NE29 50 E7
Regency Way. Pont NE20 25 A5
Regent Ave. N-u-T NE3 39 B1
Regent Centre Sta. N-u-T NE3 39 C2
Regent Ct. Blyth NE24 17 D7
Regent Ct. Gates NE8 72 C2
Regent Ct. Hebb NE31 75 D5
Regent Ct. Lbtn NE12 29 B2
Regent Ct. S Shs NE33 51 C1
Regent Ctr The. N-u-T NE3 39 C2
Regent Dr. Whick NE16 86 F4
Regent Farm Ct. N-u-T NE3 39 C1
Regent Farm Fst Sch. N-u-T NE3 39 A2
Regent Farm Rd. N-u-T NE3 39 B2
Regent Rd. Jarrow NE32 76 C6
Regent Rd. N-u-T NE3 39 C1
Regent Rd. Ryhope SR2 117 A5
Regent Rd. Walls NE28 49 A3
Regent Rd N. N-u-T NE3 39 C1
Regent St. Blyth NE24 17 E8
Regent St. H le H DH5 119 A5
Regent Terr. Gates NE8 72 B2
Regent Terr. N Shs NE29 50 E6
Regent Terr. Sland SR2 110 C2
Regents Ct. Walls NE28 48 B4
Regents Dr. Tyne NE30 32 C1
Regents Pk. Walls NE28 48 B3
Regina Sq. Sland SR5 92 D3
Reginald St. Boldon NE35 91 F8
Reginald St. Gates NE8 73 B1
Reginald St. Sland SR4 104 C3
Reid Ave. Walls NE28 49 B3
Reid Park Cl. N-u-T NE2 46 C2
Reid Park Ct. N-u-T NE2 46 C2
Reid Park Rd. N-u-T NE2 46 C2
Reid St. Mpeth NE61 9 A8
Reid's La. Seg NE23 22 E1
Reigate Sq. Cram NE23 22 B7
Rekendyke Ind Est. S Shs NE33 51 D1
Rekendyke La. S Shs NE33 51 B1
Relton Ave. N-u-T NE6 74 A4
Relton Cl. Fence DH4 118 A7
Relton PL. W Bay NE25 31 E5
Relton Terr. C le S DH3 112 C2
Relton Terr. W Bay NE25 31 E5
Rembrandt Ave. White NE34 77 C2
Remington Ave. Tyne NE30 32 C1
Remscheid Way. Ashgn NE63 6 C1
Remus Ave. H-o-t-W NE15 34 D2
Remus Cl. B Vill NE13 28 B5
Rendel St. Duns NE11 70 C1
Rendle Rd. N-u-T NE6 75 B4
Renforth St. Duns NE11 87 F8
Renfrew Cl. Tyne NE29 50 C8
Renfrew Gn. N-u-T NE5 43 B3
Renfrew Pl. Birt DH3 100 D2
Renfrew Rd. Sland SR5 92 D3
Rennie Rd. Sland SR5 92 B3
Rennie Sq. Sland SR5 92 B3
Rennington. Gates NE10 90 A5
Rennington Cl. Mpeth NE61 9 B5
Rennington Cl. Tyne NE30 32 C1
Rennington Pl. N-u-T NE5 44 A2
Renoir Gdns. White NE34 77 D2
Renwick Ave. N-u-T NE3 38 B2
Renwick Rd. Blyth NE24 17 D7
Renwick St. N-u-T NE6 68 A2
Renwick Wlk. Mpeth NE61 8 E8
Rescue Station Cotts. H-le-Sp DH5 118 F6
Resida Cl. N-u-T NE15 62 C8
Retford Gdns. N Shs NE29 50 D4
Retford Rd. Sland SR5 92 D3
Retford Sq. Sland SR5 92 D3
RetreatThe. Newb NE15 61 F8
Retreat The. Sland SR2 105 B2
Revell Terr. N-u-T NE5 44 B1
Revelstoke Rd. Sland SR5 92 C3
Revesby St. S Shs NE33 77 C6
Reynolds Ave. Kill NE12 29 B2
Reynolds Ave. Wash NE38 101 E4
Reynolds Ave. White NE34 77 D3
Reyrolle Ct. Hebb NE31 75 D5
Rheims Ct. Sland SR4 104 A3
Rheydt Ave. Walls NE28 48 C2
Rhoda Terr. Sland SR2 110 C1
Rhodes St. N-u-T NE6 75 A5
Rhodesia Rd. Sland SR5 92 D3
Rhondda Rd. Sland SR5 92 B3
Rhuddlan Ct. N-u-T NE5 43 B4
Rhyl Par. Jarrow NE31 76 A2
Rhyl Sq. Sland SR5 92 E3
Ribble Rd. Sland SR5 92 C2
Ribble Wlk. Hedw NE32 76 C2
Ribbledale Gdns. N-u-T NE7 47 B3
Ribblesdale. Pens DH4 114 B7
Ribblesdale. Walls NE28 48 C4
Ribblesdale Ave. Blyth NE24 17 B6
Richard Ave. Sland SR4 & SR2 109 A4
Richard Avenue Prim Sch. Sland SR4 109 A4
Richard Browell Rd. Tley NE15 35 E1
Richard St. Blyth NE24 17 E7
Richard St. H le H DH5 119 A3
Richardson Ave. 2 S Shs NE34 76 F4
Richardson Dees Fst Sch. Walls NE28 49 D2
Richardson Rd. N-u-T NE1 & NE2 65 C3
Richardson St. N-u-T NE6 67 C4
Richardson St. Walls NE28 49 C2
Richardson Terr. Chopw NE17 84 B1
Richardson Terr. 6 Ryhope SR2 117 A6
Richardson Terr. 5 Wash NE37 101 D8
Richmond. Ryhope SR2 116 D7
Richmond Ave. Gates NE10 75 C2
Richmond Ave. Wash NE38 101 D6
Richmond Ave. Whick NE16 69 B1
Richmond Cl. Bed NE22 10 E2
Richmond Ct. Gates NE8 72 C1
Richmond Ct. 1 Gates NE9 88 F4
Richmond Ct. Jarrow NE32 76 A7
Richmond Gdns. N-u-T NE5 43 B3
Richmond Gdns. Walls NE28 49 E3
Richmond Gr. N Shs NE29 50 E5
Richmond Mews. N-u-T NE3 45 B3
Richmond Pk. Walls NE28 48 B3
Richmond Rd. S Shs NE34 77 C6
Richmond St. Sland SR5 105 C4
Richmond Terr. Gates NE8 72 B1
Richmond Terr. 10 Gates NE10 89 D8
Richmond Terr. Hasw DH6 121 F3
Richmond Terr. W Bay NE26 31 F7
Richmond Terr. Walb NE15 35 F1
Richmond Way. Cram NE23 22 A3
Richmond Way. Pont NE20 25 A5
Rickaby St. Sland SR1 106 C4
Rickgarth. Gates NE10 89 F5
Rickleton Ave. C le S DH3 112 D5
Rickleton Prim Sch. Wash NE38 112 F8
Rickleton Way. Wash NE38 101 A1
Riddell Ave. N-u-T NE15 63 C1
Riddell Ct. 5 C le S DH2 112 C2
Riddings Rd. Sland SR5 92 D3
Riddings Sq. Sland SR5 92 D3
Ridge Ct. Hazle NE13 28 B4
Ridge Terr. Bed NE22 10 E1
Ridge The. Ryton NE40 61 C4
Ridge Villas. Bed NE22 10 E1
Ridge Way. S Del NE25 23 E1
Ridge Way The. N-u-T NE3 44 C4
Ridgely Cl. Pont NE20 26 A6
Ridgely Dr. Pont NE20 26 A6
Ridgeway. Ashgn NE63 7 A2
Ridgeway. Birt DH3 100 C6
Ridgeway. Gates NE10 90 B6
Ridgeway. N-u-T NE4 64 B4
Ridgeway. Ryhope SR2 116 C6
Ridgeway. Stake NE62 11 A8
Ridgeway Cres. Sland SR3 109 B3
Ridgeway Cty Jun & Inf Sch. S Shs NE34 77 F4
Ridgeway The. S Shs NE34 77 F3
Ridgewood Cres. N-u-T NE3 40 C1
Ridgewood Gdns. N-u-T NE3 40 B1
Ridgewood Villas. N-u-T NE3 40 B1
Riding Barns Way. Sunn NE16 87 A2
Riding Cl. Craw NE40 60 E3
Riding Dene. M Sq NE43 58 F1
Riding La. Kibble DH9 & NE11 99 B4
Riding Lea. Blay NE21 62 A1
Riding Mill Sta. R Mill NE44 80 F8
Riding Terr. M Sq NE43 58 F1
Riding The. N-u-T NE3 44 B3
Ridings Ct. Craw NE40 60 E3
Ridings The. W Bay NE25 31 C6
Ridley Ave. Blyth NE24 17 F7
Ridley Ave. C le S DH2 112 B2
Ridley Ave. Sland SR2 116 F7
Ridley Ave. Walls NE28 50 B4
Ridley Cl. Hexham NE46 53 F3
Ridley Cl. Mpeth NE61 8 E8
Ridley Cl. N-u-T NE3 38 C4
Ridley Gdns. Whick NE16 69 A1
Ridley Gr. S Shs NE34 78 A7
Ridley Mill Cotts. Stocks NE43 82 B6
Ridley Mill Rd. Stocks NE43 82 B5
Ridley Pl. N-u-T NE1 & NE99 66 A2
Ridley St. Blyth NE24 17 F8
Ridley St. Cram NE23 22 C5
Ridley St. Gates NE8 88 E8
Ridley St. Sland SR5 93 B2
Ridley Terr. Cam NE24 12 D4
Ridley Terr. Gates NE10 89 E8
Ridley Terr. Sland SR2 106 C1
Ridsdale. Prud NE42 59 B1
Ridsdale Ave. N-u-T NE5 36 E1
Ridsdale Cl. S Del NE25 23 C3
Ridsdale Cl. Walls NE28 49 C4
Ridsdale Ct. Gates NE8 72 A1
Ridsdale Sq. Ashgn NE63 6 C3
Rievaulx. Wash NE38 101 C4
Riga Sq. Sland SR5 92 C3
Riggs The. Crbdge NE45 55 F7
Riggs The. H-le-Sp DH5 118 F8
Rignall. Wash NE38 102 A5
Riley St. Jarrow NE32 76 A7
Ringmore Ct. Sland SR2 109 C2
Ringway. Sland SR5 103 A4
Ringway. Stake NE62 6 A1
Ringway Cty Fst Sch. Stake NE62 10 F8
Ringwood Dr. Cram NE23 22 B7
Ringwood Gn. Lbtn NE12 41 C3
Ringwood Rd. Sland SR5 92 D3
Ringwood Sq. Sland SR5 92 D3
Rink St. Blyth NE24 17 F8
Ripley Ave. N Shs NE29 50 E4
Ripley Ct. Gates NE9 89 B1
Ripley Dr. Cram NE23 22 A3
Ripley Terr. N-u-T NE6 68 B2
Ripon Cl. Cram NE23 21 F3
Ripon Gdns. N-u-T NE2 67 A4
Ripon Gdns. Walls NE28 49 E3
Ripon Sq. Hedw NE32 & NE35 91 B8
Ripon St. C le S DH3 112 C1
Ripon St. Gates NE8 72 B1
Ripon St. Sland SR6 93 E1
Rise The. Gates NE8 73 B1
Rise The. N-u-T NE3 44 B4
Rise The. Pont NE20 25 B2
Rise The. Ryton NE21 62 A4
Rise The. S Slu NE26 24 E4
Rishton Sq. Sland SR5 92 C3
Rising Sun Cotts. Walls NE28 49 B5
Rising Sun Ctry Pk. Walls NE28 49 B6
Ritson Cl. N Shs NE29 50 E7
Ritson St. Sland SR6 93 E4
River Bank. Stake NE62 11 C8
River Bank E. Stake NE62 11 C8
River Dr. S Shs NE33 51 C4
River Garth. Sland SR1 106 B3
River La. Ryton NE40 61 C6
River View. B Mill NE17 95 B6
River View. Beb NE22 11 D1
River View. Blay NE21 62 B2
River View. Lmth NE61 2 A3
River View. N Shs NE30 51 C6
River View. Oham NE42 59 A4
River View. Prud NE42 59 C2
River View. Ryton NE40 61 E5
River View Cl. Beb NE22 11 D1
Riverbank Rd. Sland SR5 92 D2
Riverdale. Sland SR5 103 B4
Rivermead. Wash NE38 101 E1
Rivermede. Pont NE20 25 F7
Riversdale. B Mill NE17 95 B6
Riversdale Ave. Stake NE62 11 A8
Riversdale Ct. N-u-T NE15 62 C6
Riversdale Ct. Stake NE62 11 A7
Riversdale Terr. Sland SR2 105 B1
Riversdale Way. N-u-T NE15 62 C6
Riverside. Pont NE20 25 E6
Riverside Ave. G Post NE62 10 D7
Riverside Cl. Newb NE15 61 E7
Riverside Ct. Duns NE11 71 A1
Riverside Ct. S Shs NE33 51 B2
Riverside Pk. Sland SR4 103 B3
Riverside Rd. Sland SR5 92 E2
Riverside The. Hebb NE31 75 C7
Riverside Way. Duns NE16 69 C3
Riverview Lodge. N-u-T NE4 70 A4
Roachburn Rd. N-u-T NE5 36 E2
Robert Owen Gdns. Gates NE10 89 C7
Robert St. Blyth NE24 17 E7
Robert St. N Silk SR3 116 B7
Robert St. S Shs NE33 51 D1
Robert St. Sland SR4 105 A3
Robert Terr. H Spen NE39 84 F4
Robert Terr Cotts. H Spen NE39 84 F4
Robert Wheatman Ct. Sland SR2 110 B2
Roberts St. N-u-T NE15 63 A1
Roberts Terr. Jarrow NE32 76 B5
Robertson Rd. Sland SR5 92 B2
Robertson Sq. Sland SR5 92 B3
Robin Ct. E Rain DH5 118 C3
Robin Gr. Sland SR5 92 C1
Robin La. E Rain DH4 & DH5 38 C2
Robin La. W Rain DH4 & DH5 118 C2
Robinson Gdns. Walls NE28 50 A3
Robinson Gdns. Whit SR6 78 F1
Robinson St. N-u-T NE6 67 C2
Robinson St. 8 S Shs NE33 51 D2
Robinson Terr. Burnop NE16 97 A4
Robinson Terr. N Silk SR3 116 B7
Robinson Terr. Sland SR2 106 C1
Robinson Terr. Wash NE38 101 F4
Robinswood. 8 Gates NE9 88 F5
Robsheugh Pl. N-u-T NE5 63 C4
Robson Dr. Hexham NE46 53 F3
Robson Pl. 10 Ryhope SR2 117 A6
Robson St. 7 Gates NE9 88 F5
Robson St. N-u-T NE6 67 A2
Robson Terr. H Spen NE39 85 B3
Robson Terr. Tant DH9 96 F1
Rochdale Rd. Sland SR5 92 D3
Rochdale Sq. Sland SR5 92 D3
Rochdale St. H le H DH5 119 A2
Rochdale St. Walls NE28 49 B1
Rochdale Way. Sland SR5 92 D3
Roche Ct. Wash NE38 101 C4
Rochester Cl. Ashgn NE63 7 A2
Rochester Gdns. Duns NE11 88 A8
Rochester Sq. Hedw NE32 76 B1
Rochester St. N-u-T NE6 75 A4
Rochester Terr. Gates NE10 89 E8
Rochford Gr. Cram NE23 22 A3
Rochford Rd. Sland SR5 92 C3
Rock Gr. 4 Gates NE9 88 F5
Rock Lodge Gdns. Sland SR6 93 F3
Rock Lodge Rd. Sland SR6 93 F3
Rock Terr. N-u-T NE2 66 C2
Rock Terr. 9 Wash NE37 101 E8
Rockcliffe. S Shs NE33 & NE34 51 E1
Rockcliffe. W Bay NE26 32 C5
Rockcliffe Ave. W Bay NE26 32 C4
Rockcliffe Fst Sch. W Bay NE26 32 C4
Rockcliffe Gdns. N-u-T NE15 62 F7
Rockcliffe Gdns. W Bay NE26 32 C4
Rockcliffe St. W Bay NE26 32 C4
Rockcliffe Way. Gates NE9 89 D1
Rocket Way. Lbtn NE12 42 C4
Rockhope. Wash NE38 112 F8
Rockingham Rd. Sland SR5 92 C3
Rockingham Sq. Sland SR5 92 C3
Rockmore Rd. Blay NE21 62 C1
Rockville. Sland SR6 93 E4
Rockwood Gdns. Green NE40 60 E1
Rockwood Hill Est. Green NE40 84 E8
Rockwood Hill Rd. Green NE40 60 F1
Rockwood Terr. Green NE40 60 F1
Rodin Ave. White NE34 77 D2
Rodney Cl. Ryhope SR2 116 C6
Rodney Cl. Tyne NE30 51 D7
Rodney Ct. W Bay NE26 31 D7
Rodney St. N-u-T NE6 67 B1
Rodney Way. W Bay NE26 31 D7
Rodsley Ave. Gates NE8 & NE9 88 F8
Roeburn Way. N-u-T NE3 44 C3
Roedean Rd. Sland SR5 92 E3
Roehedge. Gates NE10 90 B6
Roger St. N-u-T NE6 67 B2
Rogerson Terr. N-u-T NE5 36 E3
Rogues La. H Spen NE39 85 A5
Rokeby Ave. N-u-T NE15 62 D6
Rokeby Dr. N-u-T NE3 44 C4
Rokeby St. N-u-T NE15 62 D6
Rokeby St. Sland SR4 105 B2
Rokeby Terr. N-u-T NE6 47 C1
Rokeby View. Gates NE9 89 A1
Roker Ave. Sland SR6 93 E1
Roker Ave. W Bay NE25 31 F3
Roker Baths Rd. Sland SR6 93 E2
Roker Park Rd. Sland SR6 93 E3
Roker Park Terr. Sland SR6 93 F2
Roker Pk (Sunderland FC). Sland SR6 93 E2
Roker Terr. Sland SR6 93 F3
Rokerby Ave. Whick NE16 87 C6
Roland Rd. Walls NE28 49 E2
Roland St. Wash NE38 101 E4
Rollesby Ct. N-u-T NE5 43 B4
Romaldskirk Cl. Sland SR4 103 B1
Roman Ave. C le S DH3 112 D3
Roman Ave. N-u-T NE6 68 B2
Roman Mews. W Rain DH4 118 A2
Roman Rd. S Shs NE33 51 D4
Roman Rd N. S Shs NE33 51 C4
Roman Road Jun Mix Sch. Gates NE10 90 A5
Roman Way. Crbdge NE45 55 F6
Roman Way The. N-u-T NE5 62 D8
Romford Cl. Cram NE23 22 A3
Romford Pl. Gates NE9 89 A8
Romford St. Sland SR4 104 C2
Romilly St. S Shs NE33 51 D2
Romley Gr. Gates NE10 90 D7
Romney Ave. Sland SR2 110 B3
Romney Ave. Wash NE38 101 E4
Romney Ave. White NE34 77 D3
Romney Cl. S Row DH4 114 C5
Romney Gdns. Gates NE9 89 B7
Romsey Cl. Cram NE23 22 B7
Romsey Dr. Boldon NE35 91 E8
Romsey Gr. N-u-T NE15 62 C8
Ronald Dr. N-u-T NE15 63 A2
Ronald Gdns. Hebb NE31 75 D4
Ronald Sq. Sland SR6 93 D2
Ronaldsay Cl. 4 Sland SR2 116 E8
Ronsdorf Ct. Jarrow NE32 76 B6
Rookery Cl. Blyth NE24 17 B7
Rookery La. Whick NE16 86 E4
Rooksleigh. 5 Blay NE21 62 B1
Rookswood. Mpeth NE61 9 A6
Rookswood Gdns. R Gill NE39 85 E3
Rookwood Dr. S Burn NE13 28 C8
Rookwood Rd. N-u-T NE5 63 A4
Ropery La. Bourn DH3 112 F3
Ropery La. C le S DH3 112 D2
Ropery La. Hebb NE31 75 D6
Ropery La. Walls NE28 49 F2
Ropery Rd. Gates NE8 88 B8
Ropery Rd. Sland SR4 105 B4
Ropery The. N-u-T NE6 74 A4
Rosa St. S Shs NE33 51 D2
Rosalind Ave. Bed NE22 11 B1
Rosalind St. Ashgn NE63 6 E4
Rosamond Pl. Blyth NE24 17 F7
Rose Ave. Cram NE23 21 F8
Rose Ave. Fence DH4 113 F1
Rose Ave. Whick NE16 87 B7
Rose Cotts. Burnop NE16 96 E5
Rose Cres. Bourn DH4 113 D3
Rose Cres. Whit SR6 78 F2
Rose Ct. Hebb NE31 75 D5
Rose Gdns. Kibble NE11 99 C6
Rose Gdns. Walls NE28 49 B4
Rose Hill Way. N-u-T NE5 43 C1
Rose St. Gates NE8 71 C2
Rose St. 7 H-le-Sp DH4 118 D8
Rose St. Hebb NE31 75 D5
Rose St. Sland SR4 105 B3
Rose St E. Pens DH4 114 B8
Rose St W. Pens DH4 114 B8
Rose Terr. Green NE40 61 C2
Rose Terr. N-u-T NE5 44 B1
Rose Villa La. Whick NE16 87 B7
Rosebank Cl. Sland SR2 116 E8
Rosebank Hall. Walls NE28 49 F2
Roseberry Grange. Lbtn NE12 30 A1
Roseberry Pl. N-u-T NE2 66 C4
Roseberry Terr. 1 Boldon NE35 76 E1
Rosebery Ave. Blyth NE24 17 D7
Rosebery Ave. Gates NE8 89 A8
Rosebery Ave. S Shs NE33 51 E1
Rosebery Ave. Tyne NE29 51 A8
Rosebery Cres. N-u-T NE2 67 A4
Rosebery St. Sland SR5 93 D1
Rosedale. Bed NE22 10 E1
Rosedale. Walls NE28 48 C4
Rosedale Ave. Sland SR6 93 E6
Rosedale Cres. Burn DH4 114 C2
Rosedale Ct. N-u-T NE5 36 D2
Rosedale Rd. Craw NE40 60 F3
Rosedale St. H le H DH5 118 E1
Rosedale St. Sland SR1 105 B2
Rosedale Terr. N Shs NE30 51 B7
Rosedale Terr. N-u-T NE2 66 C3
Rosedale Terr. Sland SR6 93 E4
Roseden Ct. Lbtn NE12 41 C3
Rosedene Villas. Cram NE23 22 D6
Rosefinch Lodge. Gates NE9 88 F5
Rosegill. Wash NE37 101 B6
Rosehill. Walls NE28 49 E2
Rosehill Rd. Walls NE28 49 F2
Rosehill Terr. Walls NE28 49 E2
Roselea. Hedw NE32 76 C1
Roselea Ave. Ryhope SR2 116 F7

144 Ros – St P

Rosemary Gdns. Gates NE9 .. 89 D2
Rosemary Terr. Blyth NE24 ... 17 F6
Rosemount. Mpeth NE61 ... 9 A7
Rosemount. N-u-T NE5 ... 36 F2
Rosemount. Sland SR4 ... 103 A1
Rosemount Ave. Gates NE10 . 90 B7
Rosemount Cl. Wash NE37 ... 90 C2
Rosemount Ct. Boldon NE36 .. 92 B7
Rosemount Way. N-u-T NE7 .. 41 C1
Rosemount Way. W Bay NE25 31 C5
Roseneath Ct. Ashgn NE63 ... 6 D3
Roseville St. Sland SR4 ... 105 B1
Rosewell Pl. Whick NE16 ... 87 A4
Rosewood. Kill NE12 ... 29 F3
Rosewood Ave. N-u-T NE3 ... 40 B2
Rosewood Cres. N-u-T NE6 ... 48 C1
Rosewood Cres. S Slu NE26 . 24 D4
Rosewood Gdns. C le S DH2 112 B5
Rosewood Gdns. Gates NE9 .. 89 B5
Rosewood Gdns. N-u-T NE3 .. 44 C4
Rosewood Sq. Sland SR4 ... 107 A2
Rosewood Terr. Birt DH3 ... 100 B5
Rosewood Terr. Walls NE28 .. 50 A2
Roseworth Ave. N-u-T NE3 ... 46 A3
Roseworth Cl. N-u-T NE3 ... 46 A4
Roseworth Cres. N-u-T NE3 ... 46 A3
Roseworth Terr. N-u-T NE3 ... 45 C4
Roseworth Terr. Whick NE16 87 B7
Roslin Pk. Bed NE22 ... 11 C1
Roslin Way. Cram NE23 ... 22 A3
Ross. Ouston DH2 ... 100 A1
Ross Ave. Duns NE11 ... 70 C1
Ross Gr. Cram NE23 ... 21 F7
Ross Lea. S Row DH4 ... 114 A5
Ross St. Sland SR5 ... 93 C1
Ross Way. N-u-T NE3 ... 38 C4
Ross Way. W Bay NE26 ... 31 E7
Rosse Cl. Wash NE37 ... 101 B8
Rossendale Pl. Lbtn NE12 ... 40 C2
Rosslyn Ave. Gates NE9 ... 89 A6
Rosslyn Ave. N-u-T NE3 ... 38 B1
Rosslyn Ave. Ryhope SR2 ... 116 F7
Rosslyn Mews. Sland SR4 ... 105 A2
Rosslyn Pl. Birt DH3 ... 100 D2
Rosslyn St. Sland SR4 ... 105 A2
Rosslyn Terr. Sland SR4 ... 105 A2
Rosyth Rd. Sland SR5 ... 92 E3
Rosyth Sq. Sland SR5 ... 92 E3
Rotary Parkway. Ashgn NE63 .. 6 B4
Rotary Way. Blyth NE24 ... 17 F5
Rotary Way. N Shs NE29 ... 50 E3
Rothay Pl. N-u-T NE5 ... 43 C2
Rothbury. Ryhope SR2 ... 116 D6
Rothbury Ave. Blyth NE24 ... 17 B6
Rothbury Ave. Gates NE10 ... 75 A1
Rothbury Ave. Hebb NE32 ... 76 A4
Rothbury Ave. N-u-T NE3 ... 39 B2
Rothbury Cl. C le S DH2 ... 112 A1
Rothbury Cl. Kill NE12 ... 29 C4
Rothbury Gdns. Duns NE11 ... 88 A5
Rothbury Gdns. W Open NE13 28 C6
Rothbury Gdns. Walls NE28 ... 49 F3
Rothbury Rd. Sland SR5 ... 92 D3
Rothbury Terr. N Shs NE29 ... 50 D4
Rothbury Terr. N-u-T NE6 ... 68 A4
Rotherfield Cl. Cram NE23 ... 22 B7
Rotherfield Gdns. Gates NE9 89 A2
Rotherfield Rd. Sland SR5 ... 92 C3
Rotherfield Sq. Sland SR5 ... 92 C3
Rotherham Cl. H-le-Sp DH5 118 D6
Rotherham Rd. Sland SR5 ... 92 C3
Rothesay. Ouston DH2 ... 99 F1
Rothesay Terr. Bed NE22 ... 11 C2
Rothlea Gdns. Stake NE62 ... 11 A8
Rothley. Wash NE38 ... 101 F2
Rothley Ave. Ashgn NE63 ... 6 D2
Rothley Ave. N-u-T NE5 ... 63 C3
Rothley Cl. N-u-T NE3 ... 40 A1
Rothley Cl. Pont NE20 ... 25 D7
Rothley Ct. Kill NE12 ... 29 D3
Rothley Gdns. Tyne NE30 ... 32 B1
Rothley Gr. S Del NE25 ... 23 C3
Rothley Terr. Medom DH8 ... 95 B1
Rothley Way. W Bay NE26 ... 31 E7
Rothsay Terr. N-b-t-S NE64 ... 7 D3
Rothwell Rd. N-u-T NE3 ... 39 C1
Rothwell Rd. Sland SR5 ... 92 C2
Roundhill. Hedw NE32 ... 76 D1
Roundhill Ave. N-u-T NE5 ... 43 C2
Roundway The. Lbtn NE12 ... 41 B3
Row's Terr. N-u-T NE3 ... 40 B1
Rowan Ave. Wash NE38 ... 101 C1
Rowan Cl. Bed NE22 ... 10 F2
Rowan Cl. Sland SR4 ... 103 B1
Rowan Ct. Blyth NE24 ... 17 D6
Rowan Ct. Lbtn NE12 ... 42 C4
Rowan Ct. [4] S Shs NE34 ... 77 A4
Rowan Dr. H le H DH5 ... 118 F4
Rowan Dr. N-u-T NE3 ... 38 C2
Rowan Dr. Pont NE20 ... 25 E7
Rowan Gr. Prud NE42 ... 59 B2
Rowanberry Rd. Lbtn NE12 ... 41 B2
Rowans The. Gates NE9 ... 89 D2
Rowantree Rd.
N-u-T NE28 & NE6 ... 49 A1
Rowanwood Gdns. Duns NE11 88 B5
Rowedge Wlk. N-u-T NE5 ... 43 A2
Rowell Cl. Ryhope SR2 & SR3 116 C6
Rowes Mews. N-u-T NE6 ... 73 C4
Rowlands Gill Cty Inf Sch.
R Gill NE39 ... 85 F3
Rowlands Gill Jun Sch.
R Gill NE39 ... 85 F3
Rowlandson Cres. Gates NE10 89 D8
Rowlandson Terr. [9]
Gates NE10 ... 89 D8
Rowlandson Terr. Sland SR2 110 B4
Rowley St. Blyth NE24 ... 17 E7
Rowlington Terr. Ashgn NE63 . 6 D2
Rowntree Way. N Shs NE29 ... 51 A5
Rowsley Rd. Jarrow NE32 ... 76 C5
Roxburgh Cl. Blay NE21 ... 86 A8
Roxburgh House. W Bay NE26 32 A5
Roxburgh Pl. N-u-T NE6 ... 67 B3
Roxburgh St. Sland SR6 ... 93 D2
Roxburgh Terr. W Bay NE26 .. 32 A5
Roxby Gdns. N Shs NE29 ... 50 E5
Royal Arc. N-u-T NE1 ... 66 B1
Royal Cres. N-u-T NE4 ... 64 B4
Royal Ind Est. Hebb NE32 ... 75 F8
Royal Victoria Infmy.
N-u-T NE2 ... 65 C3
Royalty The. Sland SR2 ... 105 B2
Roydon Ave. Sland SR2 ... 110 B3
Royle St. Sland SR2 ... 110 C2
Royston Terr. N-u-T NE6 ... 75 A4
Ruabon Cl. Cram NE23 ... 22 A3
Rubens Ave. White NE34 ... 77 D3
Ruby St. New DH4 ... 114 D2
Rudby Cl. N-u-T NE3 ... 40 A4
Rudchester Pl. N-u-T NE5 ... 63 C4
Ruddock Sq. N-u-T NE6 ... 73 C4
Rudyard Ave. Sland SR2 ... 110 B3
Rudyerd Ct. N Shs NE29 ... 51 B5
Rudyerd St. [13] N Shs NE29 ... 51 A5
Rugby Gdns. Gates NE9 ... 89 C3
Rugby Gdns. Walls NE28 ... 49 E3
Ruislip Pl. Cram NE23 ... 21 F3
Ruislip Rd. Sland SR4 ... 103 A1
Runcorn. Ryhope SR2 ... 116 C7
Runcorn Rd. Sland SR5 ... 92 C3
Runhead Est. Ryton NE40 ... 61 D4
Runhead Gdns. Ryton NE40 .. 61 D5
Runhead Terr. Ryton NE40 ... 61 E5
Runnymede. Ryhope SR2 ... 116 D7
Runnymede Gdns.
Chopw NE17 ... 95 B7
Runnymede Rd. Pont NE20 ... 25 C5
Runnymede Rd. Sland SR5 ... 92 D3
Runnymede Rd. Whick NE16 . 87 A6
Runnymede Way. Sland SR5 92 D3
Runswick Ave. Lbtn NE12 ... 40 C2
Runswick Cl. N Silk SR3 ... 116 C7
Rupert Sq. Sland SR5 ... 92 E3
Rupert St. Whit SR6 ... 78 F1
Rupert Terr. Newb NE15 ... 61 F8
Rushall Pl. Lbtn NE12 ... 41 B2
Rushbury Ct. Bworth NE27 ... 30 C5
Rushford. Ryhope SR2 ... 116 D6
Rushie Ave. N-u-T NE15 ... 63 C1
Rushley Cres. Blay NE21 ... 62 C3
Rushsyde Cl. Whick NE16 ... 86 E5
Rushton Ave. Sland SR2 ... 110 B3
Rushyrig. Wash NE37 ... 101 A6
Ruskin Ave. Ashgn NE63 ... 6 F2
Ruskin Ave. Duns NE11 ... 70 C1
Ruskin Ave. E Lane DH5 ... 121 D8
Ruskin Ave. Lbtn NE12 ... 29 D1
Ruskin Cl. Prud NE42 ... 59 B1
Ruskin Cres. B Hall NE34 ... 77 B3
Ruskin Dr. Boldon NE35 ... 92 A8
Ruskin Rd. Birt DH3 ... 100 C4
Ruskin Rd. Gates NE10 & NE9 . 89 B7
Ruskin Rd. Whick NE16 ... 87 A8
Russel Ct. N-u-T NE2 ... 46 C2
Russell Ave. S Shs NE34 ... 78 A6
Russell Ct. Gates NE8 ... 71 C1
Russell Sq. S Burn NE13 ... 28 B8
Russell St. Jarrow NE32 ... 76 C7
Russell St. [8] N Shs NE29 ... 51 A5
Russell St. S Shs NE33 ... 51 C3
Russell St. Sland SR1 ... 106 B3
Russell St. Wash NE37 ... 101 C8
Russell Terr. Bed NE22 ... 15 F8
Russell Terr. Birt DH3 ... 100 B6
Russell Terr. N-u-T NE1 & NE2 66 C2
Ruswarp Dr. Silk SR3 ... 116 B6
Ruth Ave. Blay NE21 ... 62 C2
Rutherford Ave. Seaham SR7 116 F1
Rutherford Cl. G Post NE62 ... 10 E7
Rutherford Cl. Mpeth NE61 ... 8 E7
Rutherford Rd. Sland SR5 ... 92 B3
Rutherford Rd. Wash NE37 ... 90 E2
Rutherford Sch. N-u-T NE4 ... 64 A2
Rutherford Sq. Sland SR5 ... 92 B3
Rutherford St. Blyth NE24 ... 17 D7
Rutherford St. N-u-T NE1 ... 65 C1
Rutherford St. Walls NE28 ... 50 B3
Rutherglen Rd. Sland SR5 ... 92 E3
Rutherglen Sq. Sland SR5 ... 92 E3
Rutland Ave. N Silk SR3 ... 115 F7
Rutland Ave. N-u-T NE6 ... 75 A7
Rutland Pl. N Shs NE29 ... 50 F6
Rutland Pl. Wash NE37 ... 90 D2
Rutland Rd. Hebb NE31 ... 75 F3
Rutland Rd. Walls NE28 ... 49 A1
Rutland Sq. Birt DH3 ... 100 B5
Rutland St. Ashgn NE63 ... 6 C3
Rutland St. H le H DH5 ... 118 F4
Rutland St. Sland SR4 ... 104 C3
Rutland Terr. Hasw DH6 ... 121 E1
Ryal Cl. Blyth NE24 ... 17 C7
Ryal Cl. S Del NE25 ... 23 E3
Ryal Terr. N-u-T NE6 ... 68 C1
Ryal Wlk. N-u-T NE3 ... 44 A4
Ryall Ave. Hazle NE13 ... 28 A4
Rydal. Gates NE10 ... 90 A8
Rydal Ave. E Lane DH5 ... 121 C8
Rydal Ave. Tyne NE30 ... 32 A2
Rydal Cl. Boldon NE36 ... 92 C8
Rydal Cl. Kill NE12 ... 29 F3
Rydal Cres. Blay NE21 ... 86 B8
Rydal Gdns. S Shs NE34 ... 77 E6
Rydal Mount. N-b-t-S NE64 ... 7 C4
Rydal Mount. Sland SR5 ... 93 C3
Rydal Mount. Sland SR5 ... 103 A4
Rydal Rd. C le S DH2 ... 112 C1
Rydal Rd. N-u-T NE3 ... 40 A1
Rydal Rd. N-u-T NE15 ... 62 D8
Rydal St. Gates NE8 ... 72 B1
Rydal Terr. W Open NE13 ... 28 B4
Ryde Pl. Cram NE23 ... 22 B7
Ryde Terr. Duns NE11 ... 71 A1
Rye Cl. Tley NE15 ... 35 E1
Rye Hill. N-u-T NE4 ... 71 B4
Rye Hill. N-u-T NE4 ... 71 C4
Rye Terr. Hexham NE46 ... 53 F5
Rye View Rd. Sland SR2 ... 116 F7
Ryedale. Sland SR6 ... 93 F7
Ryedale. Walls NE28 ... 42 C1
Ryedale Cl. Ashgn NE63 ... 6 B2
Ryedale Ct. S Shs NE34 ... 77 A4
Ryehaugh. Pont NE20 ... 25 F6
Ryehill View. E Rain DH5 ... 118 C5
Ryemount Rd. Ryhope SR2 .. 116 D7
Ryhope Gdns. Gates NE9 ... 89 D4
Ryhope General Hospl.
Ryhope SR2 ... 116 F5
Ryhope Grange Ct.
Sland SR2 ... 110 C1
Ryhope Inf Sch. Ryhope SR2 116 F7
Ryhope Jun Sch.
Ryhope SR2 ... 116 F7
Ryhope Rd. Ryhope SR2 ... 117 A7
Ryhope Rd. Sland SR2 ... 110 B3
Ryhope St. H-le-Sp DH5 ... 118 F8
Ryhope St. Ryhope SR2 ... 116 E7
Ryhope St. Sland SR2 ... 110 C2
Ryhope St S. Ryhope SR2 ... 116 F7
Ryhope Village C of E Prim Sch.
Ryhope SR2 ... 116 F6
Ryton Comp Sch. Ryton NE40 61 B5
Ryton Ct. S Shs NE33 ... 51 D1
Ryton Golf Course. Craw NE40 60 F7
Ryton Hall Dr. Ryton NE40 ... 61 C6
Ryton Ind Est. Ryton NE21 ... 61 F5
Ryton Inf Sch. Ryton NE40 ... 61 A5
Ryton Jun Sch. Ryton NE40 ... 61 A5
Ryton Sq. Sland SR2 ... 110 B3
Ryton Terr. N-u-T NE6 ... 74 C4
Ryton Terr. Shire NE27 ... 30 D1

Sackville Rd. N-u-T NE6 ... 47 C1
Sackville Rd. Sland SR3 ... 108 B3
Sacred Heart Comp Sch.
N-u-T NE4 ... 64 C2
Sacred Heart Comp Upper Sch.
N-u-T NE4 ... 64 A3
Sacred Heart RC Mid Sch.
N-u-T NE4 ... 64 B3
Sacred Heart RC Prim Sch.
B Vill NE13 ... 28 A5
Sacred Heart RC Prim Sch.
N-u-T NE4 ... 64 A3
Sacriston Ave. Sland SR3 ... 108 C3
Sacriston Gdns. Gates NE9 ... 89 C2
Saddleback. Wash NE37 ... 101 B7
Saffron Pl. N-u-T NE6 ... 75 A5
Saga Ct. N-u-T NE6 ... 48 C1
Sage Cl. N-u-T NE15 ... 62 C8
Saint Ct. Silk SR3 ... 116 A5
Saint Wilfrid's RC Comp Sch.
S Shs NE34 ... 77 D6
Saints Peter & Paul RC Prim Sch.
S Shs NE33 ... 77 B6
St Agnes' Gdns. Craw NE40 ... 60 E4
St Agnes' Gdns N. Craw NE40 60 E4
St Agnes' Gdns W. Craw NE40 60 E4
St Agnes Prim Sch.
Craw NE40 ... 60 E4
St Aidan's Ave. Sland SR2 ... 110 C2
St Aidan's Ave. Walls NE12 ... 30 D1
St Aidan's Cl. Tyne NE29 ... 50 D8
St Aidan's Cres. Mpeth NE61 .. 9 A6
St Aidan's Ct. Tyne NE30 ... 51 C7
St Aidan's RC Fst Sch.
Ashgn NE63 ... 6 D1
St Aidan's RC High Sch.
Walls NE28 ... 50 A5
St Aidan's Rd. S Shs NE33 ... 51 D4
St Aidan's Rd.
Walls NE28 & NE6 ... 49 A1
St Aidan's Sch. Sland SR2 ... 109 C4
St Aidan's Sch & Unit for Autistic
Children. N-u-T NE5 ... 36 D2
St Aidan's Sq. Walls NE12 ... 30 C1
St Aidan's St. Gates NE8 ... 72 A1
St Aidan's Terr. N Herr DH4 114 E6
St Alban's Cl. Ears NE25 ... 31
St Alban's Cres. Gates NE10 .. 89 C7
St Alban's Cres. N-u-T NE6 ... 48 A2
St Alban's Pl. Gates NE10 ... 89 C7
St Alban's RC Sch.
Gates NE10 ... 75 A1
St Alban's RC Sch. N-u-T NE6 68 C2
St Alban's St. Sland SR2 ... 110 C3
St Alban's Terr. Gates NE8 ... 72 C1
St Albans Cl. Ashgn NE63 ... 7 A2
St Albans View. Shire NE27 ... 30 F2
St Aldate's Ct. Sland SR4 ... 107 A2
St Aloysius RC Jun Mix Sch.
Hebb NE31 ... 75 E7
St Aloysius View. Hebb NE31 75 D6
St Andrew"s Terr. Ashgn NE63 6 E4
St Andrew's Ct. Lbtn NE7 ... 41 C1
St Andrew's Dr. Gates NE9 ... 88 E3
St Andrew's La. Oving NE42 .. 58 E4
St Andrew's Rd. Hexham NE46 54 A4
St Andrew's Rd. Tanf L DH9 . 97 F1
St Andrew's St. Hebb NE31 ... 75 C7
St Andrew's St. N-u-T NE1 ... 65 C1
St Andrew's Terr. Sland SR6 . 93 F2
St Andrews. Fence DH4 ... 118 B8
St Andrews Ave. Wash NE37 101 B8
St Andrews Ct. [4] Tyne NE29 50 F8
St Ann's Cl. N-u-T NE1 ... 67 A1
St Ann's St. N-u-T NE1 ... 66 C1
St Anne's Convent Prim Sch.
N-u-T NE1 ... 71 C4
St Anne's Ct. W Bay NE25 ... 31 E3
St Anne's RC Prim Sch.
Gates NE9 ... 89 B2
St Anne's RC Prim Sch.
Sland SR4 ... 103 B1
St Anselm Cres. Tyne NE29 ... 50 C7
St Anselm Rd. Tyne NE29 ... 50 C7
St Anselm's RC High Sch.
Tyne NE29 ... 50 D7
St Anthony's C of E Prim Sch.
N-u-T NE6 ... 74 C3
St Anthony's Ct. N-u-T NE6 ... 68 C2
St Anthony's House.
N-u-T NE6 ... 74 C3
St Anthony's RC Sch.
Sland SR2 ... 105 C1
St Anthony's Rd. N-u-T NE6 ... 74 B4
St Anthony's Wlk. N-u-T NE10 74 C3
St Asaph Cl. N-u-T NE12 ... 48 A4
St Austell Cl. N-u-T NE5 ... 43 C4
St Austell Gdns. Gates NE9 ... 88 F2
St Barnabas. Bourn DH4 ... 113 D3
St Barnabas Way. Sland SR2 106 C1
St Bartholomew's C of E Prim
Sch. Lbtn NE12 ... 42 A2
St Bartholomews Cl.
Ashgn NE63 ... 6 F5
St Bartholomews Cl.
Cress NE61 ... 2 A7
St Bede's. Boldon NE36 ... 92 D7
St Bede's Cl. H le H DH5 ... 119 A4
St Bede's Dr. Gates NE8 ... 72 C2
St Bede's Inf Sch.
Jarrow NE32 ... 76 C7
St Bede's Pk. Sland SR2 ... 106 A1
St Bede's RC Jun Sch.
Jarrow NE32 ... 76 C7
St Bede's RC Prim Aided Sch.
Bed NE22 ... 15 E8
St Bede's RC Prim Sch.
N-u-T NE15 ... 63 A2
St Bede's RC Prim Sch.
S Shs NE33 ... 51 D2
St Bede's RC Prim Sch.
Wash NE37 ... 90 D1
St Bede's Terr. Sland SR2 ... 106 A1
St Bedes Pl. Blyth NE24 ... 17 B4
St Bedes Rd. Blyth NE24 ... 17 B4
St Benedict's Rc Mid Sch.
Ashgn NE63 ... 6 F3
St Benet Biscop RC High Sch.
Bed NE22 ... 15 E8
St Benet's RC Jun Mix Inf Sch.
Ouston DH2 ... 99 F1
St Benet's RC Sch (Prim).
Sland SR6 ... 106 A4
St Benets RC Prim Sch.
Sland SR6 ... 93 D2
St Bernadette's Fst Sch.
Walls NE28 ... 49 B5
St Buryan Cres. N-u-T NE5 ... 43 C4
St Catherine's RC Prim Sch.
N-u-T NE1 ... 67 A4
St Catherines Gr. N-u-T NE2 . 66 C4
St Chad's Cres. Sland SR3 ... 115 B7
St Chad's Rd. Sland SR3 ... 115 B7
St Chad's Villas. Boldon NE36 92 D7
St Christopher Way.
N Shs NE29 ... 50 C2
St Christopher's House.
Mpeth NE61 ... 8 E8
St Christopher's Rd.
Sland SR3 ... 109 A2
St Christophers Cl. Ashgn NE63 6 F5
St Clements Cl. Ashgn NE63 ... 7 A2
St Clements Ct. N-u-T NE3 ... 38 C4
St Columba's Ct. Sland SR5 ... 93 C2
St Columba's Fst Sch.
Walls NE6 ... 49 A2
St Cuthbert Ave. C le S DH3 112 D3
St Cuthbert's Ave. S Shs NE34 78 A8
St Cuthbert's Cl. H le H DH5 119 A4
St Cuthbert's Ct. Gates NE8 .. 72 A2
St Cuthbert's Ct. N-u-T NE3 .. 39 A1
St Cuthbert's Dr. Gates NE10 89 F7
St Cuthbert's Gn. N-u-T NE5 . 63 C3
St Cuthbert's High Sch.
N-u-T NE15 ... 63 B2
St Cuthbert's La.
Hexham NE46 ... 54 A4
St Cuthbert's Pl. Gates NE8 .. 72 A1
St Cuthbert's Prim RC Sch (Jun &
Inf). Sland SR4 ... 108 A3
St Cuthbert's RC Prim Sch.
N Shs NE29 ... 51 A5
St Cuthbert's RC Prim Sch.
N-u-T NE5 ... 44 A4
St Cuthbert's Rd. NE12 ... 30 C1
St Cuthbert's Rd. Gates NE8 . 72 A2
St Cuthbert's Rd. Gates NE8 . 72 B3
St Cuthbert's Rd.
N Herr DH4 ... 114 F7
St Cuthbert's Rd.
N-u-T NE15 & NE5 ... 63 B3
St Cuthbert's Rd. N-u-T NE5 .. 63 C4
St Cuthbert's Rd. New DH4 114 D3
St Cuthbert's Rd. Sunn NE16 . 98 B7
St Cuthbert's Rd. Walls NE28 49 E3
St Cuthbert's Terr.
Hexham NE46 ... 54 A4
St Cuthbert's Terr.
Sland SR4 ... 105 B3
St Cuthbert's Wlk.
C le S DH3 ... 112 C3
St Cuthberts C of E Sch.
Gates NE8 ... 71 C1
St Cuthberts Cl. Hexham NE46 54 A4
St Cuthberts Cl. Prud NE42 ... 59 C2
St Cuthberts Ct. Blyth NE24 ... 17 F7
St Cuthberts Lower Sch.
N-u-T NE15 ... 63 C2
St Cuthberts Pk. Sunn NE16 ... 98 A8
St Cuthberts Way. Blay NE21 62 D3
St David's Cl. W Bay NE26 ... 31 F8
St David's Way. Hedw NE32 ... 76 C1
St David's Way. W Bay NE26 . 31 F8
St Davids Cl. Ashgn NE63 ... 6 F5
St Ebba's Way. Ebch DH8 ... 94 E3
St Edmund Campion Sch.
Gates NE9 ... 89 D4
St Edmund's Ct. Gates NE8 ... 73 A1
St Edmund's Dr. Gates NE10 . 89 F7
St Edmund's Rd. Gates NE8 .. 72 C1
St Edmunds Aided Prim Sch.
Bworth NE27 ... 30 D3
St Etienne Ct. Gates NE10 ... 74 A1
St Gabriel's Ave. N-u-T NE6 .. 47 B1
St Gabriel's Ave. Sland SR4 104 C1
St George's Ave.
S Shs NE33 & NE34 ... 77 E8
St George's Bells Close RC Sch.
N-u-T NE15 ... 62 D5
St George's Cl. N-u-T NE2 ... 46 B2
St George's Cres. N Shs NE29 50 F5
St George's Est. Wash NE38 101 C1
St George's Hospl.
Mpeth NE61 ... 4 A2
St George's Pl. N-u-T NE15 ... 62 E5
St George's Rd. Hexham NE46 54 A4
St George's Rd. N-u-T NE15 .. 62 E5
St George's Rd. Tyne NE30 ... 32 C3
St George's Terr. Boldon NE36 92 D7
St George's Terr. N-u-T NE2 . 46 B2
St George's Terr. N-u-T NE15 62 E5
St George's Terr. Sland SR6 .. 93 F2
St George's Way. Sland SR2 106 A1
St Georges Cres. W Bay NE25 31 F4
St Georges Ct. Gates NE10 ... 90 B7
St Gregory's Ct. S Shs NE34 .. 77 F5
St Gregory's RC Jun Mix & Inf
Sch. S Shs NE34 ... 78 A7
St Helen's Cres. Gates NE9 ... 88 E5
St Helen's St. Crbdge NE45 ... 55 F6
St Hilda Ind Est. S Shs NE33 .. 51 C2
St Hilda St. S Shs NE33 ... 51 C2
St Hilda's Ave. Walls NE28 ... 49 E3
St Hilda's RC Sch. Sland SR5 93 A2
St Hilda's Rd. Hexham NE46 .. 54 A4
St Ignatius Cl. Sland SR2 ... 106 B1
St Ives Way. N-u-T NE5 ... 43 C4
St James Cl. R Mill NE44 ... 80 F7
St James' Cres.
N-u-T NE15 & NE4 ... 70 A4
St James Ct. Gates NE8 ... 73 B1
St James' Gdns. N-u-T NE15 . 64 A1
St James Lodge. N-u-T NE4 .. 64 A1
St James' Mall. Hebb NE31 ... 75 D5
St James' Pk (Newcastle Utd
F.C.). N-u-T NE99 ... 65 C2
St James RC Jun Mix Sch.
Hebb NE31 ... 75 F4
St James Rd. Gates NE8 ... 73 A2
St James' Rd. N-u-T NE15 ... 64 A1
St James Sq. Gates NE8 ... 73 A2
St James St. N-u-T NE3 ... 40 B1
St James' St. N-u-T NE1 ... 65 C2
St James Sta. N-u-T NE1 ... 65 C1
St James' Terr. N Shs NE29 .. 50 D3
St James Terr. R Mill NE44 ... 81 A7
St John Bosco RC Prim Sch.
Sland SR5 ... 92 A4
St John Boste RC Prim Sch.
Wash NE38 ... 101 A5
St John St. N-u-T NE1 ... 66 A1
St John & St Patrick's Church
Sch.
Sland SR1 ... 106 C3
St John the Baptist's RC Jun Mix
Inf Sch. Gates NE10 ... 89 D8
St John Vianney RC Prim Sch.
N-u-T NE5 ... 36 D1
St John's Ave. Hebb NE31 ... 75 D5
St John's Cl. W Bay NE26 ... 31 F8
St John's Cres. Bed NE22 ... 11 D3
St John's Ct. Bworth NE27 ... 30 C5
St John's Gn. N Shs NE29 ... 50 D3
St John's Mall. Hebb NE31 ... 75 D5
St John's Pl. Bed NE22 ... 11 D3
St John's Pl. Birt DH3 ... 100 C4
St John's Pl. W Bay NE26 ... 31 F8
St John's Rd. Bed NE22 ... 11 D2
St John's Rd. H Pitt DH6 ... 120 B5
St John's Rd. N-u-T NE4 ... 70 B4
St John's St. N Shs NE29 ... 50 D3
St John's Terr. Boldon NE36 . 92 E7
St John's Terr. Jarrow NE32 . 76 B7
St John's Terr. N Shs NE29 ... 50 D3
St John's Terr. [3]
Seaham SR7 ... 116 E1
St John's W. Bed NE22 ... 11 D3
St John's Wlk. Hebb NE31 ... 75 E5
St John's Wlk. N Shs NE29 ... 50 D3
St John's Wlk. N-u-T NE4 ... 70 B4
St Johns Pl. Gates NE10 ... 89 D8
St Johns Rd. Hexham NE46 ... 54 A3
St Johns Vale. Sland SR4 ... 107 A4
St Joseph's Ct. [7] Birt DH3 100 C5
St Joseph's Ct. Hebb NE31 ... 75 D3
St Joseph's Prim Sch.
Blay NE21 ... 62 B3
St Joseph's RC Aided Sch.
R Gill NE39 ... 85 B2
St Joseph's RC Comp Sch.
Hebb NE31 ... 75 D2
St Joseph's RC Prim Sch.
Gates NE8 ... 72 C2
St Joseph's RC Sch.
N-u-T NE4 ... 70 A4
St Joseph's RC Sch.
Sland SR4 ... 105 A3
St Joseph's RC Sec Sch.
Kill NE12 ... 29 D2
St Joseph's Way. Hedw NE32 76 C1
St Josephs RC Mid Sch.
Hexham NE46 ... 53 F4
St Jude's Terr. S Shs NE33 ... 77 C8
St Julien Gdns. N-u-T NE7 ... 48 A2
St Julien Gdns. Walls NE28 ... 50 B3
St Just Pl. N-u-T NE5 ... 43 C4
St Keverne Sq. N-u-T NE5 ... 43 C4
St Kitt's Cl. W Bay NE26 ... 31 F8
St Lawrence's RC Prim Sch.
N-u-T NE6 ... 67 C2
St Lawrence Cl. H Pitt DH6 . 120 C5
St Lawrence Rd. Gates NE6 ... 73 C2
St Lawrence Rd. H Pitt DH6 120 B5
St Lawrence Sq. N-u-T NE6 ... 67 B1
St Leonard St. Sland SR2 ... 110 C4
St Leonard's La. Mford NE61 . 3 B2
St Leonard's RC Prim Sch.
N Silk SR3 ... 116 B7
St Leonard's Wlk. Mpeth NE61 3 C2
St Lucia Cl. Sland SR2 ... 106 B1
St Lucia Cl. W Bay NE26 ... 31 E8
St Luke's Rd. N Shs NE29 ... 50 D3
St Luke's Rd. Sland SR4 ... 104 A3
St Luke's Terr. Sland SR4 ... 104 C3
St Lukes Cl. Ashgn NE63 ... 7 A5
St Lukes Rd. Hexham NE46 ... 54 A4
St Margaret's Ave. Sland SR5 92 A1
St Margaret's Dr. Tanf DH9 .. 97 D4
St Margaret's Rd. N-u-T NE15 69 A4
St Margarets Ave.
Lbtn NE12 ... 42 A2
St Mark's Cl. N-u-T NE6 ... 67 C3
St Mark's Cres. Sland SR4 .. 105 B2
St Mark's Ct. N Shs NE29 ... 50 D2
St Mark's RC Aided Prim Sch.
N-u-T NE5 ... 36 F4
St Mark's Rd. Sland SR4 ... 105 B2
St Mark's Rd N. Sland SR4 .. 105 A2
St Mark's St. Mpeth NE61 ... 3 E1
St Mark's St. N-u-T NE6 ... 67 C3
St Mark's St. Sland SR4 ... 105 B2
St Mark's Terr. Sland SR4 ... 105 B2
St Mark's Way. S Shs NE33 ... 51 C1
St Marks Ct. Bworth NE27 ... 30 E3
St Marks Rd. Hexham NE46 ... 54 A3
St Martin's Cl. W Bay NE26 ... 31 E7
St Martin's Ct. W Bay NE26 ... 31 E7
St Mary Magdalene Hospl.
N-u-T NE2 ... 65 B4
St Mary's Ave. S Shs NE34 ... 77 F6
St Mary's Ave. W Bay NE26 ... 31 F7
St Mary's Chare.
Hexham NE46 ... 54 B4
St Mary's Church (Mus).
Lmth NE63 ... 7 C6
St Mary's Coll. N-u-T NE4 ... 64 B3
St Mary's Ct. Gates NE8 ... 72 C2
St Mary's Ct. S Shs NE33 ... 77 B7
St Mary's Dr. Blyth NE24 ... 17 B6
St Mary's Field. Mpeth NE61 ... 8 F7
St Mary's Fst Sch.
Hexham NE46 ... 54 A4
St Mary's Gn. Whick NE16 ... 87 B7
St Mary's Hospl. Stann NE61 . 13 C7
St Mary's Infs Sch. Gates NE8 72 B3
St Mary's Lodge. W Bay NE26 31 F5
St Mary's Pl. N-u-T NE1 ... 66 A2
St Mary's Pl. Walb NE15 ... 35 E2
St Mary's Pl E. N-u-T NE1 ... 66 A2
St Mary's Prim Sch.
Sland SR2 ... 109 B4
St Mary's RC Cath. N-u-T NE1 71 C4
St Mary's RC Prim Sch.
Tyne NE30 ... 32 A2
St Mary's RC Schs. N-u-T NE6 68 C3
St Mary's Sch. N-u-T NE7 ... 41 A1
St Mary's St. N-u-T NE1 ... 66 C1
St Mary's Terr. Boldon NE36 .. 92 E7
St Mary's Terr. Ryton NE40 ... 61 B5
St Mary's Terr. S Shs NE33 ... 77 B7
St Mary's Training & Enterprise
Ctr. N-u-T NE4 ... 65 B1
St Mary's Way. Sland SR1 ... 106 A3
St Mary's Wynd.
Hexham NE46 ... 54 B4
St Marys C of E Jun Mix & Inf
Sch.
S Shs NE33 ... 77 B7
St Marys Cl. C le S DH2 ... 112 B1
St Marys Dr. Ashgn NE63 ... 6 F5
St Marys RC Prim Sch.
Whick NE16 ... 87 C7
St Matthew's RC Fst Sch.
Prud NE42 ... 59 C2
St Matthew's RC Jun Mix & Inf
Sch. Jarrow NE32 ... 76 B6
St Matthew's Terr. New DH4 114 D4
St Matthews Rd. Hexham NE46 53 F3
St Matthews View.
N Silk SR3 ... 116 A7
St Michael's Ave.
E Cram NE25 & NE26 ... 23 D6
St Michael's Ave. S Shs NE33 51 E1
St Michael's Ave N.
S Shs NE33 ... 51 D1
St Michael's Mount. N-u-T NE6 .. 67
C1
St Michael's RC Jun & Inf Schs.
H-le-Sp DH5 ... 118 E7
St Michael's RC Jun Sch.
N-u-T NE4 ... 70 C4
St Michael's Rd. N-u-T NE6 ... 67 B1
St Michael's Way.
Whick NE11 & NE16 ... 69 C1
St Michaels. Fence DH4 ... 118 B8
St Michaels RC Inf Sch.
N-u-T NE4 ... 71 A3
St Michaels Way. Sland SR1 105 C2
St Michaels Workshops.
N-u-T NE6 ... 67 B1
St Nicholas Ave. N-u-T NE3 ... 45 C4
St Nicholas Ave. N-u-T NE3 ... 46 A4
St Nicholas Ave. Sland SR3 ... 109 B3
St Nicholas' Bldgs. N-u-T NE1 72 A4
St Nicholas' Church Yd.
N-u-T NE1 ... 66 A1
St Nicholas Cl. Ashgn NE63 ... 6 F5
St Nicholas Hospl. N-u-T NE3 39 A1
St Nicholas Hospl (Collingwood
Clinic). N-u-T NE3 ... 39 B1
St Nicholas Rd. Boldon NE36 . 92 A7
St Nicholas Rd. Hexham NE46 54 A4
St Nicholas' Sq. N-u-T NE1 ... 66 A1
St Nicholas' St. N-u-T NE1 ... 72 A4
St Nicholas View.
Boldon NE36 ... 92 A7
St Omers Rd. Duns NE11 ... 70 C2
St Oswald's Ave. N-u-T NE6 ... 68 B2
St Oswald's Gn. N-u-T NE6 ... 68 B3
St Oswald's RC Prim Sch.
Gates NE9 ... 89 C3
St Oswald's RC Prim Sch.
N-u-T NE3 ... 40 A3
St Oswald's Rc Prim Sch.
White NE34 ... 77 D3
St Oswald's Rd.
Hebb NE31 & NE32 ... 75 F7
St Oswald's Rd. Hexham NE46 54 A4
St Oswald's Rd. Walls NE28 .. 49 E4
St Oswald's Terr. [4]
S Row DH4 ... 114 B6
St Oswin's Ave. Tyne NE30 ... 32 C3
St Oswin's Pl. Tyne NE30 ... 51 D7
St Oswin's St.
S Shs NE33 & NE34 ... 77 D7
St Patrick's Cl. Gates NE10 ... 89 D8
St Patrick's Garth.
Sland SR1 ... 106 B3
St Patrick's RC Jun Mix & Inf Sch.
Ryhope SR2 ... 116 F6
St Patrick's Wlk. Gates NE10 89 D8
St Paul's C of E Prim Sch.
N-u-T NE4 ... 71 B4
St Paul's Gdns. W Bay NE25 .. 32 A4
St Paul's Pl. N-u-T NE4 ... 65 A1
St Paul's RC Fst Sch.
Cram NE23 ... 22 B5
St Paul's Rd. Jarrow NE32 ... 76 C7
St Paul's Terr. [5]
Ryhope SR2 ... 116 F6
St Pauls Cl. Ashgn NE63 ... 6 F5
St Pauls Ct. Gates NE8 ... 71 C1
St Pauls Dr. Pens DH4 ... 113 E8
St Pauls Rd. Hexham NE46 ... 53 F4
St Peter's Ave. S Shs NE34 ... 77 E7
St Peter's Ct. N-u-T NE6 ... 67 C1
St Peter's Quayside E.
N-u-T NE6 ... 74 A4
St Peter's Quayside W.
N-u-T NE6 ... 73 C3
St Peter's RC Prim Sch.
Gates NE9 ... 89 A6
St Peter's Rd. N-u-T NE6 ... 67 C1
St Peter's Rd. N-u-T NE6 ... 73 C4
St Peter's Rd. Walls NE28 ... 49 D3
St Peter's View. Sland SR6 . 106 A4
St Peter's Wharf. N-u-T NE6 . 73 C4

St Peters Sch. N-u-T NE3 46 C4
St Peters' Way. Sland SR6 106 B4
St Philip's RC Jun Mix & Inf Sch. Duns NE11 88 A8
St Philips Cl. N-u-T NE4 65 B1
St Philips Way. N-u-T NE4 65 B1
St Robert of Newminster RC Sch. Wash NE38 101 D2
St Robert's of Newminster RC Fst Sch. Mpeth NE61 8 E8
St Rollox St. Hebb NE31 75 D5
St Ronan's Dr. S Slu NE26 24 B7
St Ronan's Rd. W Bay NE25 31 F4
St Ronans View. Gates NE9 89 A2
St Simon St. S Shs NE34 77 A4
St Stephen's Cl. S Del NE25 23 B3
St Stephen's RC Prim Sch. Lbtn NE12 41 B3
St Stephen's Way. N Shs NE29 50 D3
St Stevens Cl. Pens DH4 113 E8
St Teresa's RC Sch. N-u-T NE6 67 B4
St Thomas Aquinas RC Sch. Sland SR5 92 E2
St Thomas' Cres. N-u-T NE1 66 A2
St Thomas Mews. Prud NE42 59 D2
St Thomas More Sch. Blay NE21 62 B3
St Thomas' Sq. N-u-T NE1 66 A2
St Thomas St. 6 Gates NE9 89 A5
St Thomas' St. N-u-T NE1 66 A2
St Thomas' St. Sland SR1 106 A3
St Vincent Ct. Gates NE8 73 A1
St Vincent St. Gates NE8 73 A1
St Vincent St. S Shs NE33 51 E1
St Vincent St. Sland SR2 106 B1
St Vincent's Pl. W Bay NE26 31 F8
St Vincent's RC Sch. N-u-T NE6 74 B4
St Vincent's Way. W Bay NE26 31 F8
St Vincents Cl. N-u-T NE15 62 E8
St Wilfrid's RC Mid Sch. Blyth NE24 17 D7
St Wilfred's Rd. Crbdge NE45 56 A6
St Wilfrid's Inf Sch. Blyth NE24 17 E7
St Wilfrid's RC Inf and Jun Schs. Gates NE10 73 B2
St Wilfrid's Rd. Hexham NE46 54 A4
Salcombe Ave. Jarrow NE32 76 D6
Salcombe Gdns. Gates NE9 88 F2
Salem Hill. Sland SR2 106 B1
Salem St. Jarrow NE32 76 C7
Salem St. S Shs NE33 51 C3
Salem St S. Sland SR2 106 B1
Salem Terr. Sland SR2 106 B1
Salisbury Ave. C le S DH3 112 C2
Salisbury Ave. Tyne NE29 51 A7
Salisbury Cl. Ashgn NE63 6 F2
Salisbury Cl. Cram NE23 21 E6
Salisbury Gdns. N-u-T NE2 67 A4
Salisbury House. N-u-T NE6 67 A2
Salisbury Pl. S Shs NE33 51 E3
Salisbury St. Blyth NE24 17 D8
Salisbury St. Gates NE10 75 A1
Salisbury St. Mpeth NE61 9 B8
Salisbury St. S Shs NE33 51 E3
Salisbury St. Sland SR4 103 A3
Salisbury St. Sland SR1 106 B2
Salisbury Way. Hedw NE32 76 B1
Salkeld Gdns. Gates NE9 89 A8
Salkeld Rd. Gates NE9 89 A6
Sallyport Cres. N-u-T NE1 66 B1
Salmon St. S Shs NE33 51 D4
Saltburn Gdns. Walls NE28 50 B3
Saltburn Rd. Sland SR3 108 B3
Saltburn Sq. Sland SR3 108 B3
Salter's La. H le H DH5 & SR7 119 F6
Salter's La. H-le-Sp DH5 115 E1
Salter's La. Hasw DH6 121 E6
Salter's La. Hasw DH6 121 F2
Salter's La. Seaton DH5 & SR7 & DH6 119 F6
Salterfen La. Sland SR2 117 A8
Salterfen Rd. Sland SR2 117 A8
Salters Cl. N-u-T NE3 40 B2
Salters Ct. N-u-T NE3 40 B2
Salters' La. Lbtn NE3 & NE12 40 C3
Salters' Rd. N-u-T NE3 45 B4
Saltford. Gates NE9 89 A2
Saltmeadows Rd. Gates NE10 & NE8 73 B4
Saltwell Park Mansion Mus. Gates NE9 88 E6
Saltwell Pl. Gates NE8 88 D8
Saltwell Rd. Gates NE8 88 D7
Saltwell Rd S. Gates NE9 88 E4
Saltwell View. Gates NE8 & NE9 88 E7
Sam's Ct. Dud NE23 28 F8
Samson Cl. Kill NE12 29 C2
Sancroft Dr. H-le-Sp DH5 118 E7
Sandalwood. White NE34 77 E3
Sandalwood Sq. Sland SR4 107 B2
Sanderling Cl. Ryton NE40 61 D4
Sanderlings. Walls NE28 49 A4
Sanders Gdns. 3 Birt DH3 100 C5
Sanders' Memorial Homes. C le S DH3 112 C3
Sanderson Rd. N-u-T NE2 46 B2
Sanderson Rd. W Bay NE26 31 F5
Sanderson St. N-u-T NE4 70 C3
Sandfield Rd. Cam NE22 12 B4
Sandfield Rd. Tyne NE30 32 B3
Sandford Ave. Cram NE23 16 C1
Sandford Mews. B Vill NE13 28 A5
Sandgate. N-u-T NE1 66 C1
Sandgrove. Clea SR6 78 A1
Sandhill. N-u-T NE1 72 B4
Sandhill View Comp Sch. Sland SR3 108 A2
Sandholm Cl. Walls NE28 49 F5
Sandhurst Ave. Tyne NE30 32 C2
Sandiacres. Hedw NE32 76 C1
Sandison Ct. B Vill NE13 27 F6
Sandmartin Cl. Ashgn NE63 11 E8
Sandmere Pl. N-u-T NE15 63 A1
Sandmere Rd. Sland SR2 110 A1
Sandoe Gdns. N-u-T NE15 63 B1
Sandon Cl. Bworth NE27 30 C5
Sandown. W Bay NE25 31 D5
Sandown Cl. S Del NE25 23 D2
Sandown Ct. Walls NE28 50 A4
Sandown Gdns. Gates NE8 88 D8
Sandown Gdns. N Silk SR3 115 F8
Sandown Gdns. Walls NE28 49 F4
Sandpiper Cl. Blyth NE24 17 F4
Sandpiper Cl. Wash NE38 100 F2
Sandpiper Ct. Tyne NE30 51 D8
Sandpiper Way. Ashgn NE63 6 D1
Sandray Cl. Birt DH3 100 D1
Sandridge. N-b-t-S NE64 7 F5
Sandrigg Sq. S Shs NE34 77 E5
Sandringham Ave. Lbtn NE12 42 A2
Sandringham Cl. W Bay NE25 31 B4
Sandringham Cres. Sland SR3 115 F5
Sandringham Dr. Blyth NE24 17 D3
Sandringham Dr. W Bay NE25 31 C4
Sandringham Dr. Whick NE16 87 A7
Sandringham Gdns. Tyne NE29 51 A7
Sandringham Mews. Walls NE28 49 F4
Sandringham Rd. N-u-T NE3 46 B4
Sandringham Rd. N-u-T NE5 62 E8
Sandringham Rd. Sland SR6 93 D2
Sandringham Terr. Sland SR6 93 E2
Sandringham Way. Pont NE20 25 C4
Sands Ind Est The. Whick NE16 69 A1
Sands Rd. Whick NE16 69 A1
Sandsay Cl. Sland SR2 116 D8
Sandstone Cl. B Wh NE34 76 F3
Sandwell Dr. Pens DH4 113 F8
Sandwich Rd. Tyne NE29 31 F1
Sandwich St. N-u-T NE6 74 C3
Sandy Chare. Whit SR6 93 E8
Sandy Cres. N-u-T NE6 74 B4
Sandy La. Ashgn NE63 7 B2
Sandy La. B Vill NE13 27 E6
Sandy La. Dgton NE13 27 E6
Sandy La. Gates NE9 89 D1
Sandy La. R Mill NE44 80 E8
Sandy La. W Open NE3 & NE12 28 F4
Sandy Lane Ind Area. W Open NE3 28 E4
Sandyford Ave. Prud NE42 59 F3
Sandyford Pk. N-u-T NE2 66 C4
Sandyford Rd. N-u-T NE2 66 B3
Sandypath La. Burnop NE16 97 A7
Sandysykes. Prud NE42 59 B2
Sans St S. Sland SR1 106 B2
Sarabel Ave. G Post NE62 10 E7
Sargent Ave. White NE34 77 D2
Satley Gdns. Gates NE9 89 C2
Satley Gdns. Sland SR3 109 B2
Saunton Ct. New DH4 114 C3
Saville Lodge. 5 S Shs NE33 51 D3
Saville Row. N-u-T NE1 66 A2
Saville St. N Shs NE29 & NE30 51 B5
Saville St. 4 S Shs NE33 51 D3
Saville St W. N Shs NE29 51 A5
Savory Rd. Walls NE28 49 F3
Sawmill Cotts. Dipton DH9 96 E1
Saxilby Dr. N-u-T NE3 40 A4
Saxon Cl. Clea SR6 77 E1
Saxon Cres. Sland SR3 108 C3
Saxon Dr. Tyne NE30 32 C1
Saxon Way. Jarrow NE32 76 C7
Saxondale Rd. N-u-T NE3 38 B1
Saxton Gr. N-u-T NE7 47 A4
Scafell. Birt DH3 100 D1
Scafell Ct. 22 Silk SR3 115 F6
Scafell Dr. N-u-T NE5 44 A3
Scafell Gdns. Duns NE11 88 A6
Scalby Cl. N-u-T NE3 40 A4
Scales Cres. Prud NE42 59 F2
Scarborough Ct. Cram NE23 22 B5
Scarborough Ct. N-u-T NE6 68 A2
Scarborough Par. Jarrow NE31 76 A2
Scarborough Rd. N Silk SR3 115 F8
Scarborough Rd. N-u-T NE6 68 A2
Sceptre Ct. N-u-T NE4 71 A4
Sceptre Pl. N-u-T NE4 65 A1
Sceptre St. N-u-T NE4 65 A1
Schalksmuhle Rd. Bed NE22 10 F1
Schimel St. Sland SR5 93 B2
School App. S Shs NE34 78 A6
School Ave. Duns NE11 87 F8
School Ave. G Post NE62 10 F7
School Houses. R Gill NE39 96 B8
School La. H Spen NE39 85 A3
School La. Whick NE16 87 C7
School Loaning. S Shs NE34 77 B5
School Rd. Bed NE22 11 D3
School Rd. E Rain DH5 118 C4
School Row. H o t H NE43 82 F3
School St. Birt DH3 100 C4
School St. Hebb NE31 75 F7
School St. Whick NE16 87 A7
School Terr. Gr Lum DH4 113 E1
School View. E Lane DH5 121 D8
Schoolhouse La. Byer NE16 97 E7
Scorer St. N Shs NE29 50 F5
Scorer's La. Gr Lum DH3 113 B1
Scot Terr. Chopw NE17 84 B1
Scotby Gdns. Gates NE9 89 B3
Scotland Ct. Blay NE21 62 A1
Scotland Head. Blay NE21 86 A8
Scotland St. Ryhope SR2 117 A6
Scotswood Rd. N-u-T NE15 & NE4 69 B4
Scotswood View. Whick NE11 & NE16 69 C2
Scott Ave. Cram NE23 21 F8
Scott Cl. Hexham NE46 53 F2
Scott St. E Hart NE23 16 B3
Scott's Ave. 12 Craw NE40 60 F3
Scott's Ct. Gates NE10 90 B6
Scott's Terr. H le H DH5 119 A4
Scoular Dr. Ashgn NE63 7 A3
Scrogg Rd. N-u-T NE6 68 C2
Scruton Ave. Sland SR3 108 C3
Sea Banks. Tyne NE30 51 E8
Sea Beach Rd. Sland SR2 111 A3
Sea Crest Rd. N-b-t-S NE64 7 E6
Sea La. Sland SR6 93 E4
Sea Rd. S Shs NE33 51 E4
Sea Rd. Sland SR6 93 E4
Sea View. Ashgn NE63 12 A8
Sea View. Lmth NE61 2 B3
Sea View. Ryhope SR2 117 A6
Sea View Gdns. Sland SR6 93 E3
Sea View Pk. Cram NE23 22 D6
Sea View Pk. Whit SR6 93 D8
Sea View Rd. Sland SR2 110 B3
Sea View Rd W. Sland SR2 110 A2
Sea View St. Sland SR2 110 C2
Sea View Villas. Cram NE23 22 D6
Sea Way. S Shs NE33 51 E3
Seaburn Cl. Sland SR6 93 E4
Seaburn Dene Prim Sch. Sland SR6 93 D5
Seaburn Dr. 1 H-le-Sp DH4 118 C8
Seaburn Gdns. Gates NE9 89 D3
Seaburn Gdns. Sland SR6 93 E4
Seaburn Gr. S Slu NE26 24 C6
Seaburn Hill. Sland SR6 93 E4
Seaburn Sta. Sland SR5 93 C4
Seaburn Terr. Sland SR6 93 F4
Seaburn View. E Cram NE25 23 D6
Seacombe Ave. Tyne NE30 32 C3
Seacrest Ave. Tyne NE30 32 C2
Seafield Rd. Blyth NE24 17 E5
Seafield Terr. S Shs NE33 51 E3
Seafield View. Tyne NE30 51 D8
Seafields. Sland SR6 93 E5
Seaforth Rd. Sland SR3 109 A3
Seaforth St. Blyth NE24 17 E8
Seaham Cl. S Shs NE34 78 B6
Seaham Gdns. Gates NE9 89 C2
Seaham Grange Ind Est. Seaham SR7 116 F2
Seaham Northlea Sec Sch. Seaham SR7 117 A1
Seaham Rd. H-le-Sp DH5 119 A8
Seaham Rd. Ryhope SR2 117 A6
Seaham St. N Silk SR3 116 A7
Seascale Pl. Gates NE9 89 B4
Seatoller Ct. 3 Silk SR3 115 F6
Seaton Ave. Annit NE23 22 B1
Seaton Ave. Blyth NE24 17 C4
Seaton Ave. H-le-Sp DH5 119 A7
Seaton Ave. N-b-t-S NE64 7 D4
Seaton Burn Fst Sch. W Open NE13 28 B7
Seaton Burn High Sch. S Burn NE13 28 C8
Seaton Burn Sec Mod Sch. W Open NE13 28 C6
Seaton Cl. Gates NE10 90 B6
Seaton Cres. Holy NE25 23 F2
Seaton Cres. Seaham SR7 116 E1
Seaton Cres. W Bay NE25 31 E5
Seaton Croft. Annit NE23 29 C8
Seaton Delaval Cty Fst Sch. E Cram NE25 23 B4
Seaton Gdns. Gates NE9 89 C3
Seaton La. Seaham SR7 116 E1
Seaton Pl. B Vill NE13 28 A6
Seaton Pl. N-u-T NE6 74 B3
Seaton Rd. Shire NE27 31 A4
Seaton Rd. Sland SR3 108 A3
Seaton Sluice Cty Mid Sch. S Slu NE26 24 B7
Seaton Sluice South Sch. S Slu NE26 24 D5
Seaton Terr. Bed NE22 11 B1
Seatonville Cres. W Bay NE25 31 E3
Seatonville Gr. W Bay NE25 31 E3
Seatonville Rd. W Bay NE25 & NE30 31 E3
Second Ave. Ashgn NE63 6 E4
Second Ave. Blyth NE24 17 D6
Second Ave. C le S DH2 112 B2
Second Ave. C le S DH2 112 B8
Second Ave. Gates NE11 88 B6
Second Ave. Mpeth NE61 9 B7
Second Ave. N Shs NE29 50 B4
Second Ave. N-u-T NE6 67 C3
Second Row. Elling NE61 1 E4
Second Row. Linton NE61 1 A3
Second St. Gates NE8 72 A1
Sedbergh Rd. Tyne NE30 32 B2
Sedgeletch Ind Est. Fence DH4 114 A2
Sedgeletch Rd. Fence DH4 114 A2
Sedgemoor. Kill NE12 29 D4
Sedgemoor Ave. N-u-T NE15 69 A4
Sedgewick Pl. Gates NE8 72 B1
Sedley Rd. Walls NE28 49 B1
Sedling Rd. Wash NE38 101 B2
Sefton Ave. N-u-T NE6 47 C1
Sefton Ct. Cram NE23 16 C1
Sefton Sq. Sland SR3 108 B3
Segedunum Way. Walls NE28 49 B1
Seghill Cty Fst Sch. Seg NE23 22 F1
Seine Ct. Jarrow NE32 76 C6
Selborne Gdns. N-u-T NE2 67 A4
Selbourne Cl. Cram NE23 21 E6
Selbourne St. 2 S Shs NE33 51 D2
Selbourne St. Sland SR6 93 E1
Selbourne Terr. Cam NE24 12 D3
Selby Cl. Cram NE23 16 B1
Selby Ct. 2 Jarrow NE32 76 B7
Selby Gdns. N-u-T NE6 68 C4
Selby Gdns. Walls NE28 49 B3
Selby Sq. Sland SR3 108 B3
Selby's Grave. Blay NE21 85 F8
Sele Fst Sch The. Hexham NE46 54 A5
Selkirk Cres. Birt DH3 100 C6
Selkirk Gr. Cram NE23 16 C1
Selkirk Sq. Sland SR3 108 A3
Selkirk St. B Wh NE32 76 E3
Selkirk Way. Tyne NE29 50 C8
Selsdon Ave. Sland SR4 107 A2
Selsey Ct. Gates NE10 89 E6
Selwood Ct. S Shs NE34 77 F5
Selwyn Ave. W Bay NE25 31 D3
Seton Ave. S Shs NE34 76 F4
Seton Wlk. S Shs NE34 76 F4
Setting Stones. Wash NE38 113 A8
Sevenoaks Dr. Sland SR4 107 A2
Seventh Ave. Ashgn NE63 6 E2
Seventh Ave. Blyth NE24 17 D6
Seventh Ave. C le S DH2 112 B4
Seventh Ave. Gates NE11 88 D4
Seventh Ave. Mpeth NE61 9 B7
Seventh Ave. N-u-T NE6 67 C3
Seventh Row. Ashgn NE63 6 B4
Severn Ave. Hebb NE31 75 E3
Severn Ct. 8 Silk SR3 115 F6
Severn Dr. Hedw NE32 76 C2
Severn Gdns. Gates NE8 89 B8
Severs Terr. Wools NE5 36 B6
Severus Rd. N-u-T NE4 64 B3
Seymour Ct. Ashgn NE63 7 B3
Seymour Ct. Duns NE11 71 A1
Seymour Sq. Sland SR3 108 B3
Seymour St. N Shs NE29 51 A4
Seymour Terr. H le H DH5 119 B1
Seymour Terr. Ryton NE40 61 A5
Shadfen Cres. Pegs NE61 4 E3
Shadfen Park Rd. Tyne NE30 32 A3
Shadon Way. Birt DH3 100 E3
Shaftesbury Ave. Jarrow NE32 76 E5
Shaftesbury Ave. Ryhope SR2 116 E7
Shaftesbury Ave. W Bay NE26 31 F6
Shaftesbury Cres. Sland SR3 108 C3
Shaftesbury Cres. Tyne NE25 & NE30 32 A3
Shaftesbury Gr. N-u-T NE6 67 B3
Shaftesbury Wlk. Gates NE8 72 A2
Shafto Ct. N-u-T NE15 63 B1
Shafto St. N-u-T NE15 63 A1
Shafto St. Walls NE28 49 E3
Shaftoe Cl. Craw NE40 60 F3
Shaftoe Cres. Hexham NE46 54 A5
Shaftoe Ct. Kill NE12 29 D3
Shaftoe Ct. N-u-T NE3 39 A3
Shaftoe Leazes. Hexham NE46 53 F4
Shaftoe Rd. Sland SR3 108 A2
Shaftoe Sq. Sland SR3 108 A2
Shaftoe Way. Dgton NE13 27 B7
Shakespeare Ave. Hebb NE31 75 E6
Shakespeare St. H-le-Sp DH5 118 E7
Shakespeare St. Jarrow NE32 76 B8
Shakespeare St. N-u-T NE1 66 A1
Shakespeare St. 18 S Shs NE33 51 D1
Shakespeare St. Sland SR5 93 B2
Shakespeare St. Walls NE28 49 F3
Shakespeare Terr. Sland SR2 105 C1
Shalcombe Cl. Silk SR3 116 A6
Shallon Ct. Ashgn NE63 6 C2
Shalstone. Wash NE37 90 F1
Shamrock Cl. N-u-T NE15 62 C8
Shandon Way. N-u-T NE3 38 B1
Shanklin Pl. Cram NE23 21 E6
Shannon Cl. Sland SR5 92 A1
Shannon Ct. N-u-T NE3 37 C3
Shap Cl. Wash NE38 101 D3
Shap Ct. 2 Silk SR3 115 F6
Shap La. N-u-T NE5 43 A1
Shap Rd. Tyne NE30 32 A2
Sharnford Cl. Bworth NE27 30 D5
Sharon Cl. Kill NE12 29 B2
Sharpendon St. Hebb NE31 75 E7
Sharpley Dr. Seaham SR7 116 E1
Shaw Ave. B Hall NE34 77 B4
Shaw Gdns. Gates NE10 90 B8
Shaw La. Ebch DH8 & NE17 94 F4
Shaw La. Medom NE17 95 A4
Shawdon Cl. N-u-T NE5 43 B4
Shaws La. Hexham NE46 53 D4
Shaws La. Hexham NE46 53 D5
Shaws Pk. Hexham NE46 53 E6
Shearlegs Rd. Gates NE8 73 A3
Shearwater Ave. Lbtn NE12 41 A3
Shearwater Cl. N-u-T NE5 43 B4
Shearwater Way. Blyth NE24 17 F4
Sheelin Ave. C le S DH2 112 C1
Sheen Cl. W Rain DH4 118 A2
Sheen Ct. N-u-T NE5 37 B1
Sheep Hill. Burnop NE16 97 B6
Sheepfolds N. Sland SR5 106 A4
Sheepfolds Rd. Sland SR5 106 A4
Sheepfolds S. Sland SR5 106 A4
Sheepwash Ave. G Post NE62 10 E7
Sheepwash Bank. G Post NE62 10 E7
Sheepwash Rd. Ashgn NE61 5 E3
Sheldon Ct. Lbtn NE12 29 C1
Sheldon Gr. Cram NE23 16 C1
Sheldon Gr. N-u-T NE3 45 A3
Sheldon Rd. S Shs NE34 51 F1
Sheldon St. Jarrow NE32 76 B7
Shelford Gdns. N-u-T NE15 62 E7
Shelley Ave. Boldon NE35 92 A8
Shelley Ave. E Lane DH5 121 D8
Shelley Ave. S Shs NE34 78 B5
Shelley Ave. Spring NE9 89 F1
Shelley Cres. Blyth NE24 17 C5
Shelley Dr. Gates NE8 73 A2
Shelley Rd. Newb NE15 62 A7
Shepherd St. Sland SR4 105 A3
Shepherd Way. Wash NE38 101 F2
Shepherd's Quay. N Shs NE29 51 B4
Shepherds Way. Boldon NE36 92 A7
Sheppard Terr. Sland SR5 92 B1
Shepperley Ct. Silk SR3 116 A6
Shepton Cotts. Whick NE16 87 C3
Sheraton. Gates NE10 90 A5
Sheraton St. N-u-T NE2 65 B4
Sherborne Ave. Tyne NE29 50 D8
Sherburn Cty Jun & Inf Sch. Sherb DH6 120 A2
Sherburn Gn. R Gill NE39 85 F3
Sherburn Gr. Burn DH4 114 C1
Sherburn Grange N. Jarrow NE32 76 A5
Sherburn Grange S. Jarrow NE32 76 A5
Sherburn Hill Cty Mix Inf Sch. S Hill DH6 120 D1
Sherburn Park Dr. R Gill NE39 85 F3
Sherburn Terr. Gates NE9 89 C2
Sherburn Terr. Hams NE17 94 F5
Sherburn Way. Gates NE10 90 C7
Sherfield Dr. N-u-T NE7 48 A2
Sheridan Gn. Wash NE38 101 A1
Sheridan Rd. B Hall NE34 77 A3
Sheridan St. Sland SR4 104 C3
Sheriff's Highway. Gates NE9 89 A6
Sheriff's Moor Ave. E Lane DH5 121 C8
Sheriff's Rise Sch. Gates NE9 89 B8
Sheringham Ave. Tyne NE29 50 D7
Sheringham Cl. Silk SR3 116 A4
Sheringham Dr. Cram NE23 21 E6
Sheringham Gdns. Tley NE15 35 B2
Sherwood. Tyne NE27 31 B2
Sherwood Cl. Tyne NE27 31 B2
Sherwood Cl. Wash NE38 101 D5
Sherwood Ct. 5 Silk SR3 116 A6
Sherwood Pl. N-u-T NE3 28 C2
Sherwood View. Walls NE28 49 A4
Shetland Ct. 1 Silk SR3 116 A6
Shibdon Bank. Blay NE21 62 D2
Shibdon Cres. Blay NE21 62 D2
Shibdon Ct. Blay NE21 62 C3
Shibdon Park View. Blay NE21 62 D2
Shibdon Pond Nature Reserve. Blay NE21 62 E2
Shibdon Rd. Blay NE21 62 D3
Shibdon Rd. Blay NE21 62 E2
Shibdon Way. Blay NE21 62 F2
Shiel Gdns. Cram NE23 21 E6
Shield Ave. Whick NE16 69 B1
Shield Ct. Hexham NE46 54 B3
Shield Ct. N-u-T NE2 66 C3
Shield Gr. N-u-T NE3 40 A2
Shield Rd. Sland SR6 93 C5
Shield St. N-u-T NE2 66 C2
Shieldclose. Wash NE37 101 A6
Shieldfield Gn. N-u-T NE2 66 C2
Shieldfield House. N-u-T NE2 66 C2
Shieldfield La. N-u-T NE2 66 C2
Shields Rd. C le S DH3 112 D5
Shields Rd. Clea NE34 & SR6 78 A2
Shields Rd. Clea SR6 78 A3
Shields Rd. Gates NE10 89 F8
Shields Rd. Mpeth NE61 9 A7
Shields Rd. N-u-T NE6 67 C3
Shields Rd. Nedder NE22 15 C5
Shields Rd. Sland SR5 & SR6 93 B5
Shields Rd. W Bay NE25 & NE30 31 F3
Shields Rd W. N-u-T NE6 67 A2
Shillaw Pl. Kill NE23 29 B5
Shilmore Rd. N-u-T NE3 38 C1
Shilton Cl. S Shs NE34 78 B5
Shincliffe Ave. Sland SR5 92 C2
Shincliffe Gdns. Gates NE9 89 D3
Shiney Row Inf Sch. S Row DH4 114 B5
Shipcote La. Gates NE8 88 F8
Shipcote Terr. Gates NE8 88 F8
Shipley Art Gallery. Gates NE8 88 F8
Shipley Ave. N-u-T NE4 64 B2
Shipley Ave. Sland SR6 93 E4
Shipley Ct. Gates NE8 72 C1
Shipley Pl. N-u-T NE6 67 B2
Shipley Rd. Tyne NE30 51 C7
Shipley Rise. N-u-T NE6 67 C2
Shipley St. N-u-T NE15 62 C6
Shipley Wlk. N-u-T NE6 67 B2
Shipton Cl. Boldon NE35 76 E1
Shiremoor Fst Sch. Shire NE27 30 E3
Shiremoor Mid Sch. Shire NE27 30 F4
Shiremoor Sta. Shire NE27 30 F4
Shirley Gdns. Sland SR3 109 B3
Shirwood Ave. Whick NE16 87 A5
Shop Row. S Row DH4 114 C5
Shop Spouts. Blay NE21 62 C3
Shopping Ctr The. N-u-T NE5 36 C2
Shore St. Sland SR6 93 D1
Shoreham Ct. N-u-T NE3 37 C3
Shoreham Sq. Sland SR3 108 B3
Shorestone Ave. Tyne NE30 32 B3
Short Row. Wools NE5 36 B6
Shortridge St. 1 S Shs NE33 51 D3
Shortridge Terr. N-u-T NE2 46 C1
Shot Factory La. N-u-T NE1 & NE4 71 C3
Shotley Ave. Sland SR5 93 B3
Shotley Ct. Ashgn NE63 6 B2
Shotley Gdns. Gates NE9 89 A7
Shotton Ave. Blyth NE24 17 E6
Shotton La. Cram NE23 15 C2
Shotton La. Shot NE61, NE13 & NE23 20 F8
Shotton St. E Hart NE23 16 B3
Shrewsbury Cl. N-u-T NE12 48 A4
Shrewsbury Cres. Sland SR3 108 C3
Shrewsbury Dr. Bworth NE27 30 C5
Shrewsbury St. Duns NE11 87 F8
Shrewsbury Terr. S Shs NE33 77 C7
Shrigley Gdns. N-u-T NE3 38 C1
Sibthorpe St. N Shs NE29 51 B5
Side. N-u-T NE1 72 B4
Side Cliff Rd. Sland SR6 93 E3
Sidlaw Ave. C le S DH2 112 A2
Sidlaw Ave. Tyne NE29 31 F1
Sidlaw Ct. Ashgn NE63 6 E1
Sidmouth Rd. Gates NE9 88 F3
Sidmouth Rd. N Shs NE29 50 C5
Sidney Gr. Gates NE8 72 A1
Sidney Gr. N-u-T NE4 65 A2
Sidney St. Blyth NE24 17 D7
Sidney St. Boldon NE35 91 F8
Sidney St. N Shs NE29 51 A5
Silkey's La. N Shs NE29 50 F5
Silkstun Ct. 8 N Silk SR3 116 A7
Silksworth Cl. N Silk SR3 115 F8
Silksworth Gdns. Gates NE9 89 C2
Silksworth Hall Dr. Silk SR3 115 F6
Silksworth La. N Silk SR3 115 F7
Silksworth La. Sland SR3 109 A2
Silksworth Rd. N Silk SR3 116 A7
Silksworth Rd. Silk SR3 115 E6
Silksworth Rd. Sland SR3 115 C6
Silksworth Row. Sland SR1 105 C3
Silksworth Terr. N Silk SR3 116 A7
Silkwood Cl. Cram NE23 16 B1
Silkworth Way. Silk SR3 115 E6
Silloth Ave. N-u-T NE5 63 A4
Silloth Dr. Wash NE37 90 C2
Silloth Pl. Tyne NE30 32 B2
Silloth Rd. Sland SR3 108 A2
Silver Ct. 3 Gates NE9 89 A8
Silver Lonnen. N-u-T NE15 & NE5 63 B4
Silver St. Sland SR1 106 C3
Silver St. Tyne NE30 51 D7
Silverbirch Ind Est. Kill NE12 29 B4
Silverdale. Silk SR3 116 A4
Silverdale Ave. Gates NE10 90 D8
Silverdale Rd. Cram NE23 16 B1
Silverdale Terr. Gates NE8 & NE9 88 F8
Silverdale Way. B Wh NE34 76 F3
Silverdale Way. Whick NE16 86 F4
Silverhill Dr. N-u-T NE5 63 B3
Silverhill Sch The. N-u-T NE5 63 C3
Silverlink The. Shire NE27 & NE28 & NE29 50 A6
Silvermere Dr. Ryton NE40 61 D4
Silverstone. Kill NE12 29 E3
Silverstone Rd. Wash NE37 101 E8
Silvertop Gdns. Green NE40 61 A1
Silvertop Terr. Green NE40 84 F8
Silverwood Gdns. Duns NE11 88 B5
Simon Pl. B Vill NE13 28 A5
Simonburn. Wash NE38 100 F4
Simonburn Ave. N Shs NE29 50 C6
Simonburn Ave. N-u-T NE4 64 B4
Simonburn La. Ashgn NE63 6 F2
Simonside. Prud NE42 59 B1
Simonside. S Slu NE26 24 D4
Simonside Ave. Stake NE62 11 B8
Simonside Ave. Walls NE28 49 F4
Simonside Cl. Mpeth NE61 8 D7
Simonside Cl. S Slu NE26 24 D4
Simonside Cty Jun Sch. S Shs NE34 76 F5
Simonside Hall. S Shs NE34 76 F5
Simonside Ind Est. Jarrow NE32 76 E5
Simonside Jun Mix & Inf Sch. B Wh NE32 76 D4
Simonside Lodge. Blyth NE24 17 A8
Simonside Pl. Gates NE9 89 D3
Simonside Rd. Blay NE21 62 C1
Simonside Rd. Sland SR3 108 B3
Simonside Terr. N-b-t-S NE64 7 E4
Simonside Terr. N-u-T NE6 67 C4
Simonside View. Jarrow NE32 76 C4
Simonside View. Pont NE20 25 D7
Simonside Way. Kill NE12 & NE27 29 F4
Simpson Cl. Boldon NE35 91 E8
Simpson Ct. Ashgn NE63 7 A3
Simpson St. Blyth NE24 17 E8
Simpson St. N Shs NE29 50 E5
Simpson St. Sland SR4 105 B4
Simpson St. Tyne NE26 & NE30 32 C4
Simpson Terr. N-u-T NE15 36 B1
Simpson Terr. N-u-T NE1 & NE2 66 B2
Simpsons Memorial Homes. Craw NE40 61 A4
Sinclair Dr. C le S DH3 112 D8
Sinclair Gdns. S Del NE25 23 D3
Sinderby Cl. N-u-T NE3 40 A4
Sir GB Hunter Memorial Hospl. Walls NE28 49 C2
Sir Godfrey Thomson Ct. Gates NE10 89 C8
Sixth Ave. Ashgn NE63 6 E2
Sixth Ave. Blyth NE24 17 D6
Sixth Ave. C le S DH2 112 B3
Sixth Ave. Gates NE11 88 C4
Sixth Ave. Mpeth NE61 9 B7
Sixth Ave. N-u-T NE6 67 C3
Skaylock Dr. Wash NE38 101 A3
Skegness Par. Jarrow NE31 76 A2
Skelder Ave. Lbtn NE12 41 B2
Skelton Ct. N-u-T NE3 38 B4
Ski View. N Silk SR3 115 F8
Skiddaw Dr. Sland SR6 93 C5
Skiddaw Pl. Gates NE9 89 B4
Skinnerburn Rd. N-u-T NE1 & NE4 71 C3
Skipsea View. Ryhope SR2 116 D7
Skipton Cl. Cram NE23 16 C1
Skipton Gn. Gates NE9 89 B2
Skirlaw Cl. Wash NE38 101 D4
Skye Ct. 2 Silk SR3 116 A6
Skye Gr. Boldon NE32 76 E2
Slake Rd. Jarrow NE32 76 D8
Slaley. Wash NE38 101 E1
Slaley Cl. Gates NE10 90 C7
Slaley Ct. 4 Silk SR3 116 A6
Slatyford La. N-u-T NE15 & NE5 63 A4
Sled La. Prud NE40 & NE41 60 D3
Sleekburn Ave. Bed NE22 11 E3
Slingley Cl. 4 Seaham SR7 116 E1
Slingsby Gdns. N-u-T NE7 48 A3
Slipway The. Gates NE10 75 A2
Sloane Ct. N-u-T NE2 66 B3
Smailes La. R Gill NE39 85 C2
Smallholdings. N-b-t-S NE63 7 C6
Smeaton Ct. 5 Walls NE28 50 A1
Smeaton St. 2 Walls NE28 50 A1
Smith Gr. Ryhope SR2 116 E6
Smith St. Ryhope SR2 116 F6
Smith St. S Shs NE33 77 B8
Smith St S. Ryhope SR2 116 F6
Smith Terr. Gates NE8 71 B1
Smith's Terr. H le H DH5 119 B1
Smithburn Rd. Gates NE10 89 E7
Smithy La. Kibble NE11 & NE9 88 F1
Smithy St. S Shs NE33 51 C3
Smyrna Pl. Sland SR1 106 B3
Snipes Dene. R Gill NE39 85 E3
Snowdon Gdns. Duns NE11 88 A6
Snowdon Gr. Boldon NE36 92 B7
Snowdon Terr. H Spen NE39 84 F5
Snowdrop Cl. Blay NE21 62 A2
Soane Gdns. White NE34 77 D3
Softley Pl. N-u-T NE15 62 F7
Solingen Est. Blyth NE24 17 F5
Solway Ave. Tyne NE30 32 B2
Solway Rd. Hebb NE31 75 F4
Solway Sq. Sland SR3 108 B3
Solway St. N-u-T NE6 73 C4
Somerford. Spring NE9 89 F2
Somersby Dr. N-u-T NE3 38 B1
Somerset Gdns. Walls NE28 49 A3
Somerset Gr. Tyne NE29 50 D8
Somerset Pl. N-u-T NE4 65 A1
Somerset Rd. Hebb NE31 75 F3
Somerset Rd. Sland SR3 108 A3
Somerset Sq. Sland SR3 108 A3
Somerset St. N Silk SR3 116 A8
Somerton Ct. N-u-T NE3 37 C2
Sophy St. Sland SR5 93 B2
Sorley St. Sland SR4 105 A2
Sorrel Cl. Ashgn NE63 6 C2
Sorrel Gdns. White NE34 77 E3

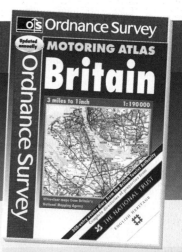

Ordnance Survey

MOTORING ATLAS

Updated annually

Britain

The best-selling *OS Motoring Atlas Britain* uses unrivalled and up-to-date mapping from the Ordnance Survey digital database. The exceptionally clear mapping is at a large scale of 3 miles to 1 inch (Orkney/Shetland Islands at 5 miles to 1 inch).

A special feature of the atlas is its wealth of tourist and leisure information. It contains comprehensive directories, including descriptions and location details, of the properties of the National Trust in England and Wales, the National Trust for Scotland, English Heritage and Historic Scotland. There is also a useful diary of British Tourist Authority Events listing more than 300 days out around Britain during the year.

Available from all good bookshops or direct from the publisher:
Tel: 01933 443863

The atlas includes:

◆ **112 pages of fully updated mapping**
◆ **45 city and town plans**
◆ **8 extra-detailed city approach maps**
◆ **route-planning maps**
◆ **restricted motorway junctions**
◆ **local radio information**
◆ **distances chart**
◆ **county boundaries map**
◆ **multi-language legend**

STREET ATLASES
ORDER FORM

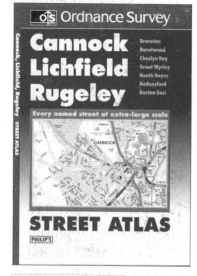

PHILIP'S

The Street Atlases are available from all good bookshops or by mail order direct from the publisher. Orders can be made in the following ways. **By phone** Ring our special Credit Card Hotline on **01933 443863** during office hours (9am to 5pm) or leave a message on the answering machine, quoting your full credit card number plus expiry date and your full name and address. **By post or fax** Fill out the order form below (you may photocopy it) and post it to: **Philip's Direct, 27 Sanders Road, Wellingborough, Northants NN8 4NL** or fax it to: **01933 443849.** Before placing an order by post, by fax or on the answering machine, please telephone to check availability and prices.

COLOUR LOCAL ATLASES

	PAPERBACK	
	Quantity @ £3.50 each	£ Total
CANNOCK, LICHFIELD, RUGELEY	☐ 0 540 07625 2	➤ ☐
DERBY AND BELPER	☐ 0 540 07608 2	➤ ☐
NORTHWICH, WINSFORD, MIDDLEWICH	☐ 0 540 07589 2	➤ ☐
PEAK DISTRICT TOWNS	☐ 0 540 07609 0	➤ ☐
STAFFORD, STONE, UTTOXETER	☐ 0 540 07626 0	➤ ☐
WARRINGTON, WIDNES, RUNCORN	☐ 0 540 07588 4	➤ ☐

COLOUR REGIONAL ATLASES

	HARDBACK	SPIRAL	POCKET	
	Quantity @ £10.99 each	Quantity @ £8.99 each	Quantity @ £5.99 each	£ Total
BERKSHIRE	☐ 0 540 06170 0	☐ 0 540 06172 7	☐ 0 540 06173 5	➤ ☐
	Quantity @ £10.99 each	Quantity @ £8.99 each	Quantity @ £4.99 each	£ Total
MERSEYSIDE	☐ 0 540 06480 7	☐ 0 540 06481 5	☐ 0 540 06482 3	➤ ☐
	Quantity @ £12.99 each	Quantity @ £9.99 each	Quantity @ £4.99 each	£ Total
DURHAM	☐ 0 540 06365 7	☐ 0 540 06366 5	☐ 0 540 06367 3	➤ ☐
EAST KENT	☐ 0 540 07483 7	☐ 0 540 07276 1	☐ 0 540 07287 7	➤ ☐
WEST KENT	☐ 0 540 07366 0	☐ 0 540 07367 9	☐ 0 540 07369 5	➤ ☐
EAST SUSSEX	☐ 0 540 07306 7	☐ 0 540 07307 5	☐ 0 540 07312 1	➤ ☐
WEST SUSSEX	☐ 0 540 07319 9	☐ 0 540 07323 7	☐ 0 540 07327 X	➤ ☐
	Quantity @ £12.99 each	Quantity @ £9.99 each	Quantity @ £5.50 each	£ Total
GREATER MANCHESTER	☐ 0 540 06485 8	☐ 0 540 06486 6	☐ 0 540 06487 4	➤ ☐
TYNE AND WEAR	☐ 0 540 06370 3	☐ 0 540 06371 1	☐ 0 540 06372 X	➤ ☐
	Quantity @ £12.99 each	Quantity @ £9.99 each	Quantity @ £5.99 each	£ Total
BIRMINGHAM & WEST MIDLANDS	☐ 0 540 07603 1	☐ 0 540 07604 X	☐ 0 540 07605 8	➤ ☐
BUCKINGHAMSHIRE	☐ 0 540 07466 7	☐ 0 540 07467 5	☐ 0 540 07468 3	➤ ☐
CHESHIRE	☐ 0 540 07507 8	☐ 0 540 07508 6	☐ 0 540 07509 4	➤ ☐
DERBYSHIRE	☐ 0 540 07531 0	☐ 0 540 07532 9	☐ 0 540 07533 7	➤ ☐
EDINBURGH & East Central Scotland	☐ 0 540 07653 8	☐ 0 540 07654 6	☐ 0 540 07656 2	➤ ☐

STREET ATLASES ORDER FORM

COLOUR REGIONAL ATLASES

	HARDBACK	SPIRAL	POCKET	
	Quantity @ £12.99 each	Quantity @ £9.99 each	Quantity @ £5.99 each	£ Total
GLASGOW & West Central Scotland	☐ 0 540 07648 1	☐ 0 540 07649 X	☐ 0 540 07651 1	➤ ☐
NORTH HAMPSHIRE	☐ 0 540 07471 3	☐ 0 540 07472 1	☐ 0 540 07473 X	➤ ☐
SOUTH HAMPSHIRE	☐ 0 540 07476 4	☐ 0 540 07477 2	☐ 0 540 07478 0	➤ ☐
HERTFORDSHIRE	☐ 0 540 06174 3	☐ 0 540 06175 1	☐ 0 540 06176 X	➤ ☐
OXFORDSHIRE	☐ 0 540 07512 4	☐ 0 540 07513 2	☐ 0 540 07514 0	➤ ☐
SURREY	☐ 0 540 06435 1	☐ 0 540 06436 X	☐ 0 540 06438 6	➤ ☐
WARWICKSHIRE	☐ 0 540 07560 4	☐ 0 540 07561 2	☐ 0 540 07562 0	➤ ☐
SOUTH YORKSHIRE	☐ 0 540 06330 4	☐ 0 540 06331 2	☐ 0 540 06332 0	➤ ☐
WEST YORKSHIRE	☐ 0 540 06329 0	☐ 0 540 06327 4	☐ 0 540 06328 2	➤ ☐
	Quantity @ £14.99 each	Quantity @ £9.99 each	Quantity @ £5.99 each	£ Total
LANCASHIRE	☐ 0 540 06440 8	☐ 0 540 06441 6	☐ 0 540 06443 2	➤ ☐
NOTTINGHAMSHIRE	☐ 0 540 07541 8	☐ 0 540 07542 6	☐ 0 540 07543 4	➤ ☐
STAFFORDSHIRE	☐ 0 540 07549 3	☐ 0 540 07550 7	☐ 0 540 07551 5	➤ ☐

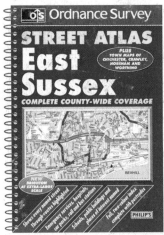

BLACK AND WHITE REGIONAL ATLASES

	HARDBACK	SOFTBACK	POCKET	
	Quantity @ £11.99 each	Quantity @ £8.99 each	Quantity @ £3.99 each	£ Total
BRISTOL AND AVON	☐ 0 540 06140 9	☐ 0 540 06141 7	☐ 0 540 06142 5	➤ ☐
	Quantity @ £12.99 each	Quantity @ £9.99 each	Quantity @ £4.99 each	£ Total
CARDIFF, SWANSEA & GLAMORGAN	☐ 0 540 06186 7	☐ 0 540 06187 5	☐ 0 540 06207 3	➤ ☐
EAST ESSEX	☐ 0 540 05848 3	☐ 0 540 05866 1	☐ 0 540 05850 5	➤ ☐
WEST ESSEX	☐ 0 540 05849 1	☐ 0 540 05867 X	☐ 0 540 05851 3	➤ ☐

Post to: Philip's Direct, 27 Sanders Road, Wellingborough, Northants NN8 4NL

◆ Free postage and packing

◆ All available titles will normally be dispatched within 5 working days of receipt of order but please allow up to 28 days for delivery

☐ Please tick this box if you do not wish your name to be used by other carefully selected organisations that may wish to send you information about other products and services

Registered Office: 2-4 Heron Quays, London E14 4JP

Registered in England number: 3597451

I enclose a cheque / postal order, for a **total** of ☐ made payable to *Octopus Publishing Group Ltd*, or please debit my

☐ Access ☐ American Express ☐ Visa ☐ Diners

account by ☐

Account no ☐☐☐☐ ☐☐☐☐ ☐☐☐☐ ☐☐☐☐

Expiry date ☐☐ ☐☐

Signature...

Name...

Address..

....

....POSTCODE

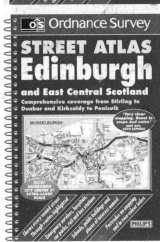